1995

RICHARD J.
DALEY

RICHARD J. DALEY

POLITICS, RACE, AND THE GOVERNING OF CHICAGO

Roger Biles

NORTHERN ILLINOIS UNIVERSITY PRESS   DeKalb   1995

© 1995 by Northern Illinois University Press

Published by the Northern Illinois University Press,

DeKalb, Illinois 60115

Manufactured in the United States using acid-free paper

Design by Julia Fauci

Library of Congress Cataloging-in-Publication Data

Biles, Roger, 1950–

    Richard J. Daley: politics, race, and the

governing of Chicago / Roger Biles.

        p.   cm.

    Includes bibliographical references and index.

    ISBN 0–87580–199–4 (cloth). —

    ISBN 0–87580–566–3 (pbk.)

    1. Daley, Richard J., 1902–1976. 2. Chicago

(Ill.)—Politics and government—1951– I. Title.

F548.54.D34B55 1995

977.3'11043'092—dc20

[B]   94-48268

          CIP

CONTENTS

PREFACE

Chicago has always been colorful: Mrs. O'Leary's cow, the Haymarket riot, the Pullman strike, Little Egypt, Charles Tyson Yerkes, Samuel F. Insull, Leopold and Loeb, Bathhouse John and Hinky Dink, Al Capone, the St. Valentine's Day massacre, Monsters of the Midway. And a great city for journalism: Ben Hecht, Nelson Algren, Studs Terkel, Mike Royko.

Chicago has also been important. The Columbian Exposition spawned the City Beautiful Movement in America. The Chicago Plan of 1909, drafted by Daniel H. Burnham and Edward H. Bennett, became the prototype for and defined city planning in the United States. The Chicago School of Architecture revolutionized the way cities looked and installed the skyscraper as a permanent feature of central business districts; Louis Sullivan, Frank Lloyd Wright, and Mies van der Rohe made the city the pacemaker in urban design. Jane Addams, Ellen Gates Starr, Florence Kelley, Mary McDowell, Mary Simkhovitch, and Graham Taylor were pioneers in social welfare for poor immigrants. Robert E. Park, Ernest W. Burgess, Louis Wirth, Harvey Zorbaugh, and others in the University of Chicago School of Sociology made the city into the great urban laboratory and defined the developing field of urban study. Chicago realtors, on the other hand, devised restrictive covenants and thereby provided the means for rigid racial residential segregation in America's cities.

Chicago. Colorful and important. So was Richard J. Daley, the city's mayor from 1955 to 1976. Short and stocky, laconic, inarticulate, and personally unimposing, Daley nevertheless produced good copy for local and national media. Often compared unfavorably with New York City's handsome, voluble, mediagenic John Lindsay, Daley was both plain and plainspoken. Daley's lack of polish and his refreshing candor made him seem more human; his fiery temper, which occasionally erupted in invective-laced verbal outbursts, underscored passionate beliefs. Sometimes, when he was angry or flustered, the words came too fast, jumbled, in memorable malapropisms.

His sophisticated critics smirked when the mayor said "I resent the insinuendos" or "They have vilified me, they have crucified me, yes, they have even criticized me," or when he exhorted an audience to "rise to ever higher and higher platitudes." The words may have been confused, the syntax garbled, the diction rough-edged, but Daley never failed to communicate effectively his meaning or his emotions.[1]

Daley was important because he stood center stage at a crucial time in the life of American cities; his impact was felt on the national as well as on the local level. He helped elect John F. Kennedy, hosted the turbulent 1968 Democratic National Convention, and remained a powerful Democrat for nearly two decades—arguably the most influential urban figure on the national scene. He also served as mayor of America's Second City for the critical years that spanned the post–World War II "urban renaissance" and the "urban crisis"—the years of urban renewal, race riots, fiscal crisis, suburban flight, and Sunbelt boom. Daley conducted Chicago's business with a steadfast resolve to oppose many of the changes that threatened to engulf his city. Utilizing his considerable administrative and political acumen, he countered (at least temporarily) many of the dominant economic and political trends that proved inexorable to other mayors. Although Daley sometimes embraced change (he modernized and professionalized the municipal bureaucracy, for example), he often resisted forward movement with all the power at his disposal, and no more so than when his atavistic racial views came into question. The ways in which this last of the big city bosses—an Irish Catholic from working-class Bridgeport—grappled with those imposing challenges, attempting to slacken the pace of history, and the degree to which his policies shaped the development of Chicago and affected its people are the subject of this book. Daley finally lost his struggle against the powerful demographic forces that were reshaping the nation's metropolises in the twentieth century. Only after the mayor's death—after ceasing to be Daley's Chicago—did the city begin to deal with the knotty problems of political representation and resource allocation that needed to be addressed on behalf of a changing, unsettled populace.

ACKNOWLEDGMENTS

My interest in Richard J. Daley arose from a conference I attended in 1977 devoted to the mayor's career, sponsored by the University of Illinois at Chicago Circle's Department of History and the Chicago Historical Society. The three-day gathering of historians, political scientists, economists, politicians, community organizers, political consultants, journalists, and architects included presentations that ranged from shameless eulogies to disinterested scholarly analyses to hard-edged criticisms. I would like to thank Professor Melvin G. Holli, who directed the Daley Conference and read this manuscript in its entirety seventeen years later. Professor Perry R. Duis sparked the conference's most memorable discussion (in colorful Wozniak's Casino, a Democratic machine stronghold) by daring to call Daley a reformer; he also read the manuscript and offered useful suggestions for revision. Archie Motley, who as curator of archives and manuscripts at the Chicago Historical Society is widely admired by urban historians, not only helped me locate sources but read the manuscript as well. Jon C. Teaford and Arnold R. Hirsch provided thoughtful comments that proved helpful in the book's revision. This book is much better for the contributions of these selfless scholars, none of whom are responsible for errors or interpretations that remain despite their advice.

Virtually all of the work for this book was done while I was a member of the history faculty at Oklahoma State University, and I would like to acknowledge my debts to the Sooner State. The College of Arts and Sciences at Oklahoma State University awarded me a sabbatical leave, and the Oklahoma Foundation for the Humanities provided a research grant that helped defray the cost of travel. During my ten years there, I had the good fortune of working in a superb department full of first-rate historians. George Moses, Bill Bryans, Rick Rohrs, Jim Huston, Elizabeth Williams, George Jewsbury, and Paul Bischoff were terrific colleagues and friends.

As always, my family merits the hardiest thanks. My father-in-law, Ed Frank, helped open doors for interviews with Chicago politicians that would have otherwise remained closed to me. My parents continued to provide unqualified support. My wife, Mary Claire, lovingly tolerates my excessive work habits and costly research trips, while managing the household and maintaining her own career. She and I find our children, Brian, Jeanne, and Grant, endlessly challenging. And the greatest joy of our lives.

RICHARD J.
DALEY

Introduction Chicago, 1945–1955

At the end of World War II, Americans faced the future with a mixture of fear and expectation, anxiety and hope. They remembered the difficult dislocations and adjustments that had plagued the nation after the First World War, and they dreaded a return of the widespread unemployment and suffering of the Great Depression. At the same time they hoped that the restoration of peace and prosperity would allow the completion of civic projects long deferred because of economic stagnation and war. In the cities, public officials drew up ambitious agendas calling for public works that would both employ millions of returning servicemen and replenish neglected infrastructures. Severe housing shortages and an enervated construction industry cried out for the resumption of home building. Antiquated and deteriorating public transit systems along with a dearth of suitable highway networks underscored the cities' inadequate transportation. Surrounded by suburbs and unable to annex or to consolidate as they had in the previous century, inner cities languished as metropolitan areas advanced across the landscape. The flight of people, industries, and wealth to the hinterlands threatened to undermine the standard of living for those who remained behind in the urban cores. Moreover, a host of new arrivals altered the demographics of the cities; possessing few resources and negligible skills, these newcomers frequently increased the pressure on existing health, education, and welfare institutions. Like the other giant industrial cities of the Midwest and the Northeast, Chicago faced an imposing series of challenges in the middle of the twentieth century.[1]

To the delight of apprehensive Chicagoans, however, the late 1940s and 1950s ushered in an era of unparalleled prosperity. The city's $1.3 billion worth of war plants (the most in any metropolitan area) fueled a peacetime industrial boom. Federal Housing Administration (FHA) loans, the Veterans Administration mortgage program, and the GI Bill made possible the dream of home ownership for a large portion of the middle and working classes, but much of the postwar growth and enrichment occurred in the region surrounding the central city. Suburbanization—an insistent process operating in Chicago virtually since its founding—accelerated after World War II. A drastic housing shortage persisted for several years after the end of the war (Chicago home builders completed an average of only 6,600 new homes annually from 1945 to 1949), so residents who had resorted to living in Quonset huts, remodeled military barracks, government-owned trailers, and even used trolley cars departed the city limits for new suburban housing developments that offered immediate home ownership. Insatiably hungry for the housing long denied them, blessed with a surplus of disposable income, and served by a new automobility that brought home and workplace conveniently closer together, families left their urban roots for crabgrass frontiers. More than 77 percent of the new homes built in the Chicago metropolitan area between 1945 and 1959 were situated beyond the city limits. Real estate developers laid out new tracts in Cook County and beyond, reaching into surrounding Lake, Will, Kane, and DuPage Counties in northeastern Illinois and Lake and Porter Counties in northwestern Indiana. The population of the Chicago Standard Metropolitan Statistical Area (SMSA) increased from 4,569,643 in 1940 to 6,220,913 twenty years later, but the city's portion of the residents declined from 74 to 57 percent.[2]

Decentralization occurred in industry as well as in population. As old facilities became outmoded and the high prices of downtown land made expansion unrealistic, business enterprises joined the centrifugal movement. Large tracts of land available on the suburban fringe allowed manufacturers to construct more efficient single-story factories with additional space for parking (a crucial concern with the growing importance of automobiles and trucks). The simultaneous appearance of residential suburbs provided housing for workers who could avoid commuting into the congested central city. In order to complement their tax bases, suburbs (and Sunbelt cities) lured businesses with promises of cheap land, lower taxes, better service delivery, and other sweetheart deals. From 1947 to 1961, Chicago's portion of the metropolitan area's industrial employment declined from 71 to 54 percent. By 1965 fewer than half of the region's manufacturing jobs remained within the city's corporate limits.[3]

Symptomatic of Chicago's manufacturing decline was the collapse of the meatpacking industry. By the end of the war, the city immortalized by Carl Sandburg as "hog butcher of the world" began to lose its primacy among U.S. communities. Whereas the railroad had concentrated the meatpacking industry in one central location in the nineteenth century, the advent of the automobile and the diesel truck, accompanied by the appearance of paved rural highways, caused the opposite effect by the middle of the twentieth century. New technologies made Chicago's sprawling base of operations unnecessary, even counterproductive. The decision to shift plant sites to Omaha, Kansas City, and a number of other smaller, western cities left Chicago's stock pens and killing houses with declining activity. In 1955 the Wilson plant closed its doors; in 1959 Armour followed, and Swift cut its production to a token amount. By 1960 all the major packers had closed their Chicago plants, and within a decade the stockyards stood completely empty. The demise of the meatpacking industry meant the loss of an estimated thirty thousand jobs in the Windy City.[4]

As Chicago lost people and employment to the suburbs, the composition of the remaining population changed significantly. In 1900 the U.S. Census Bureau identified 77 percent of Chicago's 1,698,575 people as "foreign stock"; that is, slightly more than three-fourths had been born in other countries or were native-born children of immigrant parents. Of the city's population in 1950 (3,620,962), only 45 percent were first- or second-generation immigrants. The third generation, which tended to be highly assimilable, fell outside the Census Bureau's definition of foreign stock. Members of the highly mobile second generation frequently relocated further from the city center, increasingly settling in the surrounding suburbs. Moreover, the relative size of the white ethnic groups altered as well. The Germans, the largest ethnic group in 1900, had yielded that distinction to the Poles by 1950, whereas the Irish, the second-most-populous nationality in 1900 (with 13.3 percent of the population), fell to fifth (see table 1). Although certain demographic trends were clear, most notably that Chicago's growth would no longer be fueled principally by European emigration and that later arriving groups would be increasingly influential in the future, it was still true in the mid twentieth century that the white ethnics remained the most substantial component of the population. Less cohesive and more geographically dispersed than they had been, the European immigrants and their progeny still constituted an important force in the life of Chicago.[5]

Table 1. Major Ethnic Groups in Chicago, 1900 and 1950

	1900 (%)	1950 (%)
Total population	1,698,575	3,620,962
Total "foreign stock"	1,315,307	1,628,168
Major Ethnic Groups		
Germans	428,201 (25.2)	229,230 (6.3)
Irish	225,900 (13.3)	126,940 (3.5)
Poles	111,506 (6.6)	315,504 (8.7)
Swedes	103,220 (6.1)	85,684 (2.4)
Bohemians/Czechs	77,343 (4.6)	78,135 (2.2)
USSR	40,546 (2.4)	139,504 (3.9)
Italians	27,250 (1.6)	171,549 (4.7)
Africans	30,150 (1.8)	492,265 (13.6)
Mexicans	——	24,335 (0.7)

Source: Adapted from Joseph Zikmund II, "Mayoral Voting and Ethnic Politics in the Daley-Bilandic-Byrne Era," in Samuel K. Gove and Louis H. Masotti, eds., *After Daley: Chicago Politics in Transition* (Urbana: University of Illinois Press, 1982), p. 28.

At the same time, other newcomers to the city began to increase their vital influence. Like other northern industrial cities, Chicago became a primary destination for unemployed southerners who fled impoverished rural situations in hope of greater economic opportunity. The stream of migrants began during the Second World War and, although it slowed somewhat after V-J Day, continued in the postwar decades. Many of the new arrivals hailed from the mountainous Upper South. Between 1945 and 1965, while the nation's production of coal increased, the number of workers engaged in mining decreased by three-fourths; displaced by new technology and more efficient excavation techniques, many of the unemployed headed north to seek different jobs and a higher standard of living. During the 1950s, an estimated 1,600,000 whites deserted the played-out coal mines and rutted farms of the Appalachian Mountains—an exodus of roughly one-third of eastern Kentucky and one-fifth of the entire West Virginia population. They settled in hillbilly ghettos like Dayton's East Side, Cincinnati's Over-the-Rhine, and Chicago's Uptown.[6]

Crammed into one square mile of living space, approximately one-half of the sixty thousand residents of the Uptown neighborhood had been born in the South. As they struggled to adapt to an alien environment radically different from the hills and hollows of the Appalachians, these newcomers forged networks of friends and family to ease the transition. Poor, uneducated, and possessing few marketable skills, they enjoyed little upward social mobility, and the already modest area in which they had settled became progressively seedier. Even with a 13 percent vacancy rate, Uptown ranked second among Chicago neighborhoods in population density. According to the Census Bureau, 27 percent of the area's dwellings lacked adequate plumbing facilities, and 38 percent were adjudged deteriorated. Under the pressure of the "hillbilly" migration, Uptown became one of Chicago's most abominable slums.[7]

The considerable influx of southern whites notwithstanding, the greatest change in Chicago's mid-century population occurred in the rapid rise of the black population. Also the result of a northward movement triggered by the war, the black increase eventually surpassed the Great Migration of the World War I era. In addition to the attraction of higher wages in northern industry, many black farmers, sharecroppers, and tenants left the South because of the mechanization that reduced the need for a large agricultural workforce. The erosion of the southern rural way of life gave rise to a carefully modulated black migration after World War II. Interstate highways, like railroads, became "freedom roads," and southern black families often gave bus tickets for Chicago to their children as high school graduation presents. By the 1950s and 1960s, southern blacks of all ages— but especially adolescents and young adults—headed northward to places like Chicago to join relatives, friends, and neighbors who had already established themselves in African American communities.[8]

Between 1940 and 1944, according to St. Clair Drake and Horace R. Cayton, approximately 60,000 black immigrants arrived in Chicago; during the entire decade, the city's black population increased from 278,000 to 492,000, a gain of 77 percent. A Chicago Community Inventory study revealed that in the 1940s the city's nonwhite population rose by an average of 27,000 annually, intensifying to an average yearly increase of 38,100 between 1950 and 1956. Demographers Otis Dudley Duncan and Beverly Duncan found that the vast majority of the new arrivals came from five southern states—Mississippi, Arkansas, Tennessee, Alabama, and Missouri. By 1950 only New York City had a larger black population than Chicago, and one of every thirty African Americans in the United States resided in Cook County. Chicago's black population alone would have constituted the nation's nineteenth-largest city.[9]

Yet even as thousands of blacks poured into Chicago, the city's residential neighborhoods remained rigidly segregated. The races continued to live apart, because many more African Americans found it possible to obtain housing in the existing area of black settlement than were permitted to move to other areas of the city. Situated south of downtown, the Black Belt contained the majority of black Chicagoans, with smaller settlements existing immediately west and north of the Loop. Although the U.S. Supreme Court ruled racially restrictive covenants illegal in the 1948 *Shelley v. Kraemer* decision, opponents of desegregation found other means of preserving the homogeneity of their neighborhoods. If anything, Chicago became more rigorously racially segregated after World War II: in 1940, 49 percent of the city's black inhabitants lived in entirely black census tracts; by 1950, this figure had increased to 53 percent. Whites departed from adjacent residential areas and the Black Belt expanded, but virtually no integration resulted.[10]

Overcrowding in these black communities inexorably led to worsening conditions. Whereas the number of white people in Chicago decreased between 1940 and 1950 and those who remained occupied fewer overcrowded housing units, the percentage of nonwhites forced to live in overcrowded units rose from 19 to 24 percent during the same years. Blacks commonly lived in "kitchenettes"—tiny one-room apartments equipped with gas plates in the closets—and shared bathroom facilities with several other tenant groups. Because nonwhite families earned median incomes only three-fifths those of white families and the supply of housing in Chicago remained limited, blacks found it necessary to pool incomes and to incorporate nonfamily members into the household in order to pay rents. Blacks frequently had to allocate an extraordinary proportion of their incomes for access to inferior housing while suffering the additional misfortune of overcrowding. The suffocating congestion fostered the attendant symptoms of slum life—high crime and juvenile delinquency rates, inadequate health care, deficient education, brittle family life, and finally, despair of improvement.[11]

In 1953 the *Chicago Daily News* published a ten-part exposé of slum conditions called "The City's Shame." The newspaper's investigative reporters found that as many as one thousand people lived in buildings designed for an occupancy of two hundred. In the files of the city's housing commission, they discovered over ten thousand complaints about the preponderance of rats, bugs, and other unsanitary conditions—including fifty-seven reports of rat bites within the preceding six months alone. The greatest scandal, concluded the newspaper, was the city's indifference to the widespread disregard of housing regulations. In the few cases in which tenant complaints led to arrests and trials, 60 percent of landlords were acquitted, and those who were found guilty paid at worst an average fine of $20.23. As a result of the *Daily News*'s series, the city council and the metropolitan housing council promised to investigate the situation. After the furor died down, however, conditions in the tenements remained essentially unchanged.[12]

The attempt of black Chicagoans to escape the misery of ghetto life sparked what historian Arnold R. Hirsch has called "an era of hidden violence." The years between the World War II disturbances and the race riots of the 1960s have long been described as a tranquil interlude, but Hirsch has detailed a somewhat different pattern of interracial violence occurring in Chicago during that time. Although no large-scale outbreaks involving massive destruction of property or significant loss of life resulted, the decade following the end of the war saw a continuation of territorial clashes in what Hirsch has termed "chronic urban guerilla warfare." Because one city agency— the Chicago Commission on Human Relations—was determined to conceal the public record of racial antipathy, and because Chicago's daily newspapers largely complied in this conspiracy of silence, many people living during this period of veiled violence (as well as later generations) remained ignorant of the bitter struggles going on throughout the city.[13]

The interracial violence initially involved attempted intimidation of blacks who purchased homes in white neighborhoods along the fringes of the Black Belt. From 1944 to 1946, incidents of arson, bombings, and vandalism occurred at forty-six residences newly occupied by black residents in previously all-white neighborhoods. Hooligans attacked nine of the homes twice, and one house on five separate occasions. Although the incidents were frequent and the authorities ascribed at least three deaths to the attacks, the local press provided minimal coverage and, according to Hirsch, the "white community [was] unaware of the situation."[14]

Beginning in 1946, a series of housing riots—on a large enough scale to necessitate coverage by newspapers, radio, and television—increased the racial tension in both black and white communities. When the Chicago Housing Authority (CHA) attempted to include black World War II veterans in public housing projects situated in white communities, area residents launched violent protests. The first eruption came at Airport Homes on the Southwest Side, where the CHA sought to move blacks into emergency shelters; a mob of several thousand whites battled police and destroyed property. At the CHA's Fernwood Park Homes, a crowd of five thousand people battled police details assigned to protect the project, then roamed the South Side beating black pedestrians and motorists who were unlucky enough to be cornered by the mob. The rumor that blacks had purchased a house in the South Side Englewood community triggered an outbreak of mob violence in which area residents beat Jews, University of Chicago students, labor organizers, and other whites thought to be sympathetic to integration, as well as blacks. In the struggle at Trumbull Park Homes in the South Deering community that commenced in 1953 and lasted for nearly a decade, whites harassed potential black tenants (sometimes using explosives) and staged such violent demonstrations that on one occasion the police dispatched twelve hundred officers to restore order. The most highly publicized housing riot occurred in suburban Cicero in 1951, when National Guardsmen and Cook County sheriff's police intervened to aid local authorities.[15]

During the 1950s, turf battles ensued over access to schools, parks, playgrounds, and beaches, in addition to housing. As blacks gradually gained access to housing in surrounding areas, principally on the South Side, they naturally also wanted the use of public conveniences that had previously been the exclusive domain of whites. The most violence transpired at Rainbow Beach, Bessemer Park, and Calumet Park on the city's Southeast Side; the press devoted much greater attention to these outbursts than to the earlier housing confrontations. Interracial struggles resulted from the difficult accommodation of entrenched white residents to changing neighborhood boundaries, from the painful reconfiguration of Chicago's racial borders. So long constricted in a narrow swath of land on the South Side, the black population intensified the pressure to expand into new living spaces. The end of World War II unleashed a series of forces that could not endlessly be deflected—the desire of agencies such as the Chicago Human Rights Commission and the local news media to avoid embarrassing publicity notwithstanding.[16]

In addition, the city could not ignore the related problem of slums, a cancer that continued to consume large and ever-growing portions of the local cityscape. A 1943 Chicago Plan Commission study found 242,000 substandard housing units located within a twenty-three-square-mile "blighted" zone and an additional 100,000 such units scattered throughout the city in "non-blighted" areas. In the years following the war, intense overcrowding and additional aging of these living units merely exacerbated the problem. For the most part, the worst conditions existed in an arc extending south and west from the Loop, an area where approximately one-fourth of the city's entire population resided. Ironically, the Near South Side—once Chicago's toniest residential enclave, home of the Philip Armour, Marshall Field, and George Pullman mansions on Prairie Avenue—had degenerated into the city's most pathetic slum.[17]

The first attempts to halt the degeneration of the area south of the Loop began through private initiatives. Occupying two islands in the midst of the dilapidation, the Illinois Institute of Technology (IIT) and Michael Reese Hospital (the nation's largest private medical facility at that time) took the lead in a path-breaking revitalization project in the Douglas neighborhood. The hospital created its own planning department directed by the nationally renowned Reginald R. Isaacs, while IIT appointed esteemed architect Mies van der Rohe to redesign its campus. In both cases, the institutions opted not to relocate in the suburbs but instead to affirm their commitment to the Near South Side by upgrading their existing facilities and trying to improve the surrounding neighborhood. Working in concert with the CHA, the Metropolitan Housing and Planning Council, the Roman Catholic Archdiocese of Chicago, the AFL-CIO, and two businesses (R. R. Donnelly and Sons and the Illinois Central Railroad), the two institutions formed the South Side Redevelopment Agency and opened lines of communication to local government. To stabilize the area, the board of directors proposed building a massive, middle-income, racially integrated housing development—Lake Meadows—and secured as principal investor in this development the New York Life Insurance Company. The project attracted national attention as a pioneering experiment in urban renewal based on interracial housing.[18]

The Lake Meadows project—the first buildings of which opened for occupancy in 1953—contained ten high-rise structures with over two thousand residential units on over one hundred acres of cleared land. The city participated by purchasing the necessary real estate, clearing the slums, relocating some of the displaced inhabitants, and discounting the land for sale to the investors. The $35 million project won much praise as an example of how city governments could cooperate with profit-seeking enterprises to solve the cities' housing conundrums and as proof that middle-income whites and blacks could live together amicably if they could find suitable housing. The project's vaunted success encouraged additional investments into what quickly became a transformed neighborhood. To the north of Lake Meadows, city government acquired and prepared land for the construction of the $27 million, 1,200-unit Prairie Shores housing project. Michael Reese Hospital's expansion and Mies van der Rohe's major reworking of the IIT campus—along with the enlargement of Mercy Hospital and the opening of South Commons, a privately financed residential complex on South Michigan Avenue—gave a remarkably new look to a previously decrepit wasteland.[19]

Despite the plaudits Chicago received for conducting one of the nation's first large forays into urban redevelopment, however, many problems remained and others developed. Real estate values increased and the city collected more tax revenues, but many black Chicagoans opposed the project as a boon to the middle class at the expense of the poor. In place of the 3,416 units originally occupying the site, the Lake Meadows development contained 2,033 apartments. The former area residents (none of whom could afford to live in the new facilities, which charged three times as much rent as the old units) complained bitterly of not being able to find suitable new housing elsewhere. Rather than aiding the poor, this urban renewal project merely moved them to other, less visible areas and increased congestion where they eventually settled. Some critics charged that, although integration did exist in the new projects, the residents of the Lake Meadows–Prairie Shores complex continued to live in an island of relative affluence disconnected from the surrounding sea of black poverty. The questions raised by the Near South Side urban renewal effort presaged the mixed results experienced in other cities throughout the 1950s and 1960s.[20]

Chicago's leading role in urban revitalization was underscored by another massive undertaking launched a short distance from Lake Meadows. Many of the residents who had been uprooted from the Douglas community headed south and accelerated the movement of blacks into Hyde Park, one of the city's few integrated neighborhoods and home of the University of Chicago. In 1949 concerned residents formed the Hyde Park–Kenwood Community Conference (HPKCC), and in 1952 the university created the South East Chicago Commission (SECC), both of which strove to keep the middle-class neighborhood from degenerating into a slum. By the early 1950s, fearing a wholesale exodus of whites from Hyde Park, the two organizations supported state legislation that provided for the use of government resources to prevent slum growth. The Urban Community Conservation Act of 1953 increased cities' power of eminent domain, and two years later the Chicago Land Clearance Commission began assembling sites for one of the nation's most ambitious urban renewal projects. As the neighborhood's leading property owner, the University of Chicago sought to keep too many blacks from moving in and thereby to preserve Hyde Park's racial composition. Unlike some other communities that drew the color line indelibly, Hyde Park was willing to tolerate a minority black population but fought against an influx of poor blacks. Dedicated to preserving the university environment's middle-class character, the SECC opposed any attempt to include public housing in the urban renewal scheme.[21]

Whereas private groups in Chicago took the lead quickly after the war to formulate urban redevelopment and renewal programs, city hall was less successful in establishing a partnership with the federal government to solve the housing crisis. Unlike the efforts of many other large cities to construct numerous public housing projects in the late 1940s and early 1950s, Chicago's attempts fell victim to bureaucratic conflicts and politics. In 1949 the CHA operated fewer than 8,000 low-income housing units while estimating that 272,000 families in the city lacked adequate lodging. On the very day that Congress passed the Wagner-Ellender-Taft Housing Act, which provided for a vast expansion of public housing construction, the CHA submitted a proposal to city hall to build 40,000 units of low-rent public housing over a six-year period. The CHA's plan called for building 40 percent of the public housing on vacant land; the rest of the construction would necessitate slum clearance.[22]

Prior to 1946, the CHA followed the "neighborhood composition rule," limiting the number of black residents of any particular public housing complex to the proportion of blacks in that area of the city. Desperately in need of temporary shelter for returning veterans, the CHA began construction that year on twenty-one sites in eleven wards that contained vacant land—invariably in outlying sections of white residence. To mollify white home owners fearful of a black invasion, Mayor Edward J. Kelly proposed that blacks be admitted to no more than 10 percent of the public housing vacancies citywide (their approximate proportion of Chicago's population). The CHA informally adopted this quota system, but any desegregation at all proved unacceptable to many whites residing in the bungalow belt. Token integration attempts at projects such as Airport Homes and Fernwood Park Homes led to violent resistance.[23]

After 1949 opposition to the location of public housing on vacant sites came from newly formed citizen groups such as the Southtown Planning Association, the Southwest Neighborhood Council, and the Taxpayers Action Committee. Influential citywide organizations such as the State Street Council, the Chicago Metropolitan Home Builders' Association, the Chicago Real Estate Board, the Chicago Mortgage Bankers' Association, and the Civic Federation of Chicago supported the ad hoc groups and established ties to such national federations as the National Association of Real Estate Boards, the U.S. Savings and Loan League, and the National Association of Home Builders. Such broadly based opposition including the involvement of so many powerful financial institutions made public housing a sensitive economic and political as well as social issue.[24]

In November 1949, the CHA submitted as the first installment of its construction program a list of seven sites (containing ten thousand units) to the city council, a committee of which promptly rejected five of them. Counterrecommendations made by the city council proved unacceptable to the CHA, which remained dedicated to the principle of scattered-site selection. Reflecting the desires of their constituents, the aldermen resisted the placement of low-income projects with black populations into their wards. After months of fruitless negotiations, the city council offered a compromise plan providing for 10,500 units on slum-cleared land and 2,000 units in vacant spaces, the relocation of 2,112 of the 12,465 families to be displaced, and a net gain of forty-seven units to the city's housing stock. Fearful that perpetual stalemate would result in no housing being built at all, the CHA reluctantly accepted the proposal. The federal government gave its approval in November 1951, fully two and a half years after the passage of the enabling legislation. As this episode clearly reveals, the powerful resistance to public housing in certain neighborhoods meant disappointment for the reformers hopeful of a timely amelioration of the housing crisis. By 1955 Chicago had been able to erect just twenty-six housing developments totaling 12,705 family units.[25]

The city council's crucial role in delaying public housing construction reveals how Chicago's government typically functioned at that time. At the conclusion of World War II, Mayor Edward J. Kelly still presided (if somewhat tenuously) over the powerful Democratic machine assembled by Anton Cermak in the early 1930s. Kelly had been installed in city hall when Mayor Cermak was killed in 1933 and, along with party chairman Pat Nash, had entrenched the fledgling Democratic machine in Cook County when elsewhere big city bosses were vanishing. Following the lead of Cermak (a Bohemian who had forced the party's dominant Irish element to accept other ethnic groups into his "house for all peoples"), the Kelly-Nash machine ensured loyalty by doling out patronage, favors, and political appointments to a broad spectrum of groups. Kelly nurtured Chicago's political machine by utilizing three important sources. First, he became a fervent supporter of Franklin D. Roosevelt's New Deal and kept the city solvent through the liberal use of federal funds at a time when the Great Depression provided the most serious threat to municipal governments. Second, he acquired additional financial resources from organized crime. By allowing the free operation of gambling, prostitution, and other forms of vice in his city, Kelly made Chicago a "wide-open town" and obtained more of the "grease" necessary to keep the political machine operating. Third, he actively cultivated the black vote, and his success paid huge dividends in later years when Chicago's black electorate increased dramatically.[26]

Kelly and Nash kept the fragile ethnic coalition together despite tensions inflamed most frequently by their fellow Irishmen. Mayor Kelly ruled autocratically, never needing to use the veto and only once seeing a measure he favored receive as many as twelve negative votes from the fifty-man city council. After his initial appointment to complete Cermak's unfinished term, Kelly was elected mayor in 1935, 1939, and 1943, but problems had arisen by 1947. Concerns surfaced about the septuagenarian mayor's age and flagging health, with the apparent increase in the number of scandals in municipal government (most notably in the public school system) and a rising public outcry against the highly visible presence of organized crime. But among leading Chicago Democrats, the greatest dissatisfaction with Kelly stemmed from his liberal policies on race. To the great dismay of many in the party, especially the Irish, the mayor took an uncompromising stand in favor of open housing and desegregated public schools. The party leadership persuaded Kelly not to seek reelection in 1947 and replaced him with a figurehead, civic leader Martin H. Kennelly.[27]

Although Kelly and Kennelly were both Irish Catholics from the Chicago neighborhood of Bridgeport, the two men had very little in common and behaved quite differently as mayors. Kelly had brooked no dissent and dictated policy to the city council members, who routinely rubber-stamped his initiatives. Ambitious aldermen and other party leaders who had chafed under Kelly's stern rule expected Kennelly simply to attend civic functions, to perform ceremonial duties, and to leave the business of politics and governance to the politicians. By and large, Kennelly complied. He said, "Chicago is a council-governed city. The aldermen are elected by the people of their districts. I don't think it's a function of the mayor to boss the aldermen." As a result, the locus of power shifted from the mayor's office to city council chambers. Whereas Kelly had regularly attended meetings of the key committees as well as plenary city council sessions, Kennelly absented himself from the day-to-day making of municipal policy; he seldom attended Democratic party meetings. With no political base of support and few allies in the city council, Kennelly's only influence emanated from whatever moral authority the mayor's office possessed. His leadership style was, at best, detached. As one public housing official caustically observed, "Kennelly's idea of a beautiful world is to sit around a table and have the opposing parties come to an agreement for which he would take the credit without ever opening his mouth."[28]

Disinclined to intrude in city council affairs, Kennelly rhetorically supported the attempt of the aldermen to exclude public housing from their wards. In the previous administration, Kelly guaranteed the CHA's autonomy and kept the patronage-hungry city council at bay. "They really hate us," said CHA executive secretary Elizabeth Wood, "They'd love to have that gravy." Kelly had seen the housing agency as a showplace and had enjoyed his reputation as the patron saint of public housing, but under Kennelly the situation changed radically. In 1948 black Republican alderman Archibald Carey Jr. introduced a bill that required nondiscrimination in all housing built with municipal funding or on land acquired through the city's power of eminent domain. Kennelly addressed the city council for the only time in his term to speak against the Carey ordinance, which the aldermen then defeated by thirty-one votes to thirteen.[29]

Martin Kennelly, white-haired, well groomed, and nattily dressed, seemed a dashing figure at public events, but even his admirers admitted that he contributed little of substance to city governance. With the mayor marginalized and power decentralized, the city council governed—or at least served as the arena in which the fifty aldermen defended their conflicting interests. Preoccupied with the mundane business of meeting the particular needs of their individual wards and satisfying their constituents, the aldermen seldom considered the larger issues affecting the city as a whole. A handful of the most powerful aldermen—the so-called Big Boys—made committee assignments, controlled the awarding of franchises, and regulated city business in the best interests of the Democratic party. While Mayor Kennelly looked the other way as self-interested aldermen transacted city business in a series of backroom deals, the few honest local legislators periodically registered ineffectual protestations.[30]

Mayor Kennelly's detachment had important consequences outside city hall, for he refused to address the sorry state of Chicago's public morality. Virgil Peterson of the Chicago Crime Commission said, "Mayor Kennelly is personally honest and he has stopped wide-open gambling in Chicago, but he's exerted little leadership in breaking the crime-politics alliance." Public outrage crested after the shotgun murder of a Republican ward committeeman in February 1952, an event that seemed to substantiate the suspected ties between politics and the underworld. More than 185 civic groups allied to form the Citizens of Greater Chicago, a blue-ribbon organization dedicated to destroying organized crime's influence in the police department and judicial system through legislative reform. But the Illinois General Assembly balked at passing tougher laws, and the Citizens of Greater Chicago could only promise to try again after the election of a new state legislature. As he had done throughout his years in office, Kennelly simply denied that organized crime exerted any influence in the city.[31]

At the mid-point of the twentieth century, the venal Democratic machine still ruled Chicago and, despite the election of an esteemed businessman as mayor, scandal and corruption continued to pervade local government. Martin Kennelly's apparent acquiescence to the spoilsmanship rampant in the city council and to the politicization of the school board and his stubborn refusal to acknowledge the ties between organized crime and city hall meant that the expectations of Chicago's reformers went unrealized. Postwar problems involving population and resource loss, inadequate services and facilities, crime, housing, and race plagued Chicago as they did other large U.S. cities. Especially portentous were the rising tensions between an expanding black population and a dwindling, defensive white majority. In the ten years following World War II, Chicago's political leadership provided painfully few solutions to these mounting problems. By 1955 a situation that many people saw as acute called for more effective leadership from city hall, although the source from which this new stewardship would arise remained unclear. Surely at that time few Chicagoans anticipated the launching of an urban renaissance by a Democratic machine politician, especially one as little known as the eleventh ward's nondescript Richard J. Daley.[32]

1

The Road to City Hall

Richard J. Daley hailed from Bridgeport, the cradle of Chicago mayors. Located on the south branch of the Chicago River approximately five miles southwest of downtown, Bridgeport had grown out of a settlement of Irish workers who were building the Illinois-Michigan Canal. After the canal's completion in 1848, economic activity came to center around the meat slaughtering industry. In 1865 several stockyards consolidated to form the Union Stockyards, a sprawling archipelago of cattle pens covering 355 acres. Nine railroads extended branches to serve the yards, and the invention of refrigerated cars in 1869 gave an additional boost to the expanding meatpacking industry. As Chicago became the abattoir of the nation, employment opportunities attracted numbers of immigrants to the city. After the Irish came Germans, Italians, Poles, Lithuanians, and other Eastern Europeans, each group carving out its own residential niche in the shadows of the stock pens. Other heavy industries subsequently located in Bridgeport, which over the years remained a grimy working-class community of white ethnic population that abutted the huge black community to the east.[1]

In Bridgeport's patchwork quilt of ethnic groups, tight-knit communities formed around numerous Roman Catholic parishes and a few scattered Protestant churches. Catholic churches operated parochial schools that many communicants found preferable to public education, and this reinforced the clannishness of Bridgeport's nationalistic enclaves. Similarly, the many and varied neighborhood saloons catered to homogeneous working-class clienteles. At a time when workers and their families squeezed into cramped living quarters, the saloons served as social gathering places where customers drank, ate, and exchanged gossip. Taverns also provided meeting space for organized labor groups before union halls could be built; they served as political forums, most conspicuously for the Irish whose success in attaining elective office became legendary in nineteenth-century American cities.[2]

The Irish owed their success in politics to their affinity with the English language and a wealth of experience with democratic institutions in their native land. In the 1820s, a grassroots movement in Ireland forced the British to grant Catholics political representation; as early as the 1830s, Chicagoans complained about undue Irish political activity. Following the lead of their fellow Irish in New York City and Boston, from the earliest days of settlement newcomers to Chicago embraced the Democratic party. The party of Thomas Jefferson and Andrew Jackson evinced a sincere interest in the workingmen's welfare and opposed the xenophobic Know-Nothing movement of the pre–Civil War days. The Democratic party consistently took anti-nativist, anti-abolitionist, and anti-temperance positions and repeatedly reinforced its opposition to personal liberty laws in order to appeal to many old stock voters. Unskilled jobs remained plentiful throughout the nineteenth century in Bridgeport, but many of the Irish saw politics as a more attractive avenue of upward mobility than labor. As a result, they entered careers as policemen and firemen as well as full-time politicians and thus contributed disproportionately to Chicago's growing municipal workforce.[3]

Richard J. Daley was born in Bridgeport on May 15, 1902, the only child of second-generation Irish Catholic immigrants. His father, Michael Daley, was a sheetmetal worker and business agent in the Sheet Metal Workers Union; old-timers remembered him as unassuming and taciturn. His mother, Lillian (Dunne) Daley, was eight years older than her husband and by all accounts the dominant personality in their household. Lillian Daley was a community activist who took her young son along when she marched in women's suffrage parades and spent long hours doing volunteer work for various religious and civic organizations. The family attended daily mass and communion at nearby Nativity of Our Lord Church, where Daley was baptized, took his first communion, and served as an altar boy.[4]

Young Daley attended the parochial elementary school run by the nuns at the Nativity Church and graduated in 1915. Because they had only one child to support, Daley's parents could afford to spend money on their son, and he wore newer clothing than did the other neighborhood boys. He was, said Len O'Connor, "the best-dressed kid in Bridgeport and the only one known to carry a clean handkerchief." As did most children at that time, though, Daley worked at a series of part-time and weekend jobs, hawking newspapers at streetcar stops and delivering produce from a horse-drawn vegetable cart.[5]

In 1916 Daley enrolled at De La Salle Institute, a Catholic commercial high school run by the Christian Brothers Order. At De La Salle, located several blocks east of Bridgeport in a black residential area, the predominantly Irish student body took courses in typing, bookkeeping, and shorthand, as well as in religion and in a smattering of traditional academic subjects. For poor Irish Catholic families, secretarial work presented an avenue of escape from the hog houses and tanneries; the school's alumni included four mayors, dozens of judges, commissioners, and lesser officeholders. Daley's clerical skills later proved useful in his career, as historian John M. Allswang has noted, "for it put [him] in a position where more than one superior would find him indispensable." Daley did not excel academically. Former classmates remembered him as quiet, hardworking, slightly above average in intelligence, but not a scholar by any means. His class graduated in June 1919.[6]

After completing high school, Daley began working for Dolan, Ludeman, and Company, a stockyards commission house. In the mornings he rode horses and herded cattle up the ramps to the slaughterhouses; in the afternoons he moved into the offices to perform clerical tasks. In his leisure time, Daley participated in the activities of the Hamburg Social and Athletic Club, one of many similar organizations that thrived in Chicago during the early twentieth century. Athletic clubs such as the Hamburg, Ragen's Colts, Our Flag, the Standard, and Aylwards—often referred to as youth gangs—sponsored softball teams, political debates, and other activities principally for adolescent males. Rumbles between these neighborhood gangs tarnished their image of rough respectability, but Daley swore in later years that critics unfairly exaggerated their reputation for violence. He served as the club's president for fifteen years, beginning in 1924.[7]

Five years earlier, the Hamburgers had played a leading role in one of the dramatic events of that era, the Chicago race riot of 1919, in which rioters killed fifteen whites and twenty-three blacks and burned one thousand homes. During the four-day conflagration, according to the Illinois Commission of Human Relations, 41 percent of the encounters occurred in and around Daley's Bridgeport neighborhood. Furthermore, concluded the commission, without the incendiary participation of the white athletic clubs, "it is doubtful if the riot would have gone beyond the first clash." Members of the Hamburg Club had fought in the front line against their black antagonists. Had Daley? In later years, he never responded directly to reporters' questions about the events of that summer. Neither eyewitness accounts nor arrest reports confirm his involvement; no evidence at all survives to substantiate his critics' claim that such a prominent club member surely must have been involved in the altercation. But as either a participant or an observer, the seventeen-year-old Daley could not have ignored the eruption of tribalism that suffused the Irish South Side. He understood the depth of the racial antipathies harbored by his neighbors and, considering the narrow provincialism of his Bridgeport upbringing, he probably shared them to a considerable degree.[8]

Whereas the members of the Hamburg Club quickly responded to calls to defend their turf, their primary activity was to support the Democratic party. Indeed, Daley's elevation to the club presidency indicated his coming of age politically. At the age of twenty-one, he became personal secretary to his alderman and ward committeeman, Joseph "Big Joe" McDonough. A six-foot-three-inch, three-hundred-pound former football star at Villanova University, McDonough took a liking to the young Daley and appointed him a precinct captain and city council clerk. With the powerful boss of the eleventh ward as his patron, Daley quickly established himself as a rising star in Bridgeport's Democratic party.[9]

As McDonough's personal secretary, Daley frequently tended the home fires in the eleventh ward while the alderman was busy downtown. At ward headquarters, Daley observed the lifeblood of politics: the dispensation of patronage, the awarding or withholding of favors, the martialing of the electorate, vote counting, and the exchange of money (some of it illegal) among politicians and businessmen. In city council chambers, as Mike Royko detailed, "he was able to observe how driveway permits were sold to property owners, how and why rate increases were granted to utilities and public transportation lines, how rezoning could send a piece of property spiraling in value with the stroke of a pen, and where the bottles were kept in the cloak room."[10] These were the years of a fledgling politician's education in the wheeling and dealing of a city government known for its ethical laxity.

Daley also learned about the rough-and-tumble of Chicago politics. An opportunistic pragmatist, Joe McDonough allied with Bohemian Anton Cermak in intraparty wrangles against other Irish Democrats. In the struggle for power within the party, many of the old-line pols from the more affluent communities south and west of the eleventh ward (the so-called lace-curtain Irish) looked down upon parvenus like McDonough as "pig-shit Irish." Unlike other ambitious young Irishmen, McDonough was willing to cross the ethnic boundaries, and as Cermak rose in influence so did his acolyte.[11]

In 1922 Cermak was elected president of the Cook County Board of Commissioners, a position that allowed McDonough to distribute county patronage jobs to Bridgeport loyalists. Cermak sought the mayoralty of Chicago; but under the leadership of such Irish stalwarts as Roger Sullivan and his successor, George Brennan, the Democratic party denied Cermak the nomination. In 1923 they chose reformist Judge William Dever, who promised to restore the city's good name. Incumbent Republican William Hale "Big Bill" Thompson's laissez-faire attitude toward organized crime had virtually relinquished the city to Al Capone and his henchmen, but during the next four years, Dever succeeded in driving the hoodlums out of Chicago into suburban Cicero. Unfortunately for Dever, who fashioned a very competent administration, Chicagoans longed for the greater personal liberty afforded by Thompson; they especially rued Dever's zealous enforcement of Prohibition. In 1927 Big Bill defeated Dever and restored Republican rule to city hall. Cermak's rise continued, as he won reelection as county board president and became party chairman when Brennan died in 1928.[12]

In 1930 Cermak rewarded McDonough for his loyalty, slating him to run for county treasurer. McDonough won the election and took Daley along with him to continue his secretarial duties. During the next four years Daley acted as an administrative assistant and much more, for McDonough spent little time in the county treasurer's office; he preferred, instead, to carouse in speakeasies and gamble at area racetracks. While the county treasurer enjoyed the perquisites of office and lived in the grand style, Daley the drudge became master of the counting house. Although not the elected official, Daley was doing the job, and along the way he gained invaluable experience, mastering the minutiae of budget balancing, debits, credits, and bottom lines. Much of Daley's later reputation as a mayoral financial wizard can be attributed to the experience gained during these apprenticeship years. And, of course, he also acquainted himself with the intricacies of political patronage on a larger scale than he had done before.[13]

Concurrent with his gradually ascending the lower rungs of the Democratic party ladder, Daley pursued the coveted credential sought by many Chicago politicians, a DePaul University law degree. Beginning in 1923, he attended classes in the evenings—four nights a week almost without surcease for eleven years—and graduated in 1934. (Daley nominally practiced law from 1936 to 1955, but his partner, William J. Lynch, handled most of the work.) During this time, he also pursued the hand of an Irish Catholic woman from neighboring Canaryville, Eleanor Guilfoyle, whom he began dating in 1929 and married seven years later. Deliberate, meticulous, careful, cautious, Daley progressed slowly but steadily in all areas of his life; in the quest of an educational degree, in the courtship of the woman he loved, and in his success in the competitive game of politics, he identified goals and pursued them with dogged determination. Eventually, in all these matters, his persistence paid off.[14]

In 1931 party chairman Cermak finally ran for mayor despite the misgivings of the Irish. Forging a coalition of Czechs, Poles, Germans, and Jews, in addition to the reluctant and occasionally recalcitrant Irish, Cermak put together an ethnically balanced ticket and ran on a platform of opposition to prohibition. Big Bill Thompson snidely referred to his opponent as "Pushcart Tony" and "Tony Baloney," but the nativistic slurs backfired as Chicago's heterogeneous population rallied behind the Democratic candidate. Cermak won the election handily and, seeking to mollify the Irish, chose twenty-eighth ward committeeman Patrick A. Nash to succeed him as Cook County Democratic chairman. (In fact, Cermak continued to administer party affairs while Nash served as little more than a figurehead.) This delicate coalition assembled by Cermak somehow cohered: it became the most powerful Democratic political organization in Chicago's history—and the political machine that Richard J. Daley would one day inherit.[15]

In 1933 Cermak's brief reign came to an abrupt end. A deranged assassin, aiming at president-elect Franklin D. Roosevelt, fatally shot the Chicago mayor instead. The most ambitious of the Irish—

including city council finance committee chairman and third ward alderman John S. Clark, nineteenth ward alderman John Duffy, and county commissioner Dan Ryan—along with Jewish twenty-fourth ward alderman Jacob Arvey emerged as the primary aspirants to succeed Cermak. Pat Nash was also considered a leading candidate but took himself out of the running because, at age seventy and in faltering health, he was reluctant to assume such a burdensome job. Nash did, however, assert his right as party chairman to choose the new mayor and arranged for the Democratic-controlled state legislature to pass a law authorizing the selection of a new mayor from outside the city council. Nash's choice was Edward J. Kelly. Chief engineer of the Chicago Sanitary District and president of the South Park Board, Kelly had never held elective office but had long been a leading figure in the city's Democracy. Most important, he was an Irish Catholic from Bridgeport.[16]

With Irish rule restored to the Chicago Democratic party, Kelly and Nash wisely held out olive branches to the leaders of other ethnic groups. Rather than sunder the union assembled by Cermak, they took steps to strengthen it. To the growing disparagement of some of the more chauvinistic Irishmen, the Kelly-Nash machine made available new leadership positions to Jewish, German, and Polish politicians, opening the doors to what historian John M. Allswang has called "A House for All Peoples." The new bosses' magnanimity toward Cermak's former allies benefited Daley—whose mentor, Joe McDonough, remained in the good graces of the Democratic party leaders.[17]

In 1934 Joe McDonough contracted pneumonia and died. Daley remained in the county treasurer's office for the next two years, assisting McDonough's three successors, Tom Nash, Robert Sweitzer, and Joe Gill. Although Daley may well have seen himself as the eleventh ward's next leader, the Kelly-Nash decision makers downtown thought otherwise, choosing Hugh "Babe" Connelly as the eleventh ward's committeeman and Thomas Doyle its new alderman. Daley may have been more popular and certainly more able, but Connelly and Doyle had more seniority in the party. One year later Doyle died, and Connelly installed himself as alderman. Ever patient, and a loyal company man, Daley again masked his disappointment and waited.[18]

His rise in the eleventh ward hierarchy stalled by Babe Connelly's sudden good fortune, Daley's breakthrough came in an unusual fashion. Fifteen days before the 1936 biennial elections, one of

Bridgeport's state representatives, Republican David Shanahan, died. Each Illinois district had three representatives in the state legislature, two from the majority party and one from the minority, so Shanahan's successor would have to be elected as a Republican. With Shanahan's name already printed on the ballots, Daley launched an intensive write-in campaign that resulted in his election by 5,218 votes over Republican Robert E. Rogers. Ironically, Daley won his first elective office on the Republican ticket and sat on the Democratic side of the Illinois House of Representatives only after passage of a special resolution.[19]

While serving in the state legislature in Springfield, Daley maintained his ties to Chicago. In December 1936, Cook County Clerk Michael J. Flynn appointed him chief deputy county comptroller, replacing yet another deceased Irishman, Michael O'Connor. In addition to the second paycheck it provided, Daley's job in the county clerk's office was valuable for the insights it offered him into Democratic party affairs, especially patronage allocation. Through the job, Daley earned more valuable experience in the distribution of resources in large-scale governmental bureaucracies. Most important, he saw how politicians in power used municipal funds to reward the party faithful.[20]

In 1938 death again intervened on Daley's behalf. Democratic state senator Patrick J. Carroll, whose district included part of the eleventh ward, passed away, and the young representative successfully campaigned for his seat—this time as a Democrat. Daley quickly established a good reputation as a hardworking, effective state senator, prompting the silk-stocking Legislative Voters League to observe that he "has made rather an outstanding record for a new member."[21] He served two four-year terms in the Illinois legislature's upper house, which the Republicans controlled by a three-to-one margin, and in 1941 he rose to the position of senate minority leader. Daley also served as Mayor Kelly's man in Springfield, the recognized spokesman for the interests of the Chicago Democratic machine.

Daley served for eight years in a state legislature noteworthy for its relaxed moral standards and the generally low quality of its elected officials. Springfield, Illinois, the state capital, took on a sybaritic air when the legislature convened, complete with poker games, offtrack betting, party girls, and an unending flow of alcohol. Lobbyists plied willing legislators with graft or lost handsome sums to them in friendly card games. Not all politicians were on the take, of course, but the few who shunned the illegal perquisites of elected office became the subjects of considerable comment. Daley was one of these few. State senator Botchy Connors, another member of the Kelly-Nash delegation, said of his Chicago colleague: "You can't give that guy a nickel, that's how honest he is."[22] While others lined their pockets at every opportunity, Daley went to mass daily and avoided any hint of impropriety. While others sampled the capital's lively nightlife, Daley worked in his hotel room and went on long walks with fellow Chicago state senators Abe Marovitz and Ben Adamowski. While others set up housekeeping with nubile young typists, the newly wedded Daley called home nightly and remained faithful to his wife. He was a Roman Catholic Puritan in Babylon.

Despite its sordid reputation for graft and corruption, the Kelly-Nash machine exhibited a brand of New Deal liberalism that often made it the most progressive force for change in the Illinois legislature, and Daley acted as its chief spokesman. He argued for the reduction of regressive sales taxes on several occasions and in 1939 introduced a bill requiring a 2 percent levy on individual and corporate income to reduce the tax burden on the lower classes. (The bill was defeated, and Illinois failed to adopt a state income tax until thirty years later.) Perhaps his greatest achievement in Springfield—and arguably the seminal contribution of Ed Kelly's fourteen-year mayoralty—was the unification of Chicago's bankrupt surface and elevated train lines into one public transportation system. As Kelly's point man in Springfield, Daley oversaw the legislation that created the Chicago Transit Authority. In 1945 political columnist Milburn P. Akers said of Daley, "[He] is probably the best exhibit of the hard-working, decent, honest organization politician that the Kelly machine can produce."[23]

By the end of World War II, the presence of a reputable office-holder in the increasingly infamous Chicago Democratic machine seemed remarkable indeed. Pat Nash died in 1943, and Ed Kelly's attempt to be both mayor and party chairman met with scalding criticism from the media and high-ranking Democrats. Critics complained that the seventy-year-old Kelly, who suffered from a series of physical ailments, lacked the vitality to do the job. They also despaired at Chicago's sullied image—a result, they felt, of Kelly's inattention to municipal housekeeping. A series of scandals, most notably in the school system and the police department, and official tolerance of organized crime seemed a throwback to the wild Big Bill Thompson era of the 1920s. Most distressing to the South Side Irish,

Kelly seemed to have fallen victim to the virus of racial egalitarianism, throwing his administration's support behind open housing and public school desegregation. Scandals of every stripe had surfaced over the years and the Democratic party had always survived brief flurries of public indignation, but party insiders would not tolerate city hall's imprimatur of racial integration.[24]

The mayor's declining popularity and the taint of corruption bedeviling the Democratic party convinced Kelly of the need to field a slate of high caliber in the 1946 elections. The *Chicago Daily News* lauded Daley as one of the Democrats' "brightest stars. Together with County Chairman J. M. Arvey, Alderman George D. Kells (28th) and others, he represented the younger pro-Roosevelt element upon which the Democrats hoped to rebuild as their elder members fell by the wayside." Kelly accordingly chose Daley to run for the politically sensitive office of Cook County sheriff, which had been occupied in the past by a series of rogues, crooks, and embezzlers. Because innumerable opportunities for graft existed and the sheriffs could not be reelected, most of them (in the words of Mike Royko) "got in, got it, and got out." Daley's record of integrity made him a perfect candidate for sheriff, and Kelly chose him hoping to salvage the machine's sinking fortunes in what was shaping up to be a Republican year. Daley must surely have had misgivings about running for a position that had frequently been a political dead end—Cook County sheriffs got rich or indicted, but seldom advanced to higher offices—while giving up his secure state senate seat. But he bowed to the will of his superiors and dutifully campaigned against his opponent, Republican Elmer Walsh. He lost his only election, a setback that hurt deeply at the time but that in the long run doubtlessly helped his career. Escaping the albatross of the Cook County sheriff's office, Daley continued as deputy county comptroller and awaited new opportunities for advancement.[25]

The 1946 election debacle, in which Republicans won a host of offices in addition to county sheriff, further damaged Kelly's declining reputation as a party leader. As a result, the party chose as its new chairman the city council finance committee chairman Jacob Arvey. Because the Jewish vote was dwindling in Chicago, Arvey lacked substantial electoral support and the anti-Kelly Irish saw little likelihood of him amassing greater power; he would serve as a custodian until one of the other aspirants could supplant Kelly. In 1947 Arvey and other party leaders persuaded the mayor not to seek reelection, showing him the results of public opinion polls detailing his fallen popularity. To burnish the Democrats' lackluster image, Arvey chose nonpartisan civic reformer Martin Kennelly to replace Kelly. A wealthy moving van magnate and another Bridgeport Irish Catholic, Kennelly had become well known as vice president of the Chicago Association of Commerce and Industry, Red Cross fund drive chairman, DePaul University trustee, and member of the Federal Reserve Bank's industrial advisory committee. The politically inexperienced Kennelly could serve as a caretaker in city hall while the real contenders continued to jockey for position. Because no faction had the power to seize control, the professional politicians patiently indulged Kennelly's lofty campaign rhetoric, privately referred to him as "Snow White" and "Fartin' Martin," and publicly applauded his election.[26]

Daley's ascent continued in 1947. He convened a meeting of eleventh ward precinct captains, at which they ratified his replacement of the indolent Babe Connelly as ward committeeman. Citing poor health, Connelly bowed to the fait accompli and resigned shortly thereafter. At long last, Daley possessed a seat on the Cook County Democratic Central Committee, the organization of fifty ward committeemen and thirty suburban township committeemen that charted the party's course. Because the eleventh ward routinely turned out huge vote majorities for Democratic candidates, its committeeman enjoyed special status. The forty-five-year-old Daley immediately joined the ranks of the central committee's elite inner circle.[27]

In 1947 Chairman Arvey bought himself some time with the election of a Democratic mayor, but no one doubted the precariousness of his tenure. Lack of success in the 1948 elections could jeopardize Arvey's position, and because of Republicanism's national resurgence the eager Irish anticipated a repeat of 1946. Following his earlier success of slating an apolitical reformer, Arvey confounded the party sachems by recommending two blue-ribbon candidates at the head of the 1948 ticket: public-spirited lawyer and grandson of a former U.S. vice president, Adlai E. Stevenson, for governor; and University of Chicago economist and liberal city council gadfly, Paul H. Douglas, for U.S. senator. A majority of the central committee reluctantly went along with the selections, perhaps because they considered defeat imminent and knew that Arvey would take the blame. To virtually everyone's surprise, Stevenson and Douglas won easily, and huge victory margins in Cook County helped President Harry Truman carry Illinois. Political pundits throughout the nation hailed

Arvey as a genius, a progressive machine politician with savvy and vision. Momentarily derailed, the South Side Irish grudgingly set aside their plans for revolt.[28]

Arvey recommended several people for critical jobs in Governor Stevenson's new administration, including Richard J. Daley for the position of state director of revenue. Daley's extensive financial experience in the Cook County comptroller's office and his solid record as a state senator made him the ideal nominee for the governor's cabinet, and Stevenson enthusiastically appointed him. Unlike so many other products of the Kelly-Nash machine, Daley had managed to keep his reputation unsoiled, and the press applauded the governor's choice. Milburn P. Akers of the anti-machine *Chicago Sun-Times* said, "If Adlai Stevenson can induce a few more men of Daley's unique qualifications—ability, political experience and integrity—to associate themselves with him for the next four years he will do much to assure the success of his administration."[29]

At Arvey's behest, Daley also acted as a liaison between the neophyte governor and the members of the Cook County legislative delegation. Refined, cultured, and somewhat reticent, Stevenson had little in common with most Chicago politicians, and his attempts at communication tended to be strained—especially with senate Democratic leader Botchy Connors, a salty pol of the old school. But with a foot firmly planted in each of two worlds, in the patronage-hungry Chicago wards and the corridors of Springfield government buildings, Daley kept the communication lines open and proved an invaluable asset to the governor. By all accounts, Stevenson appreciated Daley's efforts and also genuinely liked him. Adlai Stevenson III called the link between his father and the state revenue director "a close relationship, an important relationship from my father's standpoint." The younger Stevenson recalled, "it was close enough, and enough mutual respect and confidence, if not friendship, developed that that relationship developed well beyond the gubernatorial years."[30]

Daley served as state revenue director for fifteen months before a better opportunity opened up for him in Chicago. Once again, death claimed another influential Democrat—this time, Cook County Clerk Michael J. Flynn. The county clerk supervised elections, recorded births and deaths, issued marriage licenses, and maintained other vital statistics. Although these matters hardly seem important, Chicago politicians coveted the position because of its generous salary and control of three hundred patronage workers. The

Cook County Board appointed the trustworthy Daley to fill the remaining year of Flynn's term. The sudden promotion allowed Daley to return to Chicago, where his ambitions truly lay, and he eagerly prepared to retain the office in the regular election the following November.[31]

Daley won easily in 1950, an otherwise disastrous year for Chicago Democrats. Several months before the election, U.S. senator Estes Kefauver's Committee to Investigate Organized Crime in Interstate Commerce held hearings in the city as part of its highly publicized national fact-finding tour. For the first several days, the closed-door sessions produced no sensational disclosures (at least nothing that became public knowledge). But shortly before the election, an enterprising newspaper reporter published a copy of the secret testimony given the committee by a Chicago police captain, Daniel "Tubbo" Gilbert. The Democratic candidate that year for Cook County sheriff, Gilbert had volunteered to testify and proceeded to explain how he had become a wealthy man on a modest civil servant's salary. He owed his good fortune, including negotiable securities valued at $360,000, to extraordinary success at gambling. No, he unabashedly admitted to his interrogators, his betting on baseball games, prize fights, and political elections was not legal. Moreover, Gilbert artlessly commented, he felt that there was nothing wrong in his actions and the situation that permitted them.[32]

The newspapers quickly dubbed Gilbert the "World's Richest Cop," and the scandal became front page news nationwide. With an admitted crook on the verge of becoming Cook County's top law enforcement officer, all the ignominy of the not-so-distant Kelly years resurfaced in the minds of Chicago voters. An outraged electorate defeated Gilbert, along with the Democratic candidates for a host of other offices. Without Cook County support, U.S. Senate majority leader Scott Lucas lost to little-known downstate Republican Everett M. Dirksen. Admired only a short time before as a political wizard, party chairman Jacob Arvey was suddenly seen as the blunderer who slated Tubbo Gilbert and consequently brought down the whole Democratic ticket in Illinois. Only county clerk Daley emerged unscathed.[33]

As Arvey's support in the central committee evaporated, Daley hoped to supplant him, but other contenders also had designs on the party chairmanship. Daley's loyalty to Kelly and Arvey had paid dividends in his gradual rise in the party ranks, but not all of the South Side Irish were so enamored of the recent party leadership's liberal acceptance of other ethnic voting blocs. Nineteenth ward boss Tom Nash, city council finance committee chairman John Duffy, fourteenth ward alderman Clarence Wagner, and former fourteenth ward alderman Judge James McDermott united in opposition to Daley's advance. In the wake of the 1950 electoral disaster, Democratic leaders wanted to avoid a public power struggle and chose sixty-six-year-old municipal court clerk Joe Gill to replace Arvey; Gill, an unthreatening party elder, agreed to serve through the 1952 presidential election. Daley, who counted Gill among his allies in the party, settled for the office of first vice chairman.[34]

Daley's inability to seize the chairmanship of the central committee meant that he did not have the support to run for mayor—but neither did his rivals. So the Democrats resigned themselves in 1951 to accepting Martin Kennelly for another term. In many respects, Kennelly's four years in city hall had served the party well. Personally popular, the silver-haired mayor cut a dashing figure snipping ribbons, speaking at official functions, and giving bland speeches extolling civic rectitude. His list of achievements included the establishment of an independent school board, the creation of a central purchasing system for city government, and the launching of several urban renewal projects. Because of his naïveté, Kennelly remained unaware of much that went on in Chicago, and the city council enjoyed a free hand to legislate in the best interests of the Democratic machine. In one particular instance, however, Kennelly's behavior nettled party leaders. Taking his own reformist rhetoric seriously, the mayor avidly pursued civil service reform, and his efforts to reduce the number of patronage workers on the city payroll resulted in the removal of approximately twelve thousand jobs from machine control. But such mischief notwithstanding, party leaders enjoyed considerable freedom because of Kennelly's hands-off style of management and believed that they could tolerate him for a while longer.[35]

Not so William Levi Dawson, the powerful black U.S. congressman from Illinois's first congressional district. Second ward committeeman and the dominant politician in the sprawling South Side ghetto, Dawson commanded considerable respect in the Cook County Central Committee; and he despised Kennelly. In keeping with his reformist image, Kennelly had initiated police campaigns to root out two illegal activities in the black community. First, he targeted the unlicensed "jitney" cabs, owned by blacks, that operated on the South Side where the city's regulated cab companies pro-

vided irregular service. Blacks argued that they relied on these renegade cabs, which also created jobs for taxi drivers who were not
hired by downtown companies, but Kennelly would not overlook
their failure to obtain expensive city licenses. He also took aim at the
policy operation, an illegal lottery that thrived in the South Side.
With no efforts being made to curtail comparable forms of betting in
white neighborhoods, Dawson charged, this was an affront to the
black community. By targeting only black policy wheels, Kennelly
allowed the syndicate to assume control of the numbers game that
had long constituted a significant part of the black underground
economy. The mayor's crusade damaged Dawson's political fortunes, because policy wheel operators contributed considerable
sums of protection money to the ward organizations. Compounding
his offense, Kennelly dismissed Dawson's complaints with haughty
contempt. So, when the central committee met to renominate the
mayor, Dawson's representative calmly announced that the congressman found Kennelly unacceptable. Two other black leaders—
third ward committeeman Christopher Wimbish and twentieth
ward committeeman Kenneth Campbell—joined Dawson's revolt.[36]

Dawson returned from Washington for a special meeting with
Kennelly and sternly lectured the chastened mayor on the realities
of Chicago politics. Pacing the floor on his wooden leg, Dawson
screamed, "Who do you think you are? I bring in the votes. I elect
you. You are not needed, but the votes are needed. I deliver the votes
to you, but you won't talk to me?" After a lengthy harangue that left
Kennelly shaken and humiliated, Dawson privately agreed with
party leaders to allow the mayor one more term—but only one
more. Although Kennelly did not know it, he would begin his second term as a lame duck.[37]

Daley knew it, however, and resumed his quest for the party
chairmanship as the stepping stone to the mayoralty. With the support of municipal court clerk Joe Gill and municipal court bailiff Al
Horan, county clerk Daley controlled most of the party's patronage.
On July 8, 1953, Gill tendered his resignation at a plenary meeting of
the Cook County Democratic Central Committee, which immediately took up the business of choosing a successor. Arvey and Gill
lobbied in Daley's behalf, but in a lengthy and acrimonious meeting,
the South Side Irish clique of Tom Nash, John Duffy, Clarence Wagner, and Jim McDermott managed to forestall a decision. While Kennelly had routinely busied himself with ceremonial functions, finance committee chairman Wagner had virtually run the city

council since 1950, and his mayoral aspirations presented the greatest obstacle to Daley's claim on the chairmanship. Wagner's motion for a two-week postponement passed, and Daley's elevation, which had seemed assured just hours before, suddenly appeared problematical. Before the next meeting, however, Wagner died in an automobile accident and with him perished the insurgency. On July 21, 1953, the central committee met again and without fanfare quietly elected Daley.[38]

At the age of fifty-one, after thirty years in politics, with two successful tours of duty in Springfield and varied experience in different municipal posts in Cook County, Richard J. Daley became the head of Chicago's Democratic party. Although the general public did not appreciate Martin Kennelly's tenuous status, political insiders recognized Daley as the party's likely mayoral candidate in 1955 and cursorily dismissed his pledge that "I am not now or have I been a candidate for mayor." Still largely detached from party affairs, Kennelly blithely assumed he would be renominated, even though he had not been asked to speak at party fund-raisers and rallies in the fall of 1954. On December 1, 1954, Kennelly called a press conference to announce his intention to run for reelection and on December 14 opened his reelection headquarters downtown. Asked if he would make the party chairman's customary visit to the opening of the headquarters, Daley replied: "No, I have to take my kids to see Santa Claus."[39]

The Chicago newspapers understood the mayor's situation, even if he himself did not. The *Chicago Tribune* sourly observed, "The grafters and fixers, the policy racketeers and others who can't do business with Kennelly and his department heads are yearning for a city administration they can do business with." The paper also identified Daley as the machine's likely mayoral candidate, adding that the party chairman—a good family man and dedicated public servant—would be the unwitting dupe of the party's worst elements. Daley would be "the candidate of those who wish to load the city's offices once again with political payrollers and thus undo the great work of Mayor Kennelly in giving the City a real merit system of appointments and promotions."[40]

On December 15, 1954, Kennelly appeared before the Cook County Democratic party's slate-making committee, a rite of orthodoxy necessary for all aspiring candidates. Chairman Daley attended even though he was not on the twelve-member committee. As his audience sat stoically, Kennelly read a six-paragraph statement and then put away his text. An awkward silence followed. Kennelly asked if there were questions. More silence. Finally, committee chairman Joe Gill said, "Thank you, Mr. Mayor." Kennelly departed three minutes and fifty-six seconds after entering the conference room. Pale and shaken, he made a few perfunctory remarks to the press and headed back to city hall. When asked why he had attended the conclave, Daley told reporters, "My office as chairman is next door to the room where the committee is meetin'; I pop in now and then." Was he a candidate for mayor? "That's up to the committee," he replied.[41]

On December 20, the slate-making committee made its recommendations to the fifty Democratic ward committeemen. Joe Gill announced that the committee had "drafted" Daley to run for mayor, a choice ratified by a vote of forty-nine to one (Cook County assessor Frank Keenan voted for Kennelly). At last fully roused against the party bosses and determined to fight for renomination, an indignant Kennelly said, "The issue is now out in the open. The phony 'draft' is over. The question is whether the people of Chicago will rule or be ruled by the willfull, wanton inner-circle of political bosses at the Morrison Hotel." Daley expressed gratification at his selection and answered reporters' questions briefly. Why had the mayor been dumped after two terms? Because he had failed to unite the people, said Daley. In what way? "Where hasn't he failed?" came Daley's quick retort. He denied Kennelly's charges of duplicity in the nominating process. "In all the words that have been written about me in the daily press," Daley asserted, "I am proud that not a single one has criticized my conduct in public or private life."[42]

Because politicians believed that a great advantage accrued to the candidate who had his name listed first on the ballot and that distinction went to the first candidate to file nominating petitions on the designated day, Kennelly's men oversaw the opening of the U.S. mailbags at the city clerk's office as soon as the doors opened on December 29. Confidently, they watched as a deputy clerk stamped the time of arrival on the Kennelly petitions. Moments later, however, they saw a separate mailbag containing Daley's petitions, which had been brought into the office through a side door and stamped with an earlier arrival time. Kennelly's men protested the apparent chicanery but could prove nothing. The political machine was already taking care of even the smallest details of Daley's campaign.[43]

Kennelly's election strategy became apparent immediately. He intended to lead an old-fashioned crusade of the city's best elements against the benighted forces of bossism and corruption while defending the achievements of his eight years in office against the ravenous designs of the boodlers and spoilers primed to raid the public till. Kennelly would have to appeal to the Republican "newspaper wards" on the city's periphery to counter the inner-city "river wards," traditionally the area of greatest machine strength. With the support of the city's corporate moguls, he had no difficulty raising a sizable war chest; money was never a problem for Kennelly. The mayor used television often and effectively, his dignified manner and oratorical skills put to good use, but the question remained whether Kennelly's broadcast eloquence could offset the machine's patronage army that was motivated by self-interest. "Television is our precinct captain," proudly proclaimed one of the mayor's aides. "Can you ask your television set for a favor?" countered Daley.[44]

Kennelly repeatedly charged that his opponent would dismantle the set of civil service reforms so carefully assembled during the past eight years, politicize the public schools, and tolerate police corruption so that gambling, prostitution, and other organized crime might flourish. Despite Daley's apparently enviable public record, charged the mayor, he was a product of the Democratic machine; he owed his nomination to the cabal of scheming politicians who directed its activities and, if elected, would always be beholden to its grasping precinct captains. Daley heatedly denied any intention of tampering with civil service, pledged to protect the schools' autonomy, and promised to safeguard the integrity of the police commissioner by moving his office from city hall to central police headquarters. He approved of the Kennelly reforms and intended to expand on them for the greater good of all the citizenry. Daley's image also benefited from the support of Adlai Stevenson, who as governor had not worked harmoniously with Kennelly. Much to the dismay of Chicago's lakeshore liberals, Stevenson recounted Daley's splendid service as state revenue director and heartily endorsed him for mayor.[45]

Kennelly also dragged racial issues into the campaign, linking the Democratic machine, organized crime, and the black community in what an earlier machine critic called the "dictatorship from the dark." The mayor singled out Congressman Dawson as the man responsible for the machine's decision not to renominate him (an analysis endorsed by the local media). The *Chicago Defender* excoriated Kennelly for his tacit endorsement of segregated public housing and the racially discriminatory practices of his police department. Daley defended his association with Dawson, saying, "Why is it that when a man becomes successful in politics he becomes a boss? I say Bill Dawson is a real leader. Never in my fifteen years in political life has he asked me to do anything that wasn't right."[46]

The *Chicago Tribune* reported that Daley intended to resign as party chairman during his mayoral campaign. Daley neither affirmed nor denied the report (just as he had remained mute when Jacob Arvey advised him not to appear unduly ambitious by pursuing both offices), but the belief that he planned to resign gained currency in the following weeks and defused fears that he would amass enough power as both mayor and party chief to dominate the city in the classic boss fashion. Undoubtedly, party leaders feared the concentration of too much power in one man's hands because of the loss of influence it would mean for them; public-spirited citizens feared bossism for its certain damage to democratic institutions. In any event, Daley's campaign sought to distance the candidate from the more odious practices of boss politics, and the rumor of his impending resignation as Democratic party chairman aided in that effort.[47]

Daley waged an energetic campaign, giving speeches at ward organizations and labor union halls throughout the city. Hardly an eloquent speaker, he plodded through standard political boilerplate, appealing to party loyalty and civic pride. He defended the Democratic organization against charges of corruption and scored his opponent as an elitist. Daley loyalists made much of his continued residence on Lowe Avenue, one block from his birthplace, whereas Kennelly had long since fled Bridgeport for the more fashionable Edgewater Beach Hotel on the affluent Far Northside. Daley repeatedly pledged to champion the cause of the neighborhoods against the "downtown interests" (a promise he was later accused of breaking). On February 14, 1955, Daley spoke to a throng of over four thousand party loyalists at the Civic Opera House and gave a rousing speech that summarized the primary theme of his campaign. He declared:

> My opponent says, "I took politics out of the schools; I took politics out of this and I took politics out of that." I say to you: There's nothin' wrong with politics. There's nothin' wrong with good politics. Good politics is good government. . . . Ladies and gentlemen of the Democratic party of the city of Chicago, let them be the State

Street candidate. Let others be the LaSalle Street candidate. I'm proud and happy to be your candidate.[48]

In the February 22 primary, the Democratic organization turned out the votes for its mayoral hopeful. Daley carried twenty-seven wards and received 364,839 votes; Kennelly carried nineteen wards with 264,775 votes; and Polish candidate Benjamin Adamowski carried four wards with 112,072 votes (see map 1). The total of 746,015 ballots cast fell far short of the million the Kennelly forces had estimated they would need to offset the machine's assured patronage vote. Although the dissidents spent much time and money urging Republicans to cross over and vote in the Democratic primary, the election returns showed little evidence of this in the outlying wards. Voter apathy and a solid performance by the Democratic machine doomed Kennelly's insurgency.[49]

Of the victory margin of 100,064 votes, Daley collected 98,859 from eleven machine-dominated wards on the Near West and South Sides of the city. The five wards in the South Side ghetto (the second, third, fourth, sixth, and twentieth wards) provided Daley with a plurality of 45,562 (81.4% of the votes cast there). In the rapidly changing West Side, white aldermen turned out large machine votes in the predominantly black twenty-fourth, twenty-seventh, and twenty-ninth wards. Blacks repaid Kennelly for his harsh policies, while Daley—largely an unknown quantity in black enclaves—benefited by default. Scanning the returns on election night, the crestfallen mayor exclaimed, "Unbreakable. Just unbreakable, aren't they?"[50]

Daley's Republican opponent in the April election was Robert Merriam, a former Democrat and an ardent reformer. Merriam served as alderman of the fifth ward, the home of the University of Chicago and the traditional haven of much of the city's liberal establishment. Dubbed the "WASP Prince of Chicago," the thirty-six-year-old Merriam was in many ways a very attractive candidate. Son of a renowned political science professor and former fifth ward alderman who had run unsuccessfully for mayor in 1911, holder of a master's degree in public administration from the University of Chicago, and author of an autobiographical account of his own heroism in World War II's Battle of the Bulge, Merriam had for years fought the good fight for reform in the city council. Unlike the laconic Daley, he was an articulate and forceful public speaker whose youthful good looks attracted a fervent following of idealistic young

1955 Mayoral Primary Election

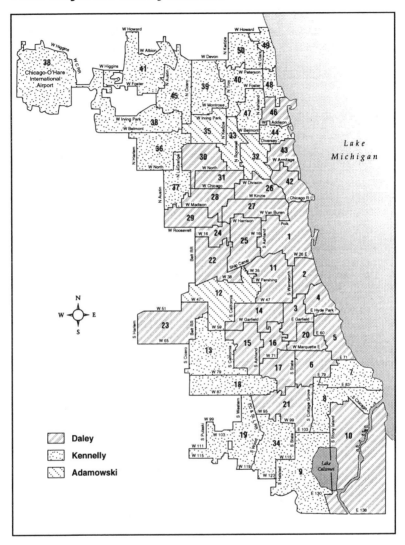

volunteers—in short, he was a sort of protestant John F. Kennedy. With solid financial backing from the Republican business establishment, Merriam presented a formidable challenge to the Democrats.[51]

Like Kennelly, Merriam aggressively attacked his opponent as a tool of the perfidious Democratic machine. He especially focused on its connections with the Capone mob's legatees, claiming that Daley's election would drag Chicago back to the infamous, lawless 1920s, when the criminal underworld had run the city. Merriam hit hard on the issue of vote fraud, seconding Kennelly's charges that widespread electoral irregularities had decided the recent Democratic primary. At the Republican candidate's urging, an eccentric character named Admiral LeRoy produced photographs of a West Side Democratic precinct captain, "Short Pencil" Sidney Lewis, erasing votes cast for Kennelly and substituting Daley X's. In the face of this incontrovertible evidence, however, the Democratic-controlled election board censured Merriam and Admiral LeRoy. Merriam also sent over thirty thousand letters to registered voters in key Democratic precincts; almost three thousand came back stamped "unclaimed" or "moved, left no address." On the basis of this sample, Merriam estimated that the Democratic primary had unfairly counted the ballots of as many as a hundred thousand ghost voters. The newspapers dutifully reported the findings, but the election board took no action.[52]

Another scandal seemingly damaging to the Democrats surfaced during the campaign, but Daley weathered it as well. The Chicago Bar Association brought charges against the party's candidate for city clerk—alderman Ben Becker—for allegedly accepting payoffs and kickbacks. Daley acted swiftly and replaced Becker on the ticket with John Marcin, who had been slated to run for city treasurer. To replace Marcin, he chose clothier Morris B. Sachs, a beloved Horatio Alger figure and longtime sponsor of the "Morris B. Sachs Original Amateur Hour," who had lost to the machine candidate in the primary. The night of their loss Sachs had cried on Kennelly's shoulder, and the photograph had appeared on the newspaper front pages the next day and had added to Sachs's stature as a local folk hero. With the addition of Sachs, the Democratic ticket emerged stronger than before from the brief contretemps.[53]

While Daley took the high road in the campaign, affirming his commitment to clean up municipal government and denying allegations of subservience to sinister forces in the party, others in the Democratic machine went after the Republican candidate without compunction. Merriam's first marriage had failed after his return from World War II, and copies of his divorce decree surfaced in the city's many Roman Catholic neighborhoods. Thirty-first ward alderman Thomas Keane said on television that "Daley has seven children and they are all his own," an unmistakable reference to Merriam's two stepchildren and his first marriage. Rumors also spread in white ethnic neighborhoods that his second wife, a native of France, was a mulatto. Letters from the fictitious "American Negro Civic Association" appeared in these neighborhoods extolling Merriam's commitment to open housing.[54]

Merriam had the backing of three of the city's four major newspapers (only the Chicago *American* endorsed the Democratic candidate) and also of the good government zealots who had favored Kennelly, including the local affiliate of the Americans for Democratic Action, the Independent Voters of Illinois. However, Adlai Stevenson's support again helped to obviate the image of Daley as just another organization hack. The Democratic candidate also received generous praise from Elizabeth Wood, the deposed executive secretary of the CHA, whose progressive credentials compared favorably with Merriam's. She said:

> I have learned to distinguish between those who make headlines and those who carry out programs. I have learned to distinguish between those who come to our help when aid is needed and those who have other business at the moment when a crisis is at hand. That is why, in distinguishing between the two candidates, I speak for Daley.

Liberal U.S. senator Paul Douglas added, "I greatly prefer Dick Daley."[55]

On April 5, 1955, Daley carried twenty-nine wards and received 708,222 votes to Merriam's 581,555. As in the February primary, the eleven hard-core machine wards did their job, giving Daley a decisive plurality of 125,179 votes (see map 2). The victory margin was modest, and Daley's running mates—John C. Marcin for city clerk, Morris B. Sachs for city treasurer, and Edward M. Koza for municipal court judge—compiled larger vote majorities. The mayor-elect spoke briefly to television crews and newspaper reporters at party headquarters, saying, "I promise no miracles—no bargains—but with unity, cooperation, and teamwork we will continue to build a better city for ourselves and our children. . . . As mayor of Chicago, I shall embrace charity, love mercy, and walk humbly with my God."

1955 Mayoral General Election

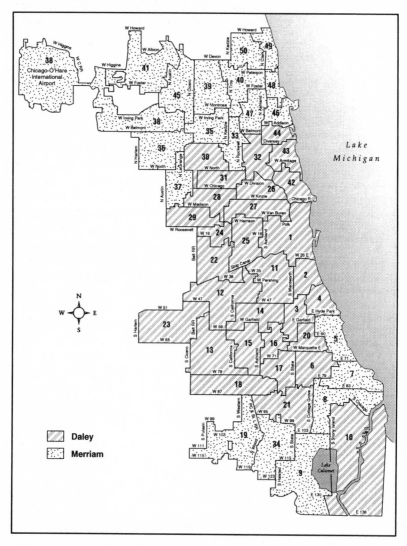

Earthy forty-third ward alderman Mathias "Paddy" Bauler crowed that "Chicago ain't ready for reform." He also rather indelicately assessed the incoming mayor, "[Thirty-first ward alderman Tom] Keane and them fellas—Jack Arvey, Joe Gill—they think they are gonna run things. . . . They're gonna run nothin'. They ain't found it out yet, but Daley's the dog with the big nuts, now that we got him elected. You wait and see; that's how it's going to be."[56]

Daley's rise to the top of Chicago politics and government was a triumph of hard work, forbearance, resilience, resolution, and luck. More than thirty years of service to the Democratic party laid the foundation for his mayoral victory. Whereas flashier politicians rose and fell, Daley stayed the course, avoided scandal, and for the most part moved steadily upward. In many instances, he simply outlived potential rivals. He carefully cultivated a reputation for party loyalty and personal integrity; his image was that of a good family man and devout Roman Catholic who, if he would never enthrall the masses, would never bring disgrace on the party. Uncomfortable before a microphone and generally lacking in oratorical skills, Daley felt more at ease with ledger books and financial statements. Indeed, his many years as a government fiscal officer constituted his greatest strength as a political candidate. Richard J. Daley was the colorless apparatchik who, after many years of service, became the leader. In 1955 the party bellwethers who backed him and the civic leaders, newspaper editors, and LaSalle Street Republicans who opposed him wondered what type of mayor this quiet, plodding Irishman from back-of-the-yards would be. Certainly, no one imagined what would follow.

2

The New Mayor

The dire privations of the Great Depression and the postponement of capital improvements necessitated by the Second World War left American cities in miserable condition by the late 1940s. The return of prosperity finally allowed cities to retire much of their antebellum debt burden, but progress came gradually for municipalities hamstrung by financial and political problems. Big city mayors—most of whom, in the wake of the New Deal, were Democrats—encountered hostility from state legislatures gerrymandered to safeguard the prerogatives of shrinking rural populations and also from the Republican Washington, D.C., of the Eisenhower years. By the mid 1950s, however, a new breed of mayors emerged to forge partnerships with local business communities in the quest for an urban renaissance. The provision of federal funds for the fledgling urban renewal program, in conjunction with the issuance of bonds and large-scale borrowing, provided the capital for the ambitious plans undertaken in cities nationwide.[1]

The new-breed mayors, who usually held college degrees in business or law, brought impressive credentials and support from a variety of constituencies to their civic improvement tasks. In Philadelphia, Mayors Joseph Clark and Richard Dilworth utilized a new city charter granting expanded executive authority to spearhead downtown development. Detroit Mayor Albert Cobo built a new civic center and convention hall to anchor the central business district. In

St. Louis, Mayor Raymond Tucker (a former engineering professor) allied with Civic Progress Incorporated (a coalition of corporate executives) to secure a $110 million bond issue for expressways, slum clearance, road improvements, and hospital construction. New Orleans Mayor DeLesseps Morrison bested an entrenched political machine before implementing his reform design. In New York City, Robert Wagner represented good government interests despite his connections with the Tammany Hall Democratic organization. In Pittsburgh, Mayor David Lawrence (whom the press dubbed a "good boss") worked closely with steel and oil magnate Richard King Mellon to effect the famed Pittsburgh Renaissance. Although vulnerable to the charge that they ignored poorer neighborhoods in concentrating solely on downtown revitalization, these mayors generated much economic activity after years of stagnation; they improved the faces of their cities' central business districts and won widespread acclaim in the national media.[2]

After he had been in office only a short time, Richard J. Daley's name began cropping up among those of the other new-breed mayors. His treatment by the press was overwhelmingly positive. At the end of his first year in office, Cabell Phillips of the *New York Times* wrote, "Young Richard J. Daley, Chicago's new Mayor, was brought up in the old Kelly-Nash machine, and Cook County remains a safe Democratic stronghold under his dominion. But he is a reformer at heart rather than a Boss." The editors of *Fortune* similarly enthused about the new mayor:

> [he] has given his city increasingly good government—and a big push forward in meeting its problems—while at the same time maintaining his organization in viable if declining power. . . . When he was elected many people believed he would sell City Hall to Cicero without a qualm. Instead, Daley went along to a remarkable extent in putting into effect reform legislation that tightened and improved the structure of Chicago's city government.

He received favorable notices in a *Time* profile, and Alfred Balk in a *Coronet* article asserted, "Dick Daley, through hard work and political know-how, is becoming the best mayor in Chicago's history."[3]

Daley received surprisingly good notices from academic circles also. Whereas political scientists had traditionally cited Chicago's boss politics as the prime reason for the city's shortcomings, they visited upon Daley less strident criticisms tempered with occasional praise. Still chastising the machine for its tolerating corruption, respected social scientists such as Edward C. Banfield and James Q. Wilson characterized the new mayor as a tough-minded pragmatist who demonstrated a remarkable capacity to work with diverse constituencies on the city's behalf. In *City Politics,* Banfield and Wilson approvingly noted that Daley "presents himself as an efficient, impartial, and expert administrator." In *Political Influence,* Banfield described how the mayor effectively used the power of the Democratic machine to assemble coalitions for massive urban development programs. Wilson concluded in *The Amateur Democrat* that "with Chicago's badly fragmented government, a boss like Daley was required to clear away the political obstacles."[4]

Chicago's civic elite, braced for the Democratic machine's plundering of city hall, had to admit that the new administration seemed surprisingly good. The horse-betting parlors and whorehouses that had been ubiquitous before the war failed to reappear, and the crime rate did not rise appreciably. Daley confounded his critics by retaining almost all of Kennelly's cabinet members, including the highly regarded chief of police and commissioner of public works. Kennelly was a smart businessman who had surrounded himself with capable assistants, Daley explained to a newspaper reporter, and he added, "If I don't catch them double-crossing me, why should I change?" Daley's replacement of fire commissioner Tony Mullaney with an old Bridgeport pal, Robert Quinn, elicited few protests because of the corrupt Mullaney's reputation as the weakest link in the Kennelly administration. The new mayor had the good fortune of not having to fire the Democratic machine's bête noir, Civil Service Commission president Stephen E. Hurley, who resigned on his own; to replace him Daley appointed another lifelong friend, William Lee, who was head of the Bakery Drivers Union and the Chicago Federation of Labor. For the position of city comptroller, the mayor chose Carl Chatters, a nationally renowned former executive director of the Municipal Finance Officers Association. He also selected, as municipal agency heads, a group of idealistic young civil servants collectively known as the "Whiz Kids," whose integrity and lack of political connections added to the mayor's improving reputation.[5]

Surrounded by his blue-ribbon management team, Daley initiated a series of reforms that significantly improved the city's delivery of services. He hired an additional 2,500 policemen, 800 firemen, and 500 sanitation workers, and his installation of new mercury arc streetlights made good his assertion that "there is not a big city in the world which has street lighting that can compare to Chicago's." All these improvements necessitated an increase in property taxes but, at least initially, met with little resistance from taxpayers. As one observer commented in *Life* magazine, "Dick's great secret is that he has found out that people don't mind being taxed if they can see what they're getting for their money." Furthermore, Daley eased the tax burden somewhat when his representatives in Springfield secured legislation granting Chicago the authority to increase sales taxes and to tax public utilities.[6]

Daley quickly won the approbation of Chicago's business community by launching an ambitious building program concentrated in the Loop. The completion of the Prudential Building in 1955 marked the construction of the first downtown office building since 1934; the Inland Steel Building opened in 1957, followed by a host of others. For all his affinity with the city's corporate leaders and repeatedly stated good intentions, Martin Kennelly had in eight years done very little to revitalize the central business district. Even one of the former mayor's supporters concluded that Kennelly had "too often exercised his constitutional right to do nothing." In the few instances in which Kennelly had initiated projects (the Prudential Building, the Congress Street Expressway, and a lakeside water filtration project, for example), completion came after the 1955 election, so the new mayor presided over the ribbon-cutting ceremonies and received the accolades. Under Daley, the Department of City Planning—a municipal agency created in 1957 to supersede the work of the semi-autonomous Chicago Plan Commission—assembled a large staff and enjoyed substantial funding; by 1964 its staff had grown from twenty-four to eighty-four, its budget from $149,500 to $914,500. Its *Development Plan for the Central Area of Chicago*, released in 1958, outlined an ambitious design for a downtown devoted to finance, business management, retailing, and upper-income housing—a blueprint endorsed by the State Street Council and the Chicago Central Area Committee, an organization created in 1956 by Holman Pettibone, chairman of the Chicago Title and Trust Company. Chicago's corporate elite also applauded Daley's selection of such respected professionals as City Planning director Ira Bach and Housing and Redevelopment coordinator James Downs.[7]

In every phase of the building boom, from conceptualization to construction, Daley and city hall planners worked closely with the business community. Ira Bach's *Development Plan for the Central Area of Chicago* grew out of a close collaboration with the Central Area Committee, which underwrote much of the research and design. "We worked with him on everything," commented a Loop businessman, "from a location for the convention center to zoning." Daley met repeatedly with Chicago entrepreneurs, men such as Arthur Rubloff in real estate development and Joel Goldblatt in retailing, exploring ways the city could tailor its broad developmental plans to the specific designs of local corporations. Nothing better illustrated the mayor's desire to encourage business ventures and his power to make unilateral, binding decisions on behalf of the city than his legendary thirty-minute meeting with Sears and Roebuck chairman Gordon M. Metcalf. Daley promptly agreed to sell the retailing giant one square block of downtown land for construction of its company's corporate headquarters, on a site already slated by the city for another use. According to Len O'Connor, Daley told Metcalf, "I don't think we'll have any problem. I think it will be a great thing for the city—havin' the biggest buildin' in the world. You go ahead with the plannin'; we'll help you."[8]

The mayor's unabashed enthusiasm for large-scale construction emanated from his understanding of the many rewards these projects produced. The erection of high-rise apartments and residential skyscrapers downtown—designed in part to recapture some of the population lost to the suburbs earlier in the century—meant abundant work for construction firms and more sales for Loop merchants. New office buildings housed white-collar jobs for taxpaying middle-class citizens with considerable amounts of disposable income. In 1958, for the first time since 1930, the amount of downtown office space increased by more than one million square feet—an achievement duplicated in 1961 and 1963. Renewal of the central business district also generated revenue for the Daley machine, as expansion-minded businessmen sought political allies who could help them to acquire tax breaks, zoning changes, and the other emoluments available from city hall. The building trades and other groups dependent upon municipal beneficence offered campaign contributions to Democratic officeholders to perpetuate the sustained construction boom from which they benefited. Daley knew the value of highly visible, lavishly publicized improvements in the municipal visage. Political capital could be mined over the entire length of a construction project, from the initial unveiling of plans to the ribbon-cutting ceremony at which the smiling mayor in hard hat presided over the dedication of a sparkling new structure. Monumental in size, and enduring, these edifices served as constant reminders of a mayor's contribution to the city.[9]

To move people in and out of the city center more efficiently, construction crews labored around the clock to complete new high-speed expressways—the Dwight D. Eisenhower to the west, the John F. Kennedy to the north, the Adlai E. Stevenson to the southwest, and the Dan Ryan to the south. Nearly five hundred miles of freeways were completed during Daley's tenure. And to accommodate the increasing number of automobiles in the city, the newly created municipal parking authority supervised the downtown building of scores of parking garages. In 1958 the West Side Subway began operating within the median of the Congress (later renamed the Eisenhower) Expressway, attracting considerable attention as the nation's first public transportation line to share space with a freeway. During the Daley years, Chicago Transit Authority trains began operating in the median strips of the Ryan, Kennedy, and Eisenhower Expressways. All of these public works projects became possible after the passage of bond issue referenda, and Chicago banks eagerly purchased the lucrative bonds.[10]

City authorities planned to complete the expressway network by constructing a tollway through the southeastern portion of the city to link up with heavily industrial northwestern Indiana, but state law prohibited municipalities from operating toll roads. Paradoxically, cities could build toll bridges, with no limitations on the length of approaches, and this inconsistency provided the loophole for completion of the highway system. Barred from building a conventional toll road, Chicago constructed an elevated thoroughfare and called it a bridge, even though it transversed a body of water for only a short distance. Rising 120 feet above the ground, the Chicago Skyway extended for seven miles over the Calumet River and a large swath of the city's iron and steel belt, from the Dan Ryan Expressway at Sixty-third Street to the west end of the Indiana toll road at Hundred-sixth Street. Frustrated Republicans in Springfield could only fulminate against the Chicago Democrats' deviousness, while Daley admirers praised his creativity.[11]

Daley earned the gratitude of the influential *Chicago Tribune* by throwing his support in Springfield behind a proposal to fund a monument to Colonel Robert R. McCormick, the newspaper's recently deceased publisher. When private financial interests declined to fund the project, the state legislature authorized the purchase of $20 million worth of bonds. To the mortification of environmentalists, the

Tribune selected a lakefront site for McCormick Place, a massive convention hall and exposition center. Civic groups objected to the despoliation of a huge section of Lake Michigan shoreline and the concomitant creation of sprawling parking lots that would produce "acres of concrete ugliness," but Daley ignored their protests and continued to support the project. The completion of the structure won praise from State Street merchants, who saw it as another example of the new mayor's surprising eagerness to aid the business community.[12]

Surpassing Mayor William Hale Thompson's reputation as "Big Bill the Builder," Daley profited from the availability of federal funds. By the time he took office, the 1949 and 1954 Housing Acts had offered cities generous assistance for slum eradication and downtown rehabilitation. Both of these housing statutes had been based on the pioneering urban renewal efforts of Chicago civic leaders, who obtained for the state's municipalities the power of eminent domain and the opportunity to use public funds for private real estate development. Illinois Institute of Technology president Henry Heald, Chicago Title and Trust chairman Holman Pettibone, Marshall Field Department Store vice president Milton Mumford, and their political cohorts pushed the Blighted Areas Redevelopment Act through the state legislature in 1947. The Illinois Urban Community Conservation Act of 1953 resulted primarily from the efforts of the city's Metropolitan Housing and Planning Council, led by realty mogul and former president of the Chicago Real Estate Board Ferd Kramer and University of Chicago chancellor Lawrence A. Kimpton. Mayor Kennelly had made relatively little use of this new cornucopia of available funding, but Daley arrived in city hall at a propitious moment for federally financed improvement schemes and quickly demonstrated his eagerness to exploit the available resources.[13]

Chicago's first attempt at urban renewal occurred in the Hyde Park–Kenwood neighborhood, site of the 1893 Columbian Exposition and home of the University of Chicago. A unique area peopled by university faculty, artists, writers, and many of the city's business and cultural elite, Hyde Park–Kenwood had enjoyed a distinctiveness since Chicago annexed the two suburbs in 1889. After World War II, many wealthy inhabitants of this area left for the suburbs, real estate companies divided spacious homes into multifamily dwellings, the poor immigrated in substantial numbers, crime rose, and the remaining residents feared the degeneration of the neighborhood's desirable environment. Between 1950 and 1956, twenty thousand whites moved from the area and twenty-three thousand nonwhites arrived. The influx of a large black population led to fears that nearby slums in the South Side Black Belt would soon predominate in Hyde Park, as they had done in the Douglas and Oakland neighborhoods to the north.[14] Dedicated to preserving one of the city's few interracial neighborhoods and its own physical plant, the University of Chicago led the campaign for neighborhood conservation. The university had employed racially restrictive covenants to preserve Hyde Park's predominantly white middle-class character until the U.S. Supreme Court declared these covenants unconstitutional in 1948. Beginning in 1952, Chancellor Kimpton took the lead in creating the South East Chicago Commission (SECC), which pursued the same goal through urban renewal. In 1955 the University of Chicago itself contracted with the city to prepare an urban renewal plan.[15]

Critics charged that the resultant project design essentially preserved the community's racial composition but at the cost of additional black population; specifically, urban renewal forestalled the immigration of poor and working-class blacks into a racially mixed but predominantly white middle-class residential area. Comedian Mike Nichols sardonically commented, "This is Hyde Park, Whites and Blacks, shoulder to shoulder against the lower classes." Author-activist James Baldwin warned, "Urban renewal means Negro removal." Julian Levy, director of the SECC, rejoined, "Urban renewal is not an exercise in sociology." The archdiocese of Chicago—largely through its spokesman, Monsignor John J. Egan—criticized the plan for its racial exclusivism and its disregard for the thousands of dwellers slated for displacement when the city invoked its power of eminent domain. An ad hoc neighborhood organization, the Hyde Park–Kenwood Tenants and Home Owners Association, objected to the dislodgment of lower- and middle-income families and the destruction of rehabilitable housing. Hyde Park's (fifth ward) alderman Leon Despres lambasted the university's adamant opposition to public housing.[16]

Mayor Daley refrained from endorsing the project during his first several years in office, no doubt in part because of Monsignor Egan's activism. By 1958, however, city officials concluded that no unified opposition existed among the Catholic clergy and laity. The publication of the project's preliminary plan attracted much favorable comment nationally as well as the strong support of the

Chicago metropolitan press. Daley finally recommended the plan on October 20, 1958, saying that public and middle-income housing for the area would be constructed in the future. After a unanimous endorsement by its Housing and Planning Committee, the city council approved the plan on November 7. According to Alderman Despres, the mayor's support hinged on the promise of future political backing by the university's board of trustees. Daley promised that "relocation of displaced persons will be handled with humanity," and at least for the moment, the press applauded the plan's adoption. The Hyde Park controversy never completely subsided, but as in other cities during the early years of urban renewal, enthusiastic supporters far outnumbered dissenters. In 1958 Daley's participation in this celebrated effort generally was well received locally and nationally.[17]

The mayor scored another public relations coup with his successful handling of the negotiations necessary to open O'Hare International Airport. After World War II, Midway Airport proved incapable of handling the ten million passengers passing through Chicago each year, and in 1946 the city acquired a Douglas Aircraft Company training ground two miles northwest of the city with the intention of establishing a larger facility. Orchard Place Airport (later renamed for Butch O'Hare, a World War II air force hero) featured longer runways, parking for ten thousand automobiles, and room for expansion on its ten-square-mile expanse. In 1949 Mayor Kennelly had declared financial exigency and announced the end of construction on the airport facilities until the airlines agreed to contribute more funds to the project. No progress ensued until 1955 when Daley met with the chief executive officers of the major airlines and obtained from those corporations an agreement for an increase in landing fees that allowed the city to retire the necessary bond issues. William A. Patterson, president of United Airlines, said that the mayor "made us feel cheap about some of the things"—so cheap, in fact, that the airlines agreed to spend their own money to construct new terminals and an air cargo building (all of which would be municipally owned) and also to rent ticket and operation space from the city. The city council ratified a fifteen-year agreement with the airlines that ensured that Chicago would recover its entire investment. At last, construction resumed.[18]

During the Kennelly administration, a jurisdictional impasse had also arisen because the city had no legal access to the airport, which was encircled by suburbs. Daley suggested that the city annex a strip of land containing Higgins Road (Route 72) to form a corridor of Chicago property through the suburbs, but the affected townships— Park Ridge, Bensenville, Franklin Park, Rosemont, Schiller Park, and Des Plaines—refused to cooperate. When the mayor pressed his case, reminding suburban officials of their costly obligation to police and to maintain the portion of the expressway linking the terminal with Chicago, they relented. On March 28, 1956, the necessary land changed hands, and in 1959 construction commenced on the new facilities needed to serve jet airplanes. In 1962 the new terminal for domestic flights opened, followed by the opening of facilities for international flights in 1963. During 1958 construction crews worked on the Northwest (later renamed the Kennedy) Expressway from sixteen to twenty-four hours per day in order to accommodate the increased traffic serving the airport; the entire route from downtown to the Northwest Toll Road opened in 1960. By 1962 O'Hare International Airport had become the world's busiest airport; and Chicagoans applauded Daley's swift and decisive handling of yet another problem that had festered under Kennelly.[19]

While the business community applauded the new mayor's determination to enhance downtown development, Chicago's labor unions also found a congenial atmosphere in city hall. The flurry of construction initiated by Daley created thousands of jobs for skilled and unskilled workers, the city council passed no legislation hostile to labor, and union leaders received representation on prestigious city commissions and authorities. City workers prospered especially, as the mayor provided these laborers with top wages as well as fringe benefit packages not enjoyed by workers in private industry. Daley met annually with union representatives, who relayed information about the prevailing pay rates in private industry and helped him to establish benchmarks for municipal pay scales. The mayor's generosity slowed and sometimes halted the organizing of municipal workers and, for the better part of Daley's years in city hall, deflected the call for collective bargaining. Organized labor's lack of militance and the city's accommodating policies resulted in remarkably few strikes, almost all of which the mayor halted in short order by negotiating a settlement. The Chicago Federation of Labor, which merged with the Cook County Industrial Union Council (the local affiliate of the Congress of Industrial Organizations), essentially became an appendage of the Democratic machine.[20]

The new Chicago mayor also had the good fortune of showcasing all the activity in his bustling city as the host of the 1956 Democratic

National Convention, which was held at the International Amphitheatre, only a few blocks from his Bridgeport home. The Democrats' chance of unseating the popular President Dwight D. Eisenhower seemed slim, and the Illinois delegation was pledged again to the candidacy of its favorite son, Adlai E. Stevenson, so the convention promised little drama. For Daley, however, hosting the convention provided an opportunity to show off the vibrant Chicago of his mayoralty—the new buildings, the ongoing construction, the heightened pace of activity that presented such a contrast to the inactivity of previous years. Convention delegates and national political pundits saw for the first time the boss of Chicago's powerful Democratic machine, the enigmatic former ward heeler who had surprised observers with his heralded municipal reforms.

Whereas the convention business remained perfunctory and the Stevenson nomination proceeded without a hitch, Daley became involved in two political sideshows of some interest to Democrats. First, a scandal erupted during the convention when the press revealed that Daley's candidate for governor, Cook County treasurer Herbert C. Paschen, had illegally maintained a "flower fund" in his office, from which he had borrowed money for a trip to Europe. Although Paschen's defalcation was admittedly minor, Daley quickly decided he must be dropped from the ticket. The mayor confirmed the rumor to reporters on the convention floor, while Paschen—seated only three chairs away—knew nothing of his fate. Moments after being told by reporters, a stunned Paschen rushed over to Daley and asked for an explanation. Expressionless, staring straight ahead, Daley replied, "What did you expect?" As reporters and other observers noted of this episode, Daley acted decisively with cold-blooded dispatch—just as he would in countless other future instances when difficult decisions had to be made with political careers in the balance.[21]

Second, Daley took the lead in advocating Massachusetts senator John F. Kennedy for the vice-presidential nomination. Adlai Stevenson's unprecedented refusal to choose a running mate and his charge to the convention to select one by acclamation led to a frenzy of behind-the-scenes lobbying for candidates, and no one worked more assiduously than the Chicago mayor. Within the Illinois delegation, downstate politicians primarily favored Missouri senator Stuart Symington and, to a lesser degree, Tennessee senator Estes Kefauver; they made no effort to hide their opposition to the Irish Catholic Kennedy. Daley twisted enough arms in the Illinois delegation to secure most of the state's sixty-four votes for Kennedy, but the convention chose Kefauver by nine votes. Kennedy graciously accepted defeat and asked that Kefauver's nomination be made unanimous, earning high marks for his behavior in defeat and leaving the convention labeled as one of the party's bright stars for the future. Daley had supported an Irish Catholic for vice president and had affirmed his strong ties to the Kennedy family, whose expansive financial empire extended into the Windy City. (The Kennedys owned the twenty-four-story Merchandise Mart on the north banks of the Chicago River, purportedly the world's largest commercial establishment.) Daley had also served notice of his intention to play politics on the national scene and had come close to winning. The Chicago mayor was recognized as an emerging force in the national Democratic party.[22]

Daley's growing renown as the energetic, successful chief executive of America's second city, underscored by his election as president of the U.S. Conference of Mayors, coincided with his consolidation of power in city hall. Even as the national media were praising the neophyte mayor as a surprisingly progressive administrator, he moved swiftly and forcefully to control the city council that had enjoyed great autonomy during the Kennelly years. Remembering Ed Kelly's admonition that "either you run the machine or the machine runs you," Daley concurrently acted to strengthen his control of the Cook County Democratic organization. The days of a weak mayor and decentralized power were clearly coming to a close in Chicago.[23]

The day after his election Daley announced that, in order to devote his full attention to the mayor's office, he would soon resign as Cook County Democratic chairman. In later years Daley insisted that he actually had offered his resignation but the party leadership refused to accept it—an event that no one else recalled. Even if he seriously contemplated resignation at that time, Daley never fulfilled the promise. Although he made much of the soul-searching he endured before reaching this decision, it seems doubtful that a politician of his ambition would have voluntarily yielded so much power shortly after attaining his primary goal. Having just used the party chairmanship to force Kennelly out of the mayoralty, Daley clearly understood the need to control both offices. Unlike many Chicagoans who naively believed in a clear-cut demarcation between the administration of party affairs and the conduct of municipal business, Daley understood the symbiotic relationship between politics and city governance. As he often remarked and as he believed fervently, "Good government is good politics." Chicago's mayor could use the power of the party chairmanship to discipline unwieldy Democrats; and the party leader's control of the city council majority allowed for swifter and easier decision making. Aware of Chicago's long history of governmental fragmentation, which was due in large measure to the strong-council, weak-mayor city charter, Daley knew of the many structural hurdles he would have to clear to govern effectively. He had no intention of giving himself anything less than the fullest measure of authority possible.[24]

Daley wasted no time in displaying his resolve to control the city council, which was statutorily more powerful than the mayor. At his April 20, 1955, inauguration he immediately addressed the interplay between the legislative and executive branches, saying:

> I have no intention of interfering in any way with the proper functions of the City Council. But as mayor of Chicago, it is my duty to provide leadership for those measures which are essential to the interests of all the people and, if necessary, to exercise the power of veto against measures which would be harmful to the people.

It was a seemingly innocuous statement, but one fraught with meaning for discerning listeners able to read between the lines. Because neither Kelly nor Kennelly had used the veto during the previous twenty-two years, the very mention of it assumed significance. Daley's assumption of the mayor's right to decide which measures "would be harmful to the people" portended a shift in power from the legislative to the executive branch of Chicago's government. In the subtle phraseology of the speech, Daley gave warning of his intentions. Later in his inaugural address, the mayor referred to the recommendations of the Chicago Home Rule Commission—an ad hoc agency appointed by Kennelly that had a few months earlier published its recommendations for making the city's government more efficient. Daley seconded the commission's proposal "to relieve the [City] Council of administrative and technical duties . . . and permit the aldermen to devote most of their time to legislation." His suggestion that the scope of aldermen's activities be reduced left no doubt about which governmental agent would assume greater authority as a consequence.[25]

The Chicago City Council, which had become infamous for its carnivorous pursuit of spoils, harbored a number of opportunists whose interest in politics had little to do with disinterested public service and who agreed with local politician George Dunne's belief that "anybody who goes into politics for some other reason than making money is a fool." According to U.S. senator and former alderman Paul H. Douglas, the city council was composed of "the cunningest body of legislative bastards to be found in all of the western world." Hailing back to the legendary days of "Bathhouse John" Coughlin and Mike "Hinky Dink" Kenna, Chicago's aldermen regularly partook of both honest and dishonest graft to amass considerable fortunes at public expense. As late as the Kennelly years, council members ignored even the rudiments of decorum during legislative sessions—laughing, joking, sleeping, perusing the *Daily Racing Form*, and otherwise ignoring the official transaction of city business. Appalled at the aldermen's venal behavior and aware of their blatant contempt for him, Kennelly had attended council meetings infrequently. Daley quickly altered the situation by presiding over all council sessions as a stern chairman and demanding a more civilized deportment. If nothing else, the Chicago City Council took on the appearance of a serious deliberative body. To cement his control of legislative proceedings, the mayor had his rostrum in the city council chambers fitted with a device that could silence the microphone of any alderman who spoke too long or who posited unacceptable ideas.[26]

City council meetings became carefully scripted affairs at which the mayor seldom engaged in debate but generally presided in stony silence. For most of the Daley years, council business proceeded under the crisp direction of the mayor's floor leader, thirty-first ward alderman Thomas Keane; after Keane's conviction for mail fraud in 1974, eleventh ward alderman Michael Bilandic performed the task. The city council rarely functioned as a deliberative body, for department heads framed legislation in consultation with the mayor long before introducing bills in legislative sessions. With Daley's imprimatur, measures sailed through committees and aldermen voted accordingly. Keane and the mayor met before council sessions, set the agenda, and made the crucial decisions about pending legislation. With the exception of the few Republicans and independents in the council, the aldermen almost always rubber-stamped everything that Daley approved.[27]

The Democratic machine demanded unwavering loyalty and brooked no deviation. Sacrificing independent initiative to party unity, aldermen followed Daley's lead regardless of their constituents' needs. Dissent became acceptable, as independent alderman Dick Simpson noted, only with "papal permission" from the mayor. For example, Simpson remembered, on one occasion Alderman William Cousins introduced a resolution condemning the fire-bombing of black homes in Marquette Park. The white majority voted to send the resolution to the Rules Committee (and thereby to kill it). With only two exceptions, the black aldermen placed party loyalty above race and voted with the majority—despite the outrage of their constituents. Subsequently, a delegation of black aldermen convinced Daley that the council's approval of such a statement was necessary for their political survival. At the next council session another resolution, virtually identical to the first, was introduced under the mayor's name and passed unanimously. The episode illustrates a crucial maxim—that the machine could countenance an innocuous resolution for tactical reasons, but loyalty to the machine remained paramount.[28]

While establishing and maintaining party discipline, Daley proceeded to remove from the council much of its authority. First, a bill passed by the state legislature (championed by state senator William Lynch, Daley's close friend and law partner) deprived the council of its historic task of preparing the budget and acquired for the mayor the item veto power over appropriations bills. From his many years as city comptroller and state revenue director, the mayor had considerable experience in budget making and a keen appreciation for the power it entailed. Transferring that responsibility not only symbolized the shift of city government's epicenter from the city council to the mayor's office, but it also allowed Daley to shape the budget to his own specifications by identifying specific allocations, reductions, and increases. Through budget making the mayor could shape fiscal policy and determine priorities for allocating limited resources. Devising the budget himself also provided Daley with knowledge of each dollar spent and of who profited from each transaction, as well as with a firmer control over the dispensation of patronage jobs in the municipal workforce. Again, the mayor demonstrated his understanding that government and politics could not be divorced in the real world.[29]

Daley also succeeded in eliminating the city council's power of criminal investigation. On the mayor's behalf, finance committee chairman Parky Cullerton introduced an ordinance that shifted the responsibility for such investigative work to the mayor's office. The ordinance appropriated money for the chief executive to hire investigators and awarded him the prerogative of deciding what action, if any, would be taken against the subjects of the inquiries. The adoption of this measure meant the end of any crusading alderman's ability to pursue corruption within formal channels; it also (and perhaps this was even more important) gave Daley additional leverage over the increasingly emasculated city council. Democratic politicians could still enjoy a measure of freedom to pursue their own interests (legal or otherwise), but they knew that such license depended upon their continued fealty to the mayor who could always hold them accountable for their actions.[30]

In 1956 Daley moved to limit the aldermen's political power, especially their ability to provide constituents with extralegal services. No longer could aldermen or ward committeemen approve zoning changes, issue driveway permits, or grant other such favors. Builders of apartment houses, restaurants, and other businesses needing driveways had in the past customarily paid their elected representatives up to $20,000 for the privilege, so Daley's new policy meant for the politicians the loss of a lucrative source of income. Henceforth (the mayor informed the legislators), all such requests would be handled through his office and without the illegal exchange of money. Business transactions once expedited informally in the wards would now be handled downtown; suddenly only the mayor could grease the wheels of the burdensome city bureaucracy. Twenty aldermen broke with the mayor and voted against the ordinance that provided for executive approval of driveway permits, but an alliance of Republicans, independents, and loyal machine Democrats formed the necessary majority. In one of the few significantly divided votes of the Daley mayoralty, the city council acceded to a substantial reduction of its own authority.[31]

Any successful political machine relies on patronage, and after the civil service reforms of the previous mayoralty, Daley had to be concerned with the decreased opportunity to reward the party faithful with city jobs. The mayor faced an imposing situation, because so many appointive municipal posts had been converted to civil service. In response, he made an increasing number of temporary appointments that were not subject to civil service regulation. Under the existing statutes, agency administrators could hire temporary employees for a maximum of 120 days; if "qualified" applicants could not be identified within that time, another 120-day appointment could be made, then another, and another. As long as the appointees remained loyal and worked hard for the party at election time, their temporary status remained unchanged, and they held their jobs endlessly. As civil servants died or retired over the years, Civil Service Commission president William Lee eliminated permanent positions or filled them "temporarily" pending examinations that the commission never offered. In this manner, Daley restored a mighty patronage army by circumventing the regulations designed to establish a meritocracy. Martin Kennelly raised an occasional protest to the violence done his beloved reforms but found his remarks drowned out by the din of praise for the new mayor's bricks and mortar projects.[32]

To an unprecedented degree, Daley kept a watchful eye on patronage matters himself. Just as he kept the budget books close by and delegated little authority for financial management, the mayor micromanaged the city's personnel matters, noting each hiring and firing, each promotion and demotion, each transfer and pay raise. Reduced to mere supplicants in the new Daley hegemony, aldermen and ward committeemen needed to visit the mayor's office to get permission for each patronage action. They marveled at Daley's apparently complete knowledge of not only the patronage numbers but also the individuals involved; how could one man responsible for running a metropolis of over three million people master so much intricate information about obscure patronage matters? The answer rested with Matthew Danaher, the mayor's close friend and neighbor, whose desk in an office adjoining the mayor's held the patronage files. At a moment's notice, Danaher could apprise Daley of jobs, contracts, votes, and favors controlled by each Democratic alderman and committeeman—information that Daley could then recite to visitors as if from memory. Years later after Danaher's death, another bright young Southside Irishman, Tom Donovan, kept the patronage books.[33]

Daley's tight control of a growing patronage force allowed him to reward family, friends, and neighbors with jobs of varying status. Bridgeport residents soon held an estimated 10 percent of the appointive city jobs, a remarkable total for such a small area. William Lynch, Daley's law partner, became counsel for the Chicago Transit Authority and, subsequently, judge of the U.S. District Court. To questions about impropriety, the mayor expressed his disdain for any man who would do less for kith and kin: "Would General Motors give a contract to Chrysler?" he asked rhetorically. In later years, when he was accused of funneling city legal business to two of his sons, both lawyers, Daley exploded: "If I can't help my sons, then they can kiss my ass!" Chicagoans applauded such straightforward responses, and many agreed with the sentiments the mayor expressed. They understood how business had long been conducted in the city, and even with all the favoritism, the Daley administration still delivered the services. The periodic expressions of outrage from the marginal good-government crowd notwithstanding, cronyism and nepotism in the Daley administration never became serious issues.[34]

With patronage, as in many other areas, Daley centralized control in the mayor's office at the expense of the city council and other traditional sources of power in the Democratic hierarchy. As the city's chief executive and head of the party, Daley enjoyed unfettered license to craft his administration to his own liking. His managerial style, contrary to that of the traditional big city boss, granted considerable autonomy to the highly skilled managers and technicians he selected for critically important business positions. Although keeping his hands off the municipal experts, Daley yet maintained a tight rein on patronage and other political matters. All the while, he paid close attention to the finances of the city and the Democratic party, mastering the ledgers of both. As would be the case in future years, onlookers discerned no second in command; Daley ruled alone. The few maverick aldermen who dared to introduce legislation invariably saw their bills interred in some committee. The measures adjudged worthwhile were unearthed and—after revision, if necessary—approved and credited to the mayor. In some cases the council outvoted resolutions, only to have them resubmitted by Daley loyalists and passed readily. When Daley appointed commissions to advise him on policy matters, he flattered well-known businessmen by asking them to serve, but he always appointed a critical mass of loyal supporters such as William Lee of the Bakery Drivers Union and William McFetridge of the Flat Janitors Union to assure the outcome.[35]

Daley's tight control of Chicago's Democratic machine extended beyond the city limits. Members of Cook County's uniformly Democratic delegation to the state legislature took their marching orders from the mayor's man in Springfield, Speaker of the House John Touhy. Every morning Chicago legislators received their "idiot sheets," scraps of paper instructing them how to vote on the bills to be considered that day. As one state representative from Chicago cracked, "I don't even go to the bathroom without checking first." Although the Cook County Democrats usually found themselves outnumbered in a predominantly Republican state, the mayor controlled a united bloc of voters large enough to tip the balance in closely contested votes. As a result, he could barter and trade favors with Republican governors such as William Stratton and Richard Ogilvie. U.S. senators Paul H. Douglas and Adlai E. Stevenson III maintained that the mayor never attempted to influence their voting or made an improper request; they attributed their freedom to the absence of federal patronage and to their invariable agreement with Daley on national legislation affecting cities. In more immediate matters of state politics and governance, however, the mayor maintained firm command.[36]

During his first term, Daley rapidly mastered the political machine he had inherited, and he consolidated the mayor's authority over the city council. His first four years in office produced intense activity, and his massive building program won high praise from businessmen, civic leaders, and the newspapers. If city hall seemed to care less about the quality of life in the residential neighborhoods, particularly the poorer ones with minority populations, little protest disturbed the generally positive evaluations garnered by the mayor. Associated with other, aggressive, highly respected mayors who fought to save the cities from decades of neglect, Daley appeared to be—despite his origins in a corrupt political machine—an effective and hardworking administrator. As the 1959 mayoral election approached, therefore, the Republicans faced a daunting proposition in finding a candidate who could possibly unseat the high-riding incumbent.[37]

Unable to entice anyone into running against Daley, Republican county chairman Tim Sheehan had to make the race himself. Forty-first ward committeeman and former member of the U.S. House of Representatives, Sheehan agreed to opposed Daley in 1959 only because of a party promise that he would be slated to run against Senator Paul Douglas in 1960 (a promise party leaders later conveniently forgot). Sheehan attempted to mount a serious campaign but found it difficult in the face of the defeatism and apathy of his own party. He complained bitterly that the normally rock-ribbed Republican business community had defected to Daley's column. State Street merchants and LaSalle Street bankers formed the Non-Partisan Committee for Reelection of Mayor Daley, and the normally Republican newspapers all endorsed the incumbent. Such members of the local elite as Clair Roddewig, president of the Association of Western Railroads, and University of Chicago chancellor Lawrence A. Kimpton publicly supported the mayor. The president of Chicago-based United Airlines and member of the United Republican Fund's board of governors, William Patterson, said, "This is a two-way street. So, I as a Republican must owe a quality of leadership and loyalty to his [Daley's] program. Because he is a Democrat is no reason I should bury my head in the sand and be a good loser." The years of Daley's first term had not been besmirched by scandal, and with very little support from his fellow Republicans, Sheehan found himself with little ammunition for the contest.[38]

Serenely confident in his overwhelming popularity, Daley campaigned sparingly. He continued to cut ribbons at the dedication ceremonies of newly completed public works and boasted of the 475 garbage trucks, 174 miles of sewerage, 69,600 new streetlights, 72 downtown parking facilities, 2,000 policemen, and 400 firemen added in the previous four years. With pride he pointed to the gala events coming to Chicago within the next several months, including the visit of Queen Elizabeth II of England, the Pan-American Games, and the opening of the St. Lawrence Seaway. Clearly, Daley had given Chicagoans all the bread and circuses they could want; why would they vote for someone else? And the vast majority did not. The incumbent received 778,612 votes (71.36 percent of the total) and won in forty-nine of the fifty wards; Sheehan received 311,940 votes and carried only his own ward. In his victory speech on election night, Daley repeated humble and increasingly familiar words: "I thank the people of Chicago. With the unity, cooperation, and teamwork of all the people of this city, we will continue to build a better city for your children and mine. As mayor of Chicago, I shall embrace charity, love mercy, and walk humbly with my God."[39]

Daley's reelection in April 1959 launched a glorious year for him and for Chicago. The city welcomed Queen Elizabeth, opened the new international waterway, and hosted the athletic games, the mayor out front beaming all the while. Even his beloved White Sox won the American League pennant and brought a World Series to Chicago's South Side for the first time in a generation. The next year would be a presidential election, the end of eight years of Republican administration, and another opportunity to place a Democrat—preferably John F. Kennedy—in the White House. Daley, however, did not foresee for 1960 the eruption of a scandal, the kind that he had avoided for four years but that when it occurred threatened to rock the very foundations of his mayoralty. Nor did he anticipate in the following years the rising specter of racial tension that came to threaten the tranquillity of Chicago and the rest of urban America. By 1960 the glorious years of unqualified praise and placidity were drawing to a close.

3
Mounting Problems

Chicago's police force had always been plagued by corruption. Like other metropolises governed by political machines, the Windy City suffered periodic outbreaks of scandal as crusading newspaper editors and other reformers uncovered police tolerance of lawbreaking in exchange for financial compensation. Sensational exposés revealed criminal alliances involving policemen, organized crime, and members of local government. In the nineteenth and early twentieth centuries, the temperance movement provided many of the opportunities for graft, because the city's large immigrant working-class population demanded alcohol. For a price, police winked at the violation of closing laws, Sabbatarian restrictions, and other impingements on personal liberty. Liquor, prostitution, narcotics, and other pleasures of the flesh remained available to consumers only because of law enforcement's policy of benign neglect—a neglect that both provided remuneration for poorly paid civil servants and dovetailed with the personal predispositions of an ethnically diverse police force. Police also selectively enforced election laws, thus assuring victory to the highest bidder, and acted as strikebreakers for wealthy industrialists in labor disputes. High-level city officials, many of whom profited from lax law enforcement, ignored corruption in the police ranks, appreciating the financial needs of municipal workers and the imposing task of reform.[1]

By the mid twentieth century, Chicago's police force s̄
couraging signs of professionalization but still remained ᶅ
for widespread corruption. Changes in laws and social c̄
eliminated some avenues for graft, but dishonest policemen
found lucrative sources for extralegal moneymaking. Tavern own
continued to pay beat cops for the privilege of staying open aft
closing time, and bagmen collected payoffs from brothels, bookies,
pimps, and drug pushers. Motorists routinely bribed traffic cops to
tear up citations, avoiding the greater cost of paying fines and the in-
convenience of visiting traffic court; cynics referred to Lake Shore
Drive as the city's last outpost of collective bargaining. Merchants
customarily paid tribute to policemen to guarantee regular pa-
trolling. Such petty corruption, institutionalized and tolerated for so
long, was commonplace. As Mike Royko commented, "Most
Chicagoans considered the dishonesty of the police as part of the
natural environment. The Chicago River is polluted, the factories
belch smoke, the Cubs are the North Side team, the Sox are the South
Side team, George Halas owns the Bears, and the cops are crooked—
so what else is new?"[2]

Mayor Daley inherited this situation and seemed to accept it as
the natural order of things. Certainly, he launched no sweeping campaigns to reform the police department. The Democratic machine
maintained close ties to the police force, many of whose members
moonlighted as precinct captains. Most ward boundaries coincided
with police districts, which made it possible for Democratic committeemen to choose their station commanders. Growing up in
Bridgeport at a time when many of the Irish joined the police force
as a way out of the stockyards, Daley understood the way the system operated. He empathized with the plight of policemen struggling to support large families on inadequate salaries and appreciated the utility of an informal reward structure. He also knew
firsthand the police subculture that existed, for a considerable number of his and his wife's relatives belonged to the force. The mayor's
extensive connections to the police department made it easy for him
to overlook the shortcomings of some of its members, and he passionately came to its defense when a 1957 *Life* article called the
Chicago force "probably" the nation's most corrupt.[3]

As inured as Daley and other Chicagoans had become to impro-
bity in the police force, however, they were taken aback by the enormity of the wrongdoing revealed early in 1960. While the mayor and

owed en-
famous
stoms
still
ers

in Florida, the Chicago newspapers broke
ng on the city's North Side. Arrested and
venty-three-year-old Richard Morrison
his accomplices had been twelve po-
rdale district. He claimed that for the
in blue" had been carting away appli-
ndise in their squad cars and allowing Mor-
cash from the break-ins. Investigators found six
or stolen goods in the policemen's apartments and
s, corroborating the "babbling burglar's" accusations. A jury
ound eight of the twelve defendants guilty and sentenced five to
prison.[4]

Citizens willing to tolerate a network of petty graft balked at the
wholesale pilfering revealed in the Summerdale scandal. Moreover,
once the spigot of disclosures had been opened, a torrent of seamy
information flowed out. Police intelligence uncovered a comparable
robbery ring in the North Damen Avenue station, as well as a bur-
glary detail's partnership with fur and jewelry thieves in the swank
Gold Coast area. A Michigan Avenue clothier reported that a theft
occurred after she had called the police to report her failure to lock
the shop's doors. At roughly the same time, repeated sightings
throughout Europe of police lieutenant Anthony DeGrazio with
mafia don Tony Accardo raised again the persistent rumors of connections between the police and organized crime. A public outcry
against malfeasance in law enforcement drowned out the gently sar-
donic jokes about the new Chicago game of "cops and/or robbers."
The persistent bleating of the reformers finally found a willing, responsive audience.[5]

The scandal also served the political interests of Daley's chief rival, state's attorney Benjamin Adamowski. His ambitions checked
by Daley's rise to supremacy in the Democratic party, Adamowski
had become a Republican and had been elected state's attorney in
1956. As the county's top prosecutor, Adamowski set out to uncover any illegalities in city hall in order to boost his own mayoral
ambitions. In 1959 he unearthed two scandals, one involving traffic
court employees fixing traffic tickets and the other relating to bail
bondsmen receiving kickbacks from the municipal court. Grand
jury hearings on these two cases dragged on for weeks
(Adamowski's picture appeared on the front pages all the while)
and served as a constant reminder of the corruption endemic in
Chicago's legal system. The Summerdale imbroglio simply ratch-

eted the level of public indignation several notches higher.[6]

For the first time in his mayoralty, Daley found himself the target of hostile questions and harsh criticism. No longer could he ignore accusations against the police department, for the evidence of wrongdoing made denial impossible. Republican governor William Stratton insisted that Daley resign as Cook County Democratic chairman so that he could focus his efforts on police reform and called for the establishment of a state-run police review board that would operate independently of the tainted local government. Stung by the disapproval, Daley lashed back intemperately. At one tense press conference, he railed at reporters, yelling that people in all professions yielded to temptation at times. No one was perfect. "There are even crooked reporters," he blurted, "and I can spit on some from right here." Pressed to name names, he quietly withdrew the charge. Such outbursts of temper flashed frequently, his physical appearance deteriorated, and rumors spread that his consumption of scotch had increased dramatically. Insiders claimed that they had never seen Daley exhibiting such signs of strain.[7]

The mayor promised reform. On January 23, 1960, he called a press conference to announce the resignation of police commissioner Timothy J. O'Connor. Appointed by Martin Kennelly in 1950, O'-Connor enjoyed the reputation of an honest policeman who had risen up the ranks through hard work and dedication. If he had failed at the herculean task of rooting out the department's bad elements, he was still widely regarded as one of the best police commissioners in the city's history. Experts applauded the modernization of the department under his administration. Yet as the man in charge, he had to accept responsibility for the department's shortcomings, and the mayor quickly asked for his resignation.[8]

Next Daley announced the formation of a blue-ribbon search committee to choose a new police commissioner. The five-member panel interviewed twenty-four department members, three other Chicagoans, and ten candidates from out of state, then offered the job to its own chairman, Orlando W. Wilson. Law enforcement authorities considered the fifty-nine-year-old Wilson the top man in the field. Before becoming a professor and dean of the University of California at Berkeley criminology department, he had been chief of police in Fullerton, California, and Wichita, Kansas, and the reorganizer of thirteen police departments in cities from San Antonio, Texas, to Portland, Maine. Wilson knew the police business from the ground up, having started as a beat patrolman in Berkeley, but he also had impeccable academic credentials; he wrote widely on police administration and procedures, and his published works included the most widely heralded criminology textbook. Wilson expressed some reservations about taking the job and insisted on being given autonomy to run the force without political interference. He finally agreed to a three-year contract along with an annual salary of $30,000 (almost twice his predecessor's). The mayor announced the appointment on February 22, 1960. To underscore his sincere commitment to reform, Daley moved Wilson's office from city hall to police headquarters and upgraded his title from commissioner to superintendent.[9]

Wilson immediately began the shake-up of the police hierarchy, firing all seven of O'Connor's deputy commissioners, promoting and demoting throughout the force, and holding new civil service promotion exams. He closed stations, centralized operations, rewrote policies, and redefined procedures. Most important, he redrew district lines to conform with law enforcement concerns rather than with political boundaries, and he restructured the police department's chain of command so that district commanders reported to the superintendent rather than to their aldermen. All this activity not surprisingly was a threat to the politicians, who objected to losing control over the police in their domains. The police rank and file did not greet Wilson's changes with total support, and one captain was suspended for publicly criticizing the new commissioner. When Wilson established an internal intelligence unit to monitor police practices, an effigy bearing the sign "Orlando Wilson—Spy" appeared hanging from an elevated train station roof. The unpopularity of the reforms in some quarters notwithstanding, the pace of change continued.[10]

Daley never wavered in supporting his new police superintendent. When Wilson requested enabling legislation from state lawmakers and the city council, the mayor went to Springfield to lobby and applied his influence in city hall. When reforms cost money, Daley found the wherewithal to pay for new equipment, higher salaries, and more personnel. During Wilson's first year, the annual police budget increased by over 100 percent. On television and in the press, the mayor praised the transformation of the police department and continued to pledge his complete support. Daley's strategy worked, and what started as a calamity became a public relations coup. Again, the national media praised Chicago's mayor as a tough leader who was willing to challenge hidebound traditions and vested interests. Daley may not have cared for the quiet, cerebral Wilson and may have disagreed with him fundamentally at times, but he never publicly broke with the superintendent. In 1963, when Wilson's three-year contract expired, Daley reappointed him for "as long as I'm mayor, or as long as he wants the job." Daley benefited from his association with the estimable Wilson, who received nothing but praise from an adoring press until his retirement in 1967. Having appointed Wilson and supported him for so long, the mayor received credit as the image of the Chicago Police Department steadily improved—ironically so, because his decisions resulted more from political expediency than from any genuine desire for reform. An admiring alderman said of the mayor's performance:

> The amazing thing about the police scandal is the way Daley turned it to his own advantage. He'd been in office five years and he knew from a lifetime of experience that the cops were on the take. Then when the scandal hit, instead of Daley being held responsible, he fired O'Connor, Wilson came in, and Daley was the guy who reformed it. Anybody else would have been raked over the coals—Lindsay is always blamed for what happens in New York—but Daley wound up being treated like a hero and a reformer. He turned it to his own advantage.[11]

With the rehabilitation of his reputation well underway, in the summer of 1960 Daley's attention turned to presidential politics. Publicly, he remained uncommitted to the many Democratic presidential candidates who courted him. Because of his support of John F. Kennedy for vice president in 1956, the press speculated that Daley would back the Massachusetts senator for the presidency in 1960. To such conjecture the mayor replied, "Yes, there's quite a bit of sentiment for Kennedy in the state. But we have sentiment for [Adlai] Stevenson and [Hubert] Humphrey, and downstate there's sentiment for [Stuart] Symington." Whatever commitment Daley felt to Illinois's favorite son, Adlai Stevenson, evaporated after a spring 1960 visit to the Stevensons' Libertyville farm, thirty miles north of Chicago. There Stevenson told Daley and party elder Jacob Arvey that he had no intention of running a third time, and the mayor felt that this unequivocal denial of interest left the field wide open.[12]

In the months preceding the nominating convention, Daley remained publicly inscrutable, warmly welcoming the various presidential aspirants to Chicago, praising all the potential candidates, and disavowing any favoritism. However, because of his lingering dream of an Irish Catholic in the White House, Daley was secretly for Kennedy all the while. Daley met occasionally with the patriarch of the family, Joseph P. Kennedy, whose business interests took him to Chicago often. A Kennedy son-in-law, R. Sargent Shriver, managed the family owned Merchandise Mart, the world's largest wholesale merchandise building, and served as president of the Chicago Board of Education; he also acted as a liaison between the Kennedys and the Chicago Democrats. Early in the campaign, John and Robert Kennedy traveled to Chicago not only to firm up their ties with Daley but also to study firsthand the operation of the nation's most successful electoral machine. The brothers met with William Dawson's lieutenants, absorbed their vast knowledge of organizing and electioneering, and incorporated these findings into a campaign manual for Kennedy staffers that was distributed nationwide. The ties between the Kennedy campaign and the Chicago Democrats were indeed strong, if not widely known.[13]

Most of the Illinois Democrats went to the party's national convention in Los Angeles solidly behind Daley, and only a handful of delegates held out for a presidential candidate other than Kennedy. Daley hoped for a unanimous Illinois vote for Kennedy and might have received it without incident had not Adlai Stevenson reconsidered his pledge. Suddenly, when Stevenson equivocated and hinted that he could be drafted to run, his supporters sprang into action. Within the convention hall chants of "We want Stevenson" grew as rumors spread of the reluctant candidate's rekindled interest. Members of the "Stop Kennedy" movement saw the nascent Stevenson boom as an opportunity to derail the front-runner, as Daley and other members of the Illinois delegation received telephone calls and telegrams urging them to get behind the banner of their native son. Stevenson still refrained from decisive action, however, never formally declaring his willingness to run but at the same time failing to denounce the movement in his behalf, and the pressure on Daley mounted.[14]

Stevenson began phoning Daley to discuss the situation, but the mayor refused to accept the calls. The reluctant candidate's supporters launched a lobbying campaign, first sending the noted poet Carl Sandburg to appeal to the mayor. A call came through from Eleanor Roosevelt, the grand matriarch of the party and a Stevenson supporter, who wished to talk to Daley. He went to her hotel suite, and she implored the mayor at length to turn away from Kennedy in favor of Stevenson—in favor of the governor in whose cabinet Daley had served years before and who had spoken for him during his first run for mayor at a time when endorsements from respectable politicians had come grudgingly. She appealed to Daley's sense of loyalty, friendship, and honor, but he would not yield: "I can't change now," he insisted, "I asked Adlai whether he would run. He gave us his answer a long time ago."[15]

Back at the convention hall, Daley continued to refuse Stevenson's telephone calls. Finally, the mayor reluctantly acceded to Jacob Arvey's argument that he should call Stevenson as a matter of courtesy. Alluding to the minimal support he had in Illinois delegation caucuses (a mere 2 votes to Kennedy's 59.5, according to contemporary reports), Stevenson asked Daley if the numbers simply reflected his lack of commitment. Would Illinoisans jump on the bandwagon if he formally declared his candidacy? No, Daley replied, he simply had no support. Brusquely, the mayor reminded Stevenson of his earlier statement of no interest and informed him that the time for decisions had long passed. Gratuitously, he added that Stevenson's support within the Illinois delegation had been weak in 1956 but that Daley had ramrodded his endorsement through. All debts had been paid in full four years earlier.[16]

Without the support of his home state, Stevenson's candidacy withered and died. Both he and Daley endured an awkward and embarrassing tableau soon thereafter, as they sat close together on the convention floor and heard the cries of "We want Adlai" wafting down from the galleries. Television viewers who saw Daley ignore Stevenson's vain attempts to strike up conversation must surely have understood the candidate's predicament. The unpleasant situation came to a merciful end when the convention nominated Kennedy on the first ballot, Daley having earlier predicted exactly the final delegate vote.[17]

The Kennedy campaign named R. Sargent Shriver to coordinate activities in Illinois, but according to Shriver, for all practical purposes Daley filled that role. The task for the mayor was simple: to produce a large enough Democratic vote in Cook County to offset the overwhelmingly Republican totals that would come from the state's other 101 counties. A strong party turnout became very important for yet another reason—derailing the reelection campaign of Republican state's attorney Ben Adamowski, who had already raised such havoc with the Summerdale scandal. To oppose

Adamowski, Daley chose Daniel Ward, a political neophyte and law school dean who was sure to appeal to reform-minded voters. Cynics remarked that for most Chicago precinct captains the removal of a hostile state's attorney assumed greater significance than the election of a U.S. president and that Daley always cared more about maximizing the turnout to defeat Adamowski than to elect Kennedy. In any event, both causes would be served by manufacturing the largest possible vote on election day.[18]

For generations the ethnocultural differences between metropolitan Cook County and the rest of Illinois—which Chicagoans derisively lumped together and referred to as "downstate"—appeared with startling clarity at election time. The polyglot urban masses and the rural and small-town voters divided over prohibition, reapportionment, home rule, and a host of other issues—Catholic, Democratic, ethnic, heterogeneous Chicago versus Protestant, Republican, nativistic, homogeneous downstate. And whereas imperious denizens of Peoria, Decatur, and Rockford railed against the Chicago Democratic machine's infamous vote stealing, Daley knew from his years in Springfield that the courthouse politicians spread across the Prairie State's cornfields felt no compunction about breaking the rules to win elections. Indeed, Republicans from Little Egypt in the state's southernmost reaches to the portions of downstate north of Chicago had all contributed to Illinois's sordid tradition of crooked politics. Securing the state's twenty-seven electoral votes for a Democrat in a presidential contest—a daunting prospect in any year—became even more challenging with the nomination of a Roman Catholic, and Daley understood the need for extraordinary effort.

Chicago Democrats from Daley down to the precinct captains worked feverishly for the party ticket, and the effort paid off on election day. An amazing 89.3 percent of eligible voters turned out in Chicago on November 8, compared to 64.5 percent nationally. Kennedy carried the city by a staggering 456,312 votes, a total that was crucial to his victory margin of 8,858 votes in Illinois. The five South Side wards of the Black Belt produced a plurality of 81,554 votes, eclipsing the victory margins they had achieved for Daley in the past. So did the machine's reliable eleven inner-city wards, accumulating a cushion of 168,611 votes. Most remarkable perhaps, the other thirty-nine wards yielded 287,701 more votes for Kennedy than for his Republican opponent, Richard M. Nixon, who carried only three (the forty-first, forty-fifth, and forty-seventh) of the city's fifty wards. Even by Chicago standards, it was an incredible victory for the Democrats, who swept all the contests that autumn, electing Governor Otto Kerner, reelecting U.S. Senator Paul Douglas, and ousting State's Attorney Ben Adamowski.[19]

Chicago's role in Kennedy's election attracted the most interest, of course, casting Daley in the role of kingmaker. Because Illinois loomed as a crucial state in what promised to be a close contest, political pundits from around the country watched events in Chicago with great interest. Daley responded with cool calculation. Relying on the vast financial resources of the Kennedys, he employed an army of poll-watchers throughout the state to minimize the vote theft that was bound to occur in Republican strongholds. In Chicago, poll-watchers for both parties worked overtime to curtail illegalities. Hours after the polls closed with the election still too close to call, John F. Kennedy called Daley on the telephone for his appraisal of the situation. Calmly, quietly, Daley replied, "Mr. President, with a little bit of luck and the help of a few close friends, you're going to carry Illinois."[20]

Convinced that the Republicans would not report the election results promptly as a ploy to save enough votes for an eleventh hour surprise, Daley held back a reserve of his own. In some downstate counties, it was rumored, Republican precinct workers had taken ballot boxes home and stopped tabulations. After Will and DuPage Counties—two Republican bellwethers near Cook County—finally reported their totals well after midnight, Daley released the Chicago tallies. The last Democratic surge put Kennedy over the top in the early morning hours on the day after the election, and Daley's machinations instantly made him a legend.[21]

Immediately, accusations of vote fraud came from the Nixon quarters as well as from Illinois Republicans. Outraged Nixon partisans claimed that the Daley machine had stolen the election for Kennedy, a charge that has survived long after the affair. Even if Illinois had gone Republican, however, the shift of twenty-seven electoral votes would not have changed the outcome of the presidential contest. The state election board's unanimous certification of the election returns on December 14 failed to still the cry of protest—even though the five-member election board chaired by Republican governor William Stratton included only one Democrat. An investigation by the Joint Civic Committee on Elections uncovered some procedural irregularities in vote counting but found the outcome unaffected; a recount of the 906 Cook County paper ballot precincts discovered a margin of error of less than four-tenths of 1 percent, a sum insufficient to deny Nixon a majority of votes. Still, combative Republicans asked how twenty-two registered voters in one precinct could cast seventy-four votes for Kennedy and two for Nixon. And what of the other evidence of vote stealing in 133 precincts involving 677 election judges that had been carefully documented by the newspapers? It was clear that the Democrats had stolen votes in Chicago, just as surely as Republicans had stolen votes downstate. A statewide recount would have taken an estimated two years and cost millions of dollars, which the Republicans would have been obligated to pay, and Nixon finally declined to pursue the investigation. Fairly or not, the Democrats carried Illinois.[22]

John F. Kennedy quickly acknowledged his political debt to Chicago's powerful mayor. The day after his inauguration, the new president showed the Daley family around the White House and posed for a picture with them in the Oval Office. Shortly thereafter, Daley spent a night at the White House, the first of many he would enjoy during the Kennedy presidency. Moreover, he became good friends with many Kennedy advisers, men such as Ken O'Donnell and David Powers, Irish Catholic politicians who liked the Chicago mayor personally and admired his political acumen. They also did not forget his yeoman service in the 1960 presidential contest.[23]

Daley's highly publicized role in Kennedy's election brought him much notoriety as the sage political veteran largely responsible for putting a Democrat in the White House. In Chicago his program of public works, subsidization of private building, and prompt service delivery continued to attract generally positive reviews, with one notable exception. One of his pet urban renewal projects—the destruction of an old, primarily Italian neighborhood on the Near Southwest Side to make space for a new University of Illinois branch campus—ignited an embarrassing grassroots protest. The neighborhood dissidents' dogged determination not to succumb quietly to their removal produced the kind of lingering negative publicity that no politician enjoys and underlined the problems inherent in big cities' use of urban renewal.

Half of the University of Illinois's students hailed from Cook County, and Chicagoans desired a local branch of the state's premier institution of higher education as an alternative to sending their children 150 miles south to the twin cities of Champaign-Urbana. In 1945 State Senator Daley had introduced a bill authorizing the construction of a Chicago campus without success. Years passed with little action, primarily because of opposition from the politically powerful university administration and alumni in Springfield, who worried about the potentially deleterious effect of a new campus on the existing institution. In the meantime, thousands of Chicago-area students matriculated at a temporary facility at Navy Pier, which became increasingly inadequate as the post–World War II college population increased steadily. In 1959 the university trustees selected a suburban site—the Riverside Golf Club, west of the city—and announced plans for the construction there of a permanent campus. Daley challenged the decision, believing that the university should be located within the city and fearing that its existence in the suburbs would add to the trend of metropolitan decentralization that he opposed in all instances. Accordingly, he proposed that the city pay the difference in cost between the land at the Riverside Golf Club and any more expensive urban sites, so that the university would have no financial incentive to locate outside city limits. He was determined that his beloved Chicago would house the metropolitan area's public university.[24]

Several inner-city sites emerged, with University of Illinois officials favoring one in Garfield Park on the West Side and another next to Meigs Field on Lake Michigan's Northerly Island. Daley had other thoughts, however; he argued that as part of his overall plan to protect the downtown Loop the campus should be situated near the central business district. Developers and Loop businessmen favored reclamation of the seedy railroad terminal area, south of downtown, but negotiations bogged down because the railroads demanded a higher price for the land than the city was willing to pay. On September 27, 1960, Mayor Daley proposed a site several blocks east of the University of Illinois Medical Center, which had been established in the 1890s and had grown into the nation's largest medical complex, around the intersection of Harrison and Halstead Streets, southwest of downtown in a neighborhood known as "the Valley." Because the Harrison-Halstead area had already been chosen as an urban redevelopment site, federal money could be used to help defray the costs and construction could commence without delay. Loop merchants, although they preferred the railroad terminal area, accepted the alternative location. The solution seemed perfect, except for the unwillingness of the Harrison-Halstead area residents to go along quietly.

The University of Illinois approved the site in February 1961, sparking a strenuous protest from neighborhood residents. When legislative and administrative remedies proved unsuccessful, the Harrison-Halstead community group sought restraining orders in state and federal courts. Its members challenged the labeling of the affected neighborhoods as "slum and blighted areas," contending that strong, viable communities existed there. They questioned whether the inadequately publicized and poorly attended public hearings on the matter had been conducted in good faith. The prolonged appeal process delayed the start of construction for more than one year, but a 1963 U.S. Supreme Court decision upheld the city's power to condemn the land.

During the legal battles the Harrison-Halstead community group—composed of about three hundred families of Italian, Greek, and Spanish descent—noisily continued their public protest. Believing that their political leaders had been co-opted by the Democratic machine, neighborhood activists took their case to the press and staged demonstrations, sit-ins, and marches. The picture of the underdog battling city hall won sympathetic treatment in the news media, which emphasized that housewives and mothers usually led the protests. Daley had disingenuously promised them that urban renewal would revitalize the community, maintained the dissenters, and only later had they discovered that the university's construction would destroy the entire neighborhood. Believing the city's assurances of limited upheaval, many residents had invested in home and business improvements. Angry and feeling betrayed, the people lashed back at city hall.[25]

Florence Scala, a young housewife who emerged as the movement's leader, met with the mayor frequently during those troubled days. She recalled that in private Daley was firm but courteous; in public, he threw down the gauntlet, taking a tough position and announcing his refusal to be intimidated by illegal protests. Daley promised to construct sufficient housing to accommodate the displaced home owners but never wavered in his determination to see the project completed. Neither did the State Street council, trade unions, and other civic groups dedicated to refurbishing the land near the Loop. The plucky neighborhood protesters may have scored some public relations victories in the local media, but they lacked the political power necessary to thwart a powerful mayor who was solidly backed by the city's business leadership.[26]

The University of Illinois at Chicago Circle—so called because of its location adjacent to the circular junction of the city's major expressways—opened in 1965. The campus uprooted an estimated

8,000 people and 630 business establishments, while several thousand more residents left along with family and friends or departed out of fear of displacement. An adjacent West Side urban renewal program dislodged another 3,500 persons and 170 businesses. The Valley's housing stock fell from approximately 6,850 units in 1960 to 3,400 units in 1970. An embittered Florence Scala complained, "All that housing they were going to put up for us? I think they put up forty-four units in one place, and about fifty units in another. And most of it was too high-priced for the people who lived there." The university uneasily coexisted thereafter with the remnants of the old neighborhood (the relatively few Italians who continued to live around the western fringe of campus) and pacified some critics by rebuilding two structures in the historic Hull House complex that had been demolished. For Daley and other growth-oriented businessmen concerned with preservation of the Loop, the campus became an island of higher land values close to downtown that slowed the entry of black and Latin populations into the area.[27]

Decidedly less controversial, the Sandburg Village project sacrificed a deteriorating jumble of houses and commercial buildings in order to insulate a luxurious lakefront residential neighborhood. After World War II, the decrepitude west of Clark Street on the Near North Side began to edge closer to the tony collection of exclusive apartments and single-family dwellings along the lake that sociologist Harvey Zorbaugh termed the "Gold Coast." The Chicago Land Clearance Commission readied the site in 1960–1961 and made it available for sale to developers who agreed to build adequate shopping outlets along with residential units. In conjunction with the Greater North Michigan Avenue Association, developer Arthur Rubloff built Sandburg Village, an upper-middle-class residential complex of high-rise apartment buildings and town houses, in the North Avenue–LaSalle Street redevelopment area. Completed under the provisions of the Illinois Blighted Areas Redevelopment Act of 1947, which required no neighborhood hearings prior to clearance, the project moved from site acquisition to demolition and construction in a remarkably short time.[28]

Although the Sandburg Village project proceeded smoothly overall, some dissent surfaced. Forty-third ward alderman Paddy Bauler opposed the redevelopment effort, which occurred in his bailiwick, but Mayor Daley ignored his objections. John J. Egan, director of the Catholic Archdiocesan Conservation Council, called for a balance between middle-income units and the high-rise luxury apartments that predominated in Rubloff's plans but found Daley similarly unsympathetic. Having been promised space in a Sandburg Village commercial complex, displaced area businesses protested little, until they realized that no such arrangements were being made. Architectural purists denounced the final product as a bland replacement for the elegant old Gold Coast mansions that had disappeared from the area. These criticisms aside, however, the Near North Side redevelopment was generally given high marks. Conveniently situated just north of downtown and near North Wells Street's trendy Old Town area, the attractive Sandburg Village development generally avoided the unpleasant publicity that plagued the Chicago Circle campus and quickly attracted its capacity of middle-class tenants.[29]

The displaced residents of the Harrison-Halstead and North Avenue–LaSalle Street neighborhoods lost their homes but, in the process, raised nettlesome questions about the human cost of urban renewal. Working-class people in other neighborhoods sympathized with their peers who had lost homes and businesses, knowing that they might someday be equally powerless to protect their abodes from the city's ravenous designs. And whereas urban renewal and downtown revitalization continued to win plaudits from the business community, owners of small bungalows and apartment renters saw few tangible benefits and incurred inevitable tax increases to pay for construction. To what degree should the neighborhoods be sacrificed to enhance downtown? And how high a price were citizens willing to pay under the assumption that the benefits accrued from a strengthened central business district would trickle down to all Chicagoans?[30]

Taxpayers began to question the cost of Daley's many enterprises. During the mayor's first two terms in office, the city's property tax rate doubled; between 1958 and 1962, it rose 41 percent, more than in any other city in the nation. From 1955 to 1963, the number of city employees increased by one-third, which created a bloated patronage force and soaring taxpayer resentment. Police Superintendent Orlando Wilson's extravagant reform expenditures raised the annual police budget from $75 million to $200 million. For years Daley increased spending steadily and the citizenry gave their imprimatur by approving new taxes and bond referenda, but the cumulative effect of such spendthrift policies eventually took its toll. In 1959 the voters narrowly approved a $66 million referendum; in 1962 they rejected a $66 million bond issue earmarked for urban renewal, streetlights, sewers, municipal buildings, refuse removal, bridges, and viaducts. (The Harrison-Halstead community group campaigned actively against the 1962 bond issue and took credit for its defeat.) The rebellion by a previously pliant electorate sent Daley and his financial experts scurrying to find new sources of revenue. In deference to beleaguered home owners, he froze the property tax rate in 1970, increased levies on vehicles and utilities, and sought more aid from the state and federal governments.[31]

The 1962 taxpayers' revolt gave new hope to a Republican party faced with the daunting task of contesting Daley's reelection in 1963. Previously bereft of any solid issues with which to challenge the mayor, the Republican opposition suddenly envisioned tapping a wellspring of voter resentment toward high taxes and inefficiency in municipal government. In Benjamin Adamowski, who had been voted out of the office of state's attorney in 1960, the Republicans possessed a dynamic, aggressive candidate well suited to exploiting the issue. An emerging scandal in the Chicago Sanitary District raised Republican spirits as well. Newspaper exposure of bribery, kickbacks, biased awarding of contracts, and bogus civil service examination results led an embarrassed Mayor Daley to clean house in the Sanitary District and to appoint a new superintendent, reformer Vinton W. Bacon.[32]

On February 28, 1963, the Adamowski campaign received another boost with the gangland slaying of a Chicago alderman. Two days earlier the voters of the twenty-fourth ward had returned incumbent alderman Benjamin Lewis to office by a lopsided count of 12,179 votes to 888. The most flamboyant and controversial of the black aldermen, Lewis was rumored to have syndicate connections. Policemen found his lifeless body handcuffed to a chair in his ward office with three bullets in the back of the head after what appeared to have been a Mafia-style execution. Police investigators questioned gamblers, hit men, and other undesirables but never made any arrests. The unsolved crime gave vent to more rumors about connections between the Democratic machine and the underworld, a theme that Adamowski exploited with relish.[33]

Feeling much more vulnerable than they had four years earlier, the Democrats looked for scandal in the Republican candidate's public record. Democratic state's attorney Daniel Ward leaked to the press that his predecessor had spent the staggering sum of $833,984 from a contingency fund without accounting for the expenditures, the implication being that some of the money had gone into Adamowski's 1960 campaign fund. Adamowski explained that he had destroyed the financial records in order to protect his informants and urged the newspapers to demand the same accountability of Daley, who as mayor had access to forty-three contingency funds in city government. No criminal proceedings resulted from these charges and countercharges, but the controversy threw the challenger on the defensive and to a great extent negated the Republican's perennial charge of machine corruption.[34]

In his campaign Daley emphasized the building renaissance of the previous eight years that had won the city national acclaim. "Under Daley Chicago has a new rhythm as exciting as any in the city's lusty past," trumpeted *Time*. "A new facade is rising in steel and zeal. New buildings loom high against the slate-grey winter waters of Lake Michigan." An adulatory article in *Holiday*, titled "Mayor Daley's Chicago," painted an equally flattering picture of the city's development under the incumbent's leadership. The mayor proudly pointed to the opening of 6.5 million square feet of new office space and to the $930 million invested in the construction of commercial buildings from 1958 to 1961 as evidence of an economic rejuvenation. His mayoralty had indeed generated unparalleled downtown development.[35]

No diversions could deflect the citizenry's deep dissatisfaction with the rising tax rate, however, and Daley showed genuine concern as the election approached. Adamowski campaigned frenetically and optimistically predicted a "searing, seething blast of votes." The challenger hungrily sought white ethnic votes by publicly opposing open housing. To shake Daley's support among the city's heavily Roman Catholic population, he accused the mayor of authorizing the welfare department's distribution of birth control devices (a charge that few voters found credible in light of Daley's highly publicized devoutness). Early on election night Adamowski told a journalist, "I think you're interviewing the next mayor of Chicago." A scant two hours later he conceded defeat, bitterly lashing out at the wealthy Republicans who backed Daley with sizable financial contributions. Daley garnered 55 percent of the votes and won by 138,000, a much narrower victory than four years earlier, when he had received 71 percent and a margin of 466,000 votes. Adamowski carried eighteen wards, Daley thirty-two (see map 3).[36]

A closer electoral analysis revealed a striking fact: Adamowski actually won 51 percent of the ballots cast by white voters, receiving solid support from his fellow Polish Americans and also faring especially well in wards adjacent to the expanding Black Belt. White

1963 Mayoral General Election

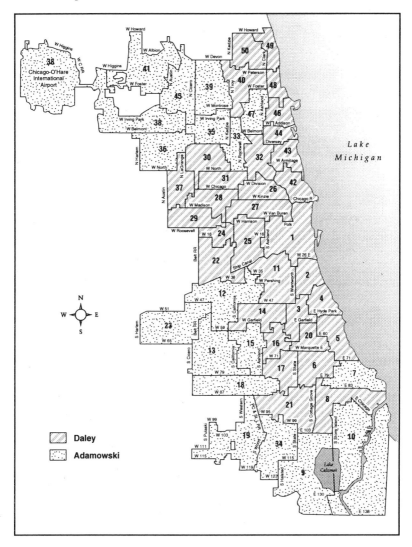

home owners resisting racial integration and escalating property taxes comprised the core of the challenger's support. Adamowski lost some wards with substantial Polish populations—the eleventh, twenty-fifth, thirty-first, and fortieth—where machine influence superseded ethnic loyalty and white backlash sentiment. Yet he fared surprisingly well in ironclad machine wards. In the syndicate-dominated first ward, Daley received 40 percent fewer votes than he had in 1959; in city council finance committee chairman Thomas Keane's thirty-first ward, half as many. The challenger even reduced by 35 percent the mayor's vote total in his own eleventh ward. In contrast, Daley won 81 percent of the black vote, carrying the twenty-fourth ward by a ratio of eighteen to one; the twenty-ninth by eight to one; the second, third, and fourth by five to one; and the sixth, seventeenth, and twentieth by four to one. The South Side Black Belt and the expanding West Side ghetto provided Daley with his winning margin.[37]

Characteristically, the mayor was quietly gracious in victory. He said, "My thoughts are one of humility, gratitude, and appreciation. As I said in 1955 and 1959, I will try to embrace charity and walk humbly with my God." He had narrowly survived against a tough and skillful opponent and needed to reassess policies in light of his eroded popularity. Holding the line against future property tax increases would help to assuage the anger of many white ethnics, but regaining the white backlash vote would require greater action. By the same token, he also needed to address the changing demographics of the Chicago electorate. At the end of World War II, only two of the river wards (the inner-city wards that traditionally provided huge vote totals for the Democratic machine) contained black voting majorities, but by 1963, ten centrally located wards had a preponderance of black voters and four others were rapidly approaching black voting majorities. Meanwhile, as the middle-class white population fled to the suburbs, working-class whites, many of them Roman Catholic supporters of the Democratic machine, left the inner wards for the distant bungalow belt on the city periphery. Ethnic succession was altering the makeup of the machine's electoral base.[38]

Black voters had turned out in great numbers, provided the margin of victory for the mayor, and rightfully expected their reward. But could Daley reallocate resources at the expense of his support in white wards and risk even greater loss of support there in the future? Or might he be better advised to ignore the blacks, who arguably had no alternative to backing the Democratic machine, and attempt to shore up the dwindling support from his white constituency? Having seen Ed Kelly's tenure in city hall end abruptly in 1947 because of his support of open housing and integrated schools, Daley recognized the political danger of supporting desegregationist policies in Chicago. The mayor faced this political choice at a critical time in the city's history—when rapid black population increase and the advance of the civil rights movement northward elevated racial tension. Thereafter, in his actions as well as in his rhetoric, the mayor began playing to his white constituency in response to a series of highly charged racial controversies. His decision to redirect the machine's support from the increasingly black river wards to the peripheral bungalow belt set the stage for the turbulent times that were to follow.[39]

4

The Challenge
to Plantation Politics

"I have lived in Chicago all my life," claimed Richard J. Daley in 1963, "and I still say we have no ghettos in Chicago." He was wrong, of course. Chicago had two sprawling African American ghettos—an older, larger area on the South Side and a newer, rapidly expanding enclave on the West Side—and remained one of the most segregated cities in the United States through the mid twentieth century. Daley's adamant refusal to recognize the state of race relations in his city was not at all remarkable for a white Chicago politician; it merely reflected a long-standing, highly successful strategy for dealing with African Americans. Like the vast majority of his predecessors, Daley consigned blacks to life in rigidly segregated residential pockets and ratified their second-class economic status. At the same time, he benefited from and relied on the overwhelming vote pluralities that the black wards turned in for Democratic candidates. Yet by the time of the Daley mayoralty, the black population was increasing rapidly and pressure was building on white home owners who lived adjacent to the bulging Black Belt. During the 1950s an average of three and a half blocks per week converted from white to black ownership, as whites departed for sprawling suburbs. The burgeoning civil rights movement, which had won some notable victories in the South, was creating a new racial militancy in the

North, as reflected in the harsher rhetoric in black Chicago neighborhoods. Although prominent black Democrats expressed little dissatisfaction with their lot, angry voices from the ghettos rejected the clientage politics that enriched a few leaders but did little for the neglected masses. Daley dismissed the talk of ghettos and racial upheaval while steadfastly defending the status quo. He could not ignore the problems forever, though, for too much demographic change and the weight of too much recent history brought Chicago belatedly into the civil rights maelstrom.[1]

Although the first permanent settler in Chicago was a black man, Jean Baptiste Pointe de Saible, the nonwhite population in the city at first grew slowly and haltingly. By the late 1840s, a small number of free blacks from elsewhere in the North and runaway slaves from the southern states established a modest community in Chicago that grew to almost one thousand by the outbreak of the Civil War. After the Great Fire of 1871, Chicago's black population became more concentrated geographically but continued to reside in racially mixed neighborhoods. The creation of a monolithic racial ghetto came at roughly the same time that southern states erected Jim Crow barriers. As their numbers grew from less than fifteen thousand in 1890 to over fifty thousand in 1915 and as they became much more noticeable in the city, blacks found hostility where they once had encountered benign neglect. As historian Allan H. Spear has shown, by the outbreak of World War I a virtually all-black ghetto on the South Side had taken shape. Shoehorned into a narrow slice of land between the railroad yards on the west and Cottage Grove Avenue on the east, the ghetto extended southward from the central business district into the Woodlawn and Englewood neighborhoods below Thirty-ninth Street.[2]

World War I triggered a mass migration of southern blacks to Chicago. Riding the Illinois Central Railroad northward, former residents of Mississippi, Louisiana, Arkansas, and other southern states poured into the city by the thousands; between 1916 and 1920, approximately fifty thousand black migrants settled in Chicago's South Side. During the decade from 1910 to 1920, Chicago's black population rose by 148 percent (from 44,103 to 109,458). The Black Belt expanded a bit farther south to accommodate the great number of newcomers but remained a narrow, densely populated strip of land. White resistance to further expansion, exacerbated by the postwar competition for jobs and rising political tensions, strained racial amity and led to the bloody 1919 race riot. Implacable white hostility kept the South Side ghetto bottled up even as the black population increased inexorably.[3]

Black migration continued in the 1920s but slowed dramatically during the Depression decade. The coming of the Second World War reinvigorated the movement of southern blacks to northern cities, and the flow of people continued thereafter. During the war, 1.6 million blacks headed northward; from 1940 to 1960, a total of 3.1 million did so. Chicago's black population rose by 77 percent during the 1940s (from 278,000 to 492,000); and in the 1950s by another 65 percent (to 813,000). The South Side ghetto expanded east into Hyde Park, Oakland, and Kenwood, west to Western Avenue, south into Woodlawn, Park Manor, Chatham, and Englewood; and its southernmost edge extended to the city limits. Again, the Black Belt expanded as whites grudgingly surrendered contiguous living spaces, but strict segregation remained the rule.[4]

On the West Side, a small colony of black settlement grew into what historian Arnold R. Hirsch has called Chicago's "second ghetto." As upwardly mobile Jews and other Eastern Europeans left the West Lawndale neighborhood west of the Loop, blacks raced in from the South Side and from outside the city to seize suddenly available housing. From 1940 to 1960, the area's white population fell from 102,048 to 10,792, whereas the number of black residents soared from 380 to 113,827. Lawndale became Chicago's new port of entry for black immigrants, and the area's black population exploded from 13 percent in 1950 to 91 percent ten years later. The black settlement spread steadily westward to the city limits and northward into the Garfield Park and Austin communities.[5]

Blockbusting realtors claimed to have a "green light" and declared "open season" on sales to black buyers. "We don't care if the whites run all the way to Hong Kong as long as they run," boasted one opportunist, "It's good business for us when they're frightened." These unscrupulous realtors infested transitional neighborhoods and incited the violence that often erupted. Urging whites to sell their homes and get out quickly, the "panic-peddlers" purchased dwellings at bargain-basement prices and then sold them to blacks at outrageous markups. Enterprising landlords divided apartment buildings and single-family homes into tiny, overpriced kitchenettes. Prosperous—if unethical—realty companies sold property "on contract," whereby home buyers paid attractively low down payments but then found themselves saddled with hefty monthly payments and discovered that they accrued no equity in the property until making the final payment. When blacks failed to meet their obligations, the realtors repossessed the houses and repeated the process with other unsuspecting customers. In the classic manner of ghetto formation, outsiders reaped substantial profits at the price of overcrowding, physical deterioration, and the resultant antisocial behavior.[6]

The creation of two sprawling ghettos to house Chicago's blacks was due in large measure to the influence of government. After World War II, the federal government endowed the cities with the wherewithal to launch urban redevelopment and renewal programs and massive public housing construction, which reinforced existing patterns of segregation. Such programs reconfigured the South Side, establishing institutional barriers to movement, replacing private dwellings with public housing monoliths, displacing thousands of poor blacks, and as a result creating the West Side ghetto. Arnold R. Hirsch concludes, "If anything, government building programs gave old enclaves a permanence never seen before, and new ones were created by the uprooted thousands who mingled—as on Chicago's West Side—with a like number of recent migrants seeking their fortune within cities still sharply divided by color."[7]

The urban renewal bonanza in Chicago began with Mayor Martin Kennelly. The darling of the city's progressive elements, Kennelly was no liberal in race relations and fully approved of residential segregation. He found little common ground with the CHA leadership bequeathed him by his predecessor, Ed Kelly; chairman Robert Taylor (a black former public housing manager) and executive secretary Elizabeth Wood favored the construction of units in white neighborhoods where vacant land could be found much more easily than in the congested Black Belt. In 1949, however, the state legislature passed a law requiring city council approval of public housing sites in cities with a population of more than five hundred thousand (a standard that described only Chicago). Acknowledging that the battle for scattered-site housing "was lost," Robert Taylor resigned in 1950. Kennelly and the city council embarked on a program to tear down slums and to erect public housing within the black ghetto. According to CHA director C. E. Humphrey, the city council, the Metropolitan Sanitary District, and the Illinois Commerce Commission all exercised the option to veto the location of public housing in white neighborhoods.[8]

When blacks trying to escape the ghetto sought housing in white communities, they met fierce resistance from neighborhood associations, mobs, and a hostile city government. White opposition to integrated housing flared at the CHA's Fernwood Park Homes in 1947, and in Park Manor and Englewood in 1949. Mayor Kennelly took no action to curb the violence and blamed the incidents on subversives. In 1951 a black family attempted to move into an apartment in suburban Cicero, and thousands of whites stormed the building. Only the intervention of the National Guard restored order. Another riot ensued in 1953 when a black family moved into a far South Side CHA project, Trumbull Park Homes. After the intimidated family fled, Elizabeth Wood secured a police detachment of a thousand men to protect the twenty new black families taking up residence in Trumbull Park. Shortly thereafter, the CHA dismissed Elizabeth Wood—whose departure meant the end of the agency's attempts to challenge the city government—and replaced her with a more malleable civil servant, retired army lieutenant general William Kean. "The Chicago Housing Authority's role in responding to the great migration from the South," notes Nicholas Lemann, "would be to try to keep as many of the migrants as possible apart from white Chicago."[9]

By the time Richard J. Daley became mayor, the city council firmly controlled housing policy; the CHA had become, in Elizabeth Wood's words, a "captive authority"; and the commitment of Chicago officialdom to racial segregation was complete. And undeniably successful. A U.S. Commission on Civil Rights report released in 1959 called Chicago the nation's most residentially segregated city. A segregation index used by demographers Karl E. Taeuber and Alma F. Taeuber—an index of dissimilarity that showed the minimum percentage of nonwhites who would need to move to produce a random racial distribution—gave Chicago a score of 92.1 in 1950 and 92.6 in 1960.[10]

Alvin Rose, Daley's choice to replace CHA executive secretary Kean, refined the cooperation between his agency and the city council to eliminate any friction in the site selection process. The mayor's appointment of compliant party loyalists to the housing board made unlikely the kind of embarrassing disagreements with the city council that had been common during the Kennelly years. The CHA cleared all housing sites with those aldermen whose wards were targeted before making recommendations to the city council. If any site recommendations introduced by the CHA or anyone else provoked opposition in city council chambers, housing coordinator James Downs recommended that consideration be deferred. In all, a smoothly functioning apparatus assured that troublesome site selection requests would be buried quietly and quickly.[11]

Fully exploiting the federal resources as Kennelly had not, Daley completed the second ghetto with remarkable dispatch. In 1955, when approximately two-thirds of the people residing in CHA projects were black, nonwhites constituted 73 percent of the families moving into public housing units. By 1959 the proportion of blacks in CHA projects had risen to 85 percent. Between 1955 and 1966, the city council approved fifty-one public housing sites, forty-nine of which were situated in the ghetto areas of the South, Near West, and Near North Sides. Of the fifty-four-family housing projects operated by the CHA in 1968, 91 percent of the units lay, by the CHA's own account, "in areas which are or soon will be substantially all Negro."[12]

In 1958 Stateway Gardens opened on State Street between Thirty-fifth Street and Pershing Road, containing 1,684 units in two seventeen-story buildings. That same year the 3,600-unit Frances Cabrini Homes extension opened, the original project having been built twenty years earlier; the 1,096-unit William Green Homes, located north and west of Cabrini, followed four years later. The Robert Taylor Homes, recognized as the largest public housing project in the world at the time of its completion in 1962, contained 4,415 units in twenty-eight identical sixteen-story buildings. Abutting Stateway Gardens and occupying a site one-fourth of a mile wide and nearly two miles long, from Pershing Road south to Fifty-fourth Street, the Robert Taylor Homes originally housed twenty-seven thousand people—of whom twenty thousand were children, all were poor, and almost all were black. Immediately upon completing McCormick Place, the construction firm that built the Robert Taylor Homes began work on the public housing poject early and, as a result, unexpectedly finished eleven months ahead of schedule. To fill the apartments rapidly, the CHA suspended its normal screening procedure and accepted tenants virtually at random. As a result, crime, juvenile delinquency, vandalism, and other problems surfaced immediately. The mammoth Robert Taylor Homes project, said architecture critic W. Joseph Black, was "one of the worst tragedies that architects have created, and surely among the world's ugliest buildings." Newspaperman M. W. Newman called it a "seventy million dollar ghetto."[13]

The Stateway Gardens–Robert Taylor Homes complex constituted a monument to big city social engineering. Extending along

State Street from Thirty-fifth to Fifty-fourth Streets in an area one-quarter of a mile wide and two miles long, the projects housed just under forty thousand poor blacks. Separating the projects from the white neighborhoods just a few blocks to the west was the Dan Ryan Expressway, a fourteen-lane demarcation between the white and black South Sides completed by Daley in 1967. Originally designed to angle sharply from the southwest to the northeast, the Dan Ryan was built as a north-south thoroughfare to conform more closely to the existing racial residential schema. For the many motorists daily traversing the "world's busiest expressway," the overwhelmingly white crowds attending Chicago White Sox baseball games at Comiskey Park on the west banks of the Dan Ryan at Thirty-fifth Street, and the thousands of white home owners in Southwest Side neighborhoods such as nearby Bridgeport, the towering projects just across the Dan Ryan Expressway were hallmarks to segregation.[14]

The mushrooming of giant public housing structures across the South Side landscape that occurred during the Daley years was as impressive to aficionados of large-scale public works construction as it would later be horrifying to critics who complained about the warehousing of the poor in cold, sterile silos. In the 1960s few such critics objected, however, for high-rise public housing (along with urban renewal in general) won favor with most liberals. Even Elizabeth Wood approved. Following the lead of such internationally renowned urbanologists as Swiss architect Le Corbusier, proponents believed that vertical development would allow for the provision of large nearby tracts of park space. With land acquisition costs prohibitively high, the economic argument for high-rises seemed compelling. For machine politicians such as Daley, the necessarily complex construction technology provided additional patronage opportunities not available with the building of low-rise dwellings. Also, the concentration of thousands of poor blacks—many of whom believed themselves dependent upon the political machine for access to the welfare system—presented an attractive political opportunity. Democratic precinct captains found public housing projects made-to-order, because they contained great numbers of registered voters under one roof; frequently, enough voters resided in such high-rise buildings to qualify as precincts by themselves. In addition, many poor blacks believed that tenancy in a public housing unit required a recommendation by that project's precinct captain—a misconception that machine politicians either encouraged or at least failed to correct.[15]

For Daley, the use of public housing to concentrate the black population in ghettos made sense for several reasons: it pleased the liberals, who saw the large-scale construction of public housing as a commitment to sheltering the poor; it maintained segregregation, which pleased his white constituency in the neighborhoods threatened by racial change; and it preserved the means by which black votes could be controlled. Maintaining the black vote—vitally important as the nonwhite population of Chicago continued to increase—was significant, but Daley had his sights on a related goal also: the emasculation of powerful black Democrat William L. Dawson. Born in Albany, Georgia, in 1886, Dawson had graduated with honors from Fisk University, served in the American Expeditionary Force during World War I, received a law degree from Northwestern University, and opened a law practice in Chicago. Entering politics as a Republican, he was elected second ward alderman in 1933. Defeated for reelection in 1939, Dawson switched to the Democratic party and became second ward committeeman with the support of the Kelly-Nash machine. Elected in 1942 to represent Illinois's first congressional district in the U.S. House of Representatives, he later became chairman of the House Committee on Expenditures and vice chairman of the Democratic National Committee.[16]

During the Kelly and Kennelly years, Dawson's power on the South Side expanded, and he became vice chairman of the Cook County Democratic Central Committee. However, Daley was unwilling to countenance any rivals, proclaiming that "there can be no organizations within The Organization." The mayor understood the role Dawson played in Kennelly's demise and must have heard the rumors that the black Democrat once proposed an alliance with a leading Polish politician to wrest control of the party machinery from Daley and his Irish supporters. Wary of the South Side leader's desire to expand his bailiwick into the increasingly black West Side, the mayor sought to decentralize authority in the hands of a number of subservient ward leaders. The use of public housing to preserve segregation neatly dovetailed with the drive to crush Dawson, because the razing of South Side slums sent thousands of his constituents to the growing West Side ghetto, where he exercised little control as yet: "Every time that iron ball bats down one of those slum buildings on the South Side," crowed Daley loyalist Benjamin Lewis, "twenty Negro families move west."[17]

Daley's campaign against Dawson seems to have been purely a

matter of practical politics, a product of the boss's desire to secure his standing against all possible competitors. There existed no animus between the two men (as there had been between Dawson and Kennelly), and they had gotten along well enough during Daley's slow rise in the Democratic party. In Springfield, Senator Daley had tutored Dawson's man Christopher Wimbish, helped him draft bills, and then lobbied for their passage. When he served as Cook County clerk, Daley had often stopped by Dawson's office on his drive home to Bridgeport and chatted for as long as an hour. As a candidate for mayor, he had paid homage to Congressman Dawson's vote-producing prowess and continued to enjoy good relations with him.[18]

Daley's ostracism of Dawson could not be explained by the fact that the emerging civil rights movement influenced Dawson's politics in any way. Always a gradualist in racial matters, Dawson appointed few blacks to the many congressional posts he controlled. In 1956, defying his black colleagues in the House and ignoring the entreaties of the NAACP, he voted against a bill prohibiting segregation in public schools. A stalwart machine politician to the end, Dawson scoffed at the more confrontational attitudes gaining force in black America. Militant young blacks accused Dawson of being a lackey for Daley and the white Democrats, of feathering his own nest and not speaking out on behalf of the poor black masses. Pilloried for avoiding the House of Representatives rostrum, Congressman Dawson said, "I don't like publicity. . . . They can't hurt you for what you don't say." Critical of the civil rights movement and its leaders, Dawson argued that traditional politics offered the most hope to urban blacks. "You want oratory, don't you?" he challenged critics in one of his few public utterances, "Well, let me tell you something. The world is full of orators, but it isn't full of organizers. In this Second Ward, we've got organizers. I don't need to make speeches to get out the vote." No dissident, William Dawson was a good company man; to Richard J. Daley, too good. He had to go.[19]

Even before becoming mayor, Daley had begun to chip away at Dawson's power. As Democratic party chairman, he vetoed Dawson's candidates for committeemen in the third, fourth, and twentieth wards and chose instead men on whose loyalty he could rely. Shortly after becoming mayor, Daley chose Claude Holman as fourth ward alderman. Holman deserted Dawson and quickly established himself as a shameless cheerleader for Daley; in city council meetings he often stood up and shouted, "God bless Richard J.

Daley, the greatest mayor in the history of the world, the best friend the black man ever had." In 1958 Holman and fifth ward alderman Leon Despres cosponsored an open occupancy bill, which Dawson roundly condemned (and presumably Daley frowned upon as well). Holman backtracked by referring the bill to the corporation counsel's office for an opinion, and there it subsequently died. Unmollified, Dawson demanded that the Democratic Central Committee punish Holman by depriving him of his patronage. Daley sided with the alderman; the results of the showdown demonstrated that Dawson's agendas carried no special weight in city hall and that the black ward leaders needed to concern themselves only with securing the mayor's blessing. After the 1963 mayoral election, Dawson shifted his residency to Washington, D.C., focused all his time on congressional business, and abdicated his role in local politics.[20]

With Dawson in self-imposed exile, the South Side black aldermen remained quietly subservient to the mayor. By Daley's second term, Chicago's black aldermen had become known as the "Silent Six" for their refusal to offer an opinion on any city council business unless receiving a signal from the mayor or finance committee chairman Tom Keane. Apart from Holman's regular paeans to the mayor, only twenty-fourth ward alderman Benjamin Lewis occasionally broke the silence and then just to vilify Dawson. Otherwise, the black Daley loyalists kept quiet and contributed their votes to the city council's automatic support of the mayor's policies: "I sometimes wonder why so many of the Negroes on the City Council are so docile in this day and age," observed a white Democrat perceptively, "and then I realize that if they weren't docile they wouldn't be there."[21]

In his study of black politics in Chicago, political scientist William J. Grimshaw noted that Daley's recruitment of black ward leaders followed some clear patterns. Spurning experienced politicians, the mayor initially chose "civic notables," men whose elevated standing in their local communities earned them a loyal following. In that fashion, Daley chose Olympic medalist Ralph Metcalfe in the third ward, prominent attorney Claude Holman in the fourth ward, affluent businessman Robert Miller in the twentieth ward, and high school athletic coach Joseph Robichaux in the twenty-first ward. As the civil rights movement intensified in the mid 1960s and the civic notables came under increasing pressure from their constituents to assert their independence from downtown, Daley began enlisting relative unknowns from the patronage ranks—men such as William

Shannon in the seventeenth ward, John Stroger in the eighth ward, and Eugene Sawyer in the twentieth ward. The preponderance of Daley's recruits were Roman Catholic, a fact that provided them with another tie to the local political machine and strikingly contrasted them to the overwhelmingly Protestant-based civil rights movement. In all cases, Daley demanded unswerving loyalty to his machine.[22]

With the exception of Lewis, the West Side wards of the second ghetto continued to be represented in the council by white aldermen. In the 1960s, long after blacks dominated the rolls of registered voters in these wards, white political organizations still predominated—in some instances, electing absentee candidates who had moved out of the neighborhoods years before. Known collectively as the "plantation wards," the wards of the black West Side provided Daley with some of his greatest vote pluralities and offered the perfect example of the cynicism inherent in machine politics. In the city's worst neighborhoods, those steeped in poverty and indeed defined by racial discrimination, black voters blandly continued to cast their ballots for a political machine apparently indifferent to their condition. Were blacks amply rewarded for their loyalty? To what degree was city government responsive to their needs? How long would it be before the rising clarion call of the civil rights movement found an audience among Chicago blacks? Could Daley still insist that there were no ghettos in his city?[23]

As such questions mounted in the early 1960s, Daley defended his record forcefully. He pointed to the number of black aldermen, committeemen, state legislators, police captains, and other government officials in Chicago—a number equal to or surpassing the number of black officials in other large cities, the mayor claimed. He spoke repeatedly of how blacks needed to replicate the successes achieved by other minorities in the past. Like the Irish, they should move up from poverty to middle-class respectability by working hard, demonstrating their loyalty to the political machine, and garnering their share of municipal jobs and other emoluments. He refused to acknowledge any significant differences involving historical circumstances or, most critically, skin color: "I think one of the real problems he has with Negroes is understanding that the Irish are no longer the out-ethnic group," observed a black Chicagoan.[24]

In addition to making political appointments, the mayor acted occasionally on behalf of blacks to secure symbolic advances. After the city council passed a statute outlawing racial discrimination in the employment of physicians in private hospitals, for example, Daley met with members of the city's medical establishment to inquire why white-only institutions refused to hire qualified black doctors. Dismissing their excuses, the mayor secured promises that the color line would be broken—and it was. Black leaders applauded the handful of appointments that resulted, but scattered among fifty or so area hospitals the change affected very few people and was inconsequential to most Chicagoans. No significant controversy resulted. Daley could clearly afford to support such policies, but he balked at tackling larger issues that potentially affected great numbers of white voters. The integration of a few hospital staffs notwithstanding, the mayor's unwillingness to challenge prevailing practices regarding public housing location, open occupancy in the private real estate market, and public school segregation left him vulnerable to charges of hostility toward fundamental civil rights issues.[25]

Problems intensified in 1963. Addressing the annual meeting of the NAACP, Daley could not finish his speech because of boos and catcalls from the conventioneers. Never before had he been treated so rudely by a black audience. Also that year, the city council considered an open housing ordinance submitted by liberal fifth ward alderman Leon Despres, which prohibited racial discrimination by real estate brokers. A joint report by Chicago's city planning and human relations commissions reviewed fair housing laws adopted in other cities and states, concluding that no significant population shifts occurred after their implementation. The city council's judiciary committee subsequently adopted a watered-down version of Despres's ordinance. The alderman complained about the changes, but real estate interests still found the measure too stringent and objected to it strongly. The morning the city council considered the bill, five thousand whites (mostly women from the Southeast, Southwest, and Northwest Side bungalow belts) marched to city hall to voice their opposition. With Daley announcing his support, the measure passed by a vote of thirty to sixteen.[26]

Immediately, the Chicago Real Estate Board filed a suit to obviate the ordinance, calling its anti-discrimination provisions unconstitutional. In 1965 the Circuit Court of Cook County ruled against the realtors and upheld the law, as did the Illinois State Supreme Court in 1967. In the meantime, as Despres predicted, the measure proved to be a paper tiger. Exempting private home owners from its strictures, the ordinance applied only to real estate brokers. Seldom invoked by the Chicago Commission on Human Relations and lacking adequate enforcement machinery, the open housing ordinance left no imprint on Chicago's racially divided cityscape. Whatever capital Daley may have earned among black voters for his support of the bill quickly evaporated amid charges of inadequacy and tokenism, whereas the impassioned reaction by white home owners to the mayor's gradualist measures underscored the rising level of racial tension in the city and presaged more conflict.[27]

As his white constituents voiced their desire to hold the line against integration, Daley was under increasing pressure from civil rights groups to institute meaningful reforms. In 1963 that pressure came primarily from The Woodlawn Organization (TWO), a neighborhood reform group founded three years earlier by famed labor organizer Saul Alinsky. Working closely with Samuel Cardinal Stritch, who shared his dream of integrating blacks into the city's socioeconomic fabric and provided necessary funds from the Roman Catholic archdiocese of Chicago, Alinsky sought to create a viable racially integrated community in the deteriorating South Side Woodlawn neighborhood. TWO's activism originally centered on opposition to the University of Chicago—whose purchases of land for expansion southward into North Woodlawn threatened to replicate the evils of other urban renewal programs—but also included attacks on the city for its poor provision of services and its operation of substandard, segregated schools.[28]

On July 10, 1963, Daley met with an eighteen-member TWO delegation led by the Reverend Arthur Brazier in hopes of heading off a march on city hall that the organization had scheduled for the next day. The discussions ranged from job discrimination to integration of the city-supported Washburne Trade School to the school board's racial policies and finally to University of Chicago expansion and urban renewal in North Woodlawn. Despite the mayor's conciliatory manner, the delegation found him unwilling to make substantive concessions and decided to go forward with the planned demonstration. On July 11, ten buses from Woodlawn containing six hundred protestors arrived at city hall. Approximately two hundred marchers conducted a brief sit-in outside the mayor's office while leaders met with Daley inside. Again the mayor was noncommittal, but shortly thereafter he agreed to halt temporarily any more demolition in Woodlawn until low-income housing was completed for the uprooted community residents.[29]

The concession on urban renewal in the South Side stilled the criticism on that issue, but TWO and other civil rights groups shifted their attention to Chicago's segregated public schools. Metropolitan demographics and the residential distribution of the baby boom generation exacerbated racial separatism, for a spate of relatively new classrooms on the predominantly white fringe contrasted sharply with classrooms in the city core, where the number of minority children overwhelmed aged facilities. Resentment among blacks about unequal educational opportunities had been simmering for years, especially since the publication of a 1958 article in the NAACP's journal, *Crisis*. The exposé revealed that 70 percent of the city's elementary schools were "predominantly white," 21 percent "predominantly black," and only 9 percent "mixed." Predominantly white elementary schools averaged 669 pupils and predominantly black schools averaged 1,275 pupils. The *Crisis* report concluded, "In cost and quality of instruction, school time, districting, and choice of sites, the Chicago Board of Education maintains in practice what amounts to a racially discriminatory policy." Dissidents also pointed to a 1962 U.S. Civil Rights Commission report that reached this determination: "From the point of view of racial discrimination or merely that of nonracial equal protection, the confinement of pupils in crowded classes when other facilities are underutilized cannot be justified." School board president Clair Roddewig countered, "If the courts would say that the neighborhood school policy violates the Constitution of the [U.S.], we would change; but the courts have not said that."[30]

The race-education conundrum revolved increasingly around the personality of one man, education superintendent Benjamin C. Willis. The superintendent arrived from Buffalo, New York, in 1953 to restore the school system's good name after his predecessor, Herold C. Hunt, caused a scandal by allowing board of education employees to write textbooks that the Chicago schools were forced to adopt. Willis enjoyed a national reputation as an effective, innovative administrator, and even his detractors admitted that he ran a scandal-free operation. He also successfully supervised $50 million bond issues in 1955, 1957, 1959, and 1961, which made possible the construction or expansion of 208 elementary schools, thirteen high schools, a junior college, and a teachers college as well as the doubling of public school teachers' salaries. But while establishing an outstanding administrative record, the superintendent also took a forthright position against public school desegregation. During Willis's first ten years in Chicago, the number of public school students mushroomed from 375,000 to 520,000. To accommodate the skyrocketing enrollment, he initiated a double-shift schedule whereby many students attended only half-days in the mornings or afternoons; significantly, blacks accounted for 90 percent of the double-shift pupils. Abjuring busing as an improper use of educational funds, Willis repeatedly upheld the tradition of neighborhood schools. When 107 black families requested transfers for their children to predominantly white schools, the superintendent denied their requests and said curtly, "They can go to school wherever they live."[31]

Blacks charged that Willis's defense of neighborhood schools amounted to more than just a preference for a sentimental ideal. They argued that Willis had constructed so many new schools in the Black Belt in order to perpetuate segregation. Because of the recent school-building boom, blacks would always have access to nearby schools even if they were overcrowded and poorly staffed. Meanwhile (Willis's detractors noted), classrooms stood empty in white schools just a few blocks away. TWO "truth squads" photographed vacant classrooms in white schools and received additional publicity when police arrested the photographers for trespassing. A Chicago Urban League study reported that black teachers earned 85 percent as much as their white counterparts earned and that the school system spent only two-thirds as much educating black pupils as whites. In 1961 Willis announced a new policy allowing black students to apply for transfers when their school's average classroom size reached forty; white schools, however, were not required to accept new students unless their classrooms averaged fewer than thirty students. A total of thirty-two students citywide qualified for transfers under this plan. In 1962 the U.S. Civil Rights Commission censured the Chicago Board of Education and the superintendent for policies retarding integration.[32]

Willis made a perfect foil for critics of the education establishment, who claimed that the haughty administrator had changed Chicago's official motto from "I Will" to "I Willis." His $48,500 annual salary made the superintendent the nation's third-highest-paid public official (trailing only President John F. Kennedy and New York governor Nelson Rockefeller), yet he appeared absolutely impervious to calls for accountability. Imperious, arrogant, and frequently inaccessible, he refused to answer questions about his policies and to provide school attendance data. In February 1963, the state legislature passed the Armstrong Act, which amended the Illinois School Code to require local school boards to dismantle segregation by redrawing attendance boundary lines. To comply with the new law, Chicago had to provide attendance figures, and although Willis continued to delay, the school board finally released the information. Belatedly acknowledging the overcrowding in ghetto schools, Willis moved black students into empty warehouses and other deserted buildings rather than into white schools. He also deployed mobile trailer classrooms, dubbed Willis Wagons, near existing schools to keep black students in their own neighborhoods. The *Chicago Defender* referred to Willis as "the Gov. Wallace of Chicago standing in the doorway of an equal education for all Negro kids in this city—a one-man educational John Birch Society, incarnate and inviolate."[33]

The rising criticism of Willis and the school board forced Daley to make a few concessions. In 1962 he added a black organization (the Cook County Physicians Association) to the list of groups that could send a representative to the mayor's advisory commission on school board nominations, and the following year he appointed Warren Bacon, a black businessman, to the school board. He would not, however, accede to the demand that Willis be fired. Although Daley appointed the members of the board of education, he piously claimed, "I have adhered strictly to the principle that there should be no interference of any kind with the policies and administration of the board of education." As a mayoral aide explained, other reasons may have accounted for Daley's reluctance to terminate Willis's employment:

> The more the blacks picked on Willis, the more popular he became among the whites. If Daley gave in, the whites would have been mad. He figured he'd always get the black vote, but the whites had already shown that they'd go for somebody else when they went for Adamowski. Besides, Willis was useful to Daley. If the civil rights people kept after Willis, it kept the heat off Daley.[34]

While the mayor did nothing, tens of thousands of black students boycotted classes. In August 1963 black demonstrators rioted, throwing molotov cocktails at one Willis Wagon and setting fire to another. Black teenagers threw bricks and bottles at policemen, who arrested fifty-six protesters. Unmoved by the violence, Daley publicly gave Willis a vote of confidence; blacks responded with a mammoth school boycott during the fall of 1963, in which two hundred thousand students missed classes for a day.[35]

On October 4, 1963, Willis suddenly announced his resignation, charging the board of education with "encroaching on his duties as superintendent." On October 7, the board voted (6–2 with one abstention) to refuse his resignation, and on October 16, Willis announced that he would abide by the board's decision and resume his duties. The protest from black Chicago came quickly and forcefully. An estimated 225,000 black students—half of Chicago's public school enrollment—boycotted classes on October 22, while another 8,000 adults encircled city hall, waving placards and shouting their displeasure. Daley claimed that the disturbances were financed by "outside sources for political reasons" and alluded vaguely to "Communist influence." A second boycott, staged on February 25, 1964, resulted in 175,000 absences and more acrimony. Daley responded tersely to reporters' questions about the demonstrations: "What did they prove?" he asked.[36]

On March 31, 1964, a group of five educators led by University of Chicago sociology department chairman Philip Hauser released a report on public education that had been mandated as part of an out-of-court settlement in the case of *Webb v. Board of Education of the City of Chicago*. Mincing no words, the report scored the school board for its complicity in segregation. Hauser took the opportunity to pillory Superintendent Willis specifically, calling him "a giant of inertia, inequity, injustice, intransigence, and trained incapacity." Six days after the report's release, the school board published a "study guide" that attempted to deflect the criticisms. Superintendent Willis declined to endorse the Hauser report, and the board of education subsequently made no effort to promote its acceptance by teachers or administrators. Having approved the study several months before when a federal court ordered the Hauser committee to assess the public schools' performance, Daley offered no comment when the furor arose over its conclusions.[37]

In June 1964, the Chicago City Council ignored the protests of dissident blacks and approved the reappointment of Lorraine Green to the board of education. A black octogenarian whose husband had been a loyal member of the Democratic machine, Mrs. Green had avidly defended Superintendent Willis's policies for years and had voted to refuse his resignation in October 1963. In her testimony before the city council, she said, "I don't know what integration means. There is no segregation in Chicago's schools. When the only question asked of a child is: 'Where do you live?' that is not segregation!" Almost alone, alderman Leon Despres spoke against the reappointment, but his eloquent remarks made no impact on Daley's city council. Amid warnings that citizen protest might escalate into mass violence, the aldermen overwhelmingly recommended Lorraine Green's reappointment. The mayor complied.[38]

A second report condemnatory of public education in Chicago was released on November 12, 1964, and kept the school segregation question on the newspaper front pages. Prepared by a committee under the guidance of University of Chicago professor Robert S. Havighurst, the 502-page report reiterated many of the charges leveled by the earlier study and made twenty-two recommendations, many of which dealt with desegregation. At his insistence, Superintendent Willis was named a member of the investigating committee, but he took no part in preparing the report. Whereas the board of education had formally responded to the Hauser document with denials, it simply ignored the Havighurst report. Again, Daley remained mute.[39]

Even as the schools controversy lingered on, other events in 1964 indicated that the civil rights question was not going to go away. A race riot in suburban Dixmoor made Chicago officials anxious about the possibility of such violence in their city, but the summer passed without incident. In October John Walsh, a white high school teacher, bought a house in Bridgeport just three blocks from the Daley home and rented it to two black college students. "I believed that it was only proper," he said, "that a Negro should live on the same street near the home of the mayor of the city of Chicago." The neighborhood residents thought otherwise. A huge crowd surrounded the building and threw bricks and rocks through the windows. The police defended the inhabitants, fought hand-to-hand with the rioters, and arrested twelve whites; four policemen were injured. The violence subsided after three days, when the police removed the black men's belongings from the house and the realtor awarded a new lease to two white tenants.[40]

Throughout the entire episode, Daley kept a low profile. Liberals urged the mayor to intercede with his neighbors and call for a cessation to the violence, but he declined to take what would have been a very unpopular position with much of his white constituency. John Walsh claimed, "I proved that Daley was guilty of passive hypocrisy. He could have prevented all the trouble. . . . Daley didn't lift a finger." The residents of Bridgeport were not ready for integration, and neither was their neighbor, the mayor.[41]

The unsettling events of 1963–1964 portended a growing challenge to white Chicago's control of a traditionally placid black population. To be sure, many blacks still supported the Democratic party, believing that the Republicans offered no viable alternative and convinced that access to government benefits depended upon continued fealty to the Daley machine. One black realist commented, "We're loyal to the organization because it works, because we know of no better way of improving our position in Chicago, and because, while it can't give everyone everything he wants, it can give most Chicago groups enough to keep them happy." But an increasing number of dissidents questioned the preservation of what they saw as an inequitable alliance—one in which black voters received disappointingly scant rewards for their electoral contributions. For the mayor and the Democratic machine he dominated, this newfound black assertiveness not only threatened patterns of segregation in public education and housing but jeopardized white political hegemony as well. With the elimination of William Dawson as an independent force in the Democratic party, Daley invested lesser amounts of power in, and received advice from, a number of black politicians equally committed to a system of clientage politics. As Dawson had done, these black aldermen concerned themselves with electioneering, patronage, and spoils to the exclusion of civil rights protest. They fiercely opposed change because of the threat it represented to their own interests, perquisites, and political fiefdoms.[42]

For Daley and the shrinking white majority in Chicago, the unwillingness to share political power, living space, schools, and (ultimately) wealth emanated from self-interest, tribalism, racism, and fear. Those critics who assailed Daley for his refusal to yield to the rising tide of black protests may have mistaken intransigence for insensitivity. The mayor, his white constituency, and a cadre of black allies became involved in a holding action against forces threatening their way of life. With Daley spearheading the resistance, the challenge to plantation politics would be met with all the resources the mighty Chicago Democratic machine could muster.

A youthful Richard J. Daley in cap and gown (Chicago Historical Society).

Richard J. Daley and Mayor Martin Kennelly (center) at an Eleventh Ward Democratic Organization Picnic on August 21, 1949. At that time, Daley was eleventh ward committeeman; in 1955 he would wrest the Democratic mayoral nomination from Kennelly (UIC—Urban Historical Collection).

Newly elected Mayor Richard J. Daley stands in front of a mural of Chicago in April 1955. In the coming years his extensive construction program would change the face of the city's downtown (Chicago Historical Society).

Mayor Daley with wife Eleanor and five of their children at the St. Patrick's Day parade in 1956. The boy in the back is future mayor Richard M. Daley (UIC—Urban Historical Collection).

Daley shakes hands with Adlai E. Stevenson, the Democratic candidate for president, in August 1956. To the consternation of many Chicago reformers, Stevenson had endorsed Daley for mayor the previous year and would again in 1959 (Chicago Historical Society).

In the company of former baseball commissioner Albert "Happy" Chandler and Massachusetts Senator John F. Kennedy at Comiskey Park, Mayor Daley cheers for his beloved Chicago White Sox during the 1959 World Series. The following year Daley would play a significant role in Kennedy's election as president. In the foreground is Richard M. Daley (*Chicago Sun-Times*).

National Guardsmen patrol West Madison Street as firemen battle blazes during the riots following the death of Martin Luther King Jr. on April 6, 1968. Following the disturbance, Daley issued his notorious "shoot-to-kill" order (Chicago Historical Society).

Helmeted Chicago police brace for a confrontation with protesters during the 1968 Democratic National Convention. Daley defended the actions of the policemen despite charges of a "police riot" (Chicago Historical Society).

Making the World Safe for Hypocrisy. No.

"Making the World Safe for Hypocrisy." Edward Sorel's 1970 King Features Syndicate cartoon caricatures Daley as a brutal policeman beating anti-war demonstrators. After the events of 1968, Chicago's mayor was widely regarded as a symbol of law-and-order and defender of the establishment (Chicago Historical Society).

A contemplative Mayor Daley presides over a city council budget debate during his last years in office. By the mid 1970s, although the Organization Democrats still maintained a comfortable majority in the city council, dissent had become more common and debate livelier (Chicago Historical Society/Photographer: Jerry Tomaselli).

5

Pressure from External Sources

Chicago's problems of race and poverty did not exist in a vacuum. City halls across urban America attempted to grapple with these intractable problems during the 1960s, usually with unsatisfactory results. Big city mayors complained that the task was frequently made more arduous by the intrusions of well-intentioned reformist groups that sought to apply uniform solutions to unique local problems. With the federal government actively implementing President Lyndon B. Johnson's Great Society programs, Washington, D.C., played a large role as financial benefactor and adviser to local governments. As the civil rights movement spilled out of the South in mid decade, northern city officials had to deal with another kind of external force—what many frustrated mayors described as "outside agitators" purveying insidious doctrines of revolution. In 1965 Mayor Richard J. Daley confronted such challenges from the federal government's War on Poverty, which offered cities great potential benefit, but at the cost of a loss of local control, and also from the Department of Health, Education, and Welfare's Office of Education, which threatened to intervene locally to force public school desegregation. He also had to deal with the Reverend Martin Luther King Jr.'s choice of Chicago as the next target of his civil rights crusade. In all these cases, Daley acted predictably by asserting the principle of home rule and showing his obvious displeasure with any outsiders intent on usurping his authority. He had no more intention of allowing federal bureaucrats to decide how government funds would be spent in his city than he had of allowing alien civil rights workers to transform Chicago institutions.

In January 1964, President Johnson declared, "This administration today, here and now, declares unconditional war on poverty in America." Later that spring, the White House sent to Congress a massive bill, the Equal Opportunity Act, whose many provisions defined the administration's anti-poverty program. The measure created the Office of Economic Opportunity (OEO) to administer a variety of projects: the Job Corps, the Volunteers in Service to America (VISTA), the Neighborhood Youth Corps, a work-study program for poor college students, loans for poor rural families and small businesses, aid to migrant workers, training for unemployed heads of households on welfare, and the vaguely defined Community Action Program (CAP). Johnson saw CAP as a modern version of the New Deal's National Youth Administration (whose Texas branch he had administered from 1935 to 1937) and expected that the federal agency would simply direct funds into the coffers of friendly Democratic city governments. It seems he either overlooked or underestimated the significance of the law's language requiring that community action programs be "developed, conducted, and administered with the maximum feasible participation of residents of the areas and members of the groups served." In congressional hearings, Mayor Daley succinctly summarized his fellow mayors' dim view of "maximum feasible participation," saying, "We think the local officials should have control of this program." Congress failed to address the mayors' misgivings and passed the bill with the original language intact.[1]

In March 1964, anticipating the passage of the bill, Chicago became one of the country's first cities to respond to President Johnson's call for a nationwide assault on poverty. To administer the CAP program, Daley created the Chicago Committee to Advance the Attack on Poverty, whose name was quickly changed to the Chicago Committee on Urban Opportunity (CCUO), an official city agency laden with trusted local bureaucrats and conspicuously lacking representatives of the poor. The "Chicago Concept," as Daley outlined it, consisted of mobilizing existing welfare agencies under the supervision of local bureaucracies; the federal government's function would be limited to providing the necessary funds, the poor's role limited to receiving them. Daley chaired the ninety-member CCUO: eighty-three members were municipal officials, corporate executives, welfare administrators, labor leaders, university presidents, clergymen, and other local luminaries; seven members represented poor neighborhood residents. As executive vice chairman of the committee, Daley installed Clair Roddewig, a highly respected railroad executive and a close friend, who functioned for all practical purposes as the board's chief administrator. Daley again made clear his opposition to "maximum feasible participation" by the poor, saying, "To throw open the poverty boards to elections in the neighborhoods would only bring conflict and bitterness which Chicago has too much of already. It is a mistake for mayors to let go of control of their programs to private groups and individuals. Local government has responsibilities it should not give up."[2]

In large measure, Daley's commitment to a tightly controlled, highly centralized program came from his experience with the federal crusade against juvenile delinquency in the cities, which had been initiated several years earlier under the Kennedy administration. The mayor concluded that the juvenile delinquency program had directed funds into civil rights organizations that attacked the city's segregated schools. Daley had fired many of the juvenile delinquency workers, created a new program that minimized community participation, and thereby relinquished eligibility for federal funding. Although his decision cost the city millions of dollars, the mayor insisted that social welfare programs be divorced from potentially divisive elements in the community. He viewed the new anti-poverty program of the Johnson administration with the same apprehension.[3]

Daley selected Dr. Deton Brooks, the black former director of research and statistics for the Cook County Department of Public Aid, to be executive director of the Chicago Committee on Urban Opportunity. Not surprisingly, Brooks's public statements mirrored the mayor's views on the committee's composition. The executive director commented, "Certainly, no one in Chicago would disagree that the poor must be involved, but I also think we should face up to the problem that there are other kinds of groups that have to be involved also." Brooks appointed the directors of the twelve neighborhood service centers that had been organized to implement the committee's programmatic decisions; the directors, in turn, chose area residents to staff the neighborhood advisory councils. The program hired one thousand poor people—most often those with letters of recommendation from Democratic precinct captains and aldermen—to serve in the vaguely defined advisory capacity of "community representative." These workers provided services to the needy but did not encourage or convey demands (the city reprimanded or fired political activists). In all, the emerging anti-poverty apparatus in Chicago cleaved tightly to the local power structure and gave the poor only token representation.[4]

Aware that the program taking shape in Daley's Chicago subverted the intentions of the War on Poverty, Washington officials quickly registered a protest. The Bureau of the Budget's William Cannon flew to Chicago to confer with the mayor and subsequently reported a stalemate. Cannon, a native Chicagoan, admitted, "I had no illusions about making radical changes in this city and I wasn't really trying to. I just wanted to see if somehow we couldn't inch forward with the notion of community participation which had been going on in Hyde Park and Back of the Yards and so on." He encountered precisely the intransigence that federal bureaucrats expected from city hall. "It was clear that there would be no poverty program without Daley running it," Cannon recalled. "He was explicit with me. I was explicit with him that there had to be local participation."[5]

Daley took his case directly to the White House. Presidential aide Bill Moyers fielded some of the mayor's telephone calls and remembered Daley railing, "What in the hell are you people doing? Does the President know he's putting MONEY in the hands of subversives? To poor people that aren't a part of the organization? Didn't the President know they'd take that money to bring him down?" Already troubled by the performance of the OEO, which seemed to be generating more complaints than accolades for his administration, Johnson listened to Daley's lamentations with a sympathetic ear. Unwilling to alienate one of the most powerful men in his party, the president took no action against Chicago's noncompliance. The CAP's director of operations Frederick Hayes recalled bitterly, "We had problems with Daley on *everything*, and he always went to the White House, and always won."[6]

Daley found in R. Sargent Shriver, the OEO's chief administrator, an ambitious politician eager to curry favor with the Chicago Democratic machine. Reputedly harboring ambitions of running for the U.S. Senate in Illinois, Shriver could not afford to alienate the state's kingmaker. Ignoring the contretemps over "maximum feasible participation," Shriver praised Daley's program for opening its neighborhood centers quickly and assembling an efficient anti-poverty bureaucracy. Indeed, he lauded Chicago for having "the model CAP in the country." While publicly criticizing Mayor John Shelley for failing to involve the poor in San Francisco's CAP program, Shriver overlooked the same shortcomings in Chicago.[7]

In 1964 The Woodlawn Organization (TWO) submitted two proposals to OEO for the creation of job-training programs, an attempt by the organization to obtain financial assistance directly from Washington, D.C. TWO claimed to be the official representative for the neighborhood and argued that, unlike municipal bureaucrats who were far removed from Woodlawn, TWO well understood how to combat poverty and joblessness. Unwilling to relinquish its control of federally funded programs, the city vigorously challenged TWO's applications. Noting Daley's opposition and his proven influence with the Johnson administration, the *Chicago Daily News* reported the assessment of a knowledgeable Washington observer that "it will be a cold day in hell before TWO gets a penny." As the newspaper predicted, OEO declined to fund TWO's proposal.[8]

In January 1965, Robert D. Shackford, the temporary head of OEO's midwest regional office, informed Brooks that Chicago was not in compliance with CAP requirements and that further funding would depend upon the total reorganization of the local organization. Following the vehement protest from Chicago that predictably resulted, OEO removed Shackford from his post. When his two successors also insisted on literal enforcement of agency regulations in Chicago, they found their tenure equally abbreviated. The subsequent appointment of a native Chicagoan with a history of amicable relations with the mayor halted the revolving door of OEO regional directors.[9]

In April 1965, the subcommittee on the War on Poverty of the U.S. House of Representatives Committee on Education and Labor held hearings on the Chicago program. The congressmen heard the president of TWO—the Reverend Lynward Stevenson—excoriate the "Chicago Concept" for its blatantly political operation. Stevenson charged, "This is maximum feasible participation of the rich. This is maximum feasible participation of precinct captains. This is maximum feasible participation of ward committeemen. Where is maximum feasible participation of the poor?" Subcommittee chairman Adam Clayton Powell followed Stevenson's testimony with a hostile cross-examination of Deton Brooks, at one point exploding, "Answer me. Who do you have? Give me the names of those on the central advisory board, council, whatever, the overall operation. Who are they? Who are poor? Have you any? Yes or no?" Dr. Brooks lamely replied, "Mr. Chairman, I say that our whole committee represents the poor." Powell scoffed that the Chicago anti-poverty organization looked like "minimum feasible participation of the poor and maximum feasible participation of the politicians." The congressional investigation received extensive coverage in the local press, but the controversy quickly subsided as the newspapers concluded that nothing would change. The *Chicago Sun-Times* expressed sympathy for the mayor's critics but assumed that Daley had already reached an agreement with Sargent Shriver that no congressional investigation could alter.[10]

At its June 1965 meeting in St. Louis, the U.S. Conference of Mayors chose Richard J. Daley to chair its new War on Poverty Committee and considered a resolution cosponsored by Democratic mayors Sam Yorty of Los Angeles and John Shelley of San Francisco urging that the OEO recognize locally approved agencies to administer CAP projects. Believing that adoption of the resolution would embarrass President Johnson, conference leaders deferred a vote and requested a meeting with administration officials. Daley and his committee promptly conferred with Theodore M. Berry (the administrator of OEO's anti-poverty program) and Vice President Hubert Humphrey (himself the former mayor of Minneapolis) to plead their case and reportedly received reassurances that the Johnson administration would continue to be attentive to the mayors' concerns. Two months later, Humphrey spoke to the National League of Cities convention about CAP. He said, "I can tell you now that your important role is assured in this program. I'm your built-in Special Agent to make sure that you are represented in this program twenty-four hours a day, 365 days a year. I've been hired for you."[11]

The friction between reform-minded OEO staffers and the Chicago CAP continued, but because of the Johnson administration's reluctance to alienate the big city mayors, "maximum feasible participation" remained decidedly minimal. Daley's minions made a few concessions, but not meaningful ones. Chicago's neighborhood advisory councils originally ignored OEO's call for the creation of neighborhood poverty councils but then relented to demonstrate literal compliance with the law. Rather than allow elections, however, the neighborhood advisory councils appointed neighborhood poverty council members who subsequently exerted little influence in policy-making. The poverty councils could "review" and "recommend" programs but had no authority in the operation of neighborhood service centers. The anti-poverty structure remained rigidly hierarchical, granting the poor virtually no voice in its operation. Deton Brooks explained, "It was decided that persons who were below the poverty line could not successfully be involved in a middle-class decision-making type of committee." Saul Alinsky grumbled that the program was a "prize piece of political pornography." In 1966 an OEO evaluation team arrived in Chicago to assess the anti-poverty program and received a personal welcome from the mayor who encouraged them to be thorough and critical. Daley also told them, however, that he would not tolerate "irresponsible charges about politics, resident participation, and segregation in the schools." The review team raised no such issues.[12]

In struggling to regulate closely the War on Poverty in his city, Richard Daley never stood alone. In addition to Sam Yorty of Los Angeles and John Shelley of San Francisco, such big city mayors as Detroit's Jerome Cavanaugh and New York City's Robert Wagner publicly opposed the OEO's strictures. As of September 1966, the poor comprised only 29 percent of the members of community action agencies nationwide. At that time Congress stipulated that only one-third of the members of neighborhood councils need be elected by the poor—a percentage roughly equivalent to the poor's representation in Chicago. According to historian Sidney Fine, the poor controlled local anti-poverty efforts in just three cities (San Francisco, Newark, and Syracuse) by the fall of 1967. That same year, Congress authorized the municipal takeover of privately operated community action agencies in tacit recognition that the mayors had won the battle for local control—a triumph many ascribed principally to Daley's unwavering efforts spanning the length of the contest.[13]

In 1965 the mayor's bureaucratic infighting with Washington attracted less attention than his ongoing battles with Chicago's increasingly aggressive civil rights organizations. As before, the focus of the turmoil continued to be Benjamin Willis's autocratic administration of the public schools. At an unofficial meeting in May, the school board voted by a seven to four margin not to extend Willis's contract for another four-year term when it expired on August 31. Ten days later at an official meeting, three board members changed their votes so that Willis was retained by a seven to four count (with the stipulation that the superintendent agree to retire on his sixty-fifth birthday in December 1966). Board member Cyrus Adams explained that such a compromise would allow adequate time for an orderly transferral of power to a new superintendent and permit Willis to remain in office during the negotiations over educational funding that were ongoing in the Illinois legislature. Black protesters anticipating Willis's imminent removal chafed at any extension, however, and suspected foul play. They believed that the three board members switched their votes on orders from Daley, who feared a white backlash to Willis's ouster. Indeed, Cyrus Adams believed that the mayor secretly intervened to ensure Willis's retention for another term.[14]

The Coordinating Council of Community Organizations (CCCO)—a confederation of local civil rights groups formed in 1962—took the lead in fashioning a protest to the school board's reversal, announcing a two-day boycott of the public schools to be held on June 10–11. On June 8, the school board obtained an injunction against the boycott, while Daley appealed to parents to send their children to school. Public housing officials, Democratic precinct captains, and other machine loyalists urged parents to keep their children in school and sometimes threatened boycotters with rent increases or removal from welfare rolls. CCCO leaders reported having been offered jobs and other bribes in return for failure to support the protest. Despite the city's efforts, however, more than one hundred thousand students ignored the injunction and marched from Soldier Field to city hall and to the board of education building on June 10. The next day police arrested 228 marchers, most of whom had halted traffic by sitting down at the intersection of Balbo and Columbus Drives. "As long as I am mayor there will be law and order," Daley affirmed. He also requested a meeting with CCCO officials, but the organization's leader, Albert Raby, refused because of the arrests. "Who is this man Raby?" Daley fumed, "He doesn't represent the people of Chicago. I've received almost a thousand phone calls from Negro mothers saying he doesn't represent them." On June 28, Daley finally met with Raby and other CCCO representatives and rejected their demands that he remove Willis immediately. In the bitter aftermath of the incident, the mayor charged that the marches had been financed by "outside sources for political reasons" and ascribed the unrest generally to "Communist influence."[15]

Along with the continuing furor over Ben Willis came the announcement that Dr. Martin Luther King Jr.'s Southern Christian Leadership Conference (SCLC) intended to take its civil rights campaign to Chicago, the "most segregated city in the North." On July 6, 1965, King paid a brief visit to Chicago; he announced his intention of launching a major desegregation effort in the city that summer and promised to return later that month. Daley's emissary, Chicago Commission on Human Relations director Edward Marciniak, met King at the airport when he returned on July 23 and tried unsuccessfully to arrange a meeting between the mayor and the civil rights leader. On July 26, King spoke to an assembly of approximately thirty thousand people at Grant Park's Buckingham Fountain, then led them on a march to city hall where he delivered another speech critical of Willis and the city fathers who supported him. Absent from the city that day to attend a mayors' conference in Detroit, Daley issued a bland rejoinder, saying, "The presentation of his position against poverty and discrimination, for which he was deservedly awarded the Nobel Prize, is a position that all right-thinking Americans should support."[16]

King quickly left Chicago, but his departure brought only a brief respite to the city, for on July 27–28, Benjamin Willis testified before a congressional committee investigating de facto racial segregation in Chicago public schools. To avoid threatened anti-desegregation demonstrations in Chicago, where the hearings had originally been scheduled, House Education and Labor Committee chairman Adam Clayton Powell Jr. moved the proceedings to Washington, D.C. Playing to an appreciative audience in his committee's conference room, Powell grilled Willis at length. The superintendent denied that his policies were intended to reinforce segregation, explaining that "housing patterns . . . pose problems in our efforts to provide opportunities for integrated education for significant numbers of children." Following Willis's testimony, University of Chicago sociologist Philip Hauser sardonically commented, "The committee should be congratulated. It is the first time that I have heard Dr. Willis say anything in twelve years in favor of integration, and I would say it is long overdue." Occurring immediately after King's visit, the highly publicized two-day hearings focused national attention again on Chicago's mounting racial crisis.[17]

Meanwhile, the anti-Willis marches that had commenced in late June continued on a reduced scale throughout the summer. Each day, from fifty to one hundred protesters carrying placards marched in front of city hall; pushing and shoving on the sidewalk often led to isolated arrests and a series of unseemly spectacles downtown as police removed the protesters. In the month following the initial demonstration, police arrested a total of seven hundred protesters. Continuous media coverage generated a steady flow of negative publicity, and some of the most prominent members of the city's business community began for the first time to question the mayor's handling of the schools crisis. Forty-eight local captains of industry submitted to the board of education a letter demanding a response to the civil rights organizations' allegations of institutionalized segregation; they received no reply.[18]

During the daily demonstrations, Chicago police followed Superintendent Wilson's instructions to exercise restraint, to employ force sparingly, and to arrest demonstrators only when necessary. The mayor, harboring no sympathy for willful lawbreakers, chafed at Wilson's permissiveness and thought the police should act more forcefully. Daley's irritation peaked that year when several Roman Catholic nuns staged a sit-in at the intersection of Madison Avenue and State Street during rush hour and he discovered that Superintendent Wilson had ordered his men to divert traffic for thirty minutes around the protesters until they voluntarily departed. Outraged that wholesale arrests had not been made, the mayor demanded an explanation of Wilson and strongly registered his disapproval. Still bound by his pledge of noninterference in police conduct, however, Daley could only vent his displeasure. Determined that minor incidents would not escalate into major crises because of excessive force employed by his officers, Wilson neither resigned nor altered his directives. The tension between the mayor and his police superintendent persisted.[19]

On August 1, civil rights organizations shifted tactics, taking their protest into the mayor's Bridgeport neighborhood. Led by black comedian Dick Gregory, approximately seventy-five protesters (including white priests and nuns as well as blacks) paraded quietly in front of the mayor's house. Hundreds of Bridgeporters initially watched in amazement, then threw eggs and tomatoes, brandished Ku Klux Klan signs, and shouted profanities at the marchers. Scores of voices sang, "Two-four-six-eight, we don't want to integrate" and "Oh, I wish I was an Alabama trooper, that is what I'd really like to be-ee-ee. Cuz if I was an Alabama trooper, I could kill the niggers legally." Miraculously, no violence ensued that first night. The next evening, the hostile crowd of onlookers grew to an estimated two thousand, and the heckling took on a more ominous tone. Some residents aimed their lawn sprinklers and hoses at the marchers; others hurled rocks and firecrackers. A large police detachment moved in, arresting sixty-five demonstrators—ostensibly for their own protection—and no area residents. Throughout the disturbances, Mayor Daley remained in his house.[20]

The next day, civil rights leaders protested the arrest of peaceful demonstrators while rock-hurling rioters remained free. Police Superintendent Wilson defended the action as the best means of averting an outbreak of uncontrollable violence. Inextricably bound to white segregationist voters, Daley came aggressively to the defense of his neighbors:

> People in their homes have a right to privacy. Surely the family of a man in public office shouldn't be subjected to this kind of action. There is no reason for this kind of marches late at night or early in the morning. I don't think it helps their cause to be marching in residential areas. I think they are surely trying to create tension. . . . Our neighbors are fine people, middle income working people. And they have no feelings one way or another about all this.[21]

Daley claimed that it was "a matter of record" that "known Communists" had fomented the trouble; later he identified the Republican party as the culprit. Leading Chicago Democrats saw the leveling of such highly dubious charges as evidence of the strain on Chicago's embattled mayor. Democratic congressman Dan Rostenkowski expressed concern to the White House over Daley's emotional health, suggesting that President Johnson find some pretext to send Daley out of the country for a week or two to defuse the tension. In any event, the mayor advised his neighbors to avoid further confrontations, to ignore the marchers when they resumed activity. An eerie calm settled over Bridgeport as the civil rights demonstrators returned for their silent vigil night after night in the sweltering August heat.[22]

The silent war of nerves ended abruptly on the night of August 12. Rushing to answer an alarm, a Chicago Fire Department hook-and-ladder truck sped away from a West Side station in the heart of the black ghetto without the tillerman who normally steered the long vehicle's tail. The truck's rear section fishtailed and uprooted a light pole, which fatally wounded a young black girl. Fueled by rumors that a drunken white fireman had killed a black girl, Chicago's first summertime race riot of the 1960s erupted. For weeks blacks had been picketing the fire station, demanding that some black firemen be employed there, and relations between the all-white firemen and the ghetto residents had deteriorated steadily. In the wake of the tragic accident of August 12, Fire Commissioner Robert Quinn rushed an all-black unit in to replace the white firemen, but it was too late to forestall the uprising.[23]

After four nights of rioting, the violence subsided. The conflagration in the Watts ghetto of Los Angeles, which occurred at roughly the same time, resulted in thirty-one deaths. Chicago officials reported eighty injuries, 169 arrests, and no fatalities. At Daley's request, Illinois governor Otto Kerner dispatched the National Guard to Chicago, but because of the successful efforts of the police and community leaders, they never left their armories. Decidedly minor in comparison with what Chicago and other cities would experience later in the decade, the riot of 1965 nevertheless caused considerable consternation among civic leaders. In public, the mayor dismissed the violence as "a question of lawlessness and hooliganism." He insisted, "I don't think the west side situation was a question of civil rights."[24]

His claims of sanguinity notwithstanding, the mayor quickly met with representatives from civil rights organizations to discuss the causes of the riot. After a two-hour exchange, the black spokesmen expressed disappointment at the lack of agreement on crucial issues. Daley steadfastly refused to discuss the termination of Education Superintendent Willis and reaffirmed his commitment to an independent school board. Equally frustrated by the lack of progress in the talks, the mayor questioned the legitimacy of the blacks' grievances. He proudly defended his administration's record on civil rights, especially in contrast with the achievements of other cities. He told one interviewer:

> Listen, when they had those riots in Harlem, the highest ranking [black] police officer in the city of New York was a lieutenant. We have three Negro commanders. We have seven Negro police captains. In the Fire Department we have two Negro deputy marshals, three battalion chiefs. We have a Negro vehicle commissioner. We have more Negro judges than New York.[25]

The chasm between black demands and Daley's willingness to respond remained wide, and the possibility of fruitful negotiations with the city government seemed remote to civil rights leaders. So, as these organizations mounted continuous demonstrations throughout the summer of 1965, they moved on other fronts as well. On July 4, 1965, the CCCO's Albert Raby submitted to U.S. Commissioner of Education Francis Keppel a complaint alleging that the Chicago Board of Education, acting in concert with the Chicago Real Estate Board and the CHA, contrived to maintain segregation in the public schools. The complaint charged specifically that the school board's policies violated Title VI Section 601 of the Civil Rights Act of 1964—which prohibited exclusion from federally funded activities on account of race, color, or national origin—as well as U.S. Department of Health, Education, and Welfare (HEW) guidelines to assure compliance with the federal law.[26]

In response to the CCCO's complaint, HEW secretary John Gardner dispatched an investigative team to assess the Chicago situation. The HEW representatives met with Benjamin Willis but found him uncooperative; he refused, for example, to provide them with the school attendance data they needed to complete their study. The Chicago superintendent further informed HEW officials that he would use the largess from the newly enacted Elementary and Secondary Education Act of 1965, which stipulated that funds be spent for students from low-income families, in white middle-class census tracts and for the purchase of additional mobile classrooms—in other words, for more Willis Wagons. Consequently, Education Commissioner Keppel decided to withhold from the Chicago public schools a $30 million appropriation from the Elementary and Secondary Education Act until resolution of the CCCO charges. On September 30, Keppel so informed Willis and Illinois superintendent of public instruction Ray Page.[27]

Chicago officials reacted swiftly and aggressively. U.S. congressman and loyal Chicago Democratic machine member Roman Pucinski questioned the legality of Keppel's action and threatened to file a lawsuit against the U.S. Office of Education. "Congress won't appropriate another nickel for education programs," threatened Pucinski, if such "arbitrary and dictatorial acts" persisted. On October 2, Superintendent Willis denied that noncompliance with the 1964 Civil Rights Act had been proved and called Keppel's decision unenforceable. Daley charged that the episode had "done irreparable damage to the whole concept of federal aid to education," adding that "he would fire Keppel if he worked for him."[28]

On October 3, Daley met with President Johnson in New York City and complained bitterly about the treatment afforded his school system. When Johnson returned to Washington, he called a meeting of HEW officials to discuss the situation and then dispatched undersecretary Wilbur Cohen to Chicago to work out a settlement. According to Cohen, Daley charged that "there is a conspiracy in the federal government of people in the OEO, the Labor Department, and HEW to embarrass him." Because Johnson already suspected OEO staffers of being disloyal, this proved to be a persuasive complaint. According to Cohen, Daley said, "You're taking away the funds from me without ever having consulted me. You never told me about the issue; you never consulted me or asked me what my views are; you never tried to get me to resolve it; all you do is you send a telegram and I read it in the newspaper."[29]

Sympathetic to Daley's charges of not being kept informed of federal government's dealings in his own backyard, Johnson promised the mayor better communication in the future. Cohen met with Daley's representative, school board chairman Frank Whiston, and within one hour the two men had worked out a face-saving agreement whereby HEW released the $30 million grant to Chicago schools and agreed to withdraw its investigators for two months while the school system looked into its own practices. Several months later, the board of education submitted to HEW an incomplete report that failed to address key questions about racial segregation. HEW's Office of Education resumed study of the situation and in January 1967 submitted its final report (a document approved in advance by Willis's successor, James F. Redmond, the Justice Department, and the White House), which issued no ultimatums and offered a series of essentially innocuous recommendations.[30]

The outcome of this episode reinforced the image of power emanating from Chicago's city hall. The mayor's vehement protests brought the resumption of federal spending just four days after the announced suspension, a compelling indication of Daley's influence with the Johnson administration. At the press conference with Wilbur Cohen announcing the negotiated settlement, Frank Whiston implied that the Office of Education was backing down because of Daley's intercession with the president. White House adviser Douglass Cater called the clash "a real embarrassment," because the Office of Education "had certainly not done the judicious thing of having informed the mayor privately, in advance, so that he would not be caught offguard by this action." Even Francis Keppel conceded that he had made a mistake in the handling of a politically sensitive situation, and he paid for the error with the loss of his job. Within a few months, both he and HEW assistant secretary James Quigley, who had zealously supported Keppel's decision to with-hold the funds, were eased out of their positions. Keppel's successor, Harold Howe II, eagerly professed his determination to maintain a good working relationship with Chicago's superintendent and mayor.[31]

The year 1965 was a troubling but, in many ways, a satisfying year for Daley. Determined to safeguard his bailiwick against outside forces, he withstood confrontations with two agencies of the federal government—the OEO and the Office of Education—that sought to impose binding restrictions on local implementation of federally funded programs. In the process, he exposed an inherent weakness in Lyndon Johnson's Great Society programs—an irreconcilable tension between reform-minded Washington bureaucrats and local politicos whose electoral strength made them crucial to the president's Democratic coalition. To appease one was to alienate the other. Daley used this leverage skillfully to retain control of such programs as the War on Poverty and federal aid to education, both of which benefited his city at no cost to the local political machine.

Yet despite these successes, Chicago's mayor could not escape the ubiquitous problem of race. Asked that year to assess the city's future, Daley confidently predicted: "You'll see a stable, harmonious city in which the people recognize the dignity and the rights of all." But the mayor's optimistic statement notwithstanding, racial tensions continued to rise. Opposition to Benjamin Willis persisted, a symptom that deeper feelings of resentment were rising to the surface. The West Side riot of August 1965 heightened the anxiety among many Chicagoans about the potential for conflict in the long hot summers to come, when temperatures would climb and tempers flare. Perhaps most troublesome, Martin Luther King's initial brief forays into the Chicago political landscape gave promise of greater immersion by national civil rights groups. Indeed, after an absence of nearly three months, King returned to the city on October 6 to assure Chicagoans that he had not forgotten his northern campaign. After the first of the year, he pledged, the SCLC would launch a full-scale assault on the forces of segregation and inequality. In a conciliatory fashion, King added, "I don't consider Mayor Daley as an enemy." But he was, of course. Achieving the kind of breakthroughs in race relations of which King spoke inevitably meant clashing with Daley and the white Chicagoans he repre- sented. The events of 1965 clearly indicated Daley's unwillingness to accept the ideas that an outsider such as King hoped to import into Chicago.[32] Changes in the city's race relations were unwel- comed, whether initiated by external forces or local agitators.

6
Confrontation with King

When the Reverend Martin Luther King Jr. took his civil rights crusade to Chicago early in 1966, more blacks lived in Cook County, Illinois, than in any other county in the nation. Not only did more blacks reside in Chicago than in the entire state of Mississippi, but more blacks occupied the city's larger public housing projects than populated Selma, Alabama—the 1965 site of King's greatest victory. Aside from the sheer numbers involved, the Windy City presented a formidable challenge to King's Southern Christian Leadership Conference (SCLC) because of the black community's complicity with the hegemony of the Daley machine. With black political power subservient to the local Democratic party, an effective organizing campaign would be extremely difficult for King to establish. Veteran civil rights leader Bayard Rustin advised King against a full-scale assault on the Chicago Democratic machine, predicting, "You won't beat Daley on his home ground and you'll come away with nothing meaningful for all your efforts." King was unpersuaded. He thought that Chicago would be a good target for civil rights reform, because unlike other northern metropolises where power was diffused and decentralized, change could be effected there with the consent of just one man. Despite its size, Chicago might be changed if Mayor Daley's opposition could be overcome. King had bested individuals who had impeded reform before—most notably Eugene "Bull" Connor in Birmingham and Sheriff Jim

Clark in Selma—and believed he could do so again. Chicago would remain the target.[1]

In anticipation of the SCLC's arrival, Daley continued to boast of his city's already considerable civil rights achievements: "We are not perfect," he asserted, "but we feel that we have done more than any other metropolitan city in the country." Although generally conciliatory in his manner, the mayor left no doubt that he resented the intrusion of outsiders who were unfamiliar with local conditions. He told the Cook County Democratic Central Committee, "We have no apology to any civil rights leaders who come into our city to tell us what to do. The record of the Democratic Party on civil rights is clear." To questions about what the city's response would be if King employed his usual tactics involving civil disobedience, Daley responded quietly but firmly: "I am hopeful and confident there will not be any reason for breaking law. All of us are for the elimination of slums. This is the number-one program of the present administration and has been for the ten years we have been here." He would, Daley said often, make sure that the city's departments cooperated fully with Dr. King, but he would not tolerate violence or other extralegal activities.[2]

In January 1966, King made three exploratory visits to Chicago. During the first two, he met with the leadership of the Coordinating Council of Community Organizations (CCCO) to outline a cooperative assault on the city's entrenched residential segregation patterns. The SCLC and local civil rights groups, which had temporarily united to form the Chicago Freedom Movement, planned to concentrate their efforts initially on a campaign to educate the public about the wretched housing conditions imposed on blacks within the de facto segregation system in northern ghettos. On his third January visit, King and his wife, Coretta Scott King, rented a four-room apartment in the heart of the city's West Side ghetto—the area just east of suburban Cicero where three hundred thousand persons were jammed into eight hundred square blocks.[3]

With much fanfare, King and his wife moved into a dilapidated building at 1550 South Hamlin Avenue in the Lawndale neighborhood known to local blacks as Slumdale. Hundreds of area residents cheered "the Pied Piper of Hamlin Avenue" as he and his entourage arrived. Inside, the Kings found a tiny, dingy apartment virtually without heat, in which, Coretta King remarked, "the smell of urine was overpowering." When the building owners had discovered the identity of their new tenant, they had quickly sent an eight-man crew to clean and repair the unit. (Media wags suggested that King could improve living conditions for the city's masses of tenement dwellers simply by changing addresses often.) Even so, the apartment's condition shocked King, who told reporters that he would lead rent strikes if slumlords failed to improve their properties immediately.[4]

Three days later, King met with Police Superintendent Orlando W. Wilson and his staff, explaining how the Chicago Freedom Movement would practice civil disobedience. Wilson received the delegation cordially, and Daley proudly proclaimed, "I believe this is the first police department in the country that [King] has met with." Repeatedly during King's early days in Chicago, the mayor and his subordinates displayed uncommon courtesy in their dealings with the civil rights personnel. The city's civil servants obligingly made every effort to accommodate the Freedom Movement's requests for action. Indeed, Daley's solicitousness made King feel that he was "fighting a pillow," creating a situation altogether different from and less satisfying than the earlier confrontations with combative southern law enforcement officers spoiling for confrontation. On February 9, without mentioning King, Daley announced a new program to clean up the city's slums by the end of 1967. The mayor implicitly agreed with the need for slum eradication and avoided public conflict with King, while emphasizing again that Chicago would take care of Chicago's problems. In the following months, the city dispatched an army of inspectors to the West Side in search of code violations, supervised repairs in thousands of dwellings in order to meet municipal housing standards, and razed hundreds of abandoned buildings. An observer said: "If Daley makes a mistake, it will not be for a lack of interest in slums. . . . Before he's through, his crusade will make King's look minor league."[5]

Determined to regain the initiative, members of the Chicago Freedom Movement seized control of a crumbling Lawndale tenement near King's apartment and announced that they were putting it in "trusteeship." They further instructed the four families residing there to pay their rent directly to King, who would use the money to make necessary repairs and forward anything left to the owner. Daley noted that this could not be done, for "there are legal and illegal ways" to aid slum dwellers. Further, he added, the city had already charged the landlord with twenty-three building code violations.

The Cook County welfare agency threatened to cancel rent-subsidy payments to any tenants who withheld their rent. King argued that, in observance of a higher morality, what the tenants had done was "supralegal"; federal district court judge James B. Parsons disagreed, calling the action "theft." Although the tenants never paid any rent, King spent $1,000 on improvements before an injunction barred the civil rights activists from entering the building.[6]

In March, Daley conferred twice with a number of the city's leading clergymen, including Roman Catholic Archbishop John P. Cody, about the problem of slum housing. Unable to be present at the first meeting, King and other members of the Freedom Movement attended the second, which lasted for a full three hours. The mayor made a lengthy and elaborate presentation, replete with fact sheets and charts, detailing all that the city government had done to address the civil rights leaders' concerns. King initiated a twenty-minute dialogue with Daley about the pervasiveness of racism in mainstream America and the "collective guilt" of Chicagoans for the fate of ghetto dwellers. Daley heatedly objected to King's sweeping indictment of white Chicago, saying, "These problems were created thousands of miles away from here in Georgia, Mississippi, and Alabama. This deprivation of education can't be laid to the people of Chicago. They had nothing to do with it."[7]

After the meeting, reporters asked King about rumors of the Chicago Freedom Movement mobilizing to contest Mayor Daley's reelection the next year. King responded quickly and decisively: "I'm not campaigning against Mayor Daley. I'm campaigning against slums." In fact, the SCLC members marveled at the mayor's dominance of the black electorate, particularly the unswerving devotion of the city's black Democratic politicians to the machine. Whatever local black insurgency existed originated outside normal political channels. When Daley suggested pointedly that King ought to return to his native Georgia, seven black ward committeemen—the most powerful black politicians in the city—seconded the suggestion.[8]

The summer's first racial disturbance came from an unexpected source, the city's tiny Puerto Rican community. Squeezed into a small area on the Near Northwest Side, the Puerto Ricans maintained a nearly invisible presence in Chicago. Although they endured the same discrimination and harsh living conditions as did Chicago's black population, the Puerto Ricans' small numbers and corresponding lack of political influence made them easy to ignore—until June 12, when a policeman shot and killed a neighborhood youth. The riot that followed left nineteen persons hospitalized and dozens more injured, seven by gunfire. Rioters burned police cars and broke storefront windows along the community's main thoroughfare, Division Street. After two days and nights, the fighting ceased. Predictably, Daley denied the existence of serious problems and blamed "outsiders."[9]

On June 25, public schools superintendent Benjamin Willis announced his resignation, a full four months earlier than anticipated. King and his cohorts were in Mississippi, participating in a march protesting the shooting of James Meredith, and offered no comment on the controversial superintendent's unexpected withdrawal from the racially charged scene. Willis's surprise announcement elicited strikingly little reaction from the CCCO, which had over the years invested so much time and effort in his removal. Even a year earlier this event might have been hailed as a milestone, but the appearance of Martin Luther King Jr. and the SCLC had upped the stakes in Chicago. Once limited to a discussion of segregated schools, dissent from the black community had become a comprehensive assault on the horrors of ghetto life. Whereas Ben Willis had once served as a lightning rod for civil rights protest, the broader-based campaign for change initiated by the Chicago Freedom Movement made the city's mayor the new focus of attention. Long before Willis's resignation, the racial struggle in Chicago had crystallized around the internationally renowned civil rights leader and the intransigent mayor.[10]

In Mississippi, King and his acolytes had argued with Stokely Carmichael and other adherents of the rising Black Power movement. The old-line civil rights leaders worried about the growing appeal to the black masses of such militant groups as the Student Nonviolent Coordinating Committee (SNCC) and the Congress of Racial Equality (CORE), both of which were expanding their activities in northern metropolises as well. Sensitive to complaints about the lack of progress made against Daley and eager to demonstrate the preferability of his methods to violent revolution, King prepared to launch large-scale civil disobedience in Chicago. The SCLC's Andrew Young explained: "We have got to deliver results—nonviolent results in a Northern city—to protect the nonviolent movement." King called for a massive rally at Soldier Field and a march to city hall on "Freedom Sunday," July 10, as the opening of a series of marches into white neighborhoods and suburbs.[11]

King hoped for a rally of one hundred thousand people on Freedom Sunday, but a much smaller crowd braved the sweltering ninety-eight-degree heat to participate. (Attendance estimates ranged from the city's twenty-three thousand to the SCLC's sixty thousand; local newspapers suggested thirty thousand to forty thousand.) After entertainment by Dick Gregory and Mahalia Jackson, James Meredith spoke briefly to the crowd. Roman Catholic auxiliary bishop Aloysius Wycislo read a message of support from Archbishop Cody, and representatives of the Union of American Hebrew Congregations and the Church Federation of Greater Chicago sat on the speaker's platform. In his keynote address, King posited the futility of violence and passionately defended the Freedom Movement's choice of peaceful civil disobedience. He affirmed his belief that nonviolence did not mean passivity and that the articulation of fully realizable goals could produce truly revolutionary changes. Summoning the full force of his indignation, he told the assemblage:

> This day we must decide to fill up the jails of Chicago, if necessary, in order to end slums. This day we must decide that our votes will determine who will be the next mayor of Chicago. We must make it clear that we will purge Chicago of every politician, whether he be Negro or white, who feels that he owns the Negro vote.

Approximately five thousand protesters followed King on the three-mile march to city hall where he taped a list of demands to the locked door. Among other demands, this truncated version of his namesake's ninety-five theses called for increased employment opportunities for minorities, a citizens review board for the police department, nondiscriminatory real estate practices, and the preparation by the city of a desegregation plan.[12]

The next day, King and ten Freedom Movement leaders met with Daley in the mayor's office to discuss the list of demands. Daley refused to endorse officially any of the items, nor would he announce his support for President Lyndon Johnson's civil rights bill that was pending in Congress. Instead, the mayor read aloud from a forty-page memorandum detailing the myriad programs devised by the city to deal with poverty and inadequate housing. Flanked by department heads and aides who fed him documents, statistics, and memoranda, the mayor coolly rebutted charges and answered questions by citing municipal initiatives already planned or just being devised. As always, Daley fell back on familiar defenses: Chicago was doing more than any other city; unfair charges ignored nascent programs; critics made sweeping indictments and spoke in generalities rather than offering specific programs as solutions. "Why don't you help us?" Daley asked the civil rights workers.[13]

Again, the meeting satisfied neither group. King told the press that Daley did not understand "the depth and dimensions of the problem we are dealing with" and that "the current programs are in good faith; they are just not broad enough to be effective." The city's designs offered "only surface changes, and the Negro community can no longer live with token changes." As a consequence, King promised, the civil rights campaign would be escalated to produce mass jailings. The mayor told reporters of his exasperation with the meeting: "We asked them, 'What would you do that we haven't done?' They had no answers. I asked for their help and suggestions, and they frankly said the answers were difficult. I asked them, 'Why can't we sit down and you tell us?' There wasn't any answer."[14]

When asked about King's threat to fill the jails with demonstrators, Daley sternly replied, "This will not be tolerated as long as I am mayor. I don't think Dr. King would violate any law. He said he was not for violence." In a more subdued manner, he added, "Dr. King is very sincere in what he is trying to do, [but] maybe, at times, he doesn't have all the facts on the local situation. After all, he is a resident of another city." Clearly, the meeting produced no results; the antagonists remained faithful to their positions and found no common ground. King prepared to take the sit-ins, boycotts, and mass demonstrations out of the central business district and lakeside civic center into the city's all-white neighborhoods where nonviolence would meet its greatest test.[15]

Before the civil rights groups could stage these marches, the rising racial tension spilled over in the worst Chicago riot since 1919. The day after the Daley-King conference, Chicago city workers began turning off fire hydrants in Lawndale where black children had turned them on to seek relief from the one-hundred-degree heat. The city justified curtailing this common practice by referring to the potentially dangerous loss of water pressure in the tinderbox created by the heat wave, yet blacks saw only another affront by a remote, insensitive white bureaucracy. With tempers frayed by the heat and after weeks of mounting irascibility, hand-to-hand struggles between firemen and residents escalated into burning, looting, and sniping. The riot consumed several square miles of the West Side, as policemen trying to protect the firemen traded gunfire with rioters. On the second day, police commissioner Orlando W. Wilson called for additional help, and the mayor sent for the Illinois National Guard. The presence of forty-two hundred National Guardsmen restored order, but during the three-day conflagration, two blacks died, more than eighty people suffered injuries, and police arrested four hundred rioters. Property damage exceeded $2 million.[16]

In the midst of the rioting Daley appeared on television and assessed blame for the turbulence. He said:

> I think you cannot charge it directly to Martin Luther King, but surely some of the people came in here and have been talking for the last year in violence and showing pictures and instructing people in how to conduct violence. They are on his staff. They are reponsible in a great measure for the instruction that has been given for the training of youngsters.

King canceled a speech in Geneva, Switzerland, to remain in Chicago. He and his cohorts roamed the fiery streets night and day, unsuccessfully trying to pacify the angry mobs. Later on the same day as Daley's television appearance, King and others met with the mayor in his office. Immediately disarming his visitors, Daley backtracked from his earlier charges, saying, "Dr. King, I want to make one thing clear. We know you did nothing to cause the disorders and that you are a man of peace and love." With both sides determined to solve the immediate crisis, they devised a series of palliatives that would be easily and quickly implemented. The city hastily attached sprinklers to hundreds of fire hydrants and trucked in portable swimming pools to the West Side. The mayor promised to apply for federal funds to build permanent swimming pools in the ghetto.[17]

Daley understandably sought quick solutions that would restore peace to his city. However, civil rights leaders saw the mayor's answers as consistent with his long-standing response to blacks' concerns—a reflexive tendency to slap Band-Aids on massive hemorrhages. Scores of water sprinklers and swimming pools could not wash away the ghetto's most severe problems, they believed; such responses only relieved the symptoms without treating the diseases. Daley's use of federal anti-poverty funds to kill rats and roaches allowed him to boast that Chicago had the country's best extermination program, but civil rights leaders remained unimpressed. They felt that such stopgap measures smacked of tokenism and avoided confronting the vital issues of desegregation in housing and the workplace. The Johnson administration's eagerness to help Daley by speeding up the delivery of federal grants similarly reflected a desire to defuse an explosive situation. The end of violence in Lawndale, therefore, brought only a brief interlude of quiet for city hall, as King looked immediately at potential sites for marches.[18]

During the following weeks, King's forces led a series of demonstrations principally into Chicago's bungalow belts on the Northwest and Southwest Sides where white home owners refused to accept black buyers and real estate agents declined to obey the city's fair housing ordinance. These whites—largely middle-class, Catholic, second- and third-generation immigrants of Polish, Lithuanian, Czech, and Italian descent—reflected the prejudices and passions of Daley's Bridgeport neighbors. Many had fled black incursions into other areas of the city and had no intention of relocating again. They prepared to defend their homes and viewed civil rights demonstrations as invading armies. Devout, church-going people, hardworking and family centered, virtuous in many ways, these white ethnics nonetheless harbored little sympathy for racial equality. They were, as Chicago blacks warned King, every bit as hateful and violent as the southern whites he had encountered in Mississippi and Alabama.

Whites greeted the Freedom Movement's first forays with a fury. On July 29, white residents of Gage Park—a blue-collar community on the Southwest Side—surrounded and heckled civil rights marchers but refrained from violence. The next day, a white mob hurled rocks and bottles at five hundred marchers in Gage Park; a small police squadron could do little to protect the protesters and made few arrests. Both Albert Raby and the Reverend Jesse Jackson were hit before the marchers made their way to safety. The following day, accompanied by several hundred policemen, the protesters assembled at a Methodist church in nearby Marquette Park. While the marchers received police protection, whites descended upon the unattended automobiles the blacks had driven to the protest site. Police reported fifteen cars set on fire and another thirty with windows and windshields smashed; angry mobs pushed two cars into the park lagoon. Police arrested eighteen and reported twenty-five injuries. Mayor Daley sent for white community leaders and warned them against violence. "Ignore the marchers and they'll go away," he advised. On August 2, demonstrators marched through the Northwest Side neighborhood of Belmont-Cragin; the following day in the same location, a crowd of approximately eight hundred harassed three hundred civil rights marchers, resulting in twenty-one arrests.[19]

On August 5, accompanied by a peace-keeping force of nine

hundred Chicago policemen, King led an integrated group of approximately six hundred protesters into Marquette Park. Hostile onlookers waving Confederate flags and sporting Nazi insignias shouted, "Nigger go home," "We want Martin Luther Coon," "Kill the Niggers," and other epithets. They hurled rocks, bottles, and bricks at the marchers; one brick struck King in the temple, temporarily sending him to his knees. A knife thrown at King struck a white bystander's shoulder. The police escort, increased to one thousand officers to offset the white mob of four thousand, formed a flying wedge around the marchers to escort them to the buses and cars waiting to take them away from the scene. Visibly staggered by the encounter, King said, "I've never seen anything like it. I've been in many demonstrations all across the south, but I can say that I have never seen—even in Mississippi and Alabama—mobs as hostile and hate-filled as I've seen in Chicago." At a march two days later in Belmont-Cragin, white onlookers pelted one thousand demonstrators with assorted missiles, and only the heroic efforts of five hundred policemen in riot gear averted a full-scale massacre.[20]

In Gage Park, Belmont-Cragin, and Marquette Park, marchers met hails of stones, firecrackers, bottles, and bricks. Frantic neighborhood whites strained against police phalanxes, spat at nuns and priests marching with blacks, and brandished signs inscribed, "Archbishop Cody and his Commie coons"; members of the American Nazi Party and other fringe groups circulated through the crowds urging greater violence. Bloodied and weary, the police continued to defend the marchers day after day, often battling their own neighbors and kinsmen. King remarked, "The people of Mississippi ought to come to Chicago to learn how to hate."[21]

The cumulative effect of the marches took its toll. The repeated clashes produced horrific images on network television and outraged editorials in the national press. At the same time, Daley came under increasing criticism from white home owners for their rough treatment by Chicago police. Why was Daley protecting the blacks? they demanded. "Get Rid of Daley" placards began to appear among the other signs bearing swastikas and racist scatology. During the Belmont-Cragin marches, whites chanted, "Don't vote for the Democrats" and "If Daley can't get rid of the marchers, let's get rid of Daley!" Democratic ward committeemen implored the mayor to end the marches or suffer defections from the party faithful who were outraged at city hall's deference to civil rights groups. Even

Archbishop Cody, who had earlier supported the demonstrations, called for the mayor to exercise leadership in bringing an end to the strife. A beleaguered Daley publicly beseeched King to halt the demonstrations, mournfully commenting on local television, "There must be some way of resolving questions without marches."[22]

Even as he continued to supply protection for the marchers and as he appealed publicly for surcease, Daley worked frantically behind the scenes to arrange negotiations with the protesters. Because of the centrality of the open housing question, Daley asked the Chicago Real Estate Board to arrange a meeting where all interested parties could seek solutions. He found the real estate board uncooperative, willing only to defend its position and determined to oppose any changes in home buying and selling practices. Daley turned to the Chicago Conference on Religion and Race, which agreed to host a meeting if King could be persuaded to attend.[23]

King announced his intention of expanding the size and scope of the demonstrations and, most notably, of taking a march into neighboring Cicero, a suburb in western Cook County outside Daley's jurisdiction. Because of Cicero's reputation as the most racist community in the area, King's announcement sent shock waves throughout the state. Governor Otto Kerner mobilized the National Guard and readied the state police for special duty. Even though supporters strongly advised King against the march, he refused to reconsider: "Not only are we going to walk to Cicero," he asserted defiantly, "we're going to work in Cicero, we're going to live in Cicero." A terrified Cicero politician replied, "Jesus, they won't make it. If they get in, they won't get out alive."[24]

Fearing a bloodbath if a civil rights demonstration entered Cicero, Daley ordered the Chicago Conference on Religion and Race to do whatever was necessary to bring King and his cohorts to the bargaining table. He also implored Chicago's labor leaders to use their influence with the Chicago Freedom Movement to call a negotiating session. Agreeing to suspend the Cicero march temporarily, King finally consented to meet with Daley and the city's business, religious, and civic elites. But even as they consented to negotiate, King and his lieutenants continued to stage demonstrations: on August 12, six hundred protesters (escorted by eight hundred policemen and a surveillance helicopter) marched in the Southwest Side near Bogan High School. On August 14, three days before the scheduled conference with city officials, the Freedom Movement simultaneously dispatched five hundred marchers to Gage Park, four hundred to Jefferson Park, and three hundred to Bogan. At each location, weary policemen strained to subdue angry white onlookers; city officials reported ten injuries (including five policemen) and the arrest of twenty-one whites. On August 16, open housing picketers descended upon downtown, marching in front of city hall and the offices of the Chicago Real Estate Board, the First Federal Savings and Loan Association, the Cook County Department of Public Aid, and the Chicago Housing Authority.[25]

On August 17, local industrialist Ben Heineman, who had earlier that year chaired the White House Conference on Civil Rights, moderated the ten-hour assembly in the parish hall of St. James Episcopal Cathedral. In his opening remarks, Daley plaintively said, "We have to do something to resolve the problems of the past few weeks." King presented nine demands, most of which dealt with enforcement of the city's open housing law and the discriminatory practices of real estate brokers. The Freedom Movement also called for an end to the concentration of high-rise public housing projects in black ghettos and to the referral of public aid recipients to available housing on the basis of race. Daley asked whether the demonstrations would stop if the demands were met. King replied, "Yes, the demonstrations in the neighborhoods might stop, but we have demands also in the areas of education and employment and you are hearing here only our demands in the area of housing." Daley responded, "If we do all we can as a city, then why can't the marches stop? I thought this was supposed to be a kickoff for a conference table." When King asked the mayor for his reaction to the itemized demands, Daley read through the list and agreed to comply with each of them. Yet CHA board chairman Charles Swibel refrained from promising that high-rise public housing construction would cease, which led to a lengthy and spirited discussion. Chicago Real Estate Board member Arthur Mohl added that realtors could abide by the city ordinance, but home sellers would ultimately dictate whether discrimination occurred.[26]

Daley's willingness to accept the Freedom Movement's demands notwithstanding, Ross Beatty—representing the Chicago Real Estate Board—balked at concluding any agreements. Beatty repeated the real estate board's unwillingness to drop its lawsuit before the Illinois Supreme Court (which challenged the state's open housing law) and argued that he was not empowered to agree to anything without his constituents' approval. When the CCCO's Albert Raby suggested an end to the day's deliberations,

Daley said, "No, let's not adjourn the meeting. The Chicago Real Estate Board should get on the phone to their members and do something about these demands now." According to John Mc-Knight, an observer from the U.S. Civil Rights Commission, Daley's order "placed a terrific burden" on the real estate board. At the mayor's suggestion, the meeting adjourned to allow Beatty to confer with the realtors he represented. As the meeting concluded, the CHA's Charles Swibel exclaimed, "We need a victory for Mayor Daley, a victory for the City of Chicago." Freedom Movement members groaned. During the recess Daley telephoned Beatty, telling him, "In the interests of the city of Chicago, you cannot come back here this afternoon with a negative answer."[27]

When the meeting reconvened that afternoon, Beatty read a lengthy, vague, and often confusing statement, part of which indicated that the real estate board would "no longer oppose open occupancy." He also said, however, that "if demonstrations do not terminate promptly we may lose control of our membership and be unable to fulfill the commitments we have here undertaken." Asked to clarify portions of his remarks, Beatty simply reread the entire document. Raby asked if brokers would be obligated to post a nondiscrimination pledge in their office windows, and Daley angrily answered, "I said already this morning that I would do that, and I keep my word." Nevertheless, the Freedom Movement's representatives thought the realtors' response incomplete and evasive, and they refused to suspend the demonstrations. Frustrated at not being able to obtain closure that day, Daley launched into a combined diatribe against his adversaries and plea for cooperation:

> I thought we were meeting to see if . . . there couldn't be a halt to what is happening in our neighborhoods. . . . I repeat, as far as the city is concerned, we are prepared to do what is asked for. I appeal to you as citizens to try to understand that we are trying. I asked why you picked Chicago? I make no apologies for our city. In the name of all of our citizens, I ask for a moratorium and that we set up a committee. We're men of good faith and we can work out an agreement. . . . What's the difference between today and a week from today with men of good faith? We're defending your rights, and also there's no question about the law. Can't you do today what you would do in a week? . . . We've got to show the City Council that you'll do something. We'll pass what we said we'd pass if we get a moratorium.[28]

The Freedom Movement representatives were unmoved. Albert Raby angrily lashed back at Daley, saying, "If I come before the Mayor of Chicago some day, I hope I can come before the Mayor of Chicago with what is just and that he will implement it because it is right rather than trading it politically for a moratorium." King remained equally cynical, later remembering, "I never got the impression [Daley] meant to do the things he was promising." To the mayor's great disappointment, the conferees could reach no mutually satisfactory agreement and decided to select a subcommittee to resume the negotiations at a later date. The subcommittee—to be chaired by Thomas Ayres, president of the Chicago Association of Commerce and Industry—consisted of five representatives from the Freedom Movement, four from the Conference on Religion and Race, four from the Commission on Human Relations, two from the real estate board, one from the Commercial Club of Chicago, and three from the mayor's office.[29]

Throughout the August 17 meeting, Daley and his staff, particularly Charles Swibel, had argued for a suspension of the demonstrations. Clearly, the threat of violence and white political backlash made the cessation of protest the mayor's primary goal. Fully aware of the pressure mounting on the city, the Freedom Movement leaders used this leverage to demand as many concessions as possible from their adversaries. The continuation of discussion caused no great hardship for the protesters and brought no relief to the city officials.

Two days later Daley obtained an injunction from Cook County Circuit Court of Appeals Judge Cornelius J. Harrington that limited civil rights protests in Chicago to one march per day involving no more than five hundred people. The city council praised the mayor's leadership; black alderman Ralph Metcalfe lauded the mayor's action as "an act of statesmanship." King accused Daley of bad faith for obtaining the injunction while negotiations were ongoing. Daley rejoined with relish that evening on local television:

> People can make all the statements that they care to about bad faith . . . I acted on the recommendation of the Superintendent of Police of Chicago. I want you to know that I was raised in a workingman's community in a workingman's home. My father was a union organizer and we did not like injunctions. I know the injustice of injunctions. But I also faced the decision of what to do with three and a half million people. Because the Superintendent of Police had said that the

crime rate was soaring as his police resources, crime fighting resources, were being thrown into protecting the Freedom Movement. He also told me that the Freedom Movement wouldn't cooperate on giving him the routes or giving him advance notice or in any way helping him in an effort to provide protection. So the decision had to be made. There were many people who were demanding that we stop the marches entirely, but we said that they had a right for the marches. The course I took was the only one that I could take. I took an oath to preserve law and order and the Constitution.[30]

Some members of the Freedom Movement urged cessation of the negotiations, but King counseled restraint. The protesters decided to stage one demonstration involving five hundred marchers within city limits and skirt the letter of the injunction by deploying additional protesters in adjacent municipalities. So, on August 21, the main protest unfolded in a working-class neighborhood in Chicago's Southeast Side, while simultaneous demonstrations occurred in suburban Chicago Heights and Evergreen Park. On August 23 came another march of limited size in the Southeast Side, which was followed by yet another the next day in West Elsdon on the Southwest Side.[31]

On August 26, the entire committee reconvened in the Walnut Room of the Palmer House Hotel in what came to be known as the "civil rights summit." All parties accepted a nine-point open housing agreement stipulating that the Chicago Real Estate Board would cease its opposition to a state fair-housing law; Chicago's Commission on Human Rights and city government would ensure enforcement of the city's fair housing ordinance; the chamber of commerce would endorse open occupancy; the CHA would implement a policy of scattered-site construction; and banks and lending agencies would make loans available to minority home purchasers. The agreement provided no timetables for implementation, notably lacked enforcement provisions, and dealt overwhelmingly with general principles, yet Freedom Movement personnel viewed it as the best pact they could obtain. Members of the summit approved the accord by unanimous vote. King announced the end of the marches, including the threatened sortie into Cicero, and called the agreement "the most significant program ever conceived to make open housing a reality in a metropolitan area." Daley triumphantly proclaimed that "Chicago, as usual, is leading the way for all other major cities."[32]

Almost immediately, the agreement came in for heated local criticism. Irate white home owners from the Northwest and Southwest Sides picketed city hall, claiming that "Daley sold out Chicago." At the same time, civil rights stalwarts condemned the pact as a toothless document signifying surrender by King and his forces. Black critics characterized the city's open housing ordinance as weak and unenforceable, dismissed the possibility of securing a worthwhile state law, minimized the impact of available mortgage money in impoverished ghettos, and most pungently, questioned the likelihood that Daley and the other members of white officialdom would honor an agreement lacking concrete proposals. One civil rights activist recalled the reaction: "We told King that we haven't won anything in this agreement. Hell, Daley and his guys are all crooks. You can't believe anything they say." Fueling the fears of the civil rights activists, city council finance committee chairman Thomas Keane soon denied the existence of an open housing agreement. The only results of the summit, he maintained, were "certain suggestions put down and goals to be sought."[33]

On October 28, King complained about the lack of action taken to implement the summit agreement and hinted at the resumption of demonstrations. Daley responded angrily, warning that King's intemperate remarks just a week before congressional and state elections might cause a "white backlash" against such liberal Democrats as Illinois senator Paul Douglas. Daley affirmed that in December after the elections, he had every intention of honoring the agreement. Nevertheless, as time passed, black Chicagoans bemoaned the continued dearth of activity on behalf of open housing. For all the drama of the Freedom Movement, it seemed nothing had changed. Albert Raby concluded wistfully, "I don't think that Martin or any of us realized what a tough town this is and how strong the Democratic organization is."[34]

The struggle between these two prominent public figures became a leading story in the nation's news media, especially because of the growing challenges to King's leadership of the civil rights movement posed by more militant activists. The contretemps in Chicago appeared to be a microcosm of the impending transferal of the civil rights movement to the North after a decade of incremental progress in the South. The question was whether the nonviolence King had employed successfully against Jim Crow could work in the northern metropolises where segregation tended to be de facto rather than de jure. Announcement of the summit agreement initially produced favorable reactions in the national media. The *Nation*'s account concluded that King had forced the powerful Chicago Democratic machine to negotiate, a noteworthy and hopeful achievement. In an article suggestively titled "Still King," the *Christian Century* portrayed the summit as a clear vindication of King's methods. *Newsweek*'s coverage of the Chicago events lauded the Freedom Movement for establishing another benchmark of racial progress and called the summit agreement "a solid vindication of Southern-style nonviolent protest in a Northern city."[35]

Such laudatory comments notwithstanding, King believed he had failed in Chicago or, at least, fallen short of the goals he had so boldly announced the preceding year. Events in the Windy City left King profoundly depressed; the hatred and violence he found there convinced him for the first time that the majority of America's whites rejected his message of integration and brotherly love. As he later told journalist David Halberstam, Chicago made him conclude that only a small minority of whites truly believed in racial equality. The only durable achievement of his prolonged involvement there seemed to be the creation of Operation Breadbasket, which produced within the next few months approximately four hundred jobs, worth more than $2 million, to the local black community. (Even so, the small scale of the program's operation in a city as large as Chicago led some to call it "Operation Drop-in-the-Bucket.") Usually unfailingly optimistic, King offered an uncharacteristically sobering analysis of his Chicago experience:

> Let's face the fact: Most of us are going to be living in the ghetto five, ten years from now. But we've got to get some things straightened out right away. I'm not going to wait a month to get the rats and roaches out of my house. . . . Morally, we ought to have what we say in the slogan, Freedom Now. But it all doesn't come now. That's a sad fact of life you have to live with.[36]

That fall, the SCLC sent a voter registration team to Chicago with the avowed goal of enrolling three thousand new black voters in time for the spring 1967 mayoral election. In December, King returned to the city to boost the flagging campaign. Because of snowy winter weather, the efficacy of the Daley machine's efforts in the ghetto, and general apathy and inertia, the SCLC workers fell far short of their goal. The actual number of newly enrolled voters was a matter of dispute, but both the SCLC and CCCO acknowledged that the registration drive had been a disappointment. In his reelection campaign, Daley excoriated the "outsiders" responsible for disturbing the city's peace. Without directly referring to his dealings with King, the mayor left little doubt about the identity of the parties responsible for Chicago's recent turmoil.[37]

Despite Ben Adamowski's strong showing four years earlier and speculation that the interminable civil rights imbroglio had eroded much of Daley's strength, the Republicans struggled to field a suitable mayoral candidate in 1967. Unwilling to accept Adamowski again and unable to recruit the kind of young articulate reformer they sought, Republican leaders resignedly chose twenty-third ward committeeman John Waner. A colorless businessman who had built a successful plumbing and air-conditioning business and had served as regional director for the U.S. Department of Housing and Urban Development, Waner ran for mayor only after receiving assurances of generous financial support from Chicago's financial community (support that failed to materialize as the campaign ensued). Spending a large amount of his own money to keep his candidacy alive, he ignored Republican ward committeemen's advice to run a "knock-the-nigger-down" campaign and confined his rhetoric to conventional municipal issues. On January 16, 1967, McCormick Place burned to the ground, raising questions about how a new, modern building could be so susceptible to fire. Talk of faulty workmanship, construction shortcuts, and payoffs surfaced immediately, but unfortunately for Waner, no investigation resulted and talk of a major scandal quickly faded. As before, the local media fell in line behind the incumbent; for the first time, all four of the city's dailies endorsed the mayor.[38]

In April, Daley defeated Waner by the lopsided count of 792,238 to 272,542. In garnering 73 percent of the vote and carrying all fifty wards, Daley received the largest number of votes he ever obtained. His victory speech sounded familiar: "I will say as I said in 1955 that I embrace charity, love mercy, and walk humbly with God as I try to give the people the finest city in the United States." Even though Waner had been the twenty-third ward Republican committeeman for years, Daley won there by one thousand votes. Not since 1935 had the Republicans lost a mayoral election so decisively.[39]

Daley appeared to emerge stronger than ever from the racial turbulence of 1966. Chicago's white home owners—some of whom had initially expressed unhappiness with the mayor for his kid-gloves handling of the Reverend Martin Luther King Jr.—approved of the way in which the civil rights summit finally had done so little to disturb existing conditions. The outcome of the 1967 mayoral election ratified Daley's earlier political decision to safeguard the insularity of the white ethnic communities when conflict arose regarding the interests of the restless black population. If Chicago's blacks resented the mayor's handling of the Freedom Movement, the April 1967 election results gave scant evidence of their discontent. Again, the Southside wards of the Black Belt—the second, third, fourth, sixth, and twentieth—produced handsome majorities for the incumbent (the five wards accumulating a net plurality of 61,552 votes). In the West Side twenty-fourth, twenty-seventh, and twenty-ninth wards, which encompassed much of the area engulfed by the previous summer's riot, the black electorate produced a total Democratic plurality of 44,581 votes. True, the number of votes for Daley from black wards decreased somewhat from 1963 to 1967—arguably a harbinger of incipient dissatisfaction with plantation politics—but overall the black wards remained among the most loyal to the mayor. Even in the face of Daley's abject appeasement of white interests, the black vote remained nearly as reliable as it had been before.[40]

In his 1967 inaugural address, Daley promised more of the same in the next four years. He vowed that "as long as I am Mayor, law and order will prevail" and that "we will be firm with those youngsters, and those families, who refuse to respect law and order." Emboldened by his electoral triumph, Daley earnestly defended his stand against the Chicago Freedom Movement and straightforwardly criticized Martin Luther King Jr. as he never had before: "He [King] is a trouble maker. He doesn't know our problems. He lives in Atlanta. We don't need him to tell us what to do. He only comes here for one purpose, or to any other city he has visited, and that is to cause trouble."[41]

Daley no longer bothered to praise King publicly while assailing him privately and stopped going to great lengths to exempt his principal adversary from criticism in blaming unnamed outside agitators for Chicago's racial turmoil. The mayor's opposition to civil rights groups hardened, and he became known as one of the greatest northern opponents of the civil rights movement. When riots broke out in the summer of 1967 in Detroit, Newark, and dozens of other cities, Chicago's mayor readied the National Guard and spoke ominously of his eagerness to thwart a national conspiracy to foment unrest. Critical of other cities' restraint in preserving order, he warned, "I can assure you there won't be any blank ammunition [in National Guard firearms]. The ammunition will be live." Chicago escaped riots that summer, but the news from the rest of urban America was alarming. King's message of nonviolent civil disobedience had been supplanted by violent protest, and Daley's prominent intransigence made Chicago an inviting—perhaps inevitable—target for black militant groups. The defeat of King's Chicago Freedom Movement merely postponed the next stage of the escalating racial conflict. As Earl Bush, Daley's press secretary, later concluded, "What Daley did was smother King. What Daley couldn't smother was the civil rights movement."[42]

7

The Law and Order Mayor

As mayor of America's second-largest city for more than a decade and as a renowned kingmaker for his supposedly decisive role in the 1960 presidential election, Richard J. Daley was by 1968 a legendary force in American politics. Widely considered an effective mayor and a cagey machine politician, Daley appeared to be a typical big city boss—practical, realistic, and for the most part, nonideological. If he had defended white Chicagoans' racial turf against civil rights advocates, in most other instances he had also dutifully supported New Deal–Fair Deal Democratic liberalism. Prior to 1968, he certainly was not considered a conservative leader of the Richard Nixon–George Wallace variety. His public image continued to be that of a hardworking mayor who retained the qualities of his humble upbringing. He still resided in the modest house at 3536 South Lowe Avenue in Bridgeport (near his parents' home at 3602 South Lowe Avenue) and exhibited no apparent desire for wealth or other trappings of power. A dedicated family man, he spent his few free hours with his wife, Eleanor, and their seven children. A devout Roman Catholic and a daily communicant, still reputed to be irreproachably honest, the mayor appeared in many respects a model public figure.

The events of 1968 both enhanced Daley's national profile and altered his public image. Because of his iron-fisted response to the riots following Martin Luther King's assassination and the events at the Democratic National Convention later that summer, Daley became in relatively short order a national symbol for the repressive state's opposition to political and social change. No longer the colorless, generally inarticulate, local pol, Daley became to many Americans a more malevolent figure—a crude bully whose eagerness to implement the rhetoric of law and order signaled a commitment to squelch dissent. The mayor unwittingly became a great hero to millions of Americans who were committed to a conservatism he opposed, and a hated villain to the liberal wing of his own beloved Democratic party. It was a transformation wrought with irony and one that left Daley hurt, defensive, and genuinely bewildered.

The turbulence of 1968 in Chicago followed an uneventful 1967, a year in which many other large American cities suffered through the worst racial rioting of modern times. During the first nine months of 1967, according to the National Advisory Commission on Civil Disorders, 164 civil disorders flared in 128 cities. State police intervened in thirty-three of the disturbances, the National Guard in eight. The most violent outbreaks occurred in Newark, New Jersey, and Detroit, Michigan. In Newark, rioters destroyed 1,029 business establishments, inflicting over $10 million in damages; authorities there reported 25 deaths and 725 injuries. During four suffocating days in July, Detroit experienced the nation's deadliest race riot in a century. After the police, National Guardsmen, and U.S. paratroopers restored order, Mayor Jerome Cavanaugh estimated the toll to be 43 fatalities, 7,000 arrests, and 1,300 buildings destroyed.[1]

For the most part, Chicago remained conspicuously absent from the list of the cities consumed by the racial fires of summer 1967. Mayor Daley faced the threat of civil disorder with a grim determination to discourage such activity in his city. When Detroit and Newark exploded in July, he quickly announced his decision to ready the National Guard. Order would be maintained and property protected, the mayor assured Chicagoans. Outside agitators who conspired to foment unrest and the radicals residing in Chicago who aided them would be dealt with peremptorily, he promised.[2]

Daley received much approbation for maintaining tranquillity during an otherwise tumultuous summer, pundits crediting his attention to poverty programs as well as his hard-nosed deterrence. Victor De Grazia, executive director of a nonprofit slum rehabilitation corporation, said, "I'll bet that Chicago has more urban-renewal projects in progress than any other city in the country." Illinois congressman and Daley acolyte Roman Pucinski noted of the absence of riots, "This was no accident. We put tens of thousands of young people to work." In a similar vein, a reporter noted admiringly, "Chicago is in on every conceivable program the Federal Government has to offer." Daley put it simply: "We have positive, constructive programs, and you do not permit anyone to violate the law or take the law into his own hands."[3]

The apparent equanimity of 1967 was misleading, however; the onlookers who hailed Mayor Daley as a municipal miracle worker mistook quiescence for contentment. The level of resentment among black Chicagoans toward the Democratic machine continued to mount, and many dissidents felt that very little had changed as a result of the previous year's much-ballyhooed summit agreement. They decried the fact that, of the 150 discrimination complaints lodged with the Chicago Commission on Human Relations in 1967, the mayor took action that may have led to suspensions of real estate licenses in only three cases. Indeed, ghetto conditions were worsening. A city official estimated that there was a shortage of fifty thousand low-income housing units in black neighborhoods, and the infant mortality rate had increased by 25 percent during the previous ten years. Although the number of blacks serving in the city council had increased to nine, only two (William Cousins and A. A. "Sammy" Rayner) exerted the independence necessary to challenge the mayor's policies. The others (collectively known as the "Silent Seven" and "Daley's Dummies") said nothing and adhered closely to the machine line on all issues. With African Americans composing nearly one-third of the city's population, blacks administered none of the municipal government's twenty-four departments and held only one of Chicago's nine congressional seats. Dissidents also resented the increased activity by police, who arrested over two hundred blacks during the summer under a state "mob action" statute adopted in 1965. The law, which the U.S. District Court later invalidated, empowered police to make arrests if they felt that a group of two or more people on the streets might be concocting trouble.[4]

Furthermore, the situation in the public school system had not improved. James F. Redmond, Ben Willis's successor as superintendent, seemed more amenable to desegregation, and his mild manner and willingness to work with different groups alleviated much of the bitterness left over from earlier years. "Gentleman Jim" (as the *Chicago Daily News* called him) moved cautiously to build a consensus for change but found little enthusiasm for his efforts elsewhere in city government. On August 23, 1967, Redmond presented a report entitled "Increasing Desegregation of Facilities, Students and Vocational Education Programs," which called for comprehensive desegregation of the schools. Willis loyalists condemned the proposal, as did the influential *Chicago Tribune*. The board of education approved the plan "in principle" but reneged in December when Redmond recommended that implementation begin by busing one thousand black students from schools in the South Shore and Austin neighborhoods to South Chicago and Belmont-Cragin.[5]

Daley refrained from opposing the proposal but indicated that he favored neighborhood schools. Asked about the Redmond plan in 1967, the mayor commented, "I said when I was first elected mayor I would not interfere in school administration. But we hope there will always be local control of schools, no matter who contributes." Later, he added, "It used to be that people wanted to see their children home for lunch, and discuss what happened in school with them." Early in 1968, Redmond proposed the busing of 573 middle-class black students to eight all-white schools on the Northwest Side. The board of education shied away from approving the plan, instead holding a series of contentious hearings that provided the backdrop for the April rioting.[6]

When five vacancies arose on the board of education in 1968, Daley appointed two members approved by an advisory commission but, breaking his long-standing pledge to abide by the commission's recommendations, appointed three who had been judged unacceptable. The appointment of these three—two of whom (board president Frank Whiston and vice president Tom Murray) were former allies of Ben Willis—maintained a majority on the board opposed to busing to achieve desegregation. A report released later that year found 80 percent of all Chicago pupils attending schools with 90 percent black or white enrollments, a situation largely unchanged since the publication of the Hauser and Havighurst studies in 1964.[7]

Blacks also continued to disparage Daley's self-serving operation of federal anti-poverty programs. In 1967, an advisor to President Johnson followed a three-day visit of Chicago ghettos with the assessment that "the poverty program does not reach the people and is controlled by the city government." Incensed that the HEW awarded a stipend to Martin Luther King Jr. for the operation in Chicago of an adult literacy program, Daley interceded with the White House to cancel the grant and refused to see presidential emissary Wilbur Cohen to discuss the matter. A 1967 OEO report lamented Daley's failure to involve the poor in the War on Poverty and warned prophetically: "A peaceful city is not enough! Meaningful change is needed!"[8]

Daley intervened in Washington, D.C., to undermine another anti-poverty program that year. On May 31, 1967, the OEO approved a $900,000 job-training program for Chicago, to be administered jointly by The Woodlawn Organization (TWO) and the Blackstone Rangers youth gang. Daley protested vigorously—arguing that the program would bypass the city's administrative unit, the Chicago Committee on Urban Opportunity—and dispatched Deton Brooks to Washington, D.C., to lobby against it. Sargent Shriver, the OEO's administrator, attempted to mollify the mayor by allowing him to approve the project's director, but Daley simply vetoed all candidates. After months of inaction, TWO appointed an acting director and attempted to commence activity. On November 15, at the urging of Daley's representative, Roman Pucinski, Congress passed an amendment to the Economic Opportunity Act stipulating that all funds for local community programs be directed through existing government agencies; in May 1968, the OEO declined to renew the TWO–Blackstone Ranger project. Although much of the public discussion focused on the questionable wisdom of legitimizing a disreputable youth gang, it is doubtful that the mayor would have approved of empowering any organization other than his own regardless of its respectability. Alderman Leon Despres saw the project's termination as "a complete victory for Mayor Daley." Despres said of the mayor, "He actually prevented a meaningful program from being conducted. I think it has great implications. It shows that as County Chairman of the Democratic party, Daley can and will block any independent group from accomplishing anything."[9]

Apparently oblivious to the rising resentment in the black community, Daley felt confident in the early months of 1968: "We will have the finest summer in the history of Chicago," the mayor predicted, as he outlined in March a program for thirty-two new swimming pools, athletic activities for seventy thousand youths, and twenty thousand new jobs in private industry for school dropouts. The optimism evaporated on Thursday, April 4, however, when an assassin fatally shot Martin Luther King Jr. in Memphis, Tennessee. The next day, Daley ordered the American flag to be flown at half-mast on city buildings and eulogized King at a special memorial service in city council chambers that was broadcast by radio and television. In that address the mayor said: "That the life of this man should be brought to a shocking end by brutal violence grieves all right-thinking citizens everywhere. Violence accomplishes nothing. . . . All of us must soften the grief of Dr. King's family and associates by demonstrating that his life was not in vain." The aldermen also heard from the Reverend Jesse Jackson, the director of the SCLC's Operation Breadbasket in Chicago. Unwilling to forget the inhospitable reception that King had received in the Windy City less than two years earlier, Jackson charged: "The blood is on the chest and hands of those that would not have welcomed him here yesterday."[10]

It quickly became apparent that many blacks shared Jackson's rancor, for the West Side rapidly ignited into an orgy of mayhem and vandalism. By noon on Friday, thousands of black children had deserted their schools and assembled in Garfield Park, heeding the exhortations of militant speakers who urged them to vent their frustrations against neighborhood businesses. The destruction began along west Madison Street, initially limited to smashing windows but soon extending to looting and arson. Chief fire alarm operator David Sullivan told reporters, "You can't tell where the fires are. They're walking west and burning as they go." At 2:00 P.M., Mayor Daley called Governor Sam Shapiro to urge him to alert the National Guard, and at 4:20 P.M., he spoke on radio and television to urge restraint: "Stand up tonight and protect the city," the mayor pleaded, "I ask this very sincerely, very personally. Let's show the United States and the world what Chicago's citizens are made of."[11]

Daley's attempts at dissuasion notwithstanding, fires burned throughout the evening. Shortly before midnight, the National Guard moved into the smoldering West Side. The next morning, the mayor inspected the carnage, stupefied by endless blocks razed by fire and the enormity of the destruction. Visibly shaken, he asked, "Why did they do this to me?" Personalizing the tragedy, the mayor struggled to understand why his policies had been found wanting. He had enjoyed a false sense of security after the peace of 1967 and could not understand why his city had suddenly been transformed into a war zone.[12]

Little rioting occurred on the Near North Side, and the older, more established South Side ghetto remained quiet due to the efforts of independent black aldermen, The Woodlawn Organization, and such street gangs as the Blackstone Rangers and the East Side Disciples. The violence resumed on the West Side on Saturday, April 6, as snipers exchanged gunfire with police and National Guardsmen while firemen sought to put out blazes. Governor Shapiro forwarded Daley's request for federal troops to Washington, D.C.; the soldiers arrived from Fort Hood, Texas, and Fort Carson, Colorado, the next day. On Saturday afternoon, the mayor announced a curfew from 7:00 P.M. to 6:00 A.M. for everyone under the age of twenty-one. When reporters asked about the possibility of shooting looters, he responded, "Well, it's a pretty serious thing to be talking about shooting looters, but I am hopeful there will be sterner action taken by the military and the Police Department today and tonight."[13]

On Sunday morning, Daley and fire commissioner Robert Quinn surveyed the damage from a helicopter circling above the West Side. Emerging from the helicopter, the mayor told reporters, "It was a shocking and tragic picture of the city. I never believed that this would happen here. I hope it will not happen again." The destruction Daley saw amounted to $14 million in insured losses. Casualties included forty-six civilians who suffered gunshot wounds, nine of whom died, and ninety policemen who were injured. Civil authorities reported 3,120 arrests—979 for disorderly conduct, 908 for burglary, 887 for curfew violation, 19 for arson, and 308 for miscellaneous charges such as aggravated battery, aggravated assault, robbery, theft, unlawful use of weapons, criminal damage, and reckless conduct.[14]

The following week, as normal activities resumed in Lawndale and the city sent bulldozers and work crews to remove the rubble from the West Side, Daley rescinded the curfew. At an April 15 press conference, he announced the creation of a nine-member committee to investigate the causes and consequences of the riot. Unwilling to await the outcome of the committee's work, however, the mayor then launched into a long discourse on the recent events. Having exercised remarkable forbearance throughout the crisis, he suddenly lost his composure and his measured, temperate public statements gave way to bitter recriminations and accusations. He blamed the riot, in part, on the breakdown of discipline in the schools, saying, "The conditions of April 5 in the schools were indescribable. The beating of girls, the slashing of teachers and the general turmoil and the payoffs and the extortions. We have to face up to this situation with discipline. Principals tell us what's happening and they are told to forget it."[15]

These references to unsafe school conditions repeated unfounded rumors circulating in Chicago about interracial clashes following the King assassination. The allusions to payoffs, extortions, and the intimidation of teachers highlighted the growing safety problems in many ghetto schools. There was obviously much truth in the mayor's undocumented, rambling reflections on the schools' deterioration, but some commentators questioned the timing of his remarks. These problems were certainly not new, said black critics, so why has the mayor suddenly become concerned? And if interracial tension existed in the city's few integrated schools, why discuss it at a time when healing was called for? Was not the mayor's rhetoric fanning the flames of racial antagonism rather than dousing them? If (as the mayor's friends suggested) he was merely blowing off steam, the stories of unacceptable school conditions served as prelude to the main target of his wrath.[16] Daley went on, in a shocking way, to evaluate the conduct of the police in the riot:

> I have conferred with the Superintendent of Police [James Conlisk, who succeeded O. W. Wilson when he retired in 1967] this morning and I gave him the following instructions, which I thought were instructions on the night of the Fifth that were not carried out: I said to him very emphatically and very definitely that an order be issued by him immediately and under his signature to shoot to kill any arsonist or anyone with a Molotov cocktail in his hand in Chicago because they're potential murderers, and to issue a police order to shoot to maim or cripple anyone looting any stores in our city. . . . I was disappointed to know that every policeman out on the beat was supposed to use his own decision and this decision was his [police superintendent James Conlisk]. In my opinion, policemen should have had instructions to shoot arsonists and looters—arsonists to kill and looters to maim and detain. . . . I assumed the instructions were given, but the instructions to the policemen were to use their own judgment. I assumed any superintendent would issue instructions to shoot arsonists on sight and to maim the looters, but I found out this morning this wasn't so and therefore gave him [Conlisk] specific instructions.[17]

In Mayor Daley's long career, this emotional outburst—rendered extemporaneously without a prepared text—became his most notable public statement. The negative fallout came quickly. Public figures such as U.S. Attorney General Ramsey Clark and New York City mayor John V. Lindsay excoriated the "shoot to kill" order. From across the nation prominent clergymen, officeholders, political liberals, and civil libertarians, whites as well as blacks, questioned how law enforcement officers could under trying circumstances always clearly distinguish arsonists and looters from innocent bystanders. Only days after praising the police for exercising commendable restraint, Daley suddenly seemed to be assailing them for applying inadequate force. And as the mayor's own investigating committee later pointed out, the police had acted in accordance with the State of Illinois's General Order 67-14, which limited the use of "deadly force" in riot situations.[18]

Battered by the swells of protest, Daley recanted: "There wasn't any shoot-to-kill order," he claimed in a hastily called press conference on April 17, "That was a fabrication." Earl Bush, the mayor's press secretary, reproached the media for irresponsibly causing the controversy: "It was damn bad reporting," he charged, "They should have printed what he meant, not what he said." Daley presented a lengthy explanation to the city council, in which he attempted to clarify his position on the use of force. Still condemning the violence of the West Side residents, the mayor claimed that he had been misunderstood. Police should maintain the peace with the minimum force necessary in keeping with state statutes and approved practices, he averred. The retraction convinced few people, however; Daley would always be remembered for the "shoot to kill" order.[19]

While claiming that the media inaccurately reported his comments, Daley also defended himself by mentioning the popular approval of the sentiments he expressed. The city's special events director, Jack Reilly, claimed that from the ten thousand letters and one thousand telegrams received at city hall it seemed the public approved of the mayor's "shoot to kill" stance by a ratio of fifteen to one. The mayor's office also released a telegram from the president of the Fraternal Order of Police expressing "our deepest respect and admiration." The *Chicago Tribune*, which praised the mayor's remarks editorially, reported that U.S. senator Cliff Hansen of Wyoming congratulated Daley and the newspaper for "the firm stand they have taken against rioting." In the age of white backlash and at a time when "law and order" became code words for racial fear and antipathy, Daley's hard line against the rioters perhaps pleased more people than it disturbed. As Mike Royko noted, "If the American Civil Liberties Union didn't approve, the white people in Gage Park and Cragin did, and they had many more votes than the ACLU."[20]

The brouhaha over Daley's "shoot to kill" order occasioned prolonged discussion, in part because the 1968 Democratic National Convention—which promised to be a particularly volatile gathering—

would be held in Chicago in August. The performance of Chicago police during the race riots in April, coupled with anti-war protesters' threats to disrupt the proceedings, seemed to set the stage for a bloody confrontation. One cop promised, "If the fight starts, don't expect it to last long. We'll win in the first round and there won't be a rematch." Equally pugnacious, Daley repeatedly vowed to control protest activities at the convention. "As long as I am mayor," he asserted, "there will be law and order in Chicago. Nobody is going to take over this city."[21]

The choice of Chicago to host the 1968 Democratic National Convention had been made long before the worrisome events of that April. Believing that the convention would bring an estimated $30–50 million to the city, the ad hoc Chicago Citizens' Committee began lobbying the Democratic National Committee in 1966. The Windy City's boosters touted Chicago's central location, the plethora of hotel accommodations, the excellent transportation, and other factors that had resulted in the city's hosting twenty-three of the previous fifty-six political party nominating conventions. Chicago hotel owners and other city fathers contributed $650,000, while Mayor Daley installed a 2.5 percent convention hotel tax that would raise another $250,000 and allow the city to tender a total bid of $900,000; runner-up Miami offered $800,000. When the Democrats made their selection late in 1967, the fact that Chicago had escaped the racial upheavals of the preceding summer also must have helped its cause.[22]

The Democrats had not held their quadrennial nominating convention in Chicago since 1956, when Daley was still a relative neophyte in office, and the mayor was eager to show off his city after the impressive downtown renaissance of the previous decade. Consequently, he used his influence with President Johnson as one of the nation's most powerful Democrats to secure the prize, meeting with the president the night before the national Democratic Site Selection Committee announced its choice. The presence of the convention in Chicago, Daley assured the president, would guarantee the delivery of Illinois's twenty-seven electoral votes in the November election. Furthermore, holding the gathering in Houston, which was rumored to be Johnson's preference, would be pointless, because Texas was already a sure Democratic state. If anti-war protesters caused trouble, Daley and Democratic governor Sam Shapiro could quickly assemble the National Guard, the mayor argued, whereas in Miami (another leading contender) the mayor would be at the mercy of Republican governor Claude Kirk. The television networks wanted Miami, so that they could save money by leaving their equipment there after the July Republican convention, but Johnson found Daley's case more persuasive. On October 8, 1967, the Democrats announced that Chicago would be the 1968 convention site.[23]

The riots following King's death and Daley's "shoot to kill" order engendered concern among many Democrats, who feared that heavy-handed police tactics in the host city could reflect negatively on the party gathering, as did a second disturbance in Chicago a few weeks later. On April 27, an estimated six thousand anti-war protesters, accompanied by five hundred policemen in riot gear, marched from Grant Park to the Civic Center plaza. Nothing untoward transpired during the orderly procession, yet when only about half the protesters had arrived at the march's termination point, the police began dispersing them. Suddenly, the police broke ranks and attacked the group, throwing some demonstrators into the plaza's reflecting pool, chasing and clubbing others. They beat downtown shoppers and other bystanders who failed to move from the scene quickly enough. Advancing in phalanxes, the police chanted, "Move, move, get out of the Loop, move, move, get out of the Loop," as they pursued their targets for blocks before subduing them. Altogether, police arrested sixty-three demonstrators, fourteen of them women.[24]

A blue-ribbon investigating commission chaired by Dr. Edward J. Sparling, president emeritus of Roosevelt University, completely exonerated the protesters and condemned the police for their unwarranted aggression. Its report concluded, "The police badly handled their task, brutalizing demonstrators without provocation. . . . The April 27th stage had been prepared by the Mayor's designated officials . . . to communicate that 'these people have no right to demonstrate or express their views.'" Asked to comment on the report's criticisms of the police, Daley replied, "Much of it is not true. I had a long conversation with Superintendent Conlisk and I know it isn't." Instead of acknowledging that law enforcement officials may have been too zealous, he commented on "the constant effort of these people to confront the police." Ignoring the committee's findings, the mayor winked at the police's excessive use of force and thereby encouraged such behavior in the future. Daley was fast becoming the symbolic champion of law and order advocates, causing increasing concern among Democratic party regulars (who feared disruption of the upcoming convention) and also raising the expectations of anti-war activists hopeful of fomenting as much disorder as possible. Clark Kissinger, coordinator of the April 27 peace march, complained of local authorities: "By making a non-violent protest impossible, they make a violent one inevitable."[25]

As Daley became more ossified in his role as archdefender of the domestic order, he presented himself as an inviting target to the hippies and Yippies bent on undermining the convention.[26] Because of his adherence to middle-class values and the political loyalty that led him to support a Democratic president's foreign policy, the Chicago mayor became the bête noir of the New Left political radicals and counterculture members who saw the nation's military involvement in Vietnam as symptomatic of the bankruptcy of American society. It is ironic that Daley abhorred America's entanglement in Southeast Asia, fearing that it would rend the Democratic party, and secretly urged Johnson to disengage the American military. According to John J. Gunther, the executive director of the U.S. Conference of Mayors, Johnson asked Daley how to extricate the nation from the Vietnam nightmare, and the Chicagoan bluntly responded, "Well, figure out how you got in. And get out the same way." But publicly the mayor never questioned the authority of his commander in chief and could not countenance others' decision to do so. Proud, stubborn, and authoritarian, Daley became the perfect foil for protesters who sought confrontation for the sake of publicity.[27]

The radical youth commenced their publicity campaign months before the convention, launching rumors of all sorts about the outrageous plans that they intended to implement in Chicago. Peace movement leaders brashly predicted that over one hundred thousand protesters would descend on the city from all over the country, a boast that officials foolishly took seriously. Threatening to take over the entire city, the Yippies sketched a number of scenarios designed to scare Chicagoans and their elected officials: hippie girls would seduce the conventioneers; "hyper-potent" male Yippies would debauch the delegates' wives, girlfriends, and daughters; revolutionaries would paint cars to look like taxis and kidnap delegates to Wisconsin; Yippie agents disguised as chefs would drug the delegates' food; and most deviously, Yippies would dissolve LSD into the water supply and turn on the entire city population. Dismissing the water and sewers department commissioner's estimate that it would require five tons of LSD (nine billion tabs) to contaminate the water, the police department increased the number of officers assigned to its "water protection brigade" around the city's water filtration plants. Even if the upcoming "Festival of Life" scheduled to be held in Lincoln Park during the convention amounted to no more than a hedonistic revelry of drugs, rock music, and sex, that would be enough to offend the moral sensibilities of Daley and many Chicagoans. And the added fillip of political protest made the impending gathering that much more intolerable.[28]

Daley and his men in Chicago's bureaucracy had no intention of cooperating with the protesters as they made their plans for convention week, and indeed, the city's various agencies threw up roadblocks whenever permits needed to be acquired or permission needed to be granted for public activities. As Earl Bush candidly explained, "Our idea was to discourage the hippies from coming." The recurring pattern of delay and obstruction began in March when the Yippies submitted requests to both the Chicago Park District and the mayor's office to use Grant Park during the convention. In the weeks that followed, they received no reply. At a meeting in early June, Deputy Mayor David Stahl hinted that their request would be denied and suggested instead that they seek permission to stage their Festival of Life at the southern end of Lincoln Park. On July 15, they submitted such a request but again received no response from the city. An early August meeting with Stahl led to another submission and, when that proved fruitless as well, to yet another inconclusive discussion with the deputy mayor. On August 22, the Yippies sought an injunction in federal court but withdrew the suit when they found out that Judge William Lynch (Daley's former law partner) would hear the case.[29]

During the same months, the National Mobilization Committee to End the War in Vietnam (MOBE) encountered similar intransigence from city hall. Beginning in June, Rennie Davis sought unsuccessfully to secure parade permits, and for weeks he failed even to obtain an appointment with anyone from the mayor's office. On August 2, he spoke briefly with David Stahl, at which time U.S. Department of Justice officials informed Davis that Mayor Daley would neither meet with him nor issue permits for sleeping in the parks. On August 12, MOBE leaders met with Stahl and the city's corporation counsel, David Elrod, but again received no permits. With only days remaining before the convention's opening, MOBE sued the city, but on August 23, Judge Lynch denied them an injunction for a march to convention headquarters at the Chicago Amphitheater. The Sunday before the convention opened, MOBE's David Dellinger went to a scheduled meeting with Stahl, but the deputy mayor failed to attend. Stahl's representative met briefly with Dellinger and exhibited no greater willingness to work with the protesters than had the deputy mayor himself.[30]

Exasperated by the unresponsiveness of local authorities, Rennie Davis complained to U.S. Attorney General Ramsey Clark, who recognized the growing probability of violence in Chicago. Clark twice sent emissaries from his office to meet with Mayor Daley; both times they offered the assistance of the Justice Department's Community Relations Service, and both times Daley rebuffed them. "The city of Chicago would take care of the city of Chicago," the mayor told the federal agents. On August 20, he announced the advance mobilization of the National Guard.[31]

The Chicago Police Department prepared to take care of the city as well. Superintendent Conlisk equipped each officer with a riot helmet and teargas dispenser and placed a shotgun in every squad car. Police officers underwent a whirlwind training course to prepare them for riot duty, instruction during which they were taught how to be strong-minded rather than strong-armed. Throughout the spring, the police increased its patrols in Old Town, the city's bohemian neighborhood along Wells Street, harassing and sometimes arresting hippies, long-haired males, and other members of the counterculture. Responding to information garnered from FBI wiretaps, the police department's intelligence division (known for years as the Red Squad) intensified its surveillance of MOBE's "Communist" leaders, Tom Hayden, David Dellinger, and Jerry Rubin.[32]

On Saturday, August 17, a week before convention delegates arrived, the hippies and Yippies began moving into Lincoln Park. Of the one hundred thousand protesters the authorities feared would come, only an estimated five thousand materialized. For the next week, they practiced techniques of civil disobedience and self-protection, held strategy sessions, and disseminated a seemingly endless stream of news releases to generate publicity. The Friday before the convention, a group of Yippies arrived at the downtown civic center and punctiliously nominated for president a 150-pound pig named Pigasus. "If our president gets out of line," they pledged, "we'll eat him." Unamused by the impromptu ceremony, police arrested six of the protesters and led Pigasus off to the Chicago Humane Society.[33]

Arrayed against the anti-war activists, in addition to the twelve-thousand-member Chicago Police Department, the mayor commanded five thousand Illinois National Guardsmen, six thousand riot-trained federal troops, hundreds of state and county police, a private security force deployed at the convention site, and a large contingent of secret service agents. The military claimed that one of every six demonstrators was an undercover federal agent. By most estimates, the forces for law and order outnumbered the dissidents five to one. As Mike Royko observed, "Never before had so many feared so much from so few."[34]

The massive security buildup also reflected Daley's concern about continued racial violence. A few days before the convention began, the *Chicago Tribune* reported rumors that revolutionaries had hired members of the Blackstone Rangers street gang to assassinate the Democratic presidential aspirants and Mayor Daley himself. A grand jury impaneled to investigate the allegations uncovered no proof, and the FBI attributed the story to "loose talk or braggadocio." Nevertheless, the local police force intensified its surveillance in ghetto neighborhoods and strongly urged Blackstone Ranger leaders to leave the city during the time of the convention.[35]

Apart from his obsession with security, Mayor Daley had a number of other concerns as the convention approached. Handling the logistics of such a massive enterprise was problematic even under ordinary circumstances, and in 1968 other difficulties arose to complicate matters. The International Brotherhood of Electrical Workers' strike impeded the city's normal telephone service and, more critically, the installation of communications equipment in convention headquarters at the International Amphitheater. A citywide taxicab strike and a walkout by transit workers threatened Chicago's transportation network. On July 22, Democratic party chairman John Bailey conferred at length with Daley in Chicago about the crippling telephone strike, then announced that the convention would not be moved to Miami. The mayor added that it would remain in Chicago no matter what, "with or without television." Daley subsequently managed to forge a temporary agreement between the electrical workers and the Illinois Bell Telephone Company, which allowed the installation of thirty-two hundred telephones and two hundred Teletype machines in the convention hall. However, the arrangement did not include the Conrad Hilton Hotel, headquarters for the Democratic National Committee and the leading presidential candidates, so inadequate telephone service continued to be a problem.[36]

Daley also clashed with the television networks. Already unhappy about having to move their equipment hundreds of miles from the Republican convention in Miami, network executives fulminated about the inconveniences caused them by the telephone strike. They bitterly protested the restrictions imposed by the Chicago mayor upon their telecasts. Citing the need for tighter security, city authorities barred the placement of cameras around the amphitheater, prohibited the use of mobile television units outside the downtown delegate hotels, and issued only seven convention floor passes to network personnel (compared to the thirty-one given in 1964). CBS political commentator Eric Sevareid on a live network broadcast excoriated Chicago for its excessive security measures, likening the atmosphere there to the repressive conditions concurrently imposed by Soviet troops in Prague, Czechoslovakia. In an August 24 meeting with network executives in his office, the mayor rolled back some of the restrictions, but the television spokesmen still bridled at not having unlimited freedom, and the tension between the networks and city hall persisted for the duration of the convention.[37]

In addition to his preoccupation with the necessary convention arrangements, Daley's powerful position within the Democratic party made him a key player in the struggle for the presidential nomination, so politics consumed much of his time as well. After President Lyndon Johnson's unforeseen announcement in February that he would not seek reelection that year, the field opened to a number of candidates and increased the possibility of Daley again becoming a kingmaker. Discussing the possibility of winning the Democratic nomination, Robert F. Kennedy said, "Daley means the ballgame," an assessment with which many politicians agreed. Kennedy's assassination in June apparently narrowed the field to vice president Hubert Humphrey, Minnesota senator Eugene McCarthy, and South Dakota senator George McGovern, and as late as the opening of the convention, Chicago's mayor refused to endorse any of the candidates. Daley's close ties to the Kennedy family spawned rumors that he might participate in an effort to draft the youngest brother, Massachusetts senator Edward Kennedy. Ignoring the speculation, Daley publicly praised all the candidates and endorsed none.[38]

Daley did indeed despair of selecting Humphrey, McCarthy, or McGovern and secretly worked to nominate Edward Kennedy. In July, Daley told reporters that he would support the youngest Kennedy if he decided to enter the race. Kennedy demurred, but Daley persisted privately in trying to convince him to run. On the eve of the convention the mayor telephoned Kennedy at the family home in Hyannis Port, Massachusetts, and urged him to reconsider.

In long-distance conversations with the senator and with his brother-in-law, Stephen Smith, Daley promised to keep the Illinois delegation uncommitted. The issue remained unresolved until well into the convention's proceedings, but despite Daley's entreaties, Kennedy never agreed to become a candidate.[39]

Juggling a host of concerns, Daley single-handedly oversaw the city's preparations for the convention. Whatever happened, whatever went right and whatever went wrong, Daley would be the impresario responsible for welcoming the nation's Democrats. From the time the delegates arrived, they saw constant reminders that they were in "Daley's Chicago." On billboards, theater marquees, posters, badges, and even the telephones in their hotel rooms, they saw the inscription, "Richard J. Daley, Mayor." The city was putting on its best face, from the unusually clean downtown streets to the wooden fences, built along the route from the Loop to the convention center, that veiled crumbling buildings, abandoned cars, and vacant weed-grown lots strewn with trash. Everywhere visitors saw the helmeted police. Intended as much to assure conventioneers of their safety as to inhibit potential lawbreakers, the ostentatious display of force nevertheless proved unsettling to many out-of-towners. As he arrived at Midway Airport on August 25, Eugene McCarthy warned his entourage that Mayor Daley "is watching over all of us."[40]

Security arrangements reached their zenith at the International Amphitheater, which took on the appearance of a medieval fortress. Encircled by a seven-foot-tall barbed-wire fence, the aged structure contained virtually every piece of sophisticated security equipment available. Bulletproof panels enclosed the building's main entrance; fifteen hundred patrolmen occupied the cordon sanitaire surrounding the edifice; policemen with rifles positioned themselves on the roofs of adjacent buildings; helicopters swooped and dived overhead. Inside the hall, ubiquitous security personnel took up highly visible positions to oversee all activities. Secret service agents and police officers with binoculars, walkie-talkies, and rifles perched on a specially constructed catwalk ninety-five feet above the convention floor.[41]

Several miles away on the Chicago lakefront, the uneasiness between the protesters and police gradually built toward the confrontation everyone expected. In Lincoln Park the Yippies staged their Festival of Life, while to the south in Grant Park the MOBE organized political speeches and rallies. On Sunday, August 25, police cleared Lincoln Park of the thousand demonstrators who had not left the grounds by the usually unenforced 11:00 P.M. curfew. Breaking ranks and pummeling the fleeing protesters, the police finally cleared the streets at about 2:00 A.M. Two policemen warned a local television reporter to "be careful, the word is out to get newsmen," and indeed, seven reporters fell victim to vicious beatings that night. Eager to silence the newsmen who might report their misdeeds, the police smashed cameras and confiscated notebooks. The hostility toward members of the press stemmed also from a resentment of the "liberal media," a perception on the part of many policemen that reporters sympathized with blacks and anti-war protesters and that their stories reflected such liberal biases. Mayor Daley defended the police and seconded their criticisms of the press, saying, "They think because they're working for a newspaper that they can do anything, they can violate any law, they can take any action because they are newsmen. This shouldn't be. This isn't any prerogative of newsmen, television or radio or anyone else."[42]

On Monday the turmoil intensified. Protesters and police skirmished during the day at a rally in Grant Park and again that evening at curfew time. In the ensuing Lincoln Park fracas that night, policemen removed their badges so they could not be identified and then went on another rampage. Attacking demonstrators and bystanders alike, shooting canisters of teargas, flailing away indiscriminately at men and women, at adolescents and the middle-aged, at clergymen and area residents, the police moved through the park chanting, "kill, kill, kill." In the neighborhood adjacent to the park, the police slashed the tires of thirty cars bearing McCarthy bumper stickers. Again, newsmen became prime targets of police violence, and twenty reporters required hospitalization for the injuries they received that evening. Newspaper and magazine editors, along with television executives, registered strong protests with city hall and met with Police Superintendent Conlisk, who issued a directive mandating better treatment of media personnel. In public, however, Daley acknowledged no wrongdoing by police. He said, "We ask that newsmen follow the orders of the police too. These men [police] are working twelve hours a day. If they ask a newsman and photographer to move, they should move as well as anyone else. How can they [the police] tell the difference [between a demonstrator and a newsman]?"[43]

Tuesday night brought more of the same in Lincoln Park. Police formations moved methodically through clusters of protesters, clearing the grounds and thrashing all those who resisted or failed to retreat quickly enough. On Tuesday, the demonstrators gave ground to the police more grudgingly than they had before, and the level of violence escalated. More than sixty protesters received medical care by the end of the evening; police reported seven injuries and one hundred arrests. Attaining all the publicity they craved, the anti-war groups grew bolder and more provocative, launching forays into Grant Park and several other sites outside the Lincoln Park area. Fully warmed to the task, the police responded savagely.[44]

As the intensifying clashes between police and anti-war dissidents created a distracting and gruesome sideshow, the events within the International Amphitheater proceeded in surreal isolation. Insulated and safe in their cocoon, yet aware of the tempest raging in the streets a few miles away, convention delegates went about the Democratic party's business of writing a platform and nominating a presidential candidate. The repression and violence seeped into the convention hall itself occasionally, as when security agents harassed anti-war delegates. Police barred New York convention delegate Allard Lowenstein from entry until he relinquished his copy of the "subversive" *New York Times*. Police arrested New York delegate Alex Rosenberg and dragged him from the convention floor for protesting too strongly an order to stop talking. When CBS reporter Mike Wallace pursued the story aggressively, another policeman punched him in the jaw. A growing number of delegates deplored the repressive atmosphere, for which they blamed the convention host.[45]

Daley remained the center of attention for another reason: his political importance in the nomination of a presidential candidate. On Sunday, the Illinois delegation chose Daley as its chairman and heard presentations from the major presidential contenders, Hubert Humphrey, Eugene McCarthy, George McGovern, and Georgia governor Lester Maddox. It was widely assumed that the Illinois group would back the front-runner, Hubert Humphrey, and that the support of this important state would start the vice president off to a certain nomination. But rather than polling the delegation and announcing its choice immediately, as expected, Daley explained that the decision would not be forthcoming until Wednesday. Lacking enthusiasm for Humphrey, whose value at the head of local and state tickets he questioned, Daley remained noncommittal in the hope of drafting Edward Kennedy. Only on Wednesday morning after Kennedy gave a final and unequivocal no to the pleas for a last-minute candidacy did Daley unenthusiastically commit to Humphrey.[46]

Highly visible in the Illinois delegation at the front near the speakers' platform, the Chicago mayor said little about his political machinations or about the events in Lincoln Park. Quiet and seemingly serene as controversy engulfed his convention, Daley seemed somnambulant at times, yet no one doubted his control over the proceedings. Giving cues to convention chairman Carl Albert from nearby, the mayor dictated the pace and length of speeches. On both Monday and Tuesday nights, he gave the signal for the termination of the sessions, the latter occasion providing one of the convention's lasting images. At 1:00 A.M., with the protracted debate over the issue of Vietnam droning on endlessly into the night, Daley signaled for adjournment. Catching the eye of Chairman Albert, he moved a finger across his neck in a dramatic sign to silence the speakers. The gesture, captured by the television cameras, graphically demonstrated how the boss was manipulating the convention. The delegates and the viewing public be damned, Daley seemed to be indicating, he would decide what was said and when. Chicago was his city, and this was his convention.[47]

On Wednesday, when the Democrats readied themselves for the selection of presidential and vice-presidential candidates, the rising tensions on the lakefront came to a boisterous climax. That afternoon, as a crowd of approximately ten thousand gathered at the Grant Park band shell to hear speeches at the only rally granted a permit by the city, police clashed with protesters when a group of young men removed an American flag from a flagpole. An estimated thirty people suffered injuries in the fifteen-minute melee that followed. Members of the crowd hurled debris at the police, who countered with smoke bombs and a full-scale assault. Officers broke ranks and used their nightsticks on demonstrators and onlookers; even medics attempting to treat the wounded became the targets of feral attacks.[48]

The main event occurred that evening, beginning shortly before 8:00 P.M. at the intersection of Michigan and Balbo Avenues in front of the Conrad Hilton Hotel. Deputy police superintendent James Rochford ordered the streets cleared of the approximately seven thousand people who were milling around the intersection. In what the Walker Commission later termed a "police riot," law enforcement officers clubbed, beat, and kicked demonstrators and onlookers, shoved hapless victims through broken restaurant windows, chased unfortunates into the hotel lobby, giving vent to the rage that had accumulated over several long days of intense riot duty. The sudden outburst lasted only about twenty minutes, after which the streets outside the hotel were emptied, but sporadic violence continued for hours thereafter.[49]

The "Battle of Michigan Avenue" resembled in most respects what had been occurring on the lakefront for the past several days. Unlike the earlier episodes, however, television crews stationed outside the main convention hotel captured the events of Wednesday night in dramatic detail. The crowd chanted, "The whole world is watching," which it soon was. Cameramen rushed the film to the convention hall, completed the editing, and broadcast the results shortly after 9:30 P.M., only an hour after the end of the confrontation. Prime-time coverage of the convention proceedings gave way to the sensational film footage, which the networks showed repeatedly, often intercut with live pictures of Mayor Daley laughing and applauding on the convention floor. The juxtaposition of the violence and Daley's joviality created the false impression that he was enjoying the downtown battle—an image the mayor and his supporters believed the television companies had created on purpose as revenge for what they perceived to be their mistreatment.[50]

As the convention delegates viewed the downtown battle on television monitors, the tension heightened in the amphitheater. The chairman of the Colorado delegation gained the floor and asked, "Is there any rule under which Mayor Daley can be compelled to suspend the police state terror being perpetrated at this minute on kids in front of the Conrad Hilton?" Cameras showed the mayor and his sons shouting at the Colorado representative. A Wisconsin delegate moved that the convention be suspended for two weeks and reconvened in another city, but the motion failed. In unsettled fashion, business continued. Delivering a nominating speech for George McGovern, Connecticut senator Abraham Ribicoff abruptly deviated from his prepared text to say, "And with George McGovern as President of the United States we wouldn't have those Gestapo tactics in the streets of Chicago. With George McGovern we wouldn't have a National Guard."[51]

Outraged, Daley and others in the Illinois delegation around him leaped to their feet and bellowed at Ribicoff. As the television cameras zoomed in for a closeup of the apoplectic mayor, he shook his fist and appeared to be shouting obscenities at the speaker. By most accounts, Daley urged Ribicoff to have carnal relations with himself.

(Daley's sons and other members of the mayor's retinue passionately argued that he had simply called Rubicoff a "faker".) Calm and composed, Ribicoff stared at the gesticulating Chicagoans and said, "How hard it is to accept the truth." Next, Frank Mankiewicz, in a speech seconding McGovern's nomination, decried the "mindless brutality on Chicago streets and on this convention floor." Daley regained his composure and attempted for a while to maintain an appearance of indifference to the anger and hostility around him, talking amiably with fellow delegates, but he left the convention hall early. He was absent when Hubert Humphrey anti-climactically accepted the presidential nomination later that evening.[52]

When delegates arrived for the Thursday session, they found on every chair a two-page handout defending the mayor and the police. The freshly minted apologia blamed the incendiary tactics of the protesters, praised the vast majority of the police for their calm detachment, and emphasized the continued use of manpower rather than firepower by the authorities. The effort to counter the negative publicity of the previous days had begun. The Democratic machine packed the galleries with loyal patronage workers carrying hundreds of "We Love Daley" signs. When the mayor entered the hall, a sea of swaying city workers chanted, "We love Daley, we love Daley." After the showing of a filmed tribute to Robert F. Kennedy, the delegates spontaneously sang "The Battle Hymn of the Republic," while the Democratic machine claque countered with a continuing chorus of "We want Daley, we want Daley." To stop the singing, Daley dispatched Ralph Metcalfe to the podium for an improvised tribute to Martin Luther King Jr. Seeking time on national television to offer his side of the story, the mayor sat for an interview with CBS's Walter Cronkite. Daley spoke darkly of assassination plots, Communist conspiracies, and other privileged information of which critics had no knowledge when they made their accusations of police brutality. Of the press's complicity, he said, "Many of them [reporters] are hippies themselves, in television and radio and everything else. They're a part of the moment. And some of them are revolutionaries, and they want these things to happen. There isn't any secret about that."[53]

Cronkite finally managed to derail one of the mayor's lengthy monologues and said:

> "Now, here's a question I want to ask you. Your police—Frank Sullivan, who is in charge of public relations for the police—said today,

'Communists.' Now is this—"

Daley interrupted, "There isn't any doubt about it. You know who they are."

"No, I don't actually," replied Cronkite.

Daley quickly continued, "Well, you know Hayden? . . . [He's] the head of the Mobilization. Surely you know Dellinger, who went to Hanoi. Why isn't anything said about those people? They're the people who even now see their cues and pick them up in Grant Park. Rennie Davis. What's Rennie Davis?"

Cronkite said, "Well, I don't know that they're Communists."

"Well, certainly, neither do I," concluded Daley.[54]

If the mayor's logic faltered at times, he succeeded in presenting his case passionately to the national television audience. Daley's references to classified information available only to him lent an appearance of authority to his defense. Rather than concede any mistakes he might have made during the previous few days, Daley responded aggressively and defended the police behavior that so many television viewers found appalling. He refused to upbraid the police, and as a consequence, their behavior persisted. Just before dawn the next morning, when someone threw some objects out of the windows of the Hilton Hotel at police on the streets below, the police stormed Eugene McCarthy's headquarters on the fifteenth floor, beat campaign workers, and forced them downstairs to the lobby. Flanked by secret service agents, McCarthy interceded to rescue his workers, and the police sullenly drifted away.[55]

The defense of Daley's Chicago continued. The police exhibited approximately one hundred "sophisticated" weapons confiscated from the demonstrators, including rocks, bricks, a Ping-Pong ball studded with nails, razor blades, baseball bats, two-by-fours, glass ashtrays, Molotov cocktails, cherry bombs, knives, and a jar containing a black widow spider—but no firearms. At a press conference following the convention, the mayor argued that the demonstrators came to Chicago solely to "assault, harass and taunt the police into reacting before the television cameras." Betraying his penchant for malapropisms, he also told reporters, "Gentlemen, get this thing straight for once and for all. The policeman isn't there to create disorder. The policeman is there to preserve disorder." Within a week, the mayor's office released "The Strategy on Confrontation," the city's official report based on the investigations of corporation counsel Ray Simon. The report emphasized the verbal and physical abuse heaped on the policemen, accused television of distorting reality through biased coverage, and reiterated the seriousness of the threats to presidential candidates posed by revolutionaries. It listed among the injured 198 policemen and only 60 demonstrators. (Voluntary medical workers reported treating over one thousand casualties.) The report contended, "Although publicity, largely unfavorable, was enormous, arrests and injuries were moderate. The Convention was not disrupted; the city was not paralyzed. Not one shot was fired; not one life lost."[56]

It would be difficult to assess the effectiveness of Daley's campaign for vindication. Many television viewers certainly remained unconvinced that the use of such force was necessary and believed "The Strategy on Confrontation" to be a whitewash. Of the roughly five thousand anti-war activists who came to Chicago, only a few hundred could be called revolutionaries, and they relied not on guns and bombs but on obscenity and mass disobedience. Demanding anonymity, an eminent Chicago businessman confessed, "A lot of people are as horrified as I am, but they see no real benefit in saying so as long as Daley remains in power." A number of professional and religious organizations—including the United Church of Christ (with two million members) and the American Psychological Association (with twenty-six thousand members)—announced the cancellation of annual conventions scheduled for Chicago. Among civil libertarians and liberal Democrats, Daley could provide no satisfactory explanation for the shocking spectacle of August 1968. The *New York Times* found the mayor guilty of "rigidity," "insensitivity," and "repression."[57]

Affirming this critical judgment, a report by the National Commission on the Causes and Prevention of Violence released in December 1968 eviscerated the city's defense. *Rights in Conflict,* compiled by Chicago lawyer Daniel Walker and a complement of 212 investigators who relied on nearly thirty-five hundred eyewitness accounts, meticulously documented "unrestrained and indiscriminate police violence." The Walker report coined the term "police riot" to describe the events along the lakefront, concluding that supervisory personnel lost control of their subordinates. Groups of policemen forgot all about the rule of law and became irrational marauders, punishing anyone and everyone in their path. Rather than challenge the report's major conclusions, Daley applauded its assessment that "the majority of policemen did act responsibly under extremely provocative circumstances." Dismissing the Walker study as insignificant, Daley concluded, "My only basic criticism is the summary, which, if used alone, would mislead the public."[58]

Daley could well be cavalier because abundant evidence existed that a majority of Americans approved of the police's stringent measures. The mayor's office claimed to have received 135,000 letters praising Daley's performance at the convention and only 5,000 in dissent. Suspicious liberals questioned the veracity of the claim, but a number of other measures of public opinion reflected the same sentiments. Radio and television stations, as well as newspapers, reported letters in support of Daley (as opposed to those against) running twenty to one. A highly respected market research team interviewed a nationwide sample of 1,194 adults and again found solid support for Chicago officials. Only 21.3 percent of the interviewees thought the police too violent, whereas 71.4 percent believed the security measures justified. Mayor Daley received a striking vote of confidence, as 61.7 percent of those interviewed thought he was doing a good job.[59]

In Chicago, the lakefront liberals and silk-stocking reformers lambasted Daley, but the denizens of the bungalow belts commended his work. Like millions of other working-class Americans, they approved of "law and order"; they wanted a chief executive who would act forcefully to quell civil unrest. Famed Chicago author Nelson Algren mused, "I don't think the clubbing represents one man. I think it represents a majority of the people of Chicago. If an election were held today, he'd win." Impatient with a permissiveness that they felt contributed to the moral breakdown of the social order, and unsympathetic to the lifestyles as well as to the cause of the anti-war protesters, the "silent majority" found a champion in Richard J. Daley. When the Chicago mayor spoke ominously of long-haired revolutionaries and assassination plots, many Americans reared on old-fashioned unquestioning patriotism found him entirely credible. When he referred derisively to left-leaning, east coast television and newsprint elitists, millions of alienated workers found their resentments and fears confirmed. The inarticulate, unassuming mayor from Irish Catholic Bridgeport became by circumstance a spokesman for the values that so many Americans felt were under seige in a confusing, threatening time. In a year notable for the Kennedy and King assassinations, student takeovers of college campuses, ghetto riots, and anarchic anti-war protests, Daley stepped forward to restore order. In the process, a man who always considered himself situated firmly within the liberal Democratic tradition became the darling of many conservatives. The mayor was surely mortified when Eugene "Bull" Connor—the Birmingham, Alabama, police superintendent who had become an international symbol of racial bigotry—cast his ballot for Daley when the convention voted for a vice-presidential candidate.[60]

Some evidence indicates that in later years Daley regretted the unfortunate occurrences of August 1968. A proud man unaccustomed to self-criticism, he never publicly repudiated his positions or admitted that the police had acted inappropriately, but privately the mayor expressed displeasure at the outcome. In confidence, he attributed the recurrent violence to lack of discipline among the police and to a dearth of leadership by Superintendent Conlisk. "That was why," he told his press secretary Frank Sullivan, "we had that disgrace over at Balbo and Michigan." Adlai Stevenson III, a persistent critic of the Chicago Democratic machine and an opponent of America's Vietnam involvement, censured Daley in the convention's aftermath. Stevenson remembered:

> He over-reacted, and I wrote a white paper a few weeks after that was published in the [Chicago] Sun-Times. It was sort of an eloquent denunciation of his heavy-handed tactics. He called me up and asked me to come over. He said, "Adlai, I know I was wrong. You're right. Forget about it. You don't have to beat a dead horse. I was wrong. We over-reacted. Now why do you have to keep complaining?"[61]

However secretly remorseful he may have been, Daley remained defiant in the weeks following the convention. His bitterness and resentment mirrored the lingering discord within the Democratic party. Hubert Humphrey left Chicago with the nomination of a divided, demoralized party that arguably never completely recovered from the convention debacle. Humphrey failed to carry Illinois in November, a crucial factor in his razor-thin loss to Republican Richard Nixon. Chicago precincts provided a victory margin for Humphrey of 421,199 votes, an insufficient amount to offset downstate totals and not even half the 1964 plurality produced for Lyndon Johnson. The additional fact that Daley's candidate for Cook County State's Attorney, Edward Hanrahan, accumulated two hundred thousand more votes than had Humphrey at the head of the Democratic ticket made it appear that the machine did less than its best on behalf of the presidential candidate.[62]

Shortly after the convention adjourned, Humphrey called it time to "quit pretending that Mayor Daley did anything that was wrong," but after losing the election, he blamed the Chicago mayor. Humphrey complained that the convention disaster saddled him with an insurmountable handicap, and afterward he charged, "Mayor Daley didn't exactly break his heart for me." In response, Daley lamented his inability to persuade Edward Kennedy to run and stated flatly that the Democrats would have won with a candidate who had "the name of a former President." He also condemned Humphrey's insistence on affirming the Johnson administration's commitments in Vietnam (conveniently forgetting that he had professed loyalty to the same policies himself). The rift between the two Democratic stalwarts never healed.[63]

In later years, Daley apologists advanced a number of explanations for the mayor's controversial actions in the summer of 1968. As mayor of Chicago, he was charged with protecting property and maintaining the peace. Snipers had to be stopped to protect firemen during the April West Side riots. The "shoot to kill" order—the unfortunate product of a momentary lapse of judgment—became much more than it should have because of the media's prejudicial reporting. The excessive security measures at the Democratic National Convention resulted from the demands of the secret service. Television highlighted the reactions of beleaguered policemen, yet ignored the provocative acts of the protesters. As mayor of Chicago, Daley had to react decisively to these crises; he found himself captive to events set in motion by others. Deputy Mayor Ken Sain later said, "I think he would have done anything to have prevented any of the disorder. Part of it was out of anyone's control."[64]

There is a measure of truth in all these reflections, of course—as well as some sadness in the mayor's feeling compelled to suppress dissent over a war he deplored. Yet for Daley the primary issues were clear, the decisions easy. No matter what his sympathies may have been for dissidents (black or white), he insisted that change be sought in an orderly fashion within the system. He understood people's frustration with an unresponsive government, but not their willingness to abandon the standard conventions of political discourse. Daley would talk with those who suggested programmatic changes through the normal give-and-take of negotiations, but he refused to deal with civil rights or anti-war rioters who spurned customary channels. His lifelong experience in machine politics taught the lessons of patience, compromise, barter, and loyalty. As a thoroughly socialized product of that politics, he felt justified in meeting force with repression.[65]

Looking back on the turbulence of the year, Daley said, "I hope to God we never see a 1968 period again. . . . The divisions were so intense." Unfortunately, the torturous issues that made 1968 so nightmarish for Chicago's mayor resurfaced in subsequent years. Two sensational jury trials dissected the Chicago Police Department's putative brutality, one resurrecting the agonies of the Democratic convention and the other examining an alleged massacre of black militants. Reform Democrats struggled to remake their crippled party and thereby wrest control from the Old Guard, with Boss Daley considered the prime target for removal. The threat of more racial violence never dissipated, and the absence of civil disorder could not disguise the rising level of dissatisfaction among black Chicagoans with a politics that they felt ignored their needs. Law and order would be no easier to sustain in the years to come.[66]

8

Daley on Trial

The unsettling events of 1968 left Mayor Daley shaken and physically drained. Acquaintances and colleagues commented on his haggard appearance and apparent lack of energy. Inattentive in conversations and easily fatigued, he seemed to be disengaged much of the time. Previously energetic and aggressive, the mayor appeared to be merely going through the motions of his job. A mild case of the flu lingered interminably, and Dr. Eric Oldberg, president of the Chicago Board of Health, commented, "He was on the brink of something serious. . . . He was in very bad shape." In addition to weathering the controversies of the recent past, Daley faced an uncertain future. The election of Richard Nixon meant that, for the first time in eight years, this most partisan of Democrats faced the prospect of dealing with a Republican president. No longer would Chicago's mayor enjoy the luxury of sleeping in Abraham Lincoln's bed in the White House during his visits to Washington or of dialing the Oval Office directly from city hall. And these amenities aside, the question of Chicago's access to federal funding, which had been so plentiful during the Kennedy-Johnson years, loomed large as well.[1]

After 1968, Daley found himself the continued center of controversy, and his leadership frequently came under question, principally through a series of well-publicized legal confrontations. In the prolonged *Gautreaux* case, which first reached the public's attention in 1969 and dragged on for nearly a decade, the courts considered the mayor's opposition to public housing desegregation. In the Chicago Seven Trial, the mayor and the city's police sought vindication for their conduct during the 1968 Democratic National Convention. Legal proceedings instigated by a lethal police raid on Black Panther headquarters kept racial tensions high and again raised nettlesome questions about the Daley administration's treatment of African Americans. For the balance of his fourth term, outside the courtroom as well as inside, Daley found his mayoralty on trial, with results that were seldom gratifying, occasionally disappointing, and most often ambiguous.

One of Daley's first tests came on the electoral front. Not only had Hubert Humphrey managed a disappointing plurality in Cook County and failed to carry Illinois in November 1968, but at the same time statewide Republican victories in the race for governor and attorney general left Daley with few allies in elective office outside Chicago. Political pundits who looked for possible signs of erosion of the mayor's power considered the six special aldermanic elections of March 1969 a barometer. Regular Democrats won handily in the eleventh, fourteenth, and thirty-second wards—areas adjoining the stockyards and the Northwest Side industrial belt whose predominantly white ethnic populations were loyal to the political machine. In the lakeside forty-second ward, an independent narrowly lost to the organization candidate. In the second ward, Bill Dawson predicted a victory for his handpicked candidate, boasting, "We're a sure winner. We always are." Nonetheless, Lawrence Woods, Dawson's administrative assistant, lost to independent Fred Hubbard, by 6,942 votes to 2,599. In the forty-fourth ward, twenty-eight-year-old independent lawyer William Singer forced a run-off with the machine candidate, deputy Cook County controller James P. Gaughan. Asked if Singer's surprisingly strong showing in Paddy Bauler's old ward represented a defeat for the machine, Daley responded, "None whatsoever," and predicted a Gaughan victory in the April 8 run-off. With the endorsement of all four major local newspapers, Singer subsequently won, with 11,983 votes to 11,780.[2]

The outcome of the special aldermanic elections portended problems for the Democratic machine. True, Daley Democrats still held a comfortable majority in the city council with thirty-seven seats—the election of Hubbard and Singer raised the total of independent Democrats to five, along with seven Republicans—but these modest gains were unprecedented during the mayor's tenure. The election of an unknown underdog like Singer who ran on an anti-Daley platform over a well-known machine regular like Gaughan would have been incomprehensible just one year earlier. Singer's victory in the comfortably upper-middle-class forty-fourth ward revealed a degree of restiveness among voters who were amenable to calls for reform. More troubling in the long term, the loss of a city council seat in Dawson's home ward threatened the breakup of the machine's suzerainty in the South Side Black Belt. In the past, the machine could arrogantly select an undistinguished figure such as Woods—who had been indicted for bribery ten years before and who continued to suffer legal entanglements with the Internal Revenue Service—and still expect no viable opposition. In 1969 Fred Hubbard won because he convinced the residents of public housing projects, who comprised 40 percent of the ward's electorate, that they would not lose their apartments or welfare eligibility by voting against Dawson's candidate. Whereas the number of Singer's North Shore liberal supporters remained insufficient to threaten the machine, the large and growing black population potentially posed a much greater challenge to the Daley machine's hegemony.[3]

Another threat came from the reformers' recurring attempt to break the mayor's monopolistic control of federal largess. On May 1, 1967, Chicago had submitted an application for developing and implementing the Great Society's new, streamlined anti-poverty plan, the Model Cities program. In the same spirit of the Equal Opportunity Act, which called for "maximum feasible participation" of the poor, the Department of Housing and Urban Development (HUD) mandated that "the development of an effective [Model Cities] application should include, from the beginning, the involvement of a cross-section of public and private groups and neighborhood residents." However, Chicago's application was written entirely by existing city agencies, and Chicago's Citizens Advisory Committee contained no residents of the four neighborhoods (Woodlawn, Lawndale, Grand Boulevard, and Uptown) targeted for Model Cities programs. Dissidents again complained that the city flouted federal eligibility requirements, and in December 1968, The Woodlawn Organization (TWO) announced the submission of its own application for a Model Cities grant.[4]

In February 1969, TWO agreed to a compromise and retracted its proposal in return for substantial representation (but not a majority) on the Model Area Planning Council (MAPC) that would administer the city's program. With TWO's capitulation, Mayor Daley could claim widespread citizen participation while still retaining majority control of the MAPC. In the citizen advisory groups for the three other project areas, Daley allowed the election of some community representatives but always maintained majority control. After the city council's Finance Committee approved Chicago's $38 million proposal by a vote of sixteen to one (with Leon Despres dissenting), the city council considered it in a three-hour discussion on April 25, 1969. Leon Despres, William Cousins, and Sammy Rayner, the three aldermen from the Woodlawn area, spoke against the measur Despres called the city's proposal "a plan of almost unlimited patronage, limited handouts and massive removal." Unmoved by these arguments, the council ratified the plan by forty-one votes to seven.[5]

HUD approved the Chicago proposal, a surprising development that TWO's Arthur Brazier attributed to a deal between incoming President Richard Nixon and Mayor Daley. It was no coincidence, Brazier charged, that Nixon's surtax bill passed the House of Representatives by five votes with last-minute support from the Chicago Democratic delegation, two days after the announcement of approval for the Model Cities grant. A likelier explanation (and one of longer-lasting significance for Daley) revolved around the Nixon administration's revised policy on Model Cities awards. New HUD secretary, George Romney, promised that in the future, "it will be up to the mayors how they spread the money," and his assistant, Floyd Hyde, spoke of "adequate" citizen participation rather than "maximum" or "widespread" public involvement. The Republican administration's handling of the Model Cities program, as part of what Nixon called the "new federalism," ensured the kind of decentralization that Daley and other big city mayors had long propounded in the dispensation of federal aid. Access to government funds remained in city hall, and this decision gave hope that relations with Nixon might be less contentious than Chicago Democrats had feared.[6]

Erwin France, who replaced Deton Brooks in 1969 as the city's administrator of Model Cities programs, noted that Daley's political influence in Washington regularly guaranteed city hall's autonomy. On one occasion, federal bureaucrats threatened to curtail funds because of Chicago's refusal to allow neighborhood involvement, and the mayor discussed with France what the city's response should be. France recalled the conversation:

> Daley said, "Talk to them." I said, "I already did." He said, "Did you get the fellas to go with you?" He meant the nine members of the Chicago congressional delegation. I called the regional director and

said, "I'd like to bring some concerned citizens to talk to you." They believe in citizen participation, right? Well, when they saw who the nine citizens were, they nearly shit. The funds didn't get cut off.[7]

The blandishments of community organizers and HUD employees to the contrary, Chicago continued to receive generous grants for the duration of the Model Cities program. In the summer of 1971, with concern about urban racial violence lingering in Washington, Erwin France mailed checks to seventy thousand people; in 1972 his office employed twenty thousand people and administered a budget of $200 million. Many residents who received Model Cities largess used their sudden windfalls to relocate to better neighborhoods, however. During the decade of the 1970s, the population of Lawndale decreased by 35 percent, Grand Boulevard by 32 percent, and Uptown by 13 percent. As those who were able to move did so, the poorest residents remained behind in a rapidly deteriorating environment. It is ironic that Chicago's ghettos became poorer as a result of federal policy—a condition that seemed to be repeated throughout urban America.[8]

Race and housing similarly figured in the first of the legal battles facing Daley, an attack on the CHA's discriminatory policies. The events of 1969 stemmed from legal actions taken against the CHA years earlier. In 1965 the city council rejected a list of public housing sites submitted by the Chicago Plan Commission (which would have involved the construction of projects in white neighborhoods) and approved nine sites submitted by the CHA (which would have been confined to ghetto areas). At the urging of the Chicago Urban League and the Metropolitan Housing and Planning Council, the West Side Federation sent a letter of protest to the Federal Public Housing Administration charging violation of the 1964 Civil Rights Act. The federal agency dismissed the complaint, ruling that local housing authorities enjoyed the right of site selection. In 1966 American Civil Liberties Union (ACLU) lawyers filed a class action suit in federal court against the CHA on behalf of Dorothy Gautreaux, three other black public housing tenants, and two black CHA applicants. *Gautreaux v. Chicago Housing Authority* charged the authority with violation of Title VI of the 1964 Civil Rights Act.[9]

According to federal judge Richard Austin, the plaintiffs needed to prove that the CHA deliberately intended to discriminate against blacks and that segregation was not coincidental. ACLU lawyer Alexander Polikoff obtained from Tamaara Tabb, the CHA's supervisor of tenant selection, an affidavit affirming that the agency "systematically excluded Negroes from the projects in white neighborhoods or admitted Negroes only on a token basis." Even more damaging to the defense, a longtime CHA employee who served as its executive director from 1968 to 1973, C. E. Humphrey, submitted a deposition that outlined collusion between the city council and the housing agency. Humphrey described the agreement forged in 1955 between CHA executive director William Kean and alderman W. T. Murphy, chairman of the city council's Housing and Planning Committee, that granted the city council veto power over site selection. Polikoff even produced the smoking gun, a memorandum confirming the Kean-Murphy understanding, which allowed him to charge that the CHA "was an active and willing partner of a segregationist City Council in a vast expansion of housing segregation in Chicago."[10]

To Judge Austin the evidence of a deliberate segregationist policy seemed as overwhelming as the regrettable results of such action. Of the fifty-four public housing projects operated by the CHA, fifty were situated within black neighborhoods and had 91 percent black occupancy. Four projects, with white occupancy ranging from 93 to 99 percent, existed outside ghetto areas. (The project with 99 percent white tenants was Bridgeport Homes, located a few blocks from the mayor's house.) This remarkable degree of segregation would have to change, Austin announced in February 1969 when he found for the plaintiffs. CHA chairman Charles Swibel argued that he was unable to change the situation: "It's up to our community leaders, our clergymen, and our business people to help us," he claimed. Mayor Daley denounced Austin's ruling, saying, "The court decision could conceivably slow up public housing construction in Chicago."[11]

On July 1, 1969, Judge Austin issued a judgment order that provided a detailed plan for complying with his February decision. The blueprint designated "Limited Public Housing Areas" (LPHAs) as census tracts with 30 percent or more nonwhite population, including a one-mile buffer zone around the tracts, and "General Public Housing Areas" (GPHAs) with virtually all-white populations, principally the North, Northwest, and Southwest neighborhoods. He ordered the CHA to build no more public housing projects in the LHPAs until it constructed seven hundred units in the GPHAs and thereafter to build on the ratio of three units in the GHPAs for every unit in the LPHAs. In the future, no census tract could contain more than 15 percent of the city's total family public housing. The order also prohibited the construction of projects more than three stories high or containing more than 120 units and denied aldermen the right to approve projects designated for location in their wards.[12]

Opponents of Austin's order predicted a calamity if the city attempted implementation. Congressman Roman Pucinski said that it "probably has dealt the death blow to public housing here." Charles Swibel lamented, "I'm not even sure [that] I *can* implement the order." Black alderman William Cousins countered, "It's not that they can't do it. It's simply that they won't." Anti-integration forces quickly mobilized to foster noncompliance. At a meeting of twenty-five home-owner associations, attorney Thomas Sutton warned, "If the construction really starts, we'll take action of some sort, and not letters or petitions. In the meantime, we'll put pressure on the aldermen to stop it. If they don't, we'll run them out of town on a rail."[13]

As Alderman Cousins feared, the city responded by refusing to build virtually any public housing at all. In the ten years following the *Gautreaux* decision, the CHA built a total of 184 units in Chicago; by the time of the next mayoral election in April 1971, none. Referring obliquely to "political considerations," Swibel did nothing about the order for the first year and then instructed the CHA's legal staff to file an appeal. Judge Austin proved to be a determined and persistent adversary, however. A former machine loyalist and legal protégé of Daley, Austin had run unsuccessfully for governor in 1956 and believed that the mayor had not supported him adequately in that contest. Many observers suspected that, alienated from the Democratic organization, he pursued the *Gautreaux* case with extraordinary zeal—a theory enhanced by the fact that the judge, who lived in the all-white conservative suburb of Flossmoor, had established no record of favoring plaintiffs in earlier desegregation cases. For the eight years preceding his death in 1977, Judge Austin pushed to force Chicago to implement his order but found the city consistently uncooperative. "It is an anomaly," said the judge, "that the 'law and order' chief executive of this city should challenge and defy the federal law." The CHA occasionally launched time-consuming legal appeals and at other times agreed to comply but took no action, all the while delaying and dissembling to forestall execution of the court order. The final effect of Judge Austin's decision remained unclear.[14]

Under fire in the *Gautreaux* case, the Daley machine took the offensive in another federal courtroom. Stung by the criticism emanating from the Democratic National Convention, Chicago officials decided to bring charges against the demonstration leaders responsible for the confrontations. Federal prosecutor Thomas Foran, a member of the Democratic machine, announced that eight radicals would be tried for violating an obscure section of the 1968 Civil Rights Act, which made it a felony to "travel in interstate commerce . . . with the intent to incite, promote, encourage, participate in and carry on a riot." The penalty for conviction would be ten years' imprisonment and a $20,000 fine. A disparate lot, the eight indicted conspirators included five demonstration organizers (Abbie Hoffman, Jerry Rubin, David Dellinger, Tom Hayden, and Rennie Davis); two lesser known protesters (John Froines and Lee Weiner); and Black Panther leader Bobby Seale. The prosecution sought to prove not that these eight men conspired together to incite a riot but that they had each come to Chicago for that purpose. Nor did the state contend that they were equally culpable; indeed, Seale's stay in the city during the convention lasted less than twenty-four hours, a time during which he gave only two inconsequential speeches.[15]

The trial commenced in September 1969 and quickly degenerated into a garish spectacle. It immediately became clear that the defendants intended to turn the courtroom into a forum for the expression of their political radicalism and that they gave little attention to the possibility that they might be found guilty. Their absolute lack of decorum within the legal system resulted from contempt for the conventions of the "establishment" of which it was a part. The defendants dressed in flamboyant costumes, draped a Vietcong flag over their table, read comic books, and ate jelly beans; they alternatively staged sudden disruptive outbursts and feigned boredom.[16]

In Judge Julius Hoffman the defendants found the perfect foil for their antics. A seventy-four-year-old native Chicagoan and graduate of Northwestern University Law School, Hoffman eagerly assumed the role of staunch defender of the establishment. A Republican appointed to the federal bench by President Eisenhower in 1953, Hoffman did not belong to the local political machine but clearly supported its side in the courtroom. Throughout the proceedings, he presided in a prejudicial and arbitrary fashion that offended legal purists regardless of political persuasion. Hoffman genuinely enjoyed the publicity and media attention that the trial provided, it seemed, as much as he relished denying Defense Attorney William Kunstler the opportunity to function as an advocate for his clients.

From the outset of the trial, Hoffman's rulings invariably favored the prosecution. During jury selection he overruled such questions to potential veniremen as "Do you support the war in Vietnam?" and "Do you know who the Jefferson Airplane are?" In front of the jury he praised U.S. Attorney Foran as "one of the finest prosecutors in the country" but spoke condescendingly to the defense lawyers. When Foran referred to Kunstler in court as a "mouthpiece," Judge Hoffman refused to consider the defense attorney's objection. "I will not only not rule on it," he insisted, "I will ignore it."[17]

As the trial progressed, the Weathermen faction of the Students for a Democratic Society (SDS) decided to demonstrate their support for the "Chicago Eight." At the same time that the defendants' outrageous behavior during the trial showed the radical left's contempt for the rule of law and order, the Weathermen sought to do the same outside the courtroom in the streets of Chicago. For several days in October, SDS's most alienated radicals staged their "days of rage." On the first day, approximately one hundred helmeted Weathermen stopped cars and beat passengers, urinated on public property, and charged into police squads, which fought back with teargas, nightsticks, and guns. By nightfall, police had arrested sixty and had shot three demonstrators. The next day, seventy Weathermen marched on an armed forces induction center; police arrested twelve demonstrators and dispersed the rest. In a subsequent march through the Loop, an estimated three hundred Weathermen broke windows and attacked bystanders. Police suffered twenty-three casualties and arrested over one hundred. At Daley's request, Governor Richard Ogilvie sent in twenty-six hundred National Guardsmen to patrol the area. Shocked by the wanton violence initiated by the protesters, the public raised few objections to the police's conduct. City hall received several hundred phone calls, many from irate Gold Coast residents fearful of the Weathermen and beholden to law enforcement authorities. To most onlookers, the days of rage bore little resemblance to the previous year's convention violence, and even the liberals had few harsh words for Mayor Daley and his police.[18]

Inside the courtroom, the defendants continued their disruptive activities and Judge Hoffman his high-handed unfairness. Because his attorney was ill and unable to attend, Bobby Seale demanded the right to cross-examine witnesses. The judge refused. Seale called Hoffman a pig, a racist, and a fascist, so the judge had him restrained with handcuffs, leg irons, and a gag. When the authorities replaced the chains with leather straps, Seale managed to wriggle free and, along with Jerry Rubin, fought with U.S. marshals. The judge cleared the courtroom, found Seale guilty of contempt, and sentenced him to a four-year prison term. The Chicago Eight thus became the Chicago Seven.[19]

The trial's most anticipated moment came when Mayor Daley testified as a defense witness on January 6, 1970. If defense attorney Kunstler hoped to goad Daley into an emotional outburst or ill-advised disclosure of impropriety, he failed completely. Throughout his three-hour testimony, Daley remained unflappable, never once showing any distemper when baited by the defense. During one twenty-minute period, Foran objected to twenty-six straight questions posed by Kunstler—and Judge Hoffman upheld the prosecutor each time. In all, Hoffman sustained seventy of the prosecution's objections. When Kunstler made a motion to have Daley declared a hostile witness (a ploy that would, if successful, allow the defense to broaden its range of questioning), the judge replied jocosely, "The mayor has been a most friendly witness." Kunstler finally gave up.[20]

At one of the few times he was allowed to answer the defense's questions, Daley claimed that he told city officials to provide "every courtesy and hospitality while they [the hippies] were in the city of Chicago." Foran's cross-examination lasted thirty seconds, during which he posed two simple questions. "Did you ever suggest to anyone that they should not issue a permit to use the city parks?" he inquired of the mayor. "No," came the reply. "Did you ever suggest to anyone that they should not issue a parade permit to anyone?" Foran asked. "No," Daley said again. Dubious as those answers may have been, the defense pressed the issue no further. The mayor's appearance, circumscribed as it was, provided virtually no information about the events of the previous August. Like the entire trial, it provided a few moments of entertainment but very little enlightenment.[21]

After four and a half months, the Chicago Seven trial limped to its conclusion in early 1970. The jury of ten men and two women deliberated for five days and then ruled that none of the defendants had conspired to violate the 1968 Civil Rights Act's anti-riot provision. The jurors found Lee Weiner and John Froines innocent of all charges but concluded that Dellinger, Hoffman, Rubin, Davis, and Hayden, although technically not guilty of participating in a conspiracy, had individually crossed state lines with intent to violate the statute. The five defendants found guilty received five-year jail sentences and $5,000 fines, plus contempt charges. It is not surprising, given Judge Hoffman's ham-handed conduct of the trial, that the sentences were later reversed on appeal. Asked if the verdict exculpated his position, Daley responded, "I look no place for vindication." The mayor's terse reply no doubt reflected his disappointment, for the jury's conclusion clearly contradicted the charges of a conspiracy. The Chicago Seven fiasco resolved nothing and only served to besmirch further the mayor's already damaged reputation.[22]

Concurrently, the legal system prepared to pass judgment on another highly publicized event of the mayor's fourth term. At 4:45 A.M. on December 4, 1969, a detachment of fourteen Chicago policemen, operating under the aegis of the state's attorney's office with a warrant authorizing the search for illegal weapons, entered a slum apartment at 2337 W. Monroe Street. The resulting eight-minute gun battle left two Black Panther officials dead—state chairman Fred Hampton and downstate organizer Mark Clark. Seven other blacks in the apartment survived the battle; four suffered multiple gunshot wounds, while the other three were left unscathed. Two policemen were treated at a nearby hospital and released. The officer in charge of the police detail, Sergeant Daniel Groth, claimed that after he and his men properly identified themselves, a woman inside the apartment fired a shotgun to initiate the battle, and the Panthers repeatedly refused to surrender. "There must have been six or seven of them firing," reported Groth. "The firing must have gone on ten or twelve minutes. If two hundred shots were exchanged, that was nothing."[23]

Within hours, however, skeptics began questioning the sergeant's tale of heroic police work. The day after the shooting, Panther deputy defense minister Bobby Rush and deputy information minister Chaka Walls took reporters on a tour of the apartment, pointing out what they believed to be evidence of an unprovoked massacre. The Black Panthers charged that the raid provided a pretext for the slaughter of their comrades, that what happened in Chicago was part of a national effort by the white establishment to eliminate black nationalist groups. Along with the Illinois Civil Liberties Union and the Afro-American Patrolmen's League, three aldermen (William Cousins, Sammy Rayner, and Leon Despres) called for an investigation.[24]

State's attorney Edward Hanrahan—whom Daley had put in charge of the city's "war on gangs" in May 1969—staunchly defended his men. Hanrahan praised the policemen's "professionalism" and "remarkable self-restraint" and displayed the cache of weapons commandeered from Fred Hampton's apartment—eighteen pistols, rifles, and shotguns, along with one thousand rounds of ammunition. In an exclusive interview with the *Chicago Tribune*, Hanrahan revealed photographic evidence that allegedly showed how the Panthers had fired first to spark the gun battle. On December 11, Hanrahan's office staged a reenactment of the raid on a half-hour locally broadcast television program. Well-known for his no-nonsense law and order views, Hanrahan aggressively defended the raid with all the resources at his disposal.[25]

The intense controversy surrounding the Panther raid resulted in four separate investigations—by a federal grand jury; a special state grand jury; the police department's internal investigation division; and a special coroner's jury. On December 19, Police Superintendent Conlisk announced that the rapidly concluded departmental query completely exonerated the officers. After a twelve-day probe, the coroner's jury ruled justifiable homicide in the Panther deaths. The sources of these rulings, as well as the remarkable haste with which they were rendered, produced charges of a whitewash and intensified the demand for a thorough, objective inquiry.[26]

On January 5, 1970, a federal grand jury was impaneled. On May 15, the grand jury released a 249-page report, a scathing condemnation of the police and a complete repudiation of the earlier investigations. According to the report, "the irreconcilable disparity between the accounts given by the officers and the physical evidence" meant the existence of "reasonable basis for public doubt of their [the investigators'] efficiency or even their credibility." Although the police claimed that the Panthers had fired at least ten to fifteen times, the grand jury reported, FBI lab reports matched only one of the (between eighty-two and ninety-nine) shots discharged to Panther weapons. The police firearms expert testified that, when threatened with losing his job if he did not sign the inaccurate report, he had lied about the results of the ballistics tests. The coroner's office had also misrepresented Hampton's wounds; the Panther leader had been shot from above while lying in bed. What had been portrayed as a heated exchange of gunfire was actually a one-sided peremptory strike.[27]

Despite its findings, the federal grand jury declined to bring indictments against the policemen, because the seven Black Panthers who survived the raid refused to testify. The Panthers declined to speak initially when they were under state indictment for attempted murder. The state dropped these charges when the FBI released the results of its investigation, but, objecting to the racial composition of the predominantly white federal grand jury, the Panthers still refused to appear as witnesses. (They did, along with the families of the victims, file a civil suit against the city; in 1982 a federal court of appeals found for the plaintiffs and awarded them a $1.85 million settlement.) But in 1970, despite the federal grand jury's damaging study, the affair seemed no closer to resolution and critics continued to call for justice.[28]

In June 1970, Mayor Daley chose Barnabas F. Sears to head the special state grand jury's investigation. A former president of the Chicago Bar Association and the American College of Trial Lawyers, Sears had an impeccable reputation for integrity and honesty. Objecting to the assumption that he was Daley's handpicked toady, Sears quickly exhibited his independence and asserted his right to prosecute the case free of political influence. After nearly one year of gathering evidence, the grand jury in April 1971 prepared indictments against State's Attorney Hanrahan and thirteen of the policemen involved in the raid. In a bizarre twist, however, Judge Joseph Power refused to sign the formal presentment. A neighbor and former law partner of the mayor, Power accused Sears of inadequately conducting the investigation and ordered the grand jury to hear testimony from Hanrahan. The state's attorney testified on several occasions for a total of twenty hours, after which Judge Power announced the appointment of a special "friend of the court" to determine whether Sears had improperly influenced the grand jury's deliberations. It appeared that Powers would do anything to keep Hanrahan from being indicted. For more than three months beginning in May 1971, Sears initiated appeals to the Illinois Supreme Court to compel Power to act on the indictment. Expressing the sense of exasperation pervasive in the city, the *Chicago Tribune* editorialized:

> The best way Judge Joseph Power . . . could serve the interests of the public and of justice would be to stop his delaying tactics and open the sealed indictment. . . . Judge Power's excessive activities on Mr. Hanrahan's behalf serve no public purpose other than to remind everyone that both he and Mr. Hanrahan are close friends of Mayor Daley and leading figures in the Democratic Machine.[29]

On August 24, 1971, the Illinois Supreme Court ordered the indictments delivered; later that day they were. The grand jury charged Hanrahan, his assistant, and twelve policemen with conspiracy to obstruct justice; Police Superintendent Conlisk was named a co-conspirator but was not charged with a criminal offense. Hanrahan ignored the call from such civic groups as the Better Government Association and the Illinois Crime Commission to take a leave of absence until the determination of his guilt or innocence. In his last official act as arraigning judge, Power reassigned the case to another Democratic judge with close connections to the Daley machine, Philip J. Romiti. The case dragged on until November 6, 1972, when Judge Romiti acquitted Hanrahan of conspiring to cover up the misdeeds of the police who had raided Fred Hampton's apartment nearly three years earlier.[30]

Once considered one of the most promising young Cook County Democrats and even a potential successor to the mayor, Edward Hanrahan fell out of favor with the party leadership. His poor judgment and impetuosity contributed to the growing racial polarization among the Democrats, and congressman Ralph Metcalfe, speaking for other black ward leaders, opposed his nomination for reelection in 1972. At first Daley agreed to support Hanrahan again, but he changed his mind when the Democratic candidates for governor (Paul Simon) and lieutenant governor (Neil Hartigan) documented downstate voters' outrage at the slating for reelection of a public official under indictment. Daley then dumped Hanrahan and replaced him with a reformer, Raymond K. Berg, only to have Hanrahan triumph in the primary. In the November election that year, Hanrahan lost as outraged black voters contributed to Republican Bernard Carey's narrow victory margin. As had occurred during the early 1960s with Benjamin Adamowski, Mayor Daley had to deal once again with a hostile state's attorney—further fallout from the disastrous December 4, 1969, Black Panther raid.[31]

Although Daley had no direct involvement in those byzantine legal proceedings, the protracted search for guilt in the Black Panther deaths reflected negatively on his reputation. The performance of Democratic jurists, particularly that of the blatantly partisan Joseph Power, underscored the close ties between the Chicago judiciary and the hegemonic political machine. Cynical blacks saw the episode as yet another example of Daley's callous disregard for their plight; civil libertarians railed against improper police behavior; and liberals caustically spoke of "business as usual" in the repressive Daley regime. The progressive elements within the Democratic party, both inside and outside Cook County, complained about the potential political consequences in upcoming elections. Could Chicago's sterling record on service delivery, its reputation as "the city that works," continue to offset the flurry of public relations disasters? Or had Daley's stubborn law and order posturing become too great a liability? Prior to launching his 1971 reelection campaign, Daley made one significant attempt to shore up his flagging relations with the Democratic party's more enlightened elements. Many of the state's Democrats favored state treasurer Adlai Stevenson III to run for the U.S. Senate against the powerful Republican incumbent, Everett M. Dirksen. In 1968 Stevenson sought the party's gubernatorial nomination, but Daley insisted that he run for the Senate instead—providing that he agree to support President Johnson's Vietnam War effort. An outspoken critic of U.S. involvement in Southeast Asia, Stevenson refused to offer the loyalty pledge and thereby lost the nomination. Persistently disparaging of Daley's "feudal" reign in Chicago, especially after the events of August 1968, Stevenson had emerged as the foremost champion of the state's good government forces. Although they remained cordial, the two politicians' disagreements on so many fundamental issues came to symbolize the huge gap between the party's liberal and conservative wings in Illinois.[32]

Laying the groundwork early for a future campaign against Dirksen, Stevenson hosted a political rally in September 1969 at the family farm outside suburban Libertyville. Hoping to build a substantial independent base, he invited fifteen thousand reform-minded Democrats, including such national figures as South Dakota senator George McGovern and Iowa senator Harold Hughes, to the hot dog and beer picnic. As the assembled liberals looked on in amazement, Daley arrived in a city limousine. His presence tantamount to an endorsement of Stevenson's candidacy, the mayor spoke glowingly of his host's political future. Even as dignitaries gave their speeches to the enthusiastic crowd, word came that Dirksen had died in Washington. Senator McGovern gave a eulogy to his deceased colleague, and Stevenson turned next to the Reverend Jesse Jackson. Stevenson remembered:

> I said, "Jesse, you get up there and pray." The whole thing ended with Jesse praying, a black choir he brought along singing "The Battle Hymn of the Republic," and everyone including Dick Daley holding hands and singing "The Battle Hymn of the Republic." Unbelievable. That time there wasn't any doubt who would be the candidate for the U.S. Senate. Daley got behind me 100 percent.[33]

State law stipulated that a special election be held to fill Dirksen's unexpired term, and Stevenson easily defeated the nondescript Republican candidate, Ralph Tyler Smith, in November 1970. Daley's dramatic appearance at the Stevenson rally, widely interpreted by the press and politicians as a fence-mending gesture, and his subsequent support of the Democrat allowed him to be on the winning side of a landslide electoral triumph. Indeed, the 1970 election results produced nothing but good news for Daley. Confounding expectations of continued Republican resurgence, Chicago Democrats won all county and state contests. After months of dire predictions, the press was again praising the mayor as a political genius. Second only to his sagacious leap onto the Stevenson bandwagon, the pundits argued, was Daley's inspired choice of Richard Elrod to run for county sheriff. The son of twenty-fourth ward committeeman Artie Elrod, thirty-six-year-old Richard graduated from Northwestern University Law School, won a seat in the state legislature, and served in the city prosecutor's office, where he helped prosecute anti-war demonstrators in 1968. During the Weathermen's days of rage, Elrod suffered paralysis from the neck down after allegedly being hit by a lead pipe. Although Elrod actually suffered the injury when tackling a fleeing protester, the mythical version of events predominated and he became a martyr for the cause of law and order. First campaigning from a wheelchair and later walking stiffly with a cane, Elrod parlayed the sympathy factor into a win. For Daley, it was part and parcel of a very gratifying election and an encouraging harbinger for the upcoming mayoral race.[34]

In December 1970, Daley's momentum slowed, however, with a new development in the *Gautreaux* case. The court of appeals affirmed Judge Richard Austin's order that the CHA submit a list of new construction sites for review by the Chicago Plan Commission. The CHA refused to comply and announced that it would appeal to the U.S. Supreme Court, which did not hear the case before adjourning in March 1971. Meanwhile, the CHA hired a public relations firm—Community Programs, Incorporated—to mount a publicity campaign emphasizing its intended compliance on site selection. Early in 1971, however, the CHA terminated its contract with the firm and reverted to its earlier opposition to the *Gautreaux* decision—at precisely the time when Mayor Daley's reelection campaign, with its opposition to public housing construction, commenced.[35]

In a more positive development, the mayor intervened in January

1971 to end a four-day public school teachers' strike. He sequestered the two negotiating teams in separate rooms in city hall and walked back and forth for twelve hours coordinating the discussions. Working comfortably with president of the teachers union John Desmond (an old friend) and school board president John Carey (whom he had appointed to the position), Daley forged an agreement and reopened the schools. Teachers received an 8 percent raise, and even though the schools were already operating in the red, Daley promised to find the additional $51 million in revenue necessary for the pay increase. *Newsweek* called the mayor's successful intervention in what had appeared to be a hopelessly bitter impasse another example of "Daley's magic."[36]

Because of Mayor Daley's extraordinary longevity in office, his 1971 campaign for an unprecedented fifth term attracted considerable attention from the national media. His age and recent involvement in so much controversy engendered speculation that the last of the big city bosses might be vulnerable, but a dearth of formidable candidates tempered the hopes of a political upset. Jesse Jackson tried to get on the ballot to oppose the mayor, but Judge William Lynch denied his petition. The Republicans chose Richard Friedman, a former Democrat who had served as First Assistant Illinois Attorney General from 1965 to 1968 and then as executive director of Chicago's Better Government Association. Launching the race with $2,500 withdrawn from a personal savings account, he raised a paltry total of $200,000 for the entire campaign—as compared to the estimated $1.5 million spent by the Democratic machine. The forty-one-year-old Friedman seemed to relish the long odds against him and admitted gamely, "I'd say I'm a 5 to 1 underdog, which is a sensational improvement over the past." Energetic and articulate, he compensated for lack of money with an eagerness to speak anywhere at any time. Most often, Friedman attacked Daley for "race politics," upbraiding the mayor for his defense of segregation and especially for his failure to comply with Judge Austin's desegregation order. How could a law and order mayor enforce the law so selectively? he asked rhetorically.[37]

Daley refused to back down on the issue of neighborhood desegregation, stubbornly maintaining his opposition to Judge Austin's mandate. Asked by a reporter if public housing would be an important issue in the election, he snapped, "Who's gonna make it one? You?" Opposing the placement of CHA projects in white neighborhoods, he said, "We're only going to build houses where people want them." While such intransigence led the Independent Voters of Illinois (IVI) to call Daley "a flagrantly racist mayor," it secured the support of conservative whites in the Southwest and Northwest bungalow belts—many of whom were Republicans who voted Democratic for the first time. The desegregation issue notwithstanding, Daley won high marks from a variety of sources for making Chicago "the city that works." Endorsing the mayor for reelection, the *Chicago Daily News* concluded, "He is a man who knows how to keep the machinery running, how to maintain and extend and improve the city's superb physical plant, how to keep it prosperous and on the move. In these achievements, he stands unique among the mayors of the nation's great cities."[38]

Chicago's apparent good health in comparison with other large cities—many saddled with nightmarish fiscal crises and appearing unable to deliver services reliably—convinced even liberal critics that, for all his shortcomings, Daley must be doing something right. Louis Masotti, a professor at the Northwestern University Center for Urban Affairs, made this observation:

> The people who criticize Daley the most have never had to live in New York or Los Angeles. What everyone wants is a philosopher-king, a mayor with both the power to govern and the wisdom to do right. But most cities end up with neither a philosopher nor a king. John Lindsay may have the wisdom, but he doesn't have the power. I greatly admire Lindsay's intent, but he's like a guy rollerskating in a herd of buffalo—he's not in control of anything. Whatever else you say about Daley, he's got the clout.

Mayoral press secretary Earl Bush defended the incumbent's record in much the same fashion: "When people say, 'Daley's not solving the problems of race, housing and education,' I simply say, 'Dammit, who the hell is?'" The voters agreed. Daley won 70 percent of the votes and carried forty-eight of the fifty wards (Friedman won the perennially reformist fifth and forty-third wards). The election produced the smallest turnout since 1935, a decline particularly noticeable in black wards, where Democratic voters unhappy with Daley's segregationist policies declined to vote Republican and stayed home in huge numbers. In the second ward (Bill Dawson's domain and for years the heart of the party's strength in the South Side), the Democratic vote decreased by 21 percent from 1967; in the neighboring seventeenth ward, by 20 percent. Assaying Friedman's lopsided defeat, one wag said, "This proves that if you put together a coalition of independents, blacks, liberals, and Republicans, there is no way Daley can keep you from getting 29 percent of the vote."[39]

Daley's landslide reelection seemed all the more remarkable after the tumult of the previous four years. Consistently in the eye of a storm, the mayor survived race riots, the furor over the Democratic National Convention, repeated attacks on the professionalism and integrity of his police force, and legal challenges to the restrictions he favored on the location of public housing. Although the local newspapers still treated him favorably overall, Daley's vendetta hardened against the national media, whose coverage of him and Chicago he considered unfairly censorious. Yet even the hostile press outside Chicago expressed grudging admiration for Daley's managerial expertise. As much as he had developed the unenviable reputation of being a mean-spirited social and political reactionary, Daley could claim for his administration fiscal solvency and service delivery unequaled by most other large U.S. cities. Uneasy race relations continued to plague the city, but results of the April 1971 election indicated that white home owners, still numerically the dominant element in the Chicago electorate, approved of the mayor's performance. In light of the alternatives apparent in other cities, Daley's conservatism looked good; the status quo he fought to preserve appeared to many people wholly desirable. "I have seen the past," remarked an envious visitor from New York City, "and it works."[40]

9

Awash in a Sea of Scandal

On May 15, 1972, Richard J. Daley celebrated his seventieth birthday. At an age when others would have already settled comfortably into retirement, the mayor showed no evidence of slowing down the brisk pace he had maintained for seventeen years on the fifth floor of city hall. The dean of the nation's mayors and the last of the big city bosses, he had surpassed by three years Ed Kelly's record for the longest tenure as Chicago's mayor and was widely hailed as the city's preeminent chief executive. He had become something of an institution in the Windy City, a figure larger than life whose ambivalent treatment by the national press did nothing to diminish his standing at home. A resounding reelection in 1971 underscored Daley's continuing hold on the electorate—a relationship that had survived scandals, unfavorable publicity, and the tensions arising from a racially divided community. At a time when urbanologists and journalists pondered whether anyone could govern America's "ungovernable" cities, Daley had not only survived but thrived.[1]

His remarkable longevity and personal popularity notwithstanding, Mayor Daley's political power showed signs of decline, however. The early 1970s proved difficult for the mayor, as his hand-picked candidates for local and state offices repeatedly lost elections and as scandals involving leading Chicago Democrats mounted with alarming frequency. Electoral setbacks and embarrassing investigations of Daley surrogates raised questions about the possible diminution of the Chicago Democratic machine's hegemony, and a hostile ruling in the landmark *Shakman* case endangered the Democrats' reliance on patronage. The unseating of the Daley delegates at the 1972 Democratic National Convention in Miami Beach, Florida, proved especially shocking, suggesting the demise of the Chicago mayor's influence in national politics. The setbacks of Daley's fifth mayoral term gave rise to questions about whether the weight of accumulated grievances and the newspapers' recurring exposés of wrongdoing had at last made the Democratic machine vulnerable.

Shortly after the April 1971 city elections, rookie alderman Dick Simpson (forty-fourth ward) challenged the Daley-dominated city council's business-as-usual methods and bravely raised the issue of corruption in municipal government. Simpson questioned the appointment of Thomas Keane Jr. (son of the powerful thirty-first ward alderman) to the zoning board of appeals. Not only was this an obvious case of nepotism, the alderman charged, but the younger Keane's status as a vice president with Arthur Rubloff and Company, one of the city's biggest and best-known real estate developers, raised serious questions regarding conflict of interests as well. For the next half hour after Simpson made these charges, a steady stream of aldermen loyally defended the nominee and roundly berated Simpson for suggesting the possibility of any impropriety. Next Mayor Daley read a maudlin poem about the bonds between fathers and sons and then launched into a five-minute tirade against anyone who dared oppose the appointment. Pacing back and forth, his face reddened with anger, Daley stabbed his finger in the air and shouted at the hushed audience. "Should I appoint strangers?" he asked sarcastically, then praised the nominee's mother, Adeline Keane, as a great Polish American woman. At last, he turned his anger on Simpson, a political science professor at the University of Illinois at Chicago Circle, saying:

> If you are a teacher, God help the students who are in your class. . . .
> I hope the halls of all the great educational institutions will stop being places for agitation and hatred against this society. And talk about the young people! With their cynical smiles and their fakery and polluted minds.

When the mayor concluded his stream-of-consciousness harangue, the aldermen confirmed the appointment by forty-four votes to two. The relatively insignificant episode engendered much comment at the time because of the mayor's sudden verbal explosion (longtime city hall watchers called it the most vitriolic outburst of temper in his career) and because it served as a harbinger to the series of controversies that surfaced during the following four years.[2]

In the early 1970s, when experts estimated that roughly one-half of Chicago's forty thousand municipal and county jobs belonged to political appointees, one of the greatest threats to the political machine came from a legal assault on patronage. In 1969 Michael Shakman, an unsuccessful candidate for the Illinois State Constitutional Convention, brought a class action suit against Mayor Daley, the city of Chicago, and the Democratic organization, charging that the patronage system infringed upon the rights of voters who worked for the city or county by compelling them to contribute funds to political campaigns and electioneer for machine candidates. The following year the U.S. Court of Appeals for the Seventh Circuit reversed a federal judge's decision and found for the plaintiff in *Shakman v. Democratic Organization of Cook County et al.* In 1972 Mayor Daley signed a consent judgment officially ending the politically motivated firing of government employees. Because the consent agreement failed to deal with politically motivated hiring practices, however, Shakman continued his legal action. In 1979 a federal judge in U.S. District Court found politically based hiring unconstitutional for its violation of the First and Fourteenth Amendments.[3]

The full impact of the 1972 ruling (Shakman I) at first appeared unclear. According to thirty-first ward alderman Thomas Keane, the knowledge that they could not be fired led many patronage workers to curtail their fund-raising activities on behalf of the Democratic party. Keane believed that greater job security eroded the fear that generated party loyalty. Even so, the freedom to hire patronage workers preserved much of the political machine's power despite limitations on firing. Moreover, before the 1979 decision (Shakman II), Daley devised several successful strategies to circumvent the first decree's intent. Through delaying tactics, sabotage, and at times outright noncompliance, the political machine minimized the impact of Shakman I. The great reduction of Chicago's huge patronage army came as a result of Shakman II, but that was years after Daley's death.[4]

In 1972 additional trouble signs came with the March Democratic primary elections. Denied renomination by the machine, state's attorney Edward Hanrahan defied Daley and stubbornly remained in the race. A federal court ruling allowed Republicans, many of whom approved of Hanrahan's extreme conservatism, to vote in the Democratic primary. At the conclusion of a fractious contest, Hanrahan won with 41 percent of the vote. (The machine candidate, Raymond Berg, received 30 percent of the vote and liberal independent Donald Page Moore 29 percent.) Daley's candidate for governor, downstater Paul Simon, lost to a renegade Democrat, Chicago corporation lawyer Daniel J. Walker. A former president of the Chicago Crime Commission and principal author of the scathing report on the 1968 Democratic National Convention, Walker ran for governor with virtually no political experience. Decrying machine politics, he worked hard to distance himself from Daley, especially when campaigning among downstate voters, and promised reform of a corrupt system of government. Informed of Walker's candidacy, Daley tersely replied that "everyone has a right to run for public office" and in public remained divorced from the primary campaign. In private Daley abhorred Walker, never forgiving him for coining the term "police riot" in 1968 and dismissing his reformist rhetoric as self-serving cant. Walker's primary victory was doubly disagreeable, for the loss to another independent both damaged the machine's reputation of invincibility and meant that Daley would have to deal with an adversarial governor in Springfield for the next four years.[5]

The same month the federal government brought suit against U.S. Court of Appeals Judge Otto Kerner, a second-generation Chicago Democratic politician and former governor of Illinois. Crusading Republican U.S. Attorney James R. Thompson indicted Kerner for mail fraud, bribery, conspiracy, income tax evasion, and perjury in connection with a sweetheart deal on racetrack stock. Several months later, Thompson charged Cook County Clerk Edward Barrett with accepting bribes from a Pennsylvania voting machine company in return for using that firm's products in Chicago elections. Barrett held an especially sensitive position, for he dealt routinely with contractors seeking city business—contractors who had been a sure source of campaign contributions to Democratic candidates for years. Although Daley was not personally implicated in either legal proceeding, both Kerner and Barrett held prominent positions in the Chicago Democratic hierarchy and their indictments again raised recurring questions about rampant corruption surrounding the mayor.[6]

Daley encountered more problems with his old nemesis, Judge Richard Austin. Still attempting to force compliance in the *Gautreaux* case, Austin reclaimed the initiative in October 1971 by ordering the

Department of Housing and Urban Development (HUD) to freeze $26 million in Model Cities funds previously earmarked for Chicago. HUD announced that the city risked losing an additional $20 million in urban renewal funds unless it approved sites for seven hundred new public housing units (to be disbursed according to Austin's 1969 formula) by December 15. Daley again challenged the judge's plan, saying, "The majority of black people want new housing, and they don't care where it is." On the Southwest Side, an angry crowd of about fifteen hundred white home owners hanged Austin in effigy.[7]

In May 1972 the U.S. Court of Appeals for the Seventh Circuit directed Judge Austin to rescind his order blocking the payment of the Model Cities money to Chicago. However, the court upheld another of the judge's orders, a January 1972 writ instructing the CHA to bypass the city council and submit directly to Austin a plan for constructing 8,500 low-income housing units—6,700 of which had to be in white neighborhoods. The city appealed the circuit court's ruling, but the U.S. Supreme Court denied certiorari. The Daley-Austin wrangle persisted, and Chicago continued to build no public housing.[8]

In addition to their continuing struggle for housing desegregation, in 1972 blacks intensified their protests against police brutality and called specifically for the firing of Police Superintendent James Conlisk. They noted that twenty-five policemen had been indicted within the last year and that Chicago law enforcement authorities had killed more people in the preceding nine months than the police in New York City, Los Angeles, and Philadelphia combined. As he had done repeatedly in the past, Daley defended the police and gave the superintendent an unequivocal vote of confidence. Conlisk remained in office for another year, and the mayor continued to deny allegations of bigotry and excessive violence directed against the police department.[9]

Daley's mounting troubles in 1972 crested with the unexpected battle over the Chicago delegation to the Democratic National Convention. After the close of the 1968 conclave, the party had established a commission to revise the procedures for the selection of convention delegates. Under the chairmanship of George McGovern, the commission drafted new guidelines to ensure broader representation within the state delegations for women, minorities, and young people by stipulating that these groups must be included in proportion to their percentage of the population. In the primary on

March 21, 1972, Chicagoans voted to select 59 of Illinois's 170 convention delegates. The winning Daley slate of fifty-nine candidates included nine black men, three black women, four white women, two Hispanic women, and five whites under the age of thirty. With women comprising 50 percent of the city's population, blacks approximately 33 percent, and Hispanics approximately 7 percent, this Chicago contingent fell far short of the demographic mix necessary to meet party strictures. "Not only did the organization fail to take the affirmative steps required to achieve fair representation of these groups," charged black alderwoman Anna Langford, "the organization deliberately used its power to assure the election of slates on which blacks, Latins, women, and young people were grossly underrepresented."[10]

Daley opponents, led by forty-third ward alderman William Singer and the Reverend Jesse Jackson, challenged the validity of the slate. In caucuses held throughout the city, the reformers staged voice-vote elections to assemble an alternative delegation. Machine loyalists frequently infiltrated the caucuses, where they heckled, disrupted, and in at least one instance started a brawl. Claiming legitimacy and buoyed by a spate of warnings from the Democratic National Committee to the Cook County organization, the Singer-Jackson forces petitioned to be seated at the national nominating convention as Chicago's representatives.[11]

Daley disdainfully repudiated the insurgents and, ignoring the McGovern committee rules, affirmed the legality of his delegation. He told the ward committeemen that he "didn't give a damn" about the reforms and believed that "once we get to the convention, no one would dare throw us out." To forestall any attempt at keeping the machine's delegation from being seated in Miami Beach, Daley filed suit in the Circuit Court of Cook County; Judge Daniel Covelli issued an injunction forbidding the Singer delegation from participation in the national convention. Anticipating a negative decision from a state court that contained a preponderance of loyal organization Democrats, the insurgents took their case to federal court. The McGovern commission filed an amicus curiae brief defending the right of the challengers to make their case at the convention, and the U.S. Supreme Court, affirming the party's right to determine its own delegate selection process, ruled on July 7 that no court should issue an injunction.[12]

A week before the start of the party gathering, the controversy moved to Washington, D.C., where the convention's Credentials

Committee heard testimony from both factions. Asked if he thought the ruling might go against his delegates, Daley told reporters, "You know they wouldn't do that to me." By a vote of seventy-one to sixty-one, with twelve abstentions, the Democratic party chose to seat the Singer-Jackson group and to deny entry to the Daley delegation. Returning from Washington, D.C., Alderman Singer triumphantly proclaimed, "*We* are the delegates now." Incredulous and outraged, Daley expressed his disbelief that the committee decided to invalidate the outcome of a legally conducted primary election: "Nine hundred thousand people participated in the election. There's no reference to that in the report. There's no reference that, although there were six to eight delegates elected in every district affected, there were fifteen to thirty-six candidates."[13]

Many disinterested onlookers, as well as party professionals, found the decision curious. Although the business-as-usual machine-politics approach used by Daley in the selection of a convention slate resulted in the election of a delegation at variance with the McGovern committee standards, questions arose about the process utilized by the alternative delegation that was approved by the Democratic party. Even political columnist Mike Royko, a persistent critic of the Cook County Democratic machine, told Singer that "your reforms have disenfranchised Chicago's white ethnic Democrats" and that Daley's delegates "come much closer to reflecting the people who vote as Democrats in Chicago than yours do." Forty-fifth ward committeeman Tommy Lyons, one of the Daley delegates who had been denied a convention seat, explained the reason for his anger:

> I was elected to it, I received about forty thousand votes, and I was replaced by someone who was chosen in a basement in a meeting attended by about twelve people. . . . The state statutes of Illinois required that the delegates be elected, so we had an election. We had opponents and we beat them, so we were elected. Then we were replaced pursuant to rules of the Democratic National Committee, in total violation of the statutes of the state of Illinois. It was anomolous, ridiculous, and, I still think today, illegal.[14]

When the convention opened in Miami Beach, the Daley delegation settled into the Diplomat Hotel in hopes that a favorable floor ruling might renounce the Credentials Committee's recommendation and expel the Singer-Jackson group. On the convention floor, colleagues of the mayor from other states lobbied to reverse the Credentials Committee's decision. Daley remained secluded in his summer home in Grand Beach, Michigan, avoiding reporters and maintaining telephone contact with his minions in Florida, most notably Illinois state Democratic chairman John Touhy. He spoke often with Lawrence O'Brien, the convention chairman and an old friend, who served as a liaison with George McGovern. Embarrassed by the whole affair yet obligated to honor the party's commitment to reform, O'Brien did little but preside objectively over the convention's deliberations. The sure Democratic presidential nominee, George McGovern, could only follow the recommendation of the Credentials Committee he had chaired—even though he must have realized how damaging the exclusion of the powerful Chicago machine would be to his campaign.[15]

Daley refused all suggestions for a compromise, including a proposal by McGovern that both Chicago delegations be seated and each of the 118 delegates be given half a vote. Perhaps the mayor still believed that at the eleventh hour the Democratic party would come to its senses and reverse the earlier decision to exclude him. Daley never wavered, because he understood that the stakes involved much more than representation at a nominating convention—especially a convention at which the likely presidential nominee spoke for a wing of the party that was alien to the boss and other old-line Democrats. Most important, any concessions the mayor might make to the reform delegation in Miami Beach would endanger his control of Chicago's Democratic party. He saw Singer and Jackson as ambitious men, eager to use their convention success as a springboard to greater influence in local politics. Daley's resolve stiffened as Jackson posited a compromise on delegate seating if five demands were met: these demands included a civilian review board to curtail police brutality, the direct allocation of federal grants to community groups without local involvement, and other departures from standard procedure that were perceived as threatening to the political machine. Daley believed that long after the Miami Beach affair was concluded, these usurpers would have to be dealt with. The dissidents might triumph in Washington, D.C., and in Miami Beach, but Chicago would be more congenial—and more important—ground on which Daley could defend the machine's interests.[16]

The fate of the Daley delegation became the convention's most compelling story, because it would serve as a litmus test for assessing several eventualities. Once again, Chicago's mayor became the center of controversy at the party's quadrennial gathering, and speculation abounded about whether the Democrats would be torn apart as they had been four year earlier. A decision on the status of the Chicago situation, along with the disputed California delegation, would demonstrate conclusively whether the reformist elements had wrested control of the party from the old professional politicians. Just as the pundits pondered the fate of the old guard at the convention, they speculated that a defeat in Miami Beach might mean the beginning of the end for Chicago's powerful mayor. Surely a victory over the last of the big city bosses, a septuagenarian who seemed to have been in office interminably, would energize Chicago's long-enervated reformers and hasten the fall of the Cook County Democratic machine.[17]

The convention's most dramatic moment occurred when the delegates voted on which Chicago faction would be seated. The pivotal vote belonged to the Massachusetts delegation, because of the belief that Daley's strong ties to Edward Kennedy and his family might prevail. When that state voted ninety-one to eleven for the dissident Chicagoans, bedlam erupted among McGovern supporters throughout the hall and specifically within the Illinois delegation. The final count was 1,486.05 to 1,371.55 against the Daleyites. Amazingly, the Democratic party had closed the door on one of its oldest and most powerful leaders. The next day, the Diplomat Hotel emptied of Chicago's organization Democrats. Daley remained incommunicado in Michigan and declined to send his congratulations to George McGovern as he customarily did to the party's presidential nominee.[18]

Despite the stirring victory that assured their right to be seated at the convention, the Singer-Jackson forces could not sustain their good fortune. Caucusing shortly after their triumph in the floor fight, the reformers argued, divided into factions, and fell into endless squabbles over minutia while attempting to conclude the crucial task of selecting three Democratic National Committee members. Still euphoric over their surprising victory and unable to focus on the urgent business at hand, they failed to cement their influence by gaining representation in the organization that would continue to make policy long after the close of the convention. Remaining in telephone contact with Daley, Illinois ex officio delegates John Touhy and Michael J. Howlett thwarted the reformers through a series of parliamentary maneuvers. Laying procedural traps, raising countless points of order, offering and seconding needless amendments, and employing a variety of tactics to prolong discussion, the Daley fifth column managed to divert the Illinois delegation from making decisions. After an exhausting sleepless night, the Illinois delegates accepted a motion at 6 A.M. to select National Committee members on August 5 in Chicago and wearily adjourned. Daley forces believed that by delaying the vote, some of the Singer delegates would become discouraged or distracted and fail to appear at the later meeting. Touhy telephoned Daley and reported, "Everything is under control again."[19]

Later that summer, in a move widely interpreted as the Mc-Governites' attempt to restore amity with the Chicago Democratic organization, six Daley loyalists were named to the Democratic National Committee. Although party reformers chafed at any overtures to machine politicians, McGovern openly sought a rapprochement with Chicago's mayor. Daley lacked any enthusiasm for McGovern and his advisers, whom he considered amateurish and ineffectual, but he welcomed the candidate graciously to Chicago and heartily endorsed him for president. Despite the humiliation suffered at the convention, Daley put the party first and remained a good soldier. Ignoring all the insulting things Daniel Walker had said about him in the party primary, Daley similarly endorsed the Democratic nominee for governor. "Daley could have taken a walk on the ticket, but he didn't do that," noted Tommy Lyons. "It just wasn't his way. Party loyalty."[20]

Convinced of McGovern's narrow appeal nationally and his limited usefulness to the local and state Democratic tickets, Daley braced for the worst in November 1972. McGovern carried Cook County but lost Illinois on the way to a landslide victory for Richard Nixon. Bernard Carey won ten of the fourteen predominantly black wards, defeating the controversial Edward Hanrahan and thereby situating a Republican in the powerful office of state's attorney for four years. The Democrats' only major victory occurred in the gubernatorial race, where Walker defeated Republican Richard Ogilvie by just seventy-seven thousand votes. Chicago Democrats, aware of Walker's anti-machine animus and purported ambitions for higher office, viewed the new administration in Springfield with trepidation. "The basis of the problem," quipped Illinois Secretary of State Michael J. Howlett, "is that we have elected a governor who hates Daley and thinks this is the way to get elected president of the United States."[21]

Mayor Daley and Governor Walker kept a wary distance during the following years, never achieving more than a polite relationship of necessity. On some occasions they clashed openly, most notably in the ongoing struggle over the proposed billion-dollar Crosstown Expressway. To relieve congestion in the existing freeway network, the twenty-two-mile Crosstown was designed to extend from the junction of the Kennedy and Edens Expressways south to Midway Airport and then east to the Dan Ryan Expressway south of the Skyway. Industries on the Far West Side and the municipal government of suburban Cicero, which was located west of the manufacturing area, sought the highway as a barrier against the sprawling Lawndale ghetto to the east. Many Lawndale residents objected to the necessary destruction of housing—more than six hundred dwellings in just over one mile at one point and approximately ten thousand altogether would be razed with the construction of the highway—and doubted Commissioner of Public Works Milton Pikarsky's promise of adequate relocation housing. As the city sought federal funds to defray the costs of construction, residents of affected communities protested in volatile meetings with Commissioner Pikarsky and other local officials. Committed, as always, to large-scale construction projects that he believed would benefit the city, Daley gave his support to the endeavor; as champion of the west-siders who fought to preserve their neighborhoods, Governor Walker spoke for the opposition. Throughout 1973, the two Democrats continued to exchange barbs in the press over the fate of the Crosstown, which in fact was never built.[22]

Overshadowing the mayor's skirmishes with the governor, a new wave of scandals in 1973 and 1974 raised concerns about corruption in the Daley machine to unprecedented levels. In January 1973, William S. Miller—the former Illinois Racing Board chairman—testified at Otto Kerner's trial that Daley had introduced him to the defendant in 1960 and "induced" him to lend Kerner $150,000 for his first gubernatorial campaign. Asked about these charges, Daley scoffed, "I don't care. I had none of it" (referring to the tainted racetrack stock). The following month came the disclosure that Daley had shifted to an Evanston firm, Heil and Heil, virtually all of the casualty insurance on Chicago's municipal buildings—and that Heil and Heil employed one of Daley's sons, John Patrick, to handle the $2 million account. The mayor initially challenged the veracity of the report and, after city comptroller David Stahl confirmed that the change had come at Daley's suggestion, steadfastly denied any impropriety. A county grand jury was impaneled to investigate. Additional charges of nepotism surfaced that year when newspapers reported that two other Daley progeny, attorneys Richard and

Michael, received preferential treatment in the city's assignment of custodianship cases. Not bothering to deny the charges, Daley exploded in parental outrage at a Cook County Democratic committee meeting. As Democratic committeemen roared their approval, Daley said, "If I can't help my sons, then they can kiss my ass. . . . I make no apologies to anyone. There are many men in this room whose fathers helped them, and they went on to become fine public officials."[23]

Although many Chicagoans applauded Daley's brassy defense of his sons and seemed willing to wink at such minor cases of nepotism, the public felt less sanguine about yet another scandal in the perennially troublesome police department. Also in 1973 came the conviction of a police traffic chief and eighteen vice detectives on charges of extortion from Near North Side tavern and nightclub owners. To quell the clamor for reform at a time when a federal grand jury had indicted thirty-seven other policemen for extortion, bribery, and income tax evasion, Daley fired Police Superintendent James Conlisk. His replacement, James Rochford, required the police department's seventy highest-ranking officers to demonstrate their integrity by taking lie detector tests. When several received failing scores on the polygraph examinations and refused to resign, Rochford summarily demoted them. The press praised the new superintendent's decisive action, but the episode revealed again clear evidence of corruption in the highest echelons of the police department—a malady that seemed to befall the city at regular intervals.[24]

The mayor and the police department attracted additional unflattering publicity over the issue of minority hiring. Whereas Chicago's black population increased substantially in the 1960s, the proportion of nonwhite police officers declined. Despite the prodding of the civil rights division of the U.S. Department of Justice and the Law Enforcement Assistance Administration, Daley refused to implement affirmative action hiring procedures. In February 1974, the Afro-American Patrolmen's League of Illinois and the NAACP asked the federal government to suspend all general revenue-sharing funds to Chicago until the police department ceased discriminating against blacks in hiring and promotions. In November, U.S. District Judge Prentice Marshall ruled against the city in a civil suit, and another federal court expropriated Chicago's federal revenue-sharing funds. Daley refused to comply with the court order and filed countersuits in several courts. Excoriating the city's "arrogant, contemptuous" behavior, Judge Marshall ended a year-long impasse by mandating hiring quotas for the Chicago police. Daley reacted vehemently, saying,

"The quota system is totally un-American. We'll continue to fight this as long as we're around." Nevertheless, a month later the mayor acknowledged that the city would comply rather than lose federal funds totaling $95 million.[25]

In early 1974, the pace of scandal disclosures quickened. In February, U.S. Attorney Jim Thompson indicted Earl Bush, the mayor's press secretary, on twelve counts of mail fraud and one count of extortion. Bush secretly owned a company whose exclusive contract with the city for all advertising and display promotion at O'Hare International Airport earned him more than $200,000 profit. Apparently, Bush had maintained this secret arrangement since 1962 without Daley's knowledge—a fact that exonerated the mayor less than it raised questions about how such defalcations could occur for so long within his immediate purview.[26]

On April 5, Thompson indicted Alderman Paul Wigoda, the law partner of city council finance committee chairman Thomas Keane, for tax evasion related to a $50,000 rezoning payoff. Five days later, a grand jury indicted county clerk Matthew Danaher on charges of conspiracy and income tax evasion. According to an investigation sponsored by the *Chicago Sun-Times* and the Better Government Association (BGA), Danaher and his brother-in-law had received over $300,000 from Chicago builders seeking zoning changes and private financing to build two subdivisions. Daley had taken Danaher, a neighbor from the eleventh ward, to city hall in 1955 and put him in charge of patronage. One of Daley's oldest, most trusted confidants (a man often mentioned as the boss's possible successor), Danaher was the biggest fish yet to be caught in Thompson's net of indictments. Visibly shaken when informed of his longtime colleague's misfortune, the mayor said, "It's a sad day for him and his family. An indictment is not a conviction."[27]

In May, Thompson struck again, indicting Thomas Keane on seventeen counts of mail fraud and one count of conspiracy. The government charged the powerful alderman with using his city council connections to obtain parcels of tax-delinquent real estate, which he reputedly sold at a profit of $135,000 to such city agencies as the Department of Urban Renewal, the CHA, the Chicago Dwelling Association, the Metropolitan Sanitary District, and the Chicago Park District. The indictment of Keane caused the greatest stir yet, for the thirty-first ward alderman was Daley's floor leader in the council and, as finance committee chairman, was widely regarded as the second most powerful politician in the city whose age alone (sixty-eight) eliminated him from consideration as the mayor's successor. Keane claimed to be a victim of Thompson's political ambitions, a theme echoed by Daley, who assailed the U.S. Attorney's "vendetta" against high-ranking Chicago Democrats. Asked if he thought that Thompson was laying the groundwork for a mayoral campaign, Daley replied, "Undoubtedly."[28]

The rapid-fire indictments created a political crisis for Daley. As Thompson moved against one after another of the mayor's closest allies, the image of corruption throughout city hall crystallized. Daley inveighed against the U.S. Attorney's granting immunity to witnesses in exchange for their damaging testimony—"Where is the justice in this?" the mayor plaintively asked—but the newspapers applauded Thompson's tactic for its proven effectiveness. Daley partisans argued that the indictments involved no wholesale looting of the public coffers and relatively small sums of money—a rather benign sort of "honest graft" whereby political insiders with privileged information enriched themselves at virtually no public expense. How dastardly, after all, were crimes involving income tax evasion and mail fraud? Yet the public outcry persisted. The general perception was that Daley remained personally honest, but evidence mounted that he paid insufficient attention to the ethics of his closest subordinates. Thompson's motives notwithstanding, the campaign against the Daley administration was taking a heavy toll.[29]

On May 6, just four days after the announcement of the indictments against Thomas Keane, Daley's health collapsed under the weight of all the bad news. Feeling a numbness in his leg and experiencing a slurring of speech, the mayor interrupted his morning schedule of meetings for an emergency visit to his physician, Dr. Thomas Coogan. Later at Presbyterian–St. Luke's Hospital, doctors concluded that Daley had suffered a mild stroke. For the first time in his long stay in city hall, the mayor's health became a concern. For nineteen years Daley's image had been that of a robust, energetic man of action, and because he seemed to keep the same frenetic pace as always, Chicagoans forgot about his advancing age. Speculation immediately arose that he would not seek another term of office in the election less than a year away. For that matter, people wondered whether the stroke was sufficiently debilitating to keep Daley from working for the remainder of the current term. For days after the event, city hall functionaries explained little about the mayor's condition; all reports remained brief and guarded.[30]

On June 2, without fanfare or advanced notice, doctors performed an endarterectomy to remove a blockage from an artery that carried blood to Daley's brain. The doctors pronounced the surgery successful and prescribed an extended period of recovery. The mayor immediately settled in at his summer home in Grand Beach, Michigan, and adopted a recuperative regimen of walking and reading, with an occasional round of golf at a nearby course. He lived in nearly total isolation for several months, his absence spawning more rumors about the degree of his incapacitation, his ability to resume the tasks of office, and his plans for the future. Business as usual proceeded at city hall, and none but a few insiders knew how much Daley kept in touch by telephone with his aides in Chicago. The summer was rife with rumor and uncertainty.[31]

As Daley convalesced in Michigan, more unsettling news came from Chicago. Having exhausted all his appeals, Otto Kerner entered the federal correctional institution at Lexington, Kentucky, to begin serving a three-year prison sentence. Emboldened by his 1972 victory in Miami Beach, Alderman William Singer announced that he would challenge Daley in the upcoming mayoral primary. Whereas this announcement had elicited little concern among organization Democrats when Singer first suggested it in October 1973, Daley's prolonged health problem and his absence from the city in 1974 encouraged reformers, who questioned both the mayor's willingness to run and his electability. In Daley's absence from the city, Singer's increased activities garnered considerable attention. Most nettlesome, after the onslaught of legal investigations into the financial affairs of the city's leading Democrats, U.S. Attorney Thompson revealed that his office had launched a probe of Daley himself—and had uncovered indications of some financial impropriety.[32]

Throughout his years in city hall, Daley appeared to be a public servant of modest means who lived frugally on his mayor's salary and eschewed the questionable moneymaking opportunities that politics inevitably provided. He once remarked, "I'm tremendously wealthy, because I have a fine family. But financially speaking, I'm not a rich man. My salary is my major source of income. I have no outside business." On July 11, however, the *Chicago Sun-Times* published an exposé entitled "$200,000 Nest Egg—Mayor Daley's Secret Firm," which alleged that for seventeen years the mayor had maintained covert ownership of a real estate and holding company for the purpose of concealing secret land trusts and other assets. Daley admitted that he and his wife owned all the stock in the Elard Realty Company, whose holdings included their summer home, a commercial building at the intersection of Thirty-seventh and Halsted Streets, two adjacent lots, and a residence near Seventy-sixth and Green Streets, but he pointed out that such an investment broke no laws. The *Sun-Times* rejoined that the Elard holdings included tax-delinquent property that had been bought by a public official, which was a violation of state law. Also, the BGA claimed, Daley had installed his own personal accountant, Peter Shannon, as president of the company, and Shannon's accounting firm received the bulk of the city's business. The BGA called for an explanation of this entangling web of interlocking interests.[33]

On September 3, after three months' absence, Daley returned to his office in city hall and promptly addressed the many questions about the Elard Company. At the urging of Chicago Corporation counsel John Melaniphy (Daley explained), he and his wife had created the company to safeguard their personal property from possible lawsuits brought against the city and, by extension, the mayor. No illegalities existed, he asserted, and the public now knew the sum total of his altogether modest assets—the mortgage-free Bridgeport home and the Elard holdings. U.S. Attorney Thompson admitted that his office's investigation uncovered no indictable offenses, and the newspaper coverage of the scandal gave way to other topics. It appeared as though the Chicago press, always vigilant to uncover scandal in the Democratic machine and especially interested in uncovering some transgressions by a mayor who had miraculously remained personally unsullied, had unearthed relatively little of consequence after all. Daley survived the Elard flap, as did his reputation for scrupulous personal conduct and financial probity.[34]

The travails of Daley's cohorts did not subside, however. In the fall of 1974, with speculation rising about the possibility of the mayor's seeking a sixth term, the newspaper headlines returned to the old stories of corruption among leading machine Democrats. On October 9, Daley testified in the trial of Earl Bush, praising his former press secretary yet denying any knowledge of the secret O'Hare Airport contracts. Indeed, Daley asserted, he fired Bush as soon as he learned that his press secretary was the sole owner of Dell Airport Advertising, Incorporated, which handled display advertising at the airport. As he emerged from the courtroom, reporters informed the mayor of Thomas Keane's conviction earlier that day. Democratic mayoral candidate William Singer moved quickly to implicate Daley, saying, "Keane is part of the system; he is what the system is all about. The mayor has to be held responsible in these convictions."

The next day a jury found Alderman Paul Wigoda guilty of income tax evasion. On October 11 came the third conviction in three days as Earl Bush was found guilty of eleven counts of mail fraud.[35]

The embarrassing publicity continued. In November, Judge Bernard Decker ignored pleas for clemency based on Thomas Keane's age and infirmity and, after rendering a scathing denunciation of public officials who betrayed the public trust, sentenced the defendant to the maximum penalty of five years for each of the eighteen counts. The next day Judge Philip Tone sentenced Earl Bush to serve one year for mail fraud; and on December 2, Paul Wigoda was sentenced to one year in prison. On December 15, Matthew Danaher died of an apparent heart attack, a month before the scheduled beginning of his trial, and Daley served as one of the six pallbearers at the funeral. For nearly one year the Chicago newspapers had featured a steady stream of stories on corruption within the Daley administration and, even as 1974 came to a close and the next mayoral election grew near, the damaging headlines persisted. After the many years of a relatively scandal-free administration, could Daley survive all the negative publicity of his fifth term? And for that matter, as a seventy-two-year-old man recuperating from a stroke who had just seen many of his oldest, closest colleagues humiliated and destroyed, would he want to continue as mayor?[36]

On December 8, 1974, Daley put to rest months of speculation, announcing his intention to run for a sixth term. By that time, his apparent vulnerability had enticed a number of Democrats to file for the February 1975 primary election. The most imposing candidate appeared to be William Singer, the brash thirty-three-year-old alderman whose triumph at the 1972 Democratic National Convention brought him instant credibility as a candidate. Darling of the lakeshore liberals and Hyde Park reformers, Singer raised over $600,000 for the primary contest. A tireless campaigner, he blamed Daley for the city's loss of two hundred thousand jobs between 1960 and 1970, for a 12 percent increase in crime during the first ten months of 1974, and for a concatenation of problems in Chicago's 584 public schools. Singer offered youthful exuberance in contrast to Daley's age and shopworn ways of conducting business, an alternative that many longtime supporters of the mayor found alluring. Ben Heineman, president of Northwest Industries and a Daley protégé for many years, endorsed Singer: "To put it purely in business terms, I would never put a man who is seventy-two and has had a stroke in charge of one of our major corporations. Expressing similar sentiments, the *Chicago Tribune* declined to endorse anyone for mayor; the *Chicago Sun-Times* and the *Chicago Daily News* came out for Singer. The *Sun-Times* charged that Daley "even faltered as a master builder," claiming that he had failed to make progress on such projects as a third airport, the Crosstown Expressway, a new multisport stadium for the city's professional teams, and another downtown subway "Clearly the Daley of today is not the Daley of four years ago," concluded the paper.[37]

Another challenge came from the political right in the person of former state's attorney Edward Hanrahan. Most recently defeated in his race for Congress in November 1974, Hanrahan was still attempting a comeback after the disastrous Black Panther raid that cast him as the white backlash champion. Hanrahan enjoyed limited appeal among most mainstream voters, who could always express their preference for a more respectable law and order candidate by voting for the mayor. Of course, Hanrahan's sulfurous personality and reputation for racial bigotry made him anathema to liberals and black voters.[38]

The issue of race loomed large in 1975, because for the first time a serious black candidate emerged in the Democratic primary to challenge Daley's renomination. Discontent with Daley had been building among Chicago's African Americans for several years, and it appeared that Ralph Metcalfe, who had replaced William Dawson as U.S. congressman in 1970, might lead the revolt. A devout party loyalist, cautious and reserved, Metcalfe finally broke with Daley over the issue of police brutality in the ghetto. No doubt influenced by his black militant son, Ralph Jr., the elder Metcalfe had become disenchanted over the years with the bigotry of the Democratic machine, and two specific incidents galvanized his determination to rebel. In both cases, Chicago police had gratuitously beaten black motorists (one of whom was a personal friend of Metcalfe), and in each case, the machine ignored the congressman's complaints and calls for investigation. A proud man, Metcalfe felt personally slighted when Daley made light of the incidents and refused to devote any attention to the matter. Severing his ties to the political organization he had served faithfully for a lifetime, Metcalfe proclaimed, "It's never too late to be black." When Edward Hanrahan won the Democratic primary for state's attorney and Daley endorsed him for reelection in 1972, Metcalfe invoked the memory of the slain Black Panthers and supported the Republican candidate, Bernard Carey. In 1975 Metcalfe organized a fund-raising effort and took preliminary steps to run for mayor, but then, claiming that Daley had pressured black businessmen into withholding contributions, he reluctantly announced his decision not to run.[39]

Metcalfe's withdrawal did not end the black insurgency, however. State senator Richard Newhouse, a handsome and articulate independent Democrat with few ties to the machine, declared his candidacy. Newhouse quickly received the backing of Operation PUSH's Jesse Jackson, but his campaign suffered from disorganization and inadequate financial backing. Realistically assessing the slim chance of a black candidate winning the party primary, many black voters despaired of cutting their ties to Daley and opted for the safer course of action. The influential *Chicago Defender* and the Johnson family publications *Ebony* and *Jet* endorsed Daley. With his ties to the organization broken and doubtful that the relatively unknown Newhouse could win, Metcalfe endorsed the liberal Singer as the best choice to unseat the mayor. The machine's hold on the black vote in Chicago was wavering by 1975, but fear, inertia, years of passive repetition, and the inability of a black candidate to attract the necessary campaign funding doomed any unified, large-scale insurrection.[40]

As combative and defiant as ever, Daley met the many challenges to his renomination eagerly. Resurrecting the controversies of his long administration, he declined to admit any mistakes and strenuously affirmed his 1968 "shoot to kill" order. Refusing to respond to specific criticisms from his foes, the mayor told reporters that his mother once advised him "to reply to political attacks by pinning some mistletoe to his coattails." Disdainful of the other candidates, whom he regularly ignored in his campaign speeches, Daley called for the election to be a referendum on his many years of leadership. Still commander of the party, he summoned the patronage army and other machine faithful to preserve the ruling class. And they did. In the February 25 primary, Daley received 432,224 votes (58 percent); Singer, 217,764 (29 percent); Newhouse, 58,548 (8 percent); and Hanrahan, 37,034 (5 percent). The mayor did especially well among white voters, besting Singer by margins of two to one citywide and three to one in the bungalow belts; with only one-third of registered African American voters making their way to the polls, Daley received a plurality of the black vote.[41]

The mayor's surprisingly easy victory in the primary dashed the hopes of the many expectant reformers who believed that the time had finally come for a new presence in city hall. These dissidents found the outcome of the Democratic contest especially disappointing, for, as usual, the anemic Republicans had failed to field a competitive candidate. Unable to entice U.S. Attorney Thompson to run, a Republican search committee had finally settled on its own chairman, forty-seventh ward alderman John Hoellen. An alderman for twenty-eight years, Hoellen had been consistently the mayor's most vocal critic in the city council and, for some of that time, its only Republican. Whereas Daley reputedly spent over $1,000,000 on his campaign, Hoellen made do with $29,000 and lamented the Republican business community's support of the incumbent. Asked why the Republican-owned city newspapers endorsed Daley yet again, columnist Mike Royko responded, "Because Daley *is* a Republican." In the first mayoral election since 1931 to attract fewer than one million voters, with only 47 percent of eligible voters participating, Daley received 536,413 votes (78 percent) to Hoellen's 136,874 (20 percent). Daley carried all fifty wards, receiving at least 60 percent of the votes in all of them and more than 90 percent in eleven. The Republican received more than 30 percent of the votes in only four wards—the fifth, forty-third, forty-seventh, and forty-eighth. Having lost his aldermanic seat as well, Hoellen forlornly concluded, "It's hard to be a Republican in Chicago."[42]

Daley's unprecedented sixth election confounded later political experts, who noted that if he had served the full four years, he would have been Chicago's mayor for twice as long as Franklin D. Roosevelt served as president of the United States. His triumph seemed all the more remarkable considering the plethora of scandals that touched the leading Democrats who worked closely with him for so long. At the same time that the Watergate misdeeds had Americans clamoring for reputable government, Daley somehow survived the crushing weight of his subordinates' convictions. Despite the best efforts of his political enemies in the U.S. Attorney's office, no evidence ever surfaced that linked Daley personally with the peccadillos of his cohorts. In the public mind, he may have been guilty of lackadaisical supervision, but nothing more insidious than that. With the Elard Realty Company scandal amounting to very little of substance, his decades-old reputation for personal probity and imperviousness to temptation remained intact. Daley may have bent the rules a bit to help his sons—an allegation he met head-on—but he remained in the minds of most Chicagoans the honest politician who lived modestly on the mayor's $35,000 salary and amassed relatively few financial assets. (The disclosure three years after his death that he also received $25,000 annually as Cook County Democratic chairman and treasurer received little attention in the press.) Daley miraculously remained in power for twenty years in a city where corruption had a long and storied tradition, and during those many years, he seemingly denied temptation at every turn. "I've never betrayed the public trust," the mayor claimed, "or they would have had me ten years ago." Spurning wealth and its trappings, Daley's only passion appeared to be for his city.[43]

10

The City That Works

For most of his tenure in city hall, Richard J. Daley was the nation's most famous big city mayor, but from 1966 to 1973, New York City's John V. Lindsay rivaled his Chicago counterpart for that distinction. Journalists and other students of urban affairs invariably noted the striking dissimilarities between the two men. Daley was rotund, stolid, a halting public speaker, an Irish Catholic product of the working class, an aging machine politician whose conservative politics and habits made him an easy target for the East Coast literati. Tall, young, handsome, eloquent, and charming, the beneficiary of prep school and Yale University educations, Lindsay seemed the perfect WASP reformer to preside over the death of New York City's crumbling Tammany Hall machine. In the racially charged atmosphere of the 1960s, Daley ordered his police to "shoot to kill" rioters and became a symbolic champion of white home owners' resistance to integration. Lindsay won national acclaim for walking the streets of Harlem in an effort to still rising passions and keep his city from igniting; he embodied the city's hope for racial harmony. By the end of his eight years in office, however, Lindsay's standing plummeted as New York City careened toward fiscal ruin and chaos; meanwhile, Daley's Chicago remained financially sound—the city that worked.[1]

Lindsay's troubles began on his first inauguration day when a transit system strike forced the cancellation of the elaborate plans for borough celebrations. Indeed, he battled incessantly for the next eight years with a series of crippling labor disputes. Teachers' strikes closed public schools, and similar walkouts and slowdowns by policemen, firemen, and sanitary workers inconvenienced New Yorkers with frustrating frequency. Historian Jon C. Teaford commented, "The mounting unrest among municipal employees reenforced New York's image as an ungovernable, unlivable metropolis in rapid decline." By contrast, Daley's control of patronage, his cozy relationship with public employee unions, and his skill as a negotiator allowed him to avoid the disastrous job actions that threatened to bring city business to a halt. C. Virgil Martin—the president of Carson, Pirie, Scott, and Company—said, "Daley is willing to negotiate. Lindsay doesn't negotiate, he talks." As Lindsay and his beleaguered parks and recreation commissioner blithely trumpeted their metropolis as "Fun City," residents of and visitors to New York City groused about high crime, suffocating traffic, unreliable mass transit, and dirty streets. In Chicago, said the conventional wisdom, garbage trucks removed refuse regularly, snow ploughs kept streets passable, expressway traffic moved at an acceptable pace, and technologically modern police and fire departments responded quickly to alarms. Lindsay's reputation unraveled with the failure of his city to deliver basic services; for all his grandiose designs and oratorical excellence, New York City's chief executive was simply not a good administrator. Baltimore Mayor William Schaefer commented, "When you need to get to the airport in Chicago, you're there in fifteen minutes. In fifteen minutes, Lindsay's still trying to find the phone on his desk."[2]

Most damaging for Lindsay was New York City's financial collapse. Although his successor, Abraham Beame, actually occupied the mayor's office when the crisis occurred in 1975, Lindsay received most of the blame for the profligate spending policies that caused the calamity. Shackled with skyrocketing service costs and shrinking revenue, New York City accumulated massive deficits and remained afloat fiscally for years only through the excessive use of short- and long-term money bonds. Exacerbating the problem, the city relied increasingly on "moral obligation bonds," which permitted unregulated borrowing in excess of legal limits. By 1975 the tightening money market convinced Wall Street banking and brokerage houses that continued purchase of city securities posed too great a financial gamble. A state-business partnership assumed control of municipal government (depriving elected local officials of the authority to make fiscal policy) and attempted to restructure the city's crippling debt. After an initial refusal to aid the city in its crisis, the federal government proffered short-term loans at unusually high interest rates. New York City could not manage to reenter the bond market until 1979 and failed to balance its budget until fiscal year 1981—and then only after drastic cuts in the municipal workforce, reductions in services, and postponement of capital improvements.[3]

New York City suffered the greatest financial disaster in American urban history, but its plight only slightly exceeded the situation in many other large cities. Detroit narrowly averted default in 1975 by laying off 10 percent of its municipal workforce and by refusing to fill twelve hundred vacant positions. To maintain fiscal solvency, Cincinnati diverted funding responsibility for the city court and the city's public university to the state. Philadelphia economized by closing its city hospital and ceasing regular street cleanings. In 1978, Cleveland's credit rating fell so low that money markets failed to accept its securities, and the city defaulted on $15.5 million in obligations to local banks. The following year, voters' passage of a 50 percent increase in the municipal income tax allowed Cleveland to regain solvency, but it suffered the ignominy of being the first American city to default since the 1930s.[4]

Alone among the nation's largest cities, Chicago shone like a beacon of fiscal responsibility during the perilous 1970s. The credit for the Windy City's heralded stability went—grudgingly, in many quarters—to its aged mayor. The man berated for a host of shortcomings was suddenly being hailed as a financial wizard, a miracle worker who kept America's second-largest city economically healthy when bankruptcy haunted urban landscapes nationwide. At a time when experts on the city bemoaned an urban crisis and questioned whether these sprawling, decaying metropolises could be kept livable, Daley's Chicago defied the conventional wisdom by maintaining a satisfactory delivery of housekeeping services. How had this singularly unimpressive man balanced the books and maintained the services when so many other big city mayors were failing to do so and calling these tasks impossible? What was Daley's secret?[5]

Chicago's remarkable financial vitality was due to several factors; some could justly be credited to Mayor Daley, whereas others existed independent of his influence. Any discussion of the city's economic stability must first recognize its natural attributes. Situated on Lake Michigan at the heart of the nation's developing east-west transportation nexus, Chicago grew with the development of the

Great Lakes canal network, rapidly becoming the hub of the burgeoning railroad system and eventually assuming the same critical position for the airline industry. Unlike such one-industry towns as Detroit, Dayton, and Gary, Chicago's economic diversity—its balance between transportation, manufacturing, and service enterprises—allowed for more flexible responses to changing economic conditions. The post–World War II Sunbelt Boom and loss of jobs to suburban sites hurt Chicago, but not to the degree evident in other large cities of the northeastern-midwestern Rustbelt. Site, location, and history buffered Chicago from the worst ravages of the emerging postindustrial society.[6]

Daley also profited from Chicago's unique municipal structure, inheriting a system whereby the city itself bore the responsibility of paying for the provision of remarkably few services. Whereas most large metropolises united service functions in one huge, costly package, a number of separate Chicago governments—each with its own autonomous legal standing, budget, taxing power, and operating costs—acted independently of one another. Long before Daley became mayor, the state of Illinois had created a number of special districts and public authorities to provide residents of Cook County with specific services, a serendipitous event that obviated the city's financial burden. Whereas, for example, New York City's corporate budget funded public health care, social welfare, mass transit, courts, correctional institutions, and public and higher education, as well as police, fire, and sanitation services, Chicago paid for no city colleges, and the county supported the only public hospital, while the money for the rest of municipal services came from other sources. The Windy City spent nothing for the operation of parks, zoos, and museums, services that were all provided by a separate park district. The board of education, with its own taxing power and a budget larger than the city's, assumed total financial responsibility for schools. In short, Chicago supplied only basic housekeeping services.[7]

Best of all for Chicago mayors (including Daley), despite having no financial responsibilities, they retained control over the various governmental agencies that served the citizenry through their appointment power and budgetary authority. For example, the mayor appointed the eleven members of the board of education, the five members of the Park District, and four of the nine members of the Regional Transit Authority (four members were chosen by suburban county board members and the eight members elected a chairman).

Of the Cook County Board of Commissioners' sixteen members, Chicago voters elected ten and suburban voters only six. Thus even as the city lost population to surrounding communities and collar counties, political power remained to a surprising extent centralized in Chicago.[8]

Daley inherited a service delivery system that diffused financial responsibility, and he also succeeded in protecting city coffers from additional claims on scarce resources. In 1970, at Daley's urging, the state legislature transferred Chicago's house of corrections to the bailiwick of the Cook County sheriff. When the city's mass transit system found it increasingly difficult to maintain service levels with a dwindling ridership, Daley avoided using city finances to subsidize the struggling enterprise and successfully urged the creation of the Regional Transit Authority (RTA), which absorbed the Chicago Transit Authority (CTA) into a state-funded agency with taxing powers. Against concerted opposition in nearby counties, where voters correctly predicted that they would pay the lion's share of the cost for a mass transit system that principally served the citizens of Chicago, the Daley machine marshaled its vast political resources for a public referendum to decide the transportation funding issue. Despite lopsided opposition in the area around Cook County (McHenry County voted 49 to 1 against the measure, for instance), the Chicago Democrats mobilized a large enough vote to prevail.[9]

Daley also scored a major coup by divesting Chicago of the responsibility for welfare costs. The burden of supporting the indigent had traditionally been shared by the county and by the Chicago Department of Public Welfare. In 1958 Cook County assumed responsibility for the administration of Aid to Families with Dependent Children (AFDC), the blind, the disabled, and the aged, as well as General Assistance. Seeking to lessen Chicago's tax load, Daley lobbied in the Illinois legislature for the state to assume the county welfare operation. In 1972 the county transferred to the state all administrative responsibility for public assistance programs, including AFDC, Medical Assistance, Social Security Supplements, and General Assistance. With the Great Society's expansion of benefits in the 1960s, with the concentration of immobile indigent populations within central cities, and with the loss of affluent taxpayers to distant suburbs, the burden of welfare increased exponentially in places such as Chicago. Daley's success at making welfare principally a federal-state responsibility in his city removed a potential albatross from the municipal budget.[10]

Daley similarly deflected costs from the municipal budget through avid use of the Public Building Commission (PBC), which the city created in 1956 to issue revenue bonds for the construction of government structures. The mayor chose six of the eleven members of the commission board; after he appointed himself, the other members elected him chairman. When the voters defeated a $66 million bond issue in a 1962 local referendum, the PBC sold $87 million of revenue bonds to begin construction of a new civic center. In subsequent years, the agency embarked on an extensive public works program, building and refurbishing a wide variety of public facilities. Critics noted that such a special agency controlled by the mayor stole from the voting public the power to decide bond issues by referendum. But most important, as political scientist Ester R. Fuchs noted, "the PBC removed capital construction costs from the city budget, reducing the city corporation's long-term debt liability and making the city's own bonds more attractive to investors."[11]

Chicago traditionally faced severe restrictions on borrowing, being limited only to tax anticipation warrants and referenda for bond issues as ways of raising revenue. New York City, which was legally empowered to borrow from banks on unsecured notes, became addicted to the practice of obtaining money based only on its promise to pay. Spared this enticement, Chicago refrained from incurring an unbearable burden of debt. Fifth ward alderman Leon Despres concluded, "By kindness of the earlier historical prohibition, Chicago had been spared the cumulative temptations to the open borrowing that felled New York." The adoption of a new state constitution in 1970 brought the city greater home rule powers, including the opportunity to float bonds with only city council approval, but no evidence indicated that Daley abused the new revenue source. Indeed, largely because of its solid reputation for fiscal management, the city attracted bids under 4 percent in its 1976 sale of $134 million in tax notes. After an easing of restrictions on Chicago's borrowing capability in Daley's last years in office, the banks and brokerage firms remained as willing as ever to buy the city's financial paper.[12]

Chicago's lofty standing in the business community stemmed in large measure from Daley's reputation as a sound financial manager and prudent investor who—again in stark contrast to his counterparts in New York City—conducted his city's fiscal affairs with thorough professionalism. He received plaudits for taking financial matters out of the grasping hands of the ward heelers and entrusting them to a professional bureaucracy. His selection of nationally renowned financial expert Carl Chatters as city comptroller won high praise, as did his choice of Chatters's successor, Clark Burrus. Years later, Burrus gave the mayor high marks for keeping politics out of the city's accounting procedures. He said of Daley:

> He had certain positions that he declared off-limits to the political infrastructure. In New York they did not distinguish financial management from any other offices that delivered services. The understanding that we had was that our office was to be apolitical. My reporting lines, my loyalty, and my commitment were to him. I had the right to hire anyone I liked professionally, and he had the right to veto. Anyone he sent over I was to review professionally, and I had the right to veto. Precinct captains never came in my office. We didn't have precinct captains, we had MBAs and CPAs. . . . I knew the people in New York who ran their business, and they were political types. That was part of their patronage system. My office was off-limits.

The lack of professionalism in New York City's fiscal office in comparison with the professionalism in Daley's Chicago occasioned comment from others as well. Adlai Stevenson III, who represented Illinois in the U.S. Senate at the time of New York City's financial crisis, said:

> I was on the Senate Banking Committee when we had to consider the bailout of New York. We couldn't get books and records. We couldn't get statements of account. We couldn't even figure out what the financial status of the city was. Never had anything like that in Chicago. Comparatively speaking, it was a well-run city.[13]

Such efficiency reflected Daley's total control of the city's decision-making apparatus. Chicago ran well because Daley and his financial managers made decisions with the full support of the municipal government. Daley's authority emanated from his political power: a power that allowed him to speak with full authority, that brought stability and confidence in Chicago's reputation as a good city to invest in, that reassured businessmen and financial experts that they could deal with one representative and know that the city's commitments would be honored. In a glowing profile of the Chicago mayor, *Business Week* reported that one of Daley's aides expressed astonishment that John Lindsay could only be certain of one vote in the city council for an upcoming proposal. "Daley can count on thirty-eight votes out of fifty," the aide proudly boasted. Such political certitude bred economic tranquillity. Chicago comptroller Clark Burrus made the same point more succinctly: "We were fortunate enough to have a political infrastructure that worked."[14]

Daley's political success depended on the support of voters who demanded service maintenance for what they perceived to be a reasonable cost. Chicago enjoyed great success selling bonds, borrowing money, and coaxing federal funds from Washington, D.C. During Daley's fourth term, at the height of Lyndon Johnson's Great Society programs, federal aid to Chicago increased by 169 percent. Even so, in 1970 the city received only 22 percent of its revenue from intergovernmental transfer payments. Like other cities, Chicago relied heavily on local taxation—an especially worrisome prospect in post–World War II America, where the suburban flight of both home owners and businesses resulted in sharp reductions in taxable property values. Sensitive to the electorate's aversion to property tax increases (especially after a dramatic 14 percent increase led to a taxpayers' revolt that almost cost him reelection in 1963), Daley held the line as firmly as he dared. During the flush days of federal subsidies in the late 1960s, he raised property taxes only 3.4 percent; during his fifth term, when the increase in federal revenues slowed and the city's taxable property value fell by an alarming 24 percent, the mayor necessarily increased the property tax rate by 12 percent. Throughout his mayoralty, Daley walked a fine line between fiscal responsibility and political exigency.[15]

At the same time, Daley fashioned an enviable record in creating new sources of revenue. He creatively devised a series of "hidden" taxes and increased rates of existing levies to forestall the politically dangerous property tax hikes. Thus the mayor raised the city's taxes on vehicles, household utility bills, and cigarettes, and he levied new taxes on hotels and motels, automobile parking, and a "head" tax that required employers to pay the city $3 per employee per month. He also obtained for Chicago a sizable portion of the revenue raised by a new state sales tax and supplied the Chicago legislative delegation's crucial votes for Republican governor Richard Ogilvie's new state income tax, the annual proceeds from which were shared with the city. With a big city mayor's scorn for suburbanites who worked downtown, availed themselves of the city's services by day, and fled to bedroom communities at night, he called repeatedly—though unsuccessfully—for a "commuter" tax.[16]

The demand for new sources of revenue intensified with the rapidly rising costs associated with keeping Chicago "the city that works." The budget required ever increasing sums of money because of escalating labor costs, a result of Chicago's maintaining a large and well-compensated municipal workforce. In other large cities, bitter clashes took place repeatedly between unionized city workers and mayors who were straining to hold down costs, to battle inflation, and to balance budgets. In 1968 alone, policemen, firemen, bus drivers, sanitary haulers, and other civil servants conducted 254 strikes involving over 200,000 employees nationwide. In New York City, the intransigent John Lindsay called city workers selfish and ineffective, and they responded militantly. Gotham's embattled mayor grappled with the Patrolmen's Benevolent Association, the United Federation of Teachers, and a host of other large, powerful municipal employee unions that staged work stoppages, disrupted the lives of millions of residents, and more often than not squeezed the concessions they desired from the city. Chicago faced the same pressure of rising labor costs, but Daley's nonconfrontational approach produced huge dividends in the absence of civic turmoil.[17]

From the outset of his mayoralty, Daley established amicable relations with organized labor and repeatedly supported handsome pay raises and benefit increases to forestall the torturous collective bargaining sessions endured by other mayors. He effectively undercut the municipal unions by guaranteeing prevailing wages for city workers and initiated the practice of sealing bargaining agreements with a handshake instead of with a written contract. Daley especially opposed granting collective bargaining rights to city policemen, and in 1974 the Northern Illinois District Court upheld his position by dismissing a complaint brought by the Confederation of Police, a national organization that represented more than half of Chicago's patrolmen. A bloated patronage workforce and generous wages meant remarkably high city payrolls, of course. In 1976 the average Chicago municipal worker earned an annual salary of $17,380, as compared to $15,066 in New York City, where the cost of living was much higher. This beneficence certainly bred contentment and political loyalty in Chicago, but did so at a price: Chicagoans paid $354.75 annually for city services whereas New Yorkers paid $286.94, a difference of $67.81. For Daley, prompt service delivery and labor tranquillity justified the expense.[18]

The city's most severe financial problems existed in public education because of the increasing aggressiveness of the Chicago Teachers Union (CTU), which grew in membership from thirteen thousand in 1966 to twenty-nine thousand in 1975. Even though the mayor could deny direct responsibility for the school budget, the importance of public education to Chicago could not be ignored. Any strategies Daley employed to keep the schools open could only endear him to the voters. Having achieved its first collective bargaining agreement in 1966, the union threatened and conducted strikes frequently thereafter to gain salary increases and additional benefits for its membership. Between 1969 and 1975, Daley intervened in union-management negotiations on four occasions, with the teachers benefiting in each instance; on the first three of these occasions, he lobbied in the state legislature to raise the funds for the necessary concessions. More interested in managing conflict than in educational policy or budgetary responsibility, the mayor could afford to support the teachers' demands. At a time when nearly one-third of the city's teachers were black and the issue of public school desegregation potentially arrayed many educators against the Democratic machine, the mayor's support for the CTU could reduce some of the hostility. Against a backdrop of sit-ins, boycotts, and other demonstrations involving the schools, avoiding teachers' strikes and forging a coalition with the powerful CTU made sound political sense. To the consternation of the city's reform elements, the grateful union endorsed the mayor for reelection in 1967 and 1971.[19]

Eager to appease the teachers, Daley greeted news of a potential strike in 1968 with the statement, "Chicago has never had a teachers' strike and I'm sure there won't be one now." At his urging, the school board averted a strike by making extensive concessions to union negotiators. In 1973, frustrated in his efforts to mediate in favor of the union, the mayor obtained from the city council a resolution authorizing him to accept resignations from school board members. His subsequent demand for the termination of any school board member blocking a settlement broke the impasse, resulted in another victory for the teachers, and placed the school board in financial straits. When the union struck in 1975, Daley abandoned all pretense of objective mediation and interrupted a school board social gathering to dictate the settlement terms. The 1975 contract produced a $100 million deficit for the public schools, a severe problem for the Chicago Board of Education, but one of no financial consequences for Daley's city budget. According to a study published in 1975, the mayor's continued generosity resulted in Chicago teachers being the nation's highest-paid instructors, and nonteaching public school employees receiving up to 30 percent higher salaries than those private-sector employees received for comparable work. Studies in the 1970s also suggested that the quality of public education—as measured by reading, math, and SAT scores—lagged behind teachers' rising salaries, especially noting the poor performance of black Chicago pupils in comparison with their peers in New York City, Philadelphia, and Baltimore.[20]

Because of the mayor's willingness to saddle public education with such massive financial obligations, few observers expressed surprise when a fiscal crisis developed in the Chicago school system in 1979. Citing the board of education's admission of a $101 million deficit, Moody's Investor Service cut the schools' Municipal Interest Grade (MIG) status from two to four, its lowest rating, thereby making the board's notes unmarketable. In January 1980, the bankrupt school system was unable to pay its fifty-two thousand employees. A bailout plan acceptable to the banks involved intervention by the state, which contributed $50 million to cover a portion of the shortfall and created a new School Finance Authority with budget veto authority and the power to issue bonds.[21]

The fiscal plight of the city's public education system, which worsened after Daley's death, underscored emerging accusations that the mayor's apparent mastery of budgetary matters was a sham. In a 1980 article entitled "The City That Survives," the *Economist* suggested, "It is increasingly apparent that Daley presided not over a 'city that works' but over a city which was better at hiding its problems than most." Daley's longtime adversary, fifth ward alderman Leon Despres, argued that the myth of Daley's financial wizardry rested on his tight control of information and his refusal to allow independent auditing firms access to the municipal ledgers. The news had been bad for some time, in other words, but the public in its ignorance had assumed the best until the mayor's death lifted the veil of secrecy. Concluding a scathing postmortem on this topic, journalist Sidney Lens said:

> So it turned out that the city that worked had worked a con game: The political machine got what it wanted—jobs (thousands of them serving no useful purpose) and power; the business community got what it wanted—low taxes and social peace; the property owners were bought off with a freeze on taxes; and the camouflaged bankruptcy was passed on to future generations.[22]

Allegations about hidden deficits and a potentially debilitating fiscal crisis increased with the election of anti-machine mayors in the 1970s and 1980s who claimed that they were paying the price for Daley's irresponsibility. Jane Byrne charged that when she became mayor in 1979, city hall was drowning in red ink. Her financial advisers claimed to have uncovered a series of debt-ridden revolving funds that were used to mask a deficit she variously estimated at between $100 and $180 million. Through the 1960s and early 1970s, according to the Byrne administration's analysis, Daley met rising costs with money from federal coffers. When these sources proved inadequate in 1972, to make up the difference he began depleting trust and agency accounts comprised of state and federal funds earmarked for such special uses as neighborhood redevelopment. The following year, charged the auditors, he spent bond proceeds allocated for capital improvements. In short, Daley was playing a kind of shell game, staying one step ahead of a shortfall by secretly spending money that had already been committed for other uses. No less a spendthrift than his peers in other big cities (charged the critics), Daley mortgaged the future rather than applying the painful service or personnel cuts necessary to balance the budget.[23]

The question remains whether Daley's creative bookkeeping damaged the city's financial standing or just represents another example of his innovating to maintain city services in an increasingly precarious financial environment. Political scientist Ester R. Fuchs argued that "the fact that Daley had diverted these funds was not real news in Chicago" and that Jane Byrne's "motives for discrediting her predecessors were blatantly political." Machine partisans suggested that the deficits were comparatively small and that they would have been easily—and quietly—managed by the banks had Daley lived. Byrne's alarmist announcements—which resulted in Moody's Investor Service downgrading Chicago bond ratings from "Aa" to "A"—proved needless, because a quick increase in the property tax eliminated the deficit. Indeed, within a year, Byrne announced the existence of a surplus in the municipal budget and the restoration of the city's credit rating. In her comparative study of Chicago's and New York City's fiscal policies, Fuchs noted that after 1963 Chicago was one of the few cities that consistently met the Municipal Finance Officers Association's standard for sound management. In general, she concluded, the Windy City was well served by Daley's financial stewardship.[24]

Donald H. Haider, Mayor Byrne's budget director at the time of the financial disclosures involving the Daley era, later concluded, "Recent notoriety and revisionists notwithstanding, Chicago was a well run and managed city during the 1970s." He attributed the deficits inherited by Mayor Byrne to an aberration in the city's usually superb financial management during the unsettled time of Daley's recovery from the stroke in 1974. "The control [Daley] had always exercised—and he understood budgets very well—was missing," Haider commented. "That period of hesitation and uncertainty, and the fact that Daley, even after his return, took a while getting things in order again, explains why these things began to happen." Haider cited as examples of the city's general financial health its modest annual budget increases, moderate debt, reduction of dependence on declining property tax revenues, and ability to exploit alternative state and federal revenue sources. Especially telling, according to Haider, the financial community consistently gave Chicago high marks for fiscal policy. Whatever Daley's shortcomings, his record in an age of deepening fiscal crisis for urban America was the envy of just about every other large city. In the popular perception, Chicago never ceased being a model of financial success.[25]

The harshest criticism that could be made of Daley was not that he secretly raided city accounts and revolving funds to plug holes in a leaky municipal treasury, but that his support of a bloated patronage army and his generosity to workers on the public payroll made such legerdemain necessary. The mayor enjoyed great success as an arbiter of labor disputes, but as political consultant Don Rose has noted, "the basis of his settlements was to give the unions basically what they wanted." Such a strategy paid political dividends but was not sound economically. With the dramatic reduction of intergovernmental payments in the 1970s and the concomitant necessity of municipal belt-tightening, Daley's munificence became harder to justify. Although the structural advantages of Chicago's government gave Daley a measure of financial latitude not shared by other big city mayors, he enjoyed no immunity to the financial exigency sweeping urban America. The formula the mayor employed for financial management through two decades increasingly became hazardous in his latter years in city hall.[26]

Because the challenges to Daley's reputation as a manager of money came after his death, his last months in office saw no such issues raised. There were, however, increasing signs of the dissolution of the Chicago Democratic machine over which Daley presided. The mayor had been reelected for an unprecedented sixth term in 1975, but for the first time he had faced a challenge in the party primary. The number of votes Daley received that year declined from his vote in 1971 by almost two hundred thousand—from 740,137 to 542,817. In the November 1976 elections, Daley's candidates for governor, attorney general, and Cook County state's attorney all lost. Perhaps most alarming for the machine, Chicago contributed only 25.7 percent of the state's total vote that year—down from 35 percent in 1960. Such a decline, reflective of ongoing demographic transformations in Illinois, raised concerns about the city's ability to defend its interests in state government—particularly against the increasingly populous, affluent suburbs of the collar counties.[27]

Close observers of Daley's years in office also perceived another unsettling development: the mayor's declining success in conceiving politically viable large-scale construction projects for Chicago. In his early years, Daley had guided several such efforts to completion and had become known as a builder mayor, but by the 1970s, his proposals met stiff opposition from the public and from rival politicians. The proposed Crosstown Expressway, which Daley defended avidly for years, united Governor Daniel Walker and a number of middle- and working-class neighborhood organizations into a coalition that prevented the project's approval. Walker's contravention also proved decisive in blocking the Franklin Street Connector, a subway extension favored by the mayor that required joint funding by the local, state, and federal governments. The governor's objections to a new subway mirrored protests from the press, which questioned the need for additional mass transit to serve the central business district, and from a distinguished citizens organization, the Business and Professional People for the Public Interest. Similar public outcries derailed Daley's plans for the location of a third airport on an island in Lake Michigan, another public university (Loop College), a new hockey arena for the Chicago Black Hawks, and a football stadium for the Chicago Bears at another lakefront site. Denied permission to relocate Soldier Field, the mayor urged an expansion and complete reconstruction of the existing facility but had to settle for more modest renovations—an outcome that indicated again his failure to bring grandiose building plans to fruition.[28]

For the organization Democrats, the increasing disaffection of black voters represented the most sobering development. By the time of Daley's death in 1976, blacks constituted almost 40 percent of Chicago's population and the number of wards headed by black committeemen had increased to fourteen (up from nine in 1968). The expanding black electoral presence expressed its dissatisfaction with the Daley administration's handling of several sensitive racial issues. The Democratic organization continued to resist public school desegregation, scattered-site public housing construction, open occupancy in the private real estate market, and affirmative action hiring in the police and fire departments. With incessant regularity, federal courts sided with black plaintiffs only to have the city government appeal, delay, or plead inability to comply with the rulings. To remind blacks of this recurring pattern, the *Gautreaux* case resurfaced in 1976, a full decade after its genesis, when the U.S. Supreme Court ordered the U.S. Department of Housing and Urban Development to take remedial action in metropolitan Chicago.[29]

During Daley's last years in office, discriminatory hiring in the police department became a persistent and troublesome issue. In 1974 the city lost a civil suit in federal court that resulted in the withholding of federal revenue-sharing funds in excess of $100 million, but Daley opposed the use of hiring quotas to achieve racial balance and borrowed $55 million from local banks to cover the shortfall in the municipal payroll. The city appealed District Judge Prentice Marshall's desegregation order to the U.S. Court of Appeals for the Seventh Circuit when Daley refused to comply with the judge's plan. For two years the mayor haggled with Marshall over an appropriate hiring strategy to correct the demographic imbalance in the police force. Until the time of his death, Daley denounced quotas and defended the hiring policies of the police department—even at the cost of tens of millions of federal dollars and his increased unpopularity in the black community.[30]

A growing sense of black political independence showed in the apostate candidacy of Ralph Metcalfe in 1976. Espousing "the liberation of the people from the Daley plantation," Metcalfe balked when the Democratic party refused to reslate him for U.S. congressman and ward committeeman. He ran a fiery campaign openly critical of Daley that resulted in a groundswell of support among black voters. Although the other black committeemen declined to join his insurgency, Metcalfe organized a large stable of volunteers who helped construct an imposing grassroots coalition. He won both elections in remarkable fashion, making history as the first black politician singled out for elimination to survive against the full power of the Democratic machine and obliterating the myth of Daley's invincibility. Metcalfe's achievement served as a harbinger of the black political uprising that would topple the Democratic machine years after Daley's death.[31]

In 1976, although some warning signs were evident to discerning political analysts, the Daley machine still seemed remarkably resilient. Some city hall watchers idly speculated about what would happen when the seventy-four-year-old mayor finally passed from the scene—an intriguing question because the boss of the last of the big city machines had been so careful not to designate a successor—but there was no indication that Daley could not continue to serve for a longer time. Reporters noticed no slackening in the mayor's brisk regimen and knew of no reason to question the completeness of his recovery from the stroke two years before. His death came suddenly, unexpectedly.

On Monday, December 20, 1976, Mayor Daley told no one on his staff that he had felt chest pains over the weekend and had scheduled an appointment with his physician, Dr. Thomas J. Coogan Jr., for later that day. Instead, he went about the typical business of the city's chief executive, attending a Cook County Democratic Committee breakfast, dispensing with routine paperwork in his city hall office, then driving to a political function in the tenth ward. After speaking at the dedication of a newly completed Park District gymnasium, he kept his 2:00 P.M.. appointment with Dr. Coogan. Concerned by the results of an electrocardiogram administered to Daley, the physician ordered that the mayor be admitted to a hospital for further tests. Before that could be done, however, the mayor suffered a massive heart attack. Frantic efforts by paramedic personnel to restimulate Daley's heart failed, and a priest who was hurriedly called to the scene administered the last rites of the Roman Catholic church. Dr. Coogan pronounced the mayor dead at 3:50 P.M.[32]

On Tuesday, a bitterly cold day whipped by icy winds, an estimated one hundred thousand Chicagoans queued up to walk by Daley's casket in Bridgeport's Nativity of Our Lord Church. A host of dignitaries, including Vice President Nelson Rockefeller, President-elect Jimmy Carter, and Senators Edward Kennedy and George McGovern, attended the funeral on Wednesday. After the ceremony, the funeral cortege proceeded to Holy Sepulchre Cemetary on the Southwest Side, where Daley was buried alongside his parents. In the intrusive glare of the national media, in the frigid grey of a Chicago winter, the life of America's last big city boss came to a close. While many Chicagoans mourned, others less enamored of the Democratic machine pondered the significance of the mayor's passing. This was, they all recognized, the end of an era—a time when Richard J. Daley, commanding the nation's last great urban political machine, had made Chicago famous for being, despite all the controversies of his twenty-one years as mayor, "the city that works."[33]

11

The Battle for Chicago

Richard J. Daley's years in city hall came at an especially precarious time for urban America. Big city mayors struggled with a variety of issues: the disappointing results of urban redevelopment and renewal programs that had raised unrealizable expectations after World War II; civil rights demonstrations that gave way to ghetto riots; rapidly deteriorating streets, buildings, bridges, and other public structures; dwindling financial resources and the resultant budgetary shortfalls; the exodus of people and industry to suburban and Sunbelt locations; and as a concomitant of all these problems, a nagging fear that local governments lacked the means to solve the "urban crisis." Amid increasing speculation about "ungovernable" cities, many mayors saw their flourishing political careers derailed by their inability to deal with these apparently intractable problems. In 1967 the decade's worst racial conflagration undermined the rise of Detroit's "golden boy" mayor, Jerome Cavanaugh; and the following year, the first black mayor of a major American city, Cleveland's Carl Stokes, suffered withering criticism for his handling of a massive race riot. Urban disasters sundered the presidential ambitions of at least two big city mayors: in the wake of the lethal Watts riot in 1965, the U.S. Civil Rights Commission condemned Los Angeles mayor Sam Yorty for "gross negligence" and for fostering a hostile racial atmosphere, while in New York City John Lindsay's crisis-plagued administration ended in his retirement from politics.

Almost alone among the prominent big city mayors, Daley escaped the pitfalls so prevalent during those perilous times.[1]

Daley not only survived but flourished. He was Chicago. Not even Fiorello LaGuardia, who became internationally renowned during his three terms as New York City's mayor, came to symbolize his city in the way that Daley did in his twenty-one-year tenure in Chicago's city hall. Perfectly typecast to lead Carl Sandburg's "city of the broad shoulders," Daley's plebeian origins, unglamorous appearance, plodding oratory, and conservative politics were ideally suited to the blue-collar city on the lake. With the exception of one, none of Chicago's mayors ever left city hall and held higher political office (the exception, Edward F. Dunne, later served as governor of Illinois), and Daley never aspired to loftier positions in Springfield or Washington, D.C. Having spent time in the state capital as a necessary part of his political advancement, he had no desire to return there as governor. Like most other Chicagoans, he viewed service in state government as part of an apprenticeship; in the city's political tradition, the Illinois legislature served the same function for Chicago's city hall that West Point did for the U.S. Army officer corps. Rumors occasionally surfaced about a possible Daley campaign for the U.S. Senate, but Democratic insiders never took them seriously. Being mayor of Chicago was his raison d'être, and whether they agreed with him or not, most Chicagoans sensed that Daley invariably acted according to his understanding of what was best for his city.[2]

Daley's chauvinistic, single-minded determination to preserve Chicago defined his mayoralty. As the chief executive of the nation's second-largest city and as boss of the last of the great urban political machines, he wielded awesome power and controlled the lives of great numbers of people. Recognized as one of the towering political figures of his age, Daley commanded respect—and fear—in the highest councils of the Democratic party and the national government. Yet for all his influence (what Chicagoans call "clout"), Daley spent the years of his mayoralty fighting a holding action against the inexorable changes overwhelming his city. Although he experienced some successes along the way and gave ground grudgingly, he incurred the same defeats that his fellow mayors had suffered more quickly and more openly. His stubborn defense of political, social, and economic conditions notwithstanding, demographic changes proceeded apace. Chicago's population peaked at 3,618,500 in 1951 and declined steadily thereafter; whites left the city and were replaced by less affluent people of color. Industries and jobs also departed Chicago. By 1976 approximately 350 factories and industrial parks existed in the metropolitan area outside Chicago, and by 1980 fewer than half of the area's workers were employed in the city itself. In his 1975 reelection campaign, the mayor flatly denied such statistical findings. Nevertheless, developments in a postindustrial service-based economy, combined with harmful national government policies, sapped Rustbelt cities such as Chicago. Urbanologist Pierre de Vise explained, "Chicago lost half a million whites but gained a third of a million blacks; lost 211,000 jobs but gained 90,000 welfare recipients; lost 140,000 private housing units but gained 19,000 public housing units." Unable to arrest or to reverse these changes, Daley concentrated on stanching the flow and minimizing the damage—as political scientist Ira Katznelson put it, "getting for the city the least bad deal."[3]

Daley's inability to alter sweeping trends in urban development did not mean that his years in city hall were uneventful, unimportant, or inconsequential to millions of Chicagoans. In many instances, his decisions and actions spanning more than two decades profoundly shaped the city's history. From the outset, he reestablished the mayor's office as the locus of power in the city after the eight years of Martin Kennelly's desultory stewardship. Seizing power from the disreputable city council, whose defalcations had earned its members the ignominious nickname "the grey wolves," Daley muted the prevailing image of venality, assumed control of the budget process, and centralized all patronage matters. Certainly one of Daley's most impressive achievements was to retain power for more than twenty years while surrounded by a changing cast of ruthless and ambitious characters who sought the party chairmanship or mayoralty. In a series of public and private challenges, he scotched the rebellious designs of the Adamowskis, Hanrahans, Singers, and the "Young Turks" Vrdolyak and Burke, Democrats who coveted the city's highest leadership positions. Because he also ruled the Democratic machine autocratically, the mayor centralized power in the city in a manner reminiscent of the Kelly-Nash era. Businessmen, government officials, labor union leaders, and national politicians knew that one man possessed the authority to speak and to act for Chicago.[4]

At the same time, Daley professionalized city government and— at least in the early years—earned the plaudits of the silk-stocking good government crowd. His modernization of the police and fire departments, installation of a new streetlighting system, and general improvement of service delivery put the mayor squarely within the structural reform tradition that bloomed in American cities in the late nineteenth and early twentieth centuries. (Structural reformers sought to improve the quality of urban life through more efficient use of resources and the broader application of sound business principles.) Complaints arose over the years about the inefficiency of the political machine's reliance on patronage, but the belief remained widespread that compared with other large U.S. cities Chicago did a better job of delivering vital services. Such structural reforms benefited all the citizenry but especially favored businessmen who valued order, security, cleanliness, and stability.[5]

Chicago's wealthiest and most influential entrepreneurs, virtually all of whom were devout Republicans, thrived under Daley's leadership and became his ardent political backers. Meanwhile, a series of Republican underdogs complained bitterly about having to run inadequately financed mayoral campaigns against Daley while their party's aristocratic leadership publicly lauded and privately bankrolled the Democratic incumbent. The LaSalle Street bankers and State Street retailers appreciated the mayor's aversion to increasing the tax burden on the elites and his success in tapping federal, state, and other local sources of revenue. Ensuring Chicago's ability to obtain loans at favorable terms, Daley was especially solicitous of the city's financial institutions. In 1971, for example, the *New York Times* reported a significant underassessment of Chicago's five largest banks, which allowed the Continental Bank alone to save $1.8 million in unpaid taxes. Like many mayors in post–World War II America, Daley believed that the survival of the nation's metropolises depended on the viability of their downtown areas, and the city's corporate leaders recognized the mayor's role in what *Chicago Daily News* owner John S. Knight called "the commercial rebirth the city was experiencing."[6]

The business community applauded Daley's immediate emergence as a builder mayor. Not since the years of William Hale Thompson (who was known by the end of his administrations as "Big Bill the Builder") had the city seen such frenetic construction activity. Thompson's legacy—based on the completion of the Michigan Boulevard link and the construction of streets, bridges, and government buildings—paled in comparison with the major alterations of the cityscape effected by Daley. The Daley years saw the opening and enlargement of O'Hare International Airport, construction of the University of Illinois campus, expansion of the city's interconnected expressway system from 53 to 506 miles, and a monumental building boom that revitalized the downtown Loop area. With the construction of such landmarks as the John F. Hancock Building, the First National Bank Plaza, the Standard Oil Building, the Marina Towers, and the Sears Tower, Chicago resumed its place as one of the architectural showplaces of the world. Architectural historian Carl W. Condit concluded, "The immense program of [public] building that began in 1955 constituted the foremost example in the U.S. of the spontaneous reconstruction of the urban core; indeed, possibly the only other city in the world that has experienced a similar remaking is Montreal."[7]

The aggrandizement of the Loop and the ubiquitous reminders of Daley's devotion to public works spending created controversy, however. Critics accused the mayor of being in the thrall of bricks and mortar projects while ignoring less visible needs, thereby ensuring his support from the merchants and leaving enduring monuments to his leadership, though at the expense of the human dimension. A spectacular skyline and immaculate lakefront parks adjacent to downtown gave Chicago one of the most striking "front yards" of any city in the nation, but the "back yards" where the vast majority of the people lived suffered from neglect. "Get off the subway anywhere in the central business area and you won't find a broken city sidewalk," charged fifth ward alderman Leon Despres. "Get off the subway almost anywhere else, and you will." Not only did the site clearance prior to construction destroy neighborhoods and uproot families with little attention to their resettlement, but other social agendas went wanting as long as construction remained the top priority. Suburban Democratic committeeman Lynn Williams said, "He had a kind of worship for the pouring of concrete. He liked physical things. He was not interested in ideas, but in getting skyscrapers into the Loop he was effective." Echoed Studs Terkel: "He's marvelous when it comes to building things like highways, parking lots, and industrial complexes. But when it comes to healing the aches and hurts of human beings, Daley comes up short."[8]

"When it comes to healing the aches and hurts of human beings," asked *Commentary*'s Joseph Epstein, "who comes up long? John Lindsay? Sam Yorty of Los Angeles? Carl Stokes of Cleveland? But then since when have mayors been charged with 'healing' to begin with?" Daley and his defenders often responded to such criticisms by asking who had done better elsewhere. Had other mayors developed some secret formula for reversing urban decay and fulfilling the aspirations of all their constituents? Which big city escaped unscathed from the red hot summers of the 1960s and responded satisfactorily to the cries for racial equality? Journalist David Halberstam observed, "It was one of the ironies of Daley's rule of Chicago that because he had succeeded so much in other areas his failures on race relations seemed so marked. Unlike other mayors, one sensed that he had the power to do something."[9]

Like so many other mayors of northern metropolises caught between defensive, dwindling white populations and swelling black populations, Daley had to deal with a deepening racial crisis in the 1960s and 1970s. And, as other political leaders typically did, he responded to racial problems only when they became too dangerous to ignore. For many years, a quiescent African American population remained loyal to the Daley machine and (although some civil rights groups assailed the city for failing to meet the black community's housing, education, and employment needs) constituted one of the key components of the Chicago Democrats' electoral coalition. Through such malleable black leaders as William Dawson and Ralph Metcalfe, the mayor funneled the rewards and incentives that made clientage politics a staple in Chicago. Cognizant of the group's numerical significance, the Daley machine gradually increased the total of black patronage appointments and candidates for elective office; by 1971, for example, the city treasurer and sixteen of the fifty aldermen were black. Still, the absence of any African Americans in the machine's uppermost ranks underscored the degree to which blacks' political recognition lagged behind their population share. More important to a new generation of blacks who were dissatisfied with the paltry gains made possible by clientage politics, the Daley machine expended insufficient effort to eradicate racial inequality and its attendant socioeconomic effects.[10]

By the mid 1960s, Daley's relations with Chicago's African American community were worsening. Heightened racial consciousness, a product of the era's civil rights movement, led blacks to demand more than Daley was able or willing to give. Political scientist Steven P. Erie has argued that Daley bought extra time for the machine by providing black Chicagoans with additional support originating in the federal government's enhanced welfare programs. Under the aegis of the local Democratic administrations, the number of black families receiving welfare increased from 18 percent in 1969 to 32 percent in 1979. Although the ward leaders and precinct captains played no role in certifying eligibility, they threatened to terminate public aid for disloyal voters and operated welfare information booths in public housing projects. In short, they did everything possible to create the impression that receipt of government assistance depended on the local Democratic organization.[11]

Daley gave blacks some of what they wanted—jobs, recognition, and welfare—and did so in increasing amounts. At the same time, however, he reserved for his white constituency what they demanded—segregation. With the Reverend Martin Luther King Jr. and other black leaders, the mayor willingly negotiated the increase of services to the black community and even the expansion of political opportunity for blacks; the mayor believed such changes possible as long as blacks remained within their own neighborhoods and schools. Open housing, the location of primarily black public housing projects in white neighborhoods, and desegregated education jeopardized the machine's viability and the city's economic equilibrium. Daley shored up his political support among the white ethnics (especially after his narrow victory over Ben Adamowski in the watershed 1963 mayoral election) by preserving the racial homogeneity of the bungalow belts while attempting to minimize the number of black renegade voters; unlikely to vote Republican, the overwhelmingly Democratic black electorate could do little but vote for the machine. At worst, they would likely not vote. Big city political machines, including the Chicago model, had always rested in large measure on the political support of the poor. As his city's disadvantaged became increasingly black, Daley catered to the interests of the third- and fourth-generation white ethnics who remained in the city. No longer reliant on the machine for jobs, socialization, and other "traditional" services, working-class whites looked to the mayor to defend their homes and social values. Thus, the Cook County Democratic machine settled onto a racial fault line and felt the portentous results of doing so after the mayor's death. Responding to white Chicagoans' concerns would presumably also anchor a population that the city administration desperately wanted to retain. In a 1967 report, Daley's board of education made clear the reasons for its segregationist policies, saying:

> The immediate short range goal must be to anchor the whites that still remain in the city. To do this requires that school authorities quickly achieve and maintain stable racial attendance proportions in changing fringe areas. . . . We . . . propose . . . that Negro enrollments in the schools in these changing sections of the city be limited and fixed immediately.[12]

The city government's dedication to segregation could be seen also in the changed role of the CHA during the Daley years. Nationally acclaimed as a spearhead for racial integration in public housing during Ed Kelly's mayoralty, the CHA became under Daley one of the nation's most persistent litigants in opposition to scattered-site public housing. In 1979, ten years after Judge Richard B. Austin ruled against the CHA in the celebrated *Gautreaux* case, an urban consultant reported to Judge John P. Crowley (Austin's successor on the federal bench) that the CHA had not made its "best efforts" to identify or to purchase sites for new construction. Testifying before a congressional investigating committee in 1978, CHA executive director Gustave W. Master said that the agency had built so little public housing primarily because of the time-consuming court proceedings resulting from its own appeals and its refusal to locate suitable sites in white residential areas. Committee chairwoman Cardiss Collins questioned Master:

> "You continued to do all this looking but you have not been able to find one vacant lot or lots on which you can build more than 184 units of nonpublic elderly housing in the past ten years?"
>
> "Yes. That's substantially correct, ma'am. That's correct," responded Master.
>
> "I must say," remarked Collins, "that's really a most dismal record for any housing authority."[13]

Despite the city's inertia, the CHA was Chicago's largest landlord—and the nation's second largest—at the time of Daley's death. In 1976 the agency operated 42,735 units of family housing with a total tenantry of 140,000 (approximately 4.5 percent of the total city population). CHA-operated units comprised less than 4 percent of Chicago's residential housing, however, and the majority of the city's poor families lived in private dwellings. The city's public housing policy in the 1960s and 1970s assumed significance not, therefore, because of its impact on a significant portion of the three million inhabitants or because experts saw the solution to Chicago's inadequate housing stock resting with the construction of massive amounts of publicly managed low-cost dwellings. Rather, the CHA's policies exacerbated a growing resentment among black citizens against a municipal government they viewed as insensitive to their needs—a condition brought into bold relief in the area of public housing, where 95 percent of tenants were black. The CHA's controversial performance and the rising rate of complaints about the quality of life in existing projects (lamentations concerning crime, drug use, juvenile delinquency, poor maintenance, and other problems) left Mayor Daley vulnerable to charges of warehousing the black poor.[14]

The CHA in fact became an unvarnished disaster during Mayor Daley's tenure. Citing the CHA's "high operating costs, deficits, and poor physical conditions," a 1982 study by the federal government rated the agency "among the worst" in the nation. The report said that under the direction of Charles Swibel (a reputed slumlord whose appointment by Daley was unfathomable to political observers), the CHA's sole purpose had become the "acquisition of as many Federal . . . dollars as possible for the creation of patronage jobs and financial opportunities." The report called Swibel's retention "unconscionable" and considered any expectation of reform under his administration "foolhardy." The disheartening decline of the quality of low-cost housing for the poor was surely one of the sorriest developments of the Daley era.[15]

An equally dispiriting result of Daley's leadership was the deterioration of the city's public education system. Beset by a deepening financial crisis in the latter years of the mayor's tenure, the schools spent as much per pupil as any big city system yet by all accounts provided a substandard education. According to the school system's own measurements, the performance of its students lagged far behind national averages and worsened with each grade. The *Chicago Sun-Times* characterized what went on in the city's schools as "the near-collapse of learning." Reformers attributed the sordid plight of the city's public schools to several factors: the excessive employment of janitors and other support personnel for patronage purposes to the detriment of spending on educational resources; the concern of the city's largely Roman Catholic leadership with parochial education and the resultant indifference to public schools; and the callous disregard for an increasingly nonwhite public school enrollment. Whatever the Daley machine's culpability, white flight and the attendant loss of tax dollars for schools became both cause and effect of the declining resources available for public education. Again, as in so many other areas, race figured in Chicago's changing fortunes.[16]

Chicago's black, Hispanic, and other minority populations occupied peripheral positions in the Democratic machine's political calculus. Mayor Daley presided over a monolith composed of business, banking, real estate, and labor organizations, all of which advanced their own interests and, to the degree that they relied on the city's viability, worked on behalf of Chicago. The mayor lacked the power simply to dictate to these groups, but because of the Democratic machine's hegemony and the decision-making power it vested in him as its leader, he could act as an influential broker. In that capacity, Daley attempted to balance the interests of Bridgeport and the Loop, workers and owners, city government and municipal employees, a secure past and an uncertain future. He did not, however, broker the interests of blacks and whites; and holding the color line became the fulcrum around which his administration turned. He resuscitated a stagnant, lifeless downtown and made Chicago a more pleasant community for its white residents—significant feats for any big city mayor in those years. But in an increasingly nonwhite city, his policies addressed the needs of too few residents. A powerful man with a great love for his city and a vast knowledge of how local and state governments operated, he dedicated himself to saving Chicago from those centrifugal forces that were eroding America's great metropolises. Daley's amazing longevity in office brought stability and at least the appearance of his being able to do what other mayors could not, yet his passing from the scene meant that the city would have to confront the serious problems he could only hold in abeyance.[17]

The abrupt end of the Daley era created uncertainty about Chicago's future. Partisans and disinterested observers alike had been speculating for years about the Cook County Democratic organization's gradual loss of power, and the boss's death raised the question of whether the last of the nation's big city political machines could survive. Deprived of the political influence enjoyed by minority populations in other U.S. cities, Chicago's black electorate could only see the end of boss rule as an unprecedented opportunity. In a city riven by racial animosity, the new municipal leadership would have to make critical choices about the allocation of resources and the resultant impact on the black and white populations. Whereas a white mayor might ignore the rising aspirations of the city's black population and attempt to maintain Daley's segregationist policies, an African American mayor might practice the politics of redistribution. As much as blacks dreaded the continuation of business as usual, whites feared the kinds of "affirmative action patronage" and set-aside programs that were utilized by black mayors elsewhere. The stakes were indeed high, for mayoral succession involved not just who held power but also how that power would be used to affect the lives of Chicago's citizens.[18]

Daley's sudden death triggered an unseemly scramble for control of the Chicago Democratic machine. Because the longtime mayor had studiously avoided selecting an heir apparent, the field seemed wide open and a number of ambitious politicians mobilized to seize control. According to the existing statutes, the city council would select an interim mayor to preside until a special election could be held. After forty years of Irish Catholic mayors from Bridgeport, during a time when the Irish population of the city had dwindled to an insignificant number, many Chicagoans expressed the strong desire for an ethnically diverse leadership that was more reflective of the metropolitan area's demographic makeup. Many of the city's nonwhite population, including the Reverend Jesse Jackson, ardently supported the candidacy of black thirty-fourth ward alderman Wilson Frost, who claimed that his status as city council president pro tempore made him acting mayor. Alderman Roman C. Pucinski of the large Northwest Side Polish community advanced his own candidacy, while the Young Turks—aldermen Edward Vrdolyak (tenth ward) and Edward Burke (fourteenth ward)—worked hard to recruit support within the council. After several days of heated negotiations in backrooms and city hall corridors outside the glare of the television lights, the contestants agreed on a temporary mayor who promised not to be a candidate in the upcoming special election, eleventh ward alderman Michael A. Bilandic. Completing the carefully crafted deal, Wilson Frost became finance committee chairman, Vrdolyak replaced Frost as president pro tempore, and the city council voted by forty-five votes to two for Bilandic.[19]

A lifelong Bridgeport resident of Croatian descent, quiet, colorless, timorous, and believed to be unambitious, Bilandic had dutifully served as Daley's surrogate in the city council since 1969 and seemed to be the perfect caretaker for Chicago. To serve as party chairman, the political insiders selected Cook County Board president George Dunne, another self-effacing loyalist who pledged not to seek the mayoralty. While the Young Turks and blacks aggressively jockeyed for positions of greater influence in the post-Daley party hierarchy, the machine recovered from the initial shock of its leader's death and rallied to maintain control of city government. Barely one week after becoming interim mayor, Bilandic reneged on his earlier pledge and announced his candidacy in the special election. In the April 1977 Democratic mayoral primary, the machine candidate faced opposition from several dissident groups. In addition to Alderman Pucinski, former state's attorney Edward Hanrahan vied for the white ethnic vote. A new black contender, State Senator Harold Washington, also emerged, but he raised little money and campaigned almost exclusively on the black South Side. He prophesied that "there is a sleeping giant in Chicago. And if this sleeping giant, the potential black vote, ever woke up, we'd control the city." At least for the moment, however, the machine's electoral strength held firm as Bilandic won with 50.4 percent of the votes and carried thirty-eight wards. In the June special election, he easily defeated Dennis Block, the city's lone Republican alderman, by 340,000 votes.[20]

The two-year Bilandic interregnum produced few changes in city hall. The new mayor found himself in a precarious position, surrounded on all sides by ambitious factions: the Old Guard machine loyalists who sought to preserve long-standing arrangements; the Young Turks, whose impatience under Daley had barely been kept in check; and the blacks, Poles, and lakefront liberals who saw in Bilandic a much more vulnerable target than Daley had ever been. Because he was not the eleventh ward committeeman, the mayor enjoyed no control over the Cook County Democratic Central Committee. Worse, Bilandic's ward committeeman was the former mayor's son, State Senator Richard M. Daley, whom many true believers envisioned as his father's rightful successor. With such a narrow power base, the mayor's hope for reelection rested largely on the number of aspiring candidates and the inability of any one of them to outdistance the others. Although his record as mayor was undistinguished, Bilandic's supporters argued, the city continued to function reasonably well after Daley's death. Bond ratings remained high and municipal budgets balanced, both good indicators of satisfactory fiscal management. As late as the fall of 1978, these modest attributes seemed sufficient and no contender emerged to threaten the incumbent seriously—certainly not the lone declared Democratic candidate, Jane Byrne.[21]

Bilandic lost the election in 1979 because of an unpredicted meteorological disaster—a series of record-breaking January snowstorms that paralyzed the city and called into question the reliability of its basic services. Stranded cars prevented snowplows and salt trucks from doing their work; the city's side streets, many of which went unplowed for the winter, froze into single-lane, two-rutted ice roads; garbage went uncollected and the rat population soared; and grocery store shelves remained bare as delivery trucks waited interminably for streets to become passable. Denying the severity of the problem, Bilandic presented to the public a business-as-usual face and belatedly announced an ineffectual snow-removal plan that cost the city $90,000 but removed very little snow. Chicagoans expressed outrage at the mayor's incompetence and arrogance. Irate black workers stood freezing on public transit platforms as commuter trains bound for the Loop sped by their stations without making scheduled stops, a consequence of Mayor Bilandic's apparent decision to serve only the white residents of outlying residential areas. The mayor's denial of responsibility for the CTA's "skip-stop" policy may have defused the charges of blatant racism but reenforced the impression of a fragmented city government whose agencies floundered without the clear direction once provided by Daley. Struggling for weeks in a campaign without any viable issues, the rejuvenated Byrne candidacy skillfully exploited the theme of administrative incapability and hammered away at other alleged instances of graft and political favoritism in city hall. The voters responded to the challenger's warnings that Chicago appeared no longer to be "the city that works" and in the February primary turned out the machine incumbent. In the April election, Byrne captured 82 percent of the popular vote and defeated Republican Wallace Johnson by the largest margin in the city's history. The Daley machine was dead, said the pundits, in the wake of a political revolution.[22]

Jane Byrne turned out to be an odd revolutionary. Although she had campaigned as an anti-machine reformer in 1979 and inveighed against the "evil cabal" of men who ran the city behind the scenes, the new mayor was very much a product of the Chicago Democratic organization. A loyal follower of Richard J. Daley, she had become under his sponsorship a member of the Democratic National Committee and cochairman of the Cook County Democratic Central Committee. In 1968 Daley appointed her the first commissioner of the city's Department of Consumer Sales, Weights, and Measures, a position she held until Bilandic cashiered her in November 1977. Indeed, Byrne's career as a reformer predated her election as mayor by the same length of time as did her candidacy. Ensconced in city hall, she promptly sought a rapprochement with the party regulars and effected a close working relationship with the same evil cabal she had pilloried only a few weeks earlier. The political experts quickly recanted their obituaries for the Cook County Democratic machine.[23]

While renewing ties with the party stalwarts, Mayor Byrne also expressed a strong desire for independence. She presided over a thorough reshuffling of city hall personnel, dismissed several department heads, clashed with powerful city agencies (most notably the park district), and rejected such pet projects of Mayors Daley and Bilandic as the Crosstown Expressway and the Franklin Street subway. For four years Mayor Byrne feuded with the press; newsmen accused her of "shooting from the lip" and called her "Calamity Jane" and "Attila the Hen." Her penchant for confrontation led to three bitter clashes with public employee unions. Whereas Daley had sealed agreements with municipal unions with a handshake rather than a formal contract and had repeatedly found the wherewithal to satisfy labor's demands, Byrne argued that the city could no longer afford the costly benefits packages customarily proffered to city workers. Talking tough and demonstrating her willingness to weather prolonged strikes, the mayor successfully challenged the demands of the transit workers, firefighters, and teachers unions. Byrne won the battles for fiscal responsibility, but the frequent disruptions caused by the strikes added to the impression of government-by-chaos. Whatever achievements the mayor managed disappeared in the atmosphere of persistent contentiousness overshadowed by what a *Chicago Tribune* reporter called "her image as a mind-changing, impulse-directed chief administrator."[24]

In her 1979 election, Byrne's voter strength came from the black middle-class wards, a result of Bilandic's overt hostility to the city's nonwhite residents. When she resumed her ties to the political machine, black voters felt betrayed, however. To keep Richard M. Daley from expanding his appeal in white ethnic communities, the mayor openly antagonized blacks—ironically utilizing the same ploy that Richard J. Daley had used to shore up his own support with the same white groups after 1963. Byrne initiated the redrawing of new boundary lines to remove black electoral majorities in three wards and reduced black representation on the school board and the public housing authority. She ignored blacks for key leadership positions in her administration, choosing less qualified white ethnics to head the school board and the police department. Rising black resentment surfaced with the decision to boycott ChicagoFest, one of Mayor Byrne's aggressively marketed and generally quite successful special events. Under the leadership of the Reverend Jesse Jackson, the boycott worked well enough to drive the once-profitable enterprise into the red. Dissatisfaction with Byrne led directly in the fall of 1982 to a vastly successful voter registration drive that enrolled 125,000 new black voters in time for the upcoming mayoral election.[25]

Black restiveness, escalating for several years under the Democratic machine's iron rule, grew exponentially under Mayors Bilandic and Byrne, both of whom seemed to play racial politics more blatantly and affront black sensibilities more openly than had Richard J. Daley. In the 1983 mayoral campaign, Harold Washington became the beneficiary of the rising discontent. Like Byrne a product of the Daley machine who had broken away to become an independent Democrat, Washington ran as a reformer in a three-cornered race against the mayor and State's Attorney Richard M. Daley. For four years the newspapers had predicted an epic showdown between the boss's son, who seemed destined to exercise his birthright and reclaim city hall for the Bridgeport faithful, and the female mayor, whose following seemed increasingly tenuous. The mayor accordingly did all she could to isolate the young Daley, to drive him out of the Democratic organization and into political oblivion. With the much-anticipated showdown between Byrne and Daley monopolizing the headlines, few people gave the relatively unknown Washington much of a chance to win the election.[26]

In one of the most remarkable campaigns in Chicago's tumultuous political history, Daley won the endorsement of the city's major newspapers and Byrne built huge leads in the public opinion polls, but Washington won the election. At the eleventh hour, Edward Vrdolyak, whom Byrne had installed as party chairman in 1982, told a rally of white Democratic precinct captains, "A vote for Daley is a vote for Washington. . . . It's a racial thing. Don't kid yourself. I am calling on you to save your city, to save your precinct. We are fighting to keep the city the way it is." In the February 22, 1983, Democratic primary, approximately four hundred thousand more voters cast ballots than in the Byrne-Bilandic contest four years earlier. Daley and Byrne split the white vote, while Washington swept the black vote in precincts that produced record voter turnouts. Washington beat Byrne by a slender margin of thirty-six thousand votes. In the general election, race continued to define the contest; only a handful of white Democratic committeemen endorsed the primary winner, and the majority openly supported the Republican candidate, Bernard Epton. Byrne announced her intention to run as a "unity" candidate to save the city but abandoned her write-in candidacy when Epton's blatantly racist campaign began to gain momentum. The Republican's slogan "Epton—Before It's Too Late" played to white fears of a black mayor, and Vrdolyak, brazenly working against his party's nominee, charged that Washington had once been arrested for child molestation. Eloquently indignant in his self-defense, Washington effectively linked Epton's candidacy with the bankrupt Democratic machine and won the election by 48,250 votes.[27]

The 1983 election, certainly one of the most sordid in Chicago's history, brought racial antipathies boiling to the surface. Unfortunately for Mayor Washington, the tensions did not recede after the election. For most of his first administration, Washington found himself embroiled in the nefarious "council wars" that brought municipal government virtually to a standstill. Led by opposition spokesman Edward Vrdolyak, the mayor's twenty-nine white aldermanic opponents constituted the necessary majority to thwart the efforts of the twenty-one loyal blacks and white liberals. The city council approved few of the mayor's appointments, rejected his budgets, refused to pass a tax increase that Washington termed necessary to avoid a budgetary shortfall, and sought his impeachment in the courts. The gridlock between the executive and legislative branches of Chicago's government from 1983 to 1986—which led the *Wall Street Journal* to refer to the city as "Beirut on the Lake"—contrasted sharply with the government-by-rubber-stamp common from 1955 to 1976. Not until the outcome of special aldermanic elections mandated by a federal court in 1986 was Washington able to govern the city; the results of those elections left the council divided evenly, twenty-five to twenty-five, with the mayor possessing the tie-breaking vote.[28]

Because of Washington's extraordinarily difficult first term, hope soared in some quarters that a white challenger could unseat him in 1987. Jane Byrne declared her candidacy a full two years early in 1985, and although both Richard M. Daley and Edward Vrdolyak hinted at seeking the Democratic nomination, neither did so. Vrdolyak relinquished his position as Democratic party chairman to run in the general election as a third-party candidate, and a Daley surrogate—Cook County Assessor Thomas Hynes—ran as an independent Democrat. The Republicans nominated a former member of Byrne's cabinet, Donald Haider. In both the primary and the general elections, Washington assumed the reform mantle and characterized his opponents as machine politicians; they, in turn, relied again on the politics of racial divisiveness. The mayor won 54 percent of the vote in the Democratic primary as well as in the general election, a slight improvement over his winning margins of 1983. He again carried the black vote overwhelmingly and did slightly better among white voters than he had done four years earlier.[29]

At last armed with an electoral mandate and a cooperative majority in the city council, Harold Washington seemed poised to implement his legislative agenda. Tragically, however, he died of a massive heart attack on November 25, 1987. Despite having grown decidedly obese while in office, the mayor had appeared healthy and robust; his death at age sixty-five came unexpectedly. The report of Washington's demise set off a massive outpouring of grief in Chicago's black community, where his stirring defeats of the Democratic machine had brought him a passionate following. Blacks and whites alike reflected sadly on his lack of opportunity finally to govern the city whose mayoralty he had twice won. They also wondered if another black politician could become mayor of Chicago, or if Washington's triumph represented the high-water mark of black political influence. Was Washington's mayoralty the harbinger of a new age or an aberration, his death the opportunity for the city's whites to reclaim control?[30]

As they had done eleven years earlier, the city council had to select from within its ranks an interim mayor to serve until a special election could be held. The Reverend Jesse Jackson returned hurriedly from the Persian Gulf to become involved in the struggle for power in Chicago and lent his name to the candidacy of fourth ward alderman Timothy Evans. Many white ethnics lined up behind Eugene Sawyer, a Richard J. Daley acolyte whom they thought to be the most malleable black alderman. As the city council deliberated, Jackson and thousands of Evans supporters demonstrated in the streets outside, chanted anti-Sawyer slogans, and in some cases threatened black aldermen whose loyalty they questioned. Although Evans supporters feared the existence of backroom deals, much of the negotiations proceeded in the city hall lobby and council gallery in front of television cameras that were broadcasting events live to rapt audiences in an estimated 480,000 households. The decision came on December 2 at 4:01 A.M. as twenty-three white and six black aldermen elected the conciliatory Eugene Sawyer over the more outspoken Timothy Evans by twenty-nine votes to nineteen.[31]

Chicago's second black mayor presided over an ephemeral coalition and, unlike Harold Washington, could not command the loyalty of a united black electorate. Sawyer's attempt to cancel a special mayoral election scheduled for 1989 met with defeat when supporters of Timothy Evans successfully challenged it in the courts. In the February 1989 Democratic primary, Sawyer's toughest challenge came from three-time Cook County State's Attorney Richard M. Daley, whose campaign contrasted sharply with his 1983 effort. Severing obvious ties to the old Democratic machine, young Daley surrounded himself with a heterogeneous group of advisers, assumed a more progressive position on many issues, and campaigned hard for the lakefront liberal vote to buttress his traditional white ethnic backing. He achieved a melding of the bungalow and condo votes while improving his standing with Hispanic and black voters and defeated Sawyer by over one hundred thousand votes. A divided black community cost Sawyer the kind of overwhelming victory margins he needed in predominantly black wards to win, and he lacked the following among white liberals that Harold Washington had achieved.[32]

Democratic nominee Daley faced two opponents in the April general election—Timothy Evans and Edward Vrdolyak, the former Democratic-party-chairman-turned-Republican. The possibility that a black candidate would attain a winning plurality because two candidates split the white vote did not materialize, for, as historian Paul M. Green concluded, "Evans was no Washington, Vrdolyak did not have the firepower or finances of Byrne, and Daley '89 was a far better candidate than Daley '83." The enervated black electorate failed to rally behind Evans, and many Sawyer partisans, unable to forget the poor treatment afforded their candidate, chose to stay at home or to vote for Daley. The result was a landslide victory for Daley, who carried thirty-one wards and won by 150,000 votes.[33]

Richard M. Daley's election in 1989, followed by his impressive reelection two years later, brought to a close the violent convulsions that followed the end of Richard J. Daley's rule in 1976. After twenty-one uninterrupted years of the elder Daley's towering presence in city hall, Chicago had five different mayors during the thirteen years following his death. Assailing the race baiting, demagoguery, and acrimony of the preceding years, the younger Daley appealed to Chicagoans as a healer who intended to work for the best interests of all groups. His low-key, button-down style had a tonic effect, and many voters undoubtedly associated his name with an earlier era of solidity and competence. Although machine old-timers spoke of the son's election in terms of a "restoration," the newly elected mayor went to great lengths to convince the electorate that he was no "Son of Boss." He readily acknowledged the demise of his father's political machine and repeatedly affirmed his commitment to a newer, more inclusive and broader-based politics. With patronage drastically reduced and nonwhite political interests impossible to ignore, Richard M. Daley would apparently have to be more of a chief executive officer than a boss.[34]

Many of the challenges facing the big city mayors of the 1990s had confronted their predecessors in the 1960s and 1970s—a stagnant economy, a hostile federal government, soaring service costs, a weakening tax base, crime, drugs, a crumbling infrastructure, and a host of other problems. Richard M. Daley would be fighting against the same forces of decay and disintegration that Richard J. Daley had confronted earlier, the problems only having grown more severe with time. Political and demographic alterations in the years since the elder Daley's death, however, ensured that the new mayor could not rely on the tactics his father had employed to combat them. It seemed impossible—if not undesirable—to replicate the kind of boss politics that characterized Chicago for much of the twentieth century. Chicagoans' election of the son represented the desire for an end to the uncertainty and disorder prevalent since the father's death, a return to an earlier time of stability. Yet Richard J. Daley's Chicago was to many people, in Carl Condit's words, "a perfect paradox of brilliant technological and architectural achievement standing beside the failure to produce a decent human environment for the majority of its citizens." His service of private capital and the white middle class, a strategy designed to preserve the city's tax base, rewarded a select group of Chicagoans but trickled down slowly and unevenly to the rest of Chicago's residents. Richard J. Daley had made Chicago "the city that works"; the challenge for Richard M. Daley would be to make it a city that worked for all its people.[35]

NOTES

Preface

1. Peter Yessne, comp., *Quotations from Mayor Daley* (New York: G. P. Putnam's Sons, 1969), pp. 124–25.

Introduction: Chicago, 1945–1955

1. Harold M. Mayer and Richard C. Wade, *Chicago: Growth of a Metropolis* (Chicago: University of Chicago Press, 1969), pp. 375–76. On post–World War II cities, see Carl Abbott, *Urban America in the Modern Age, 1920 to the Present* (Arlington Heights, Ill.: Harlan Davidson, 1987); Jon C. Teaford, *The Twentieth-Century American City: Problem, Promise, and Reality* (Baltimore: Johns Hopkins University Press, 1986); Kenneth Fox, *Metropolitan America: Urban Life and Urban Policy in the United States, 1940–1980* (Jackson: University Press of Mississippi, 1986); and John H. Mollenkopf, *The Contested City* (Princeton: Princeton University Press, 1983).

2. Mayer and Wade, *Chicago,* pp. 410–16; "Chicago's Comeback," *U.S. News and World Report* 38 (May 27, 1955), p. 38; David Halberstam, *The Fifties* (New York: Villard Books, 1993), p. 134; Arnold R. Hirsch, *Making the Second Ghetto: Race and Housing in Chicago, 1940–1960* (Cambridge: Cambridge University Press, 1983), pp. 23–28. On post–World War II suburbanization, see Kenneth T. Jackson, *Crabgrass Frontier: The Suburbanization of the United States* (New York: Oxford University Press, 1985).

3. Mayer and Wade, *Chicago,* pp. 425–28.

4. Ibid., p. 428; William Cronon, *Nature's Metropolis: Chicago and the Great West* (New York: W. W. Norton, 1991), pp. 259, 375; "Chicago's Title Threatened as Meat Processor Decentralizes," *Business Week* (August 27, 1955), p. 73; Milton Derber, *Labor in Illinois: The Affluent Years, 1945–1980* (Urbana: University of Illinois, 1989), p. 245.

5. John M. Allswang, *Bosses, Machines, and Urban Voters* (Baltimore: Johns Hopkins University Press, 1986), pp. 119–21; Joseph Zikmund II, "Mayoral Voting and Ethnic Politics in the Daley-Bilandic-Byrne Era," in Samuel K. Gove and Louis H. Masotti, eds., *After Daley: Chicago Politics in Transition* (Urbana: University of Illinois Press, 1982), pp. 27–30.

6. Todd Gitlin and Nanci Hollander, *Uptown: Poor Whites in Chicago* (New York: Harper and Row, 1970), p. xxiii; Abbott, *Urban America,* pp. 70–71; Teaford, *Twentieth-Century American City,* pp. 117–18.

7. Gitlin and Hollander, *Uptown,* pp. xviii–xix.

8. Peter Gottlieb, "Rethinking the Great Migration: A Perspective from Pittsburgh," in Joe William Trotter Jr., ed., *The Great Migration in Historical Perspective: New Dimensions of Race, Class, and Gender* (Bloomington: Indiana University Press, 1991), pp. 77–78. Also see James R. Grossman, *Land of Hope: Chicago, Black Southerners, and the Great Migration* (Chicago: University of Chicago Press, 1989); and Nicholas Lemann, *The Promised Land: The Great Black Migration and How It Changed America* (New York: Alfred A. Knopf, 1991).

9. St. Clair Drake and Horace R. Cayton, *Black Metropolis: A Study of Negro Life in a Northern City* (Chicago: Universiy of Chicago Press, 1945), p. 9; Otis Dudley Duncan and Beverly Duncan, *The Negro Population of Chicago: A Study of Residential Succession* (Chicago: University of Chicago Press, 1957), pp. 2, 23, 34, 41; Hirsch, *Making the Second Ghetto,* p. 17.

10. Duncan and Duncan, *The Negro Population of Chicago,* pp. 95–97; Hirsch, *Making the Second Ghetto,* p. 17.

11. Hirsch, *Making the Second Ghetto,* p. 24; "Divided City," *Commonweal* 50 (May 6, 1949), p. 86; Duncan and Duncan, *The Negro Population of Chicago,* pp. 82–84.

12. "Chicago's Shame," *Time* 61 (June 29, 1953), p. 75; "War on Slums," *Newsweek* 42 (November 16, 1953), pp. 90–91.

13. Hirsch, *Making the Second Ghetto,* pp. 40, 41. Also see Arnold R. Hirsch, "Race and Housing: Violence and Communal Protest in Chicago, 1940–1960," in Melvin G. Holli and Peter d'A. Jones, eds., *The Ethnic Frontier: Group Survival in Chicago and the Midwest* (Grand Rapids, Mich.: William B. Eerdmans, 1977).

14. Hirsch, *Making the Second Ghetto,* p. 53.

15. Ibid., pp. 53–63; Homer A. Jack, "Test at Trumbull Park," *Christian Century* 73 (March 21, 1956), pp. 366–68.

16. Hirsch, *Making the Second Ghetto,* pp. 63–67.

17. Ibid., p. 22; Martin Meyerson and Edward C. Banfield, *Politics, Planning, and the Public Interest* (New York: Free Press, 1955), p. 30.

18. Mayer and Wade, *Chicago,* pp. 380–82; Carl W. Condit, *Chicago, 1930–1970: Building, Planning, and Urban Technology* (Chicago: University of Chicago Press, 1974), pp. 205–6.

19. Mayer and Wade, *Chicago,* pp. 384–86; "Chicago Answers the Challenge," *American City* 69 (August 1954), pp. 92–93.

20. Mayer and Wade, *Chicago,* p. 384; Glen E. Holt and Dominic A. Pacyga, *Chicago: A Historical Guide to the Neighborhoods, the Loop, and South Side* (Chicago: Chicago Historical Society, 1979), p. 55; Condit, *Chicago, 1930–1970,* p. 206. On urban renewal, see Jon C. Teaford, *The Rough Road to Renaissance: Urban Revitalization in America, 1940–1985* (Baltimore: Johns Hopkins University Press, 1990); Scott Greer, *Urban Renewal and American Cities* (Indianapolis: Bobbs-Merrill, 1965); and James Q. Wilson, ed., *Urban Renewal: The Record and the Controversy* (Cambridge: MIT Press, 1966).

21. Hirsch, *Making the Second Ghetto*, chap. 5; "Chicago Answers the Challenge," p. 94.

22. Meyerson and Banfield, *Politics, Planning, and the Public Interest*, pp. 29–33. Also see Devereaux Bowly, *The Poorhouse: Subsidized Housing in Chicago, 1895–1976* (Carbondale: Southern Illinois University Press, 1978).

23. Meyerson and Banfield, *Politics, Planning, and the Public Interest*, pp. 124–28. On Kelly's role, see Roger Biles, *Big City Boss in Depression and War: Mayor Edward J. Kelly of Chicago* (DeKalb: Northern Illinois University Press, 1984), chap. 8.

24. Meyerson and Banfield, *Politics, Planning, and the Public Interest*, pp. 107–16.

25. Ibid., pp. 26–27, 199–200, 239, 246; "An Encroaching Menace," *Life* 38 (April 11, 1955), p. 126.

26. On Ed Kelly, see Biles, *Big City Boss*. A shorter summary can be found in Paul M. Green and Melvin G. Holli, eds., *The Mayors: The Chicago Political Tradition* (Carbondale: Southern Illinois University Press, 1987), chap. 8.

27. Biles, *Big City Boss*.

28. Kennelly quoted in John Bartlow Martin, "How Corrupt Is Chicago?" *Saturday Evening Post* 223 (March 31, 1951), p. 71; public housing official quoted in Meyerson and Banfield, *Politics, Planning, and the Public Interest*, p. 81; Edward C. Banfield and James Q. Wilson, *City Politics* (Cambridge: Harvard University Press and MIT Press, 1963), p. 107. On Kennelly, see Arnold R. Hirsch, "Martin H. Kennelly: The Mugwump and the Machine," in Green and Holli, *The Mayors*; and Peter J. O'Malley, "Mayor Martin H. Kennelly of Chicago: A Political Biography," Ph.D. dissertation, University of Illinois at Chicago, 1980.

29. Elizabeth Wood quoted in Biles, *Big City Boss*, p. 135; "Divided City," p. 88; Meyerson and Banfield, *Politics, Planning, and the Public Interest*, pp. 136–37; William J. Grimshaw, *Bitter Fruit: Black Politics and the Chicago Machine, 1931–1991* (Chicago: University of Chicago Press, 1992), p. 58.

30. Meyerson and Banfield, *Politics, Planning, and the Public Interest*, pp. 64–75.

31. Virgil Peterson quoted in Martin, "How Corrupt Is Chicago?" p. 62; "Chicago Reform," *Newsweek* 42 (July 13, 1953), p. 30; "Chicago: Lost and Leaderless," *Christian Century* 69 (March 26, 1952), pp. 358–59; Hirsch, "Martin H. Kennelly," p. 133.

32. Hirsch, "Martin H. Kennelly," pp. 135–37.

1. The Road to City Hall

1. Holt and Pacyga, *Chicago*, pp. 113–19; Mayer and Wade, *Chicago*, pp. 48–52. Also see Louise C. Wade, *Chicago's Pride: The Stockyards, Packingtown, and Environs in the Nineteenth Century* (Urbana: University of Illinois Press, 1987); James R. Barrett, *Work and Community in the Jungle: Chicago's*

Packinghouse Workers, 1894–1922 (Urbana: University of Illinois Press, 1987); and Cronon, *Nature's Metropolis.*

2. Holt and Pacyga, *Chicago,* pp. 114–16. Also see Perry R. Duis, *The Saloon: Public Drinking in Chicago and Boston, 1880–1920* (Urbana: University of Illinois Press, 1983).

3. Lawrence J. McCaffrey, Ellen Skerrett, Michael F. Funchion, and Charles Fanning, *The Irish in Chicago* (Urbana: University of Illinois Press, 1987), pp. 61–62. Also see Andrew M. Greeley, *That Most Distressful Nation: The Taming of the American Irish* (Chicago: Quadrangle Books, 1972), pp. 203–15; Steven P. Erie, *Rainbow's End: Irish-Americans and the Dilemmas of Urban Machine Politics, 1840–1985* (Berkeley: University of California Press, 1988); and Edward M. Levine, *The Irish and Irish Politicians* (Notre Dame: University of Notre Dame Press, 1966).

4. Peter J. O'Malley, "Richard J. Daley," in Melvin G. Holli and Peter d'A. Jones, eds., *Biographical Dictionary of American Mayors, 1820–1980: Big City Mayors* (Westport, Conn.: Greenwood Press, 1981), p. 93; Eugene Kennedy, *Himself! The Life and Times of Mayor Richard J. Daley* (New York: Viking Press, 1978), pp. 31–35; Len O'Connor, *Clout: Mayor Daley and His City* (New York: Avon, 1975), p. 17.

5. O'Connor, *Clout,* p. 17; Mike Royko, *Boss: Richard J. Daley of Chicago* (New York: Signet, 1971), pp. 33–34.

6. Kennedy, *Himself!* pp. 38–39; Royko, *Boss,* pp. 34–35; Allswang, *Bosses, Machines, and Urban Voters,* rev. ed. (Baltimore: Johns Hopkins University Press, 1986), p. 122.

7. Bill Gleason, *Daley of Chicago: The Man, the Mayor, and the Limits of Conventional Politics* (New York: Simon and Schuster, 1970), p. 112; Royko, *Boss,* p. 37; O'Connor, *Clout,* p. 18.

8. Royko, *Boss,* pp. 35–38; Illinois Commission of Human Relations quoted in William M. Tuttle Jr., *Race Riot: Chicago in the Red Summer of 1919* (New York: Atheneum, 1977), p. 33.

9. Kennedy, *Himself!* p. 42; O'Connor, *Clout,* p. 19.

10. Royko, *Boss,* p. 40.

11. O'Connor, *Clout,* pp. 24–25.

12. Ibid., pp. 25–26. On Cermak, see Alex Gottfried, *Boss Cermak of Chicago: A Study of Political Leadership* (Seattle: University of Washington Press, 1962). On Dever, see John R. Schmidt, *"The Mayor Who Cleaned Up Chicago": A Political Biography of William E. Dever* (DeKalb: Northern Illinois University Press, 1989).

13. Kennedy, *Himself!* pp. 55–56.

14. Royko, *Boss,* pp. 41, 44; Kennedy, *Himself!* pp. 54–55.

15. Allswang, *Bosses, Machines, and Urban Voters,* pp. 110–16; John M. Allswang, *A House for All Peoples: Ethnic Politics in Chicago, 1890–1936* (Lexington: University Press of Kentucky, 1971), pp. 156–60; Alex Gottfried, *Boss Cermak of Chicago,* pp. 347–50; "Chicago Swaps Bosses," *New Republic* 66 (April 22, 1931), pp. 260–62.

16. Biles, *Big City Boss,* pp. 14–19.

17. Ibid., pp. 43–46.

18. O'Connor, *Clout,* pp. 27–28.

19. Royko, *Boss,* pp. 45–46; Kennedy, *Himself!* pp. 63–66; Gleason, *Daley of Chicago,* p. 121.

20. Kennedy, *Himself!* p. 69.

21. Ibid.

22. Royko, *Boss,* p. 53.

23. Biles, *Big City Boss,* pp. 142–45; Milburn Akers quoted in Kennedy, *Himself!* pp. 73–74.

24. Biles, *Big City Boss,* pp. 145–48.

25. *Chicago Daily News,* November 4, 1946; Royko, *Boss,* p. 54; O'Connor, *Clout,* pp. 31–32.

26. Biles, *Big City Boss,* pp. 147–50; Levine, *The Irish and Irish Politicians,* p. 215. On Kennelly, see Hirsch, "Martin H. Kennelly"; and O'Malley, "Mayor Martin H. Kennelly of Chicago."

27. Royko, *Boss,* pp. 56–57.

28. Ibid., pp. 57–58.

29. John Bartlow Martin, *Adlai Stevenson of Illinois* (Garden City, N.Y.: Doubleday, 1976), p. 359.

30. Royko, *Boss,* pp. 58–59; Martin, *Adlai Stevenson of Illinois,* pp. 359, 391–92; interview with Adlai E. Stevenson III, March 11, 1991, Chicago, Illinois.

31. O'Connor, *Clout,* p. 72.

32. Ibid., pp. 73–74; Royko, *Boss,* pp. 59–60.

33. Royko, *Boss,* pp. 59–60.

34. Kennedy, *Himself!* p. 89.

35. Royko, *Boss,* p. 61; O'Connor, *Clout,* p. 84.

36. Robert Gruenberg, "Dawson of Illinois," *Nation* 183 (September 8, 1956), pp. 196–98; Grimshaw, *Bitter Fruit,* pp. 58–59; Biles, *Big City Boss,* pp. 97–101; Royko, *Boss,* pp. 61–62; James L. Cooper, "South Side Boss," *Chicago History* 19 (Fall–Winter 1990–1991), p. 77.

37. Kennedy, *Himself!* p. 90.

38. *Chicago Tribune,* July 9, 22, 1953; O'Connor, *Clout,* pp. 76–80.

39. Daley quoted in Joe Mathewson, *Up against Daley* (LaSalle, Ill.: Open Court, 1974), p. 49; and O'Connor, *Clout,* p. 101.

40. O'Connor, *Clout,* p. 102.

41. *Chicago Tribune,* December 16, 1954; Gill quoted in Royko, *Boss,* p. 88; Daley quoted in O'Connor, *Clout,* p. 103.

42. *Chicago Tribune,* December 21, 1954.

43. Ibid., December 30, 1954.

44. Kennedy, *Himself!* p. 110.

45. O'Connor, *Clout,* p. 107; Royko, *Boss,* p. 88; John Bartlow Martin, *Adlai Stevenson and the World* (Garden City, N.Y.: Doubleday, 1977), pp. 163–64; interview with Adlai E. Stevenson III.

46. Grimshaw, *Bitter Fruit*, p. 100.
47. *Chicago Tribune,* December 21, 1954; *Chicago Daily News,* February 23, 1955; Kennedy, *Himself!* p. 107.
48. Kennedy, *Himself!* p. 114.
49. *Chicago Tribune,* February 23, 1955.
50. O'Connor, *Clout,* p. 114; Kennelly quoted in *Chicago Daily News,* February 23, 1955.
51. Kennedy, *Himself!* pp. 116–17.
52. Ibid., p. 121; *Chicago Daily News,* February 24, 1955.
53. Royko, *Boss,* pp. 92–93.
54. Ibid., p. 94; Thomas Keane quoted in Gleason, *Daley of Chicago,* p. 205.
55. Elmer Gertz, "Chicago's Hectic Race," *Nation* 180 (April 2, 1955), p. 281; Elizabeth Wood quoted in Gleason, *Daley of Chicago,* p. 206; Paul Douglas quoted in Mathewson, *Up against Daley,* p. 53.
56. *Chicago Tribune,* April 6, 1955; quotations are from Kennedy, *Himself!* p. 131.

2. The New Mayor

1. Teaford, *Rough Road to Renaissance,* pp. 69, 80; Zane L. Miller, *The Urbanization of Modern America: A Brief History* (New York: Harcourt, Brace, Jovanovich, 1973), p. 184.
2. Teaford, *Rough Road to Renaissance,* pp. 56–60; Abbott, *Urban America,* pp. 77–78; Teaford, *Twentieth-Century American City,* p. 119; and Miller, *Urbanization of Modern America,* pp. 183–84. See also Edward F. Haas, *De-Lesseps S. Morrison and the Image of Reform: New Orleans Politics, 1946–1961* (Baton Rouge: Louisiana State University Press, 1974); and Michael P. Weber, *Don't Call Me Boss: David L. Lawrence, Pittsburgh's Renaissance Mayor* (Pittsburgh: University of Pittsburgh Press, 1988).
3. Cabell Phillips, "Exit the Boss, Enter the Leader," *New York Times Magazine,* April 15, 1956, p. 44; Seymour Freedgood, "New Strength in City Hall," in Editors of Fortune, ed., *The Exploding Metropolis* (Garden City, N.Y.: Doubleday, 1958), p. 93; "Daley Life in Chicago," *Time* 68 (July 16, 1956), p. 21; Alfred Balk, "Chicago's 'New Look' Political Boss," *Coronet* 47 (December 1959), p. 52.
4. Banfield and Wilson, *City Politics,* p. 333; Edward C. Banfield, *Political Influence* (New York: Free Press of Glencoe, 1961); James Q. Wilson, *The Amateur Democrat: Club Politics in Three Cities* (Chicago: University of Chicago Press, 1962), p. 72. See also James Q. Wilson, *Political Organizations* (New York: Free Press, 1973); and Donald S. Bradley and Mayer N. Zald, "From Commercial Elite to Political Administrator: The Recruitment of the Mayors of Chicago," *American Journal of Sociology* 71 (September 1965), pp. 153–67.
5. Interview with Tommy Lyons, May 14, 1991, Springfield, Illinois;

Daley cited in Len O'Connor, *A Reporter in Sweet Chicago* (Chicago: Contemporary Books, 1983), p. 290; Kennedy, *Himself!* pp. 137–40; *Chicago Daily News*, February 23, 1955; Freedgood, "New Strength in City Hall," p. 97.

6. Daley cited in William Bowen, "Chicago: They Didn't Have to Burn It Down after All," *Fortune* 71 (January 1965), p. 232; Keith Wheeler, "Last Big Boss on U.S. Scene," *Life* 48 (February 8, 1960), pp. 145, 146 (145); Royko, *Boss*, p. 98.

7. Condit, *Chicago, 1930–1970*, p. 84; Mayer and Wade, *Chicago*, p. 450; quotation is from Glen E. Holt, "Urban Redevelopment: The Rebuilding and Revitalization of Chicago's Loop" (paper presented at the Richard J. Daley Chicago Conference, October 13, 1977); Ira J. Bach, "Chicago Expands Its Burnham Plan," *American City* 76 (September 1961), p. 102; Larry Bennett, "Postwar Redevelopment in Chicago: The Declining Politics of Party and the Rise of Neighborhood Politics," in Gregory D. Squires, ed., *Unequal Partnerships: The Political Economy of Urban Redevelopment in Postwar America* (New Brunswick, N.J.: Rutgers University Press, 1989), p. 166; Gregory D. Squires, Larry Bennett, Kathleen McCourt, and Philip Nyden, *Chicago: Race, Class, and the Response to Urban Decline* (Philadelphia: Temple University Press, 1987), p. 201 n.; Pastora San Juan Cafferty and William C. McCready, "The Chicago Public-Private Partnership Experience: A Heritage of Involvement," in R. Scott Fosler and Renée A. Berger, eds., *Public-Private Partnership in American Cities: Seven Case Studies* (Lexington, Mass.: D. C. Heath, 1982), pp. 134–39.

8. Holt, "Urban Redevelopment"; Gerald D. Suttles, *The Man-Made City: The Land-Use Confidence Game in Chicago* (Chicago: University of Chicago Press, 1990), p. 10; Daley cited in O'Connor, *Clout*, p. 138.

9. Teaford, *Rough Road to Renaissance*, p. 132; Ralph Whitehead, "The Organization Man," *American Scholar* 46 (Summer 1977), pp. 352–53; Melvin G. Holli, "Daley to Daley: Richard J. to Richard M.," *PremierCHICAGO* (May–July 1992), pp. 16–18.

10. Bach, "Chicago Expands Its Burnham Plan," p. 103; Suttles, *The Man-Made City*, p. 35; Condit, *Chicago, 1930–1970*, pp. 235–48; Mayer and Wade, *Chicago*, pp. 440–42; Teaford, *Rough Road to Renaissance*, p. 103.

11. Condit, *Chicago, 1930–1970*, p. 237; Mayer and Wade, *Chicago*, p. 442.

12. Condit, *Chicago, 1930–1970*, p. 127; O'Connor, *Clout*, p. 133.

13. Bowen, "Chicago," p. 146; Hirsch, *Making the Second Ghetto*, pp. 136–70.

14. Holt and Pacyga, *Chicago*, pp. 73–81.

15. Peter H. Rossi and Robert A. Dentler, *The Politics of Urban Renewal: The Chicago Findings* (New York: The Free Press of Glencoe, 1961), pp. 22–89.

16. Rossi and Dentler, *Politics of Urban Renewal*, pp. 65, 221–25 (Mike Nichols quoted on p. 65); James Baldwin and Julian Levy quoted in James Dugan, "Mayor Daley's Chicago," *Holiday* 34 (December 1963), p. 190; William H. McNeill, *Hutchins' University: A Memoir of the University of*

Chicago, 1929–1950 (Chicago: University of Chicago Press, 1991), p. 167; "Clouter with Conscience," *Time* 81 (March 15, 1963), p. 35; "Slum Blight: Chicago's Number One Target," *Architectural Forum* 116 (May 1962), p. 121; Mayer and Wade, *Chicago,* pp. 388–98. For a discussion of Monsignor Egan's role, see Margery Frisbie, *An Alley in Chicago: The Ministry of a City Priest* (Kansas City: Sheed and Ward, 1991), pp. 94–113.

17. Hirsch, *Making the Second Ghetto,* pp. 135–67; Sanford D. Horwitt, *Let Them Call Me Rebel: Saul Alinsky—His Life and Legacy* (New York: Alfred A. Knopf, 1989), p. 374; Rossi and Dentler, *Politics of Urban Renewal,* pp. 250–66; Daley quoted in *Chicago Tribune,* November 8, 1958; Frisbie, *An Alley in Chicago,* p. 113; Condit, *Chicago, 1930–1970,* pp. 211–14.

18. William Patterson quoted in Richard P. Doherty, "The Origin and Development of Chicago-O'Hare International Airport" (Ph.D. dissertation, Ball State University, 1970), pp. 12–60, 165–69; Condit, *Chicago, 1930–1970,* p. 259.

19. Mayer and Wade, *Chicago,* pp. 448–50; O'Connor, *Clout,* p. 132; Condit, *Chicago, 1930–1970,* pp. 259–63; Doherty, "Chicago-O'Hare International Airport," pp. 118–19, 223–43, 325.

20. J. David Greenstone, *Labor in American Politics* (New York: Vintage Books, 1969), pp. 87–104; "Chicago's Daley: How to Run a City," *Newsweek* 77 (April 5, 1971), p. 82; David Lewin, "Mayoral Power and Municipal Labor Relations: A Three-City Study," *Employee Relations Law Journal* 6 (spring 1981), p. 651; Derber, *Labor in Illinois,* p. 238; Melvin G. Holli and Paul M. Green, *Bashing Chicago Traditions: Harold Washington's Last Campaign* (Grand Rapids, Mich.: William B. Eerdmans, 1989), p. 152.

21. Daley quoted in Kennedy, *Himself!* p. 157; O'Connor, *Clout,* pp. 143–44.

22. Kennedy, *Himself!* p. 158; O'Connor, *Clout,* pp. 144–46.

23. Dwight D. Eisenhower to Richard J. Daley, May 5, 1960 (President's Personal File 47, Dwight D. Eisenhower Presidential Library, Abilene, Kansas); Ed Kelly quoted in Hirsch, "Martin H. Kennelly," p. 135.

24. *Chicago Sun-Times,* April 18, 1958; Daley quoted in Royko, *Boss,* p. 97.

25. *Chicago Tribune,* April 21, 1955.

26. George Dunn quoted in Bill Granger and Lori Granger, *Lords of the Last Machine: The Story of Politics in Chicago* (New York: Random House, 1987), p. 6; Paul Douglas quoted in O'Connor, *Clout,* pp. 126–27; Kennedy, *Himself!* p. 161.

27. Interview with Dick Simpson, 26 May 1993, Chicago, Illinois.

28. Ibid.

29. Grimshaw, *Bitter Fruit,* p. 93; Wheeler, "Last Big Boss on U.S. Scene," p. 143; Arnold R. Hirsch, "Chicago: The Cook County Democratic Organization and the Dilemma of Race, 1931–1987," in Richard M. Bernard, ed., *Snowbelt Cities: Metropolitan Politics in the Northeast and Midwest since World War II* (Bloomington: Indiana University Press, 1990), pp. 76–77;

Kennedy, *Himself!* p. 136; Ester R. Fuchs, *Mayors and Money: Fiscal Policy in New York and Chicago* (Chicago: University of Chicago Press, 1992), p. 215.

30. Kennedy, *Himself!* p. 138; O'Connor, *Clout,* p. 127.

31. Wheeler, "Last Big Boss on U.S. Scene," p. 143; Royko, *Boss,* p. 98; Dick Simpson, "The Chicago City Council, 1971–1991" (unpublished paper in the possession of the author).

32. O'Connor, *Clout,* pp. 129–30; Milton L. Rakove, *Don't Make No Waves, Don't Back No Losers: An Insider's Analysis of the Daley Machine* (Bloomington: Indiana University Press, 1975), p. 205.

33. Granger and Granger, *Lords of the Last Machine,* p. 163.

34. O'Connor, *Clout,* pp. 132–33; Daley quoted in Kennedy, *Himself!* pp. 149, 254.

35. Grimshaw, *Bitter Fruit,* p. 12; David K. Fremon, *Chicago Politics Ward by Ward* (Bloomington: Indiana University Press, 1988), pp. 48–49; O'Connor, *Clout,* p. 134.

36. State representative quoted in "Clouter with Conscience," p. 24; interview with Adlai E. Stevenson III; Paul H. Douglas, *In the Fullness of Time: The Memoirs of Paul H. Douglas* (New York: Harcourt, Brace, Jovanovich, 1971), pp. 173, 185.

37. Grimshaw, *Bitter Fruit,* p. 12; Fremon, *Chicago Politics,* pp. 48–49; O'Connor, *Clout,* p. 134.

38. Milton L. Rakove, *We Don't Want Nobody Nobody Sent: An Oral History of the Daley Years* (Bloomington: Indiana University Press, 1979), p. 270; Allswang, *Bosses, Machines, and Urban Voters,* p. 128; *Chicago Daily News,* April 6, 1959; William Patterson quoted in Gleason, *Daley of Chicago,* pp. 283-284.

39. Speech, March 14, 1959 (Richard J. Daley Papers, University of Illinois at Chicago Library, box 2, folder 11); *Chicago Tribune,* April 8, 1959; O'Connor, *Clout,* p. 151; Daley quoted in Kennedy, *Himself!* pp. 163–64.

3. Mounting Problems

1. See Lloyd Wendt and Herman Kogan, *Bosses in Lusty Chicago: The Story of Bathhouse John and Hinky Dink* (Bloomington: Indiana University Press, 1974).

2. Robert Bendiner, "A Tale of Cops, Robbers, and the Visiting Professor," *Reporter* 23 (September 15, 1960), p. 33; Royko, *Boss,* p. 113.

3. Kennedy, *Himself!* pp. 166–67; Royko, *Boss,* p. 112; Herbert Brean, "A Really Good Police Force," *Life* 43 (September 16, 1957), p. 71.

4. Richard C. Lindberg, *To Serve and Collect: Chicago Politics and Police Corruption from the Lager Beer Riot to the Summerdale Scandal* (Westport, Conn.: Praeger, 1991), pp. 295–302; Leon Despres, "Corruption in Chicago," *Nation* 190 (March 12, 1960), p. 220; Gleason, *Daley of Chicago,* pp. 222–24.

5. Bendiner, "A Tale of Cops, Robbers, and the Visiting Professor," p. 33.

6. O'Connor, *Clout,* pp. 149, 170–71; Royko, *Boss,* p. 114.

7. Lindberg, *To Serve and Collect,* p. 322 n. 35; Royko, *Boss,* p. 118.

8. Virgil W. Peterson, "The Chicago Police Scandals," *Atlantic Monthly* 206 (October 1960), pp. 61–63; Lindberg, *To Serve and Collect,* p. 305.

9. Bendiner, "A Tale of Cops, Robbers, and the Visiting Professor," p. 34; William J. Bopp, *"O. W.": O. W. Wilson and the Search for a Police Profession* (Port Washington, N.Y.: Kennikat, 1977), pp. 84–87; Peterson, "Chicago Police Scandals," p. 64; Gleason, *Daley of Chicago,* pp. 227–28; *New York Times,* February 23, 1960; Lindberg, *To Serve and Collect,* p. 309.

10. Bendiner, "A Tale of Cops, Robbers, and the Visiting Professor," p. 35; Bopp, *"O. W.,"* pp. 101–2.

11. Daley quoted in Bopp, *"O. W.,"* p. 108; Lindberg, *To Serve and Collect,* p. 313; Royko, *Boss,* pp. 122–23 (alderman quoted on p. 123).

12. Daley quoted in Wheeler, "Last Big Boss on U.S. Scene," p. 139; Kennedy, *Himself!* pp. 169–70; Martin, *Adlai Stevenson and the World,* p. 523.

13. O'Connor, *Clout,* pp. 152–54; "Joe Kennedy Buys," *Time* 46 (July 30, 1945), p. 84; Vernon Jarrett, "An Old Pro Views Political Strategy," *Chicago Tribune,* February 8, 1974.

14. Kennedy, *Himself!* pp. 174–75.

15. Edmund F. Kallina Jr., *Courthouse over White House: Chicago and the Presidential Election of 1960* (Orlando: University of Central Florida Press, 1988), p. 58; Daley quoted in Kennedy, *Himself!* p. 175.

16. Martin, *Adlai Stevenson and the World,* p. 526; interview with Adlai E. Stevenson III; Gleason, *Daley of Chicago,* p. 256.

17. O'Connor, *Clout,* p. 155.

18. Royko, *Boss,* pp. 123–24. In *Courthouse over White House,* Edmund F. Kallina Jr. concludes that the real reason Daley supported Kennedy was that he hoped a strong candidate at the head of the ticket would attract enough votes to recapture the state's attorney's office and the governor's mansion (p. 57).

19. "Clouter with Conscience," p. 34; O'Connor, *Clout,* pp. 156–57; *New York Times,* November 10, 1960. In addition to carrying the forty-first, forty-fifth, and forty-seventh wards, Nixon narrowly lost five others—the nineteenth, thirty-eighth, thirty-ninth, forty-fourth, and forty-eighth (Kallina, *Courthouse over White House,* pp. 235–36).

20. Kennedy, *Himself!* pp. 184–85; Daley quoted in Allen J. Matusow, *The Unraveling of America: A History of Liberalism in the 1960s* (New York: Harper and Row, 1984), p. 26.

21. Kennedy, *Himself!* pp. 185–86; Kenneth P. O'Donnell and David F. Powers, *"Johnny, We Hardly Knew Ye": Memories of John Fitzgerald Kennedy* (New York: Simon and Schuster, 1973), pp. 257–58.

22. *New York Times,* December 3, 15, 1960; *Chicago Tribune,* December 1, 3, 5, 11, 1960; Kallina, *Courthouse over White House,* pp. 89–92, 119–25; "Clouter with Conscience," p. 34; John F. Kennedy to Richard J. Daley, March 23, 1961 (Executive File PL/ST 13, John F. Kennedy Library, Boston, Massachusetts).

23. Richard J. Daley to Kenneth O'Donnell, November 29, 1961 (Exec-

utive File PR6–1/D, John F. Kennedy Library); O'Connor, *Clout*, pp. 164–65; interview with Tommy Lyons.

24. The information in this and the two following paragraphs is taken from George Rosen, *Decision-Making Chicago-Style: The Genesis of a University of Illinois Campus* (Urbana: University of Illinois Press, 1980), pp. 20–59, 65–85, 112–18.

25. Royko, *Boss*, pp. 126–27.

26. Ibid., p. 128; Rosen, *Decision-Making Chicago-Style*, pp. 18–169.

27. Rosen, *Decision-Making Chicago-Style*, pp. 128–39, 160; Florence Scala quoted in Royko, *Boss*, p. 129.

28. Harvey Zorbaugh, *The Gold Coast and the Slum* (Chicago: University of Chicago Press, 1929); Bennett, "Postwar Redevelopment in Chicago," pp. 169–70; Condit, *Chicago, 1930–1970*, p. 215; Mayer and Wade, *Chicago*, pp. 388–89. The Fort Dearborn Project Papers at the University of Illinois at Chicago Library contain some information about Arthur Rubloff's role in the residential development of the area north of downtown but focus more on the construction of government buildings in the Loop.

29. Bennett, "Postwar Redevelopment in Chicago," pp. 169–70; Mayer and Wade, *Chicago*, pp. 388–89; Condit, *Chicago, 1930–1970*, pp. 215–19.

30. See Teaford, *Rough Road to Renaissance*.

31. Ibid., p. 142; Erie, *Rainbow's End*, pp. 157–61; *Chicago Tribune*, June 25, 1978.

32. Royko, *Boss*, p. 129; Condit, *Chicago, 1930–1970*, p. 254.

33. *Chicago Tribune*, March 1, 1963.

34. Condit, *Chicago, 1930–1970*, p. 338; Royko, *Boss*, p. 130.

35. "Clouter with Conscience," p. 24; Dugan, "Mayor Daley's Chicago," pp. 84–87, 90–92, 189–98, 205–11; Holt, "Urban Redevelopment."

36. Adamowski quoted in Gleason, *Daley of Chicago*, p. 339, and in *Chicago Daily News*, April 3, 1963; Allswang, *Bosses, Machines, and Urban Voters*, p. 130; O'Connor, *Clout*, pp. 177–78.

37. Grimshaw, *Bitter Fruit*, p. 115; Joseph Zikmund II, "Mayoral Voting and Ethnic Politics," pp. 37–40; Gleason, *Daley of Chicago*, p. 339; *Chicago Tribune* and *Chicago Daily News*, April 3, 1963.

38. Daley quoted in *Chicago Tribune*, April 3, 1963; Whitehead, "The Organization Man," pp. 355–56.

39. Whitehead, "The Organization Man," pp. 355–56.

4. The Challenge to Plantation Politics

1. Daley quoted in *Chicago Tribune*, July 9, 1963; Mayer and Wade, *Chicago*, p. 406.

2. Allan H. Spear, *Black Chicago: The Making of a Negro Ghetto, 1890–1920* (Chicago: University of Chicago Press, 1967), pp. 5–27.

3. Spear, *Black Chicago*, pp. 129–46; Duncan and Duncan, *The Negro Population of Chicago*, pp. 30–35. Also see Tuttle, *Race Riot*; Grossman, *Land of*

Hope; and Thomas Lee Philpott, *The Slum and the Ghetto: Neighborhood Deterioration and Middle-Class Reform, Chicago, 1880–1930* (New York: Oxford University Press, 1978).

4. Mollenkopf, *The Contested City*, p. 38; Lemann, *The Promised Land*, p. 70; Hirsch, *Making the Second Ghetto*, pp. 3–5; Paul Kleppner, *Chicago Divided: The Making of a Black Mayor* (DeKalb: Northern Illinois University Press, 1985), p. 33.

5. Hirsch, *Making the Second Ghetto*, p. 194; W. Joseph Black, "The Renewed Negro and Urban Renewal," *Architectural Forum* 128 (June 1968), p. 63; Lemann, *The Promised Land*, p. 81.

6. Realtors quoted in Kleppner, *Chicago Divided*, pp. 33, 34; Lemann, *The Promised Land*, pp. 81–82.

7. Hirsch, *Making the Second Ghetto*, pp. 253, 275 (275).

8. Interview with Devereaux Bowly Jr., April 26, 1991, Chicago; Robert Taylor quoted in Hirsch, *Making the Second Ghetto*, p. 224; *Chicago Sun-Times*, March 28, 1968.

9. Lemann, *The Promised Land*, pp. 73–74 (73); Hirsch, "Race and Housing," pp. 331–68; Hirsch, "Martin H. Kennelly," pp. 138–40; Bowly, *The Poorhouse*, p. 84; Jack, "Test at Trumbull Park," pp. 366–67.

10. Elizabeth Wood quoted in Hirsch, "Martin F. Kennelly," p. 139; Alan B. Anderson and George W. Pickering, *Confronting the Color Line: The Broken Promise of the Civil Rights Movement in Chicago* (Athens: University of Georgia Press, 1986), p. 80; Karl E. Taeuber and Alma F. Taeuber, *Negroes in Cities: Residential Segregation and Neighborhood Change* (Chicago: Aldine Publishing Company, 1965), pp. 28–39.

11. Hirsch, *Making the Second Ghetto*, pp. 241, 257; interview with Devereaux Bowly Jr.

12. Bowly, *The Poorhouse*, p. 112; CHA quoted in Kleppner, *Chicago Divided*, p. 45.

13. Pierre deVise, "Descent from the Summit: Race and Housing in Chicago since 1966" (Ph.D. dissertation, University of Illinois at Chicago, 1985), pp. 63–64; Bowly, *The Poorhouse*, pp. 115–28; William Mullen, "The Road to Hell," *Chicago Tribune Sunday Magazine*, March 31, 1985, p. 12; *Chicago Daily News*, April 15, 1965; Black, "The Renewed Negro and Urban Renewal," p. 63; M. W. Newman quoted in Condit, *Chicago, 1930–1970*, p. 160.

14. Lemann, *The Promised Land*, pp. 92–93; Mayer and Wade, *Chicago*, p. 446; interview with Don Rose, May 20, 1991, Chicago, Illinois; Royko, *Boss*, p. 137.

15. Lemann, *The Promised Land*, p. 92; interview with Devereaux Bowly Jr. See also Le Corbusier, *The Radiant City: Elements of a Doctrine of Urbanism to Be Used as the Basis of Our Machine-Age Civilization* (New York: Orion Press, 1933).

16. Cooper, "South Side Boss," pp. 68–70; Biles, *Big City Boss*, pp. 97–99.

17. William J. Grimshaw, *Black Politics in Chicago: The Quest for Leader-*

ship, 1936–1979 (Chicago: Loyola University, 1980), p. 8; Gruenberg, "Dawson of Illinois," p. 196; Milton Rakove, "Jane Byrne and the New Chicago Politics," in Gove and Masotti, *After Daley,* p. 223; Daley quoted in Grimshaw, *Bitter Fruit,* p. 12; Benjamin Lewis quoted in Hirsch, "Chicago," p. 80.

18. Dempsey Travis, *An Autobiography of Black Politics* (Chicago: Urban Research Press, 1987), p. 206; James Q. Wilson, *Negro Politics: The Search for Leadership* (New York: Free Press, 1960), p. 88.

19. Cooper, "South Side Boss," p. 73; Dawson quoted from Wilson, *Negro Politics,* p. 72, and from *Chicago Tribune,* February 8, 1974.

20. Claude Holman quoted from Fremon, *Chicago Politics,* p. 40; Grimshaw, *Black Politics in Chicago,* pp. 13–14; Grimshaw, *Bitter Fruit,* pp. 32, 108–9.

21. Travis, *Autobiography of Black Politics,* p. 235; Lemann, *The Promised Land,* p. 90; quotation is from David Halberstam, "Daley of Chicago," *Harper's* 237 (August 1968), p. 31. The Silent Six were Ralph Metcalfe, Claude Holman, William Harvey, Kenneth Campbell, Robert Miller, and George Collins.

22. Grimshaw, *Bitter Fruit,* especially chap. 6.

23. Grimshaw, *Black Politics in Chicago,* p. 28.

24. Lemann, *The Promised Land,* p. 91; quotation is from Halberstam, "Daley of Chicago," p. 26.

25. Wilson, *Negro Politics,* pp. 89–92.

26. *Chicago Tribune,* July 5, 1963; Royko, *Boss,* p. 142; Thomas M. Landye and James J. Vanecko, "The Politics of Open Housing in Illinois," in Lynn W. Eley and Thomas W. Casstevens, eds., *The Politics of Fair-Housing Legislation: State and Local Case Studies* (San Francisco: Chandler, 1968), pp. 86–91.

27. Landye and Vanecko, "The Politics of Open Housing," pp. 97–99; Chicago Commission on Human Relations, "A Report to the Mayor and City Council of Chicago on the Present Status and Effectiveness of Existing Fair Housing Practices Legislation in the U.S. as of August 31, 1967," pp. 29, 37.

28. Lemann, *The Promised Land,* pp. 97–100.

29. Horwitt, *Let Them Call Me Rebel,* pp. 440–44; James Ridgeway, "Poor Chicago," *New Republic* 152 (May 15, 1965), p. 19.

30. "De Facto Segregation in the Chicago Public Schools," *Crisis* 65 (February 1958), p. 89; John E. Coons, "Chicago," in *Civil Rights USA: Public Schools in the North and West* (Washington, D.C.: Government Printing Office, 1962), p. 232; Clair Roddewig quoted from Anderson and Pickering, *Confronting the Color Line,* p. 95; John H. Fish, *Black Power/White Control: The Struggle of The Woodlawn Organization in Chicago* (Princeton: Princeton University Press, 1973), p. 52.

31. Mary J. Herrick, *The Chicago Schools: A Social and Political History* (Beverly Hills, Calif.: Sage Publications, 1971), pp. 306–12; Lemann, *The*

Promised Land, p. 91; James R. Ralph Jr., *Northern Protest: Martin Luther King Jr., Chicago, and the Civil Rights Movement* (Cambridge: Harvard University Press, 1993), pp. 14, 19–20; Willis quoted from "Big City Schoolmaster," *Time* 78 (September 15, 1961), p. 55.

32. Betty Flynn, "The Battle of Ben Willis" (CORE Papers, box 3, folder 1965 [Jan.*-March], Chicago Historical Society, Chicago, Illinois); Herrick, *The Chicago Schools,* pp. 312–14; "The Education of Big Ben," *Time* 82 (August 30, 1963), p. 48; Fish, *Black Power/White Control,* p. 54.

33. "The Education of Big Ben," p. 48; "Big City Schoolmaster," p. 55; Anderson and Pickering, *Confronting the Color Line,* p. 107; Royko, *Boss,* p. 142; *Chicago Defender* quoted from Ralph, *Northern Protest,* p. 20.

34. Anderson and Pickering, *Confronting the Color Line,* pp. 107–8; Daley quoted in *Chicago Daily News,* October 5, 1963; aide quoted in Royko, *Boss,* p. 143.

35. "The Education of Big Ben," p. 48; Lemann, *The Promised Land,* p. 234.

36. *Chicago Daily News,* October 5, 1963; Herrick, *The Chicago Schools* (Willis quoted on pp. 317–18, Daley quoted on p. 337); "DeFacto Superintendent," *Time* 82 (November 1, 1963), p. 56; Anderson and Pickering, *Confronting the Color Line,* p. 119 (Daley quoted on p. 133).

37. *Chicago Tribune,* April 1, 1964; Herrick, *The Chicago Schools,* pp. 323–25; Philip Hauser quoted in Charles and Bonnie Remsberg, "Chicago, Legacy of an Ice Age," *Saturday Review* 50 (May 20, 1967), p. 73; O'Connor, *Clout,* p. 184; Albert Raby to Francis Keppel, July 4, 1965 (Douglass C. Cater Files, folder "Civil Rights Bill: Complaints under Title VI," Lyndon B. Johnson Presidential Library, Austin, Texas).

38. Paul E. Peterson, *School Politics Chicago Style* (Chicago: University of Chicago Press, 1976), pp. 6–7; "On the Appointment of Mrs. Green to the Board of Education," Remarks Made in the City Council, June 10, 1964, by Leon Despres (CORE Papers, box 2, folder 1964 [June], Chicago Historical Society, Chicago, Illinois).

39. *Chicago Tribune,* November 13, 1964; Anderson and Pickering, *Confronting the Color Line,* pp. 146–48; Albert Raby to Francis Keppel, July 4, 1965 (Douglass C. Cater Files, folder "Civil Rights Bill: Complaints under Title VI," Lyndon B. Johnson Presidential Library, Austin, Texas).

40. Royko, *Boss,* pp. 133–36 (John Walsh quoted on p. 133); Gleason, *Daley of Chicago,* pp. 161–62.

41. Walsh quoted in Royko, *Boss,* p. 136.

42. Black realist quoted from Andrew M. Greeley, "Take Heart from the Heartland," *Nation* 163 (December 12, 1970), p. 17; Michael F. Funchion, "The Political and Nationalist Dimensions," in McCaffrey, Skerrett, Funchion, and Fanning, *The Irish in Chicago,* pp. 89–90.

5. Pressure from External Sources

1. President Johnson quoted in Matusow, *The Unraveling of America,* p. 124; Equal Opportunity Act cited in J. David Greenstone and Paul E. Peter-

son, "Reformers, Machines, and the War on Poverty," in James Q. Wilson, ed., *City Politics and Public Policy* (New York: John Wiley and Sons, 1968), p. 273; Daley quoted in House Committee on Education and Labor, *Hearings before the Subcommittee on the War on Poverty Program of the Committee on Education and Labor,* 88th Cong., 2nd Sess., 1964, pt. 2, p. 767.

2. Trudy Haffron Bers, "Private Welfare Agencies and Their Role in Government-Sponsored Welfare Programs: The Case of the War on Poverty in Chicago" (Ph.D. dissertation, University of Illinois at Urbana-Champaign, 1973), pp. 2–3; Seymour Z. Mann, *Chicago's War on Poverty* (Chicago: Loyola University Center for Research on Urban Government, 1966), p. 1; Anderson and Pickering, *Confronting the Color Line,* p. 170; James V. Cunningham, *Urban Leadership in the Sixties* (Waltham: Brandeis University, 1970), p. 41; George J. Washnis, *Municipal Decentralization and Neighborhood Resources: Case Studies of Twelve Cities* (New York: Praegar, 1972), p. 126; Daley quoted in Cunningham, *Urban Leadership in the Sixties,* p. 42.

3. J. David Greenstone and Paul E. Peterson, *Race and Authority in Urban Politics: Community Participation and the War on Poverty* (New York: Russell Sage Foundation, 1973), pp. 22–23.

4. Ibid., p. 40; Deton Brooks quoted in U.S. Congress, House Committee on Education and Labor, *Hearings before the Subcommittee on the War on Poverty Program of the Committee on Education and Labor,* 89th Cong., 1st Sess., Examination of the War on Poverty Program, held in Washington, D.C., April 12–15, 29, 30, 1965 (Washington D.C.: Government Printing Office, 1965), p. 342; Matusow, *The Unraveling of America,* p. 249; Paul E. Peterson, "Forms of Representation: Participation of the Poor in the Community Action Program," *American Political Science Review* 64 (June 1970), p. 498.

5. William Cannon quoted from interview, May 21, 1982 (Oral History Collection, Lyndon B. Johnson Presidential Library, Austin, Texas), and from Lemann, *The Promised Land,* p. 166.

6. Bill Moyers and Frederick Hayes quoted from Lemann, *The Promised Land,* p. 167; interview with Wilbur Cohen, May 10, 1969 (Lyndon B. Johnson Presidential Library, Austin, Texas).

7. Lemann, *The Promised Land,* p. 167; R. Sargent Shriver quoted in Greenstone and Peterson, *Race and Authority in Urban Politics,* p. 23; John C. Donovan, *The Politics of Poverty* (New York: Pegasus, 1967), pp. 55–56.

8. Fish, *Black Power/White Control,* pp. 81–89; *Chicago Daily News,* May 13, 1965.

9. Greenstone and Peterson, *Race and Authority in Urban Politics,* pp. 21–22.

10. Mann, *Chicago's War on Poverty,* pp. 7–8; Stevenson, Powell, and Brooks quoted from *Hearings before the Subcommittee on the War on Poverty Program of the Committee on Education and Labor,* pp. 359, 378; Wil Haygood, *King of the Cats: The Life and Times of Adam Clayton Powell Jr.* (Boston: Houghton Mifflin, 1993), pp. 313–14; Powell quoted from Jules Witcover and Erwain Knoll, "Politics and the Poor: Shriver's Second Thoughts," *Reporter* 33 (December 30, 1965), p. 24; *Chicago Sun-Times,* July 28–29, 1965, and March 27, 1966.

11. *New York Times,* June 8, 1965; Witcover and Knoll, "Politics and the Poor," p. 23; interview with Jack T. Conway, August 13, 1980 (Oral History Collection, Lyndon B. Johnson Presidential Library); Hubert Humphrey quoted in Donovan, *The Politics of Poverty,* p. 57.

12. Peterson, "Forms of Representation," p. 496; Greenstone and Peterson, *Race and Authority in Urban Politics,* pp. 22, 23 (Brooks quoted on p. 160); Alinsky quoted in Marion K. Sanders, "Conversations with Saul Alinsky, Part 2: A Professional Radical Moves in on Rochester," *Harper's* 231 (July 1965), p. 54; Daley quoted in Cunningham, *Urban Leadership in the Sixties,* p. 44.

13. Donovan, *The Politics of Poverty,* pp. 54–57; Sidney Fine, *Violence in the Model City: The Cavanaugh Administration, Race Relations, and the Detroit Riot of 1967* (Ann Arbor: University of Michigan Press, 1989), pp. 76–78; Peterson, "Forms of Representation," p. 505.

14. Lois Wille, "Mayor Daley Meets the Movement," *Nation* 201 (August 30, 1965), pp. 92–93; Cyrus Adams to Wayne C. Booth, June 1, 1965 (Cyrus Adams Papers, box 11, folder 4, Chicago Historical Society, Chicago, Illinois); audio tape, Cyrus Adams Papers, box 38.

15. Daley quoted in *Chicago Tribune,* June 12, 1965 ("law and order"), and in Ralph, *Northern Protest,* p. 28 ("who is Raby?"); Remsberg, "Chicago, Legacy of an Ice Age," p. 75; David J. Garrow, *Bearing the Cross: Martin Luther King Jr. and the Southern Christian Leadership Conference* (New York: William Morrow, 1986), p. 433; Daley after the riot quoted in Herrick, *The Chicago Schools,* p. 337.

16. King quoted in Gleason, *Daley of Chicago,* p. 36; Garrow, *Bearing the Cross,* pp. 433, 534; Daley quoted in Kennedy, *Himself!* p. 193.

17. Gary Orfield, *The Reconstruction of Southern Education: The Schools and the 1964 Civil Rights Act* (New York: Wiley-Interscience, 1969), pp. 165–66; Haygood, *King of the Cats,* p. 315; quotations are from U.S. Congress, House Committee on Education and Labor, *Investigation of DeFacto Racial Segregation in Chicago's Public Schools: Hearings before a Special Subcommittee of the Committee on Education and Labor,* July 27, 28, 1965, 89th Cong., 1st sess. (Washington, D.C.: Government Printing Office, 1965), pp. 43, 114; *New York Times,* June 28, 29, 1965.

18. *New York Times,* July 12, 1965; Kevin P. Buckley and Richard Cotton, "Chicago: The Marchers and the Machine," *Reporter* 33 (November 4, 1965), p. 30; O'Connor, *Clout,* p. 191.

19. Bopp, "*O. W.,*" p. 116.

20. Wille, "Mayor Daley Meets the Movement," p. 94; Royko, *Boss,* pp. 144–45 (quotations from p. 144); *Chicago Tribune,* August 3, 1965.

21. Royko, *Boss,* p. 145; Wille, "Confrontation in Chicago," *Nation* 201 (August 30, 1965), pp. 92–95; Daley quoted from Kennedy, *Himself!* p. 196.

22. Daley quoted from Royko, *Boss,* pp. 145–46; Larry O'Brien to Lyndon B. Johnson, August 11, 1965 (memorandum, executive file LG/Chicago LE/LG HU2/ST13 FG400/ST13 PR8-3/D*, Lyndon B. Johnson Presidential Library).

23. *Chicago Tribune*, August 14, 1965.
24. Daley quoted from *Chicago Tribune*, August 17, 1965.
25. Royko, *Boss*, p. 147.
26. Albert Raby to Francis Keppel, July 4, 1965 (Douglass C. Cater files, folder "Civil Rights Bill: Complaints under Title VI," Lyndon B. Johnson Presidential Library).
27. Orfield, *The Reconstruction of Southern Education*, pp. 177–81; Francis Keppel to Joseph A. Califano Jr., memorandum, October 4, 1965; Francis Keppel to Benjamin C. Willis, September 30, 1965; and Francis Keppel to Ray Page, September 30, 1965 (all in Douglass C. Cater files, folder "Civil Rights Bill: Complaints under Title VI," Lyndon B. Johnson Presidential Library).
28. Pucinski quoted from *Chicago Daily News*, October 2, 1965; press release by Benjamin C. Willis, October 2, 1965 (Cyrus Adams Papers, box 13, folder 4, Chicago Historical Society, Chicago, Illinois); Daley quoted from Anderson and Pickering, *Confronting the Color Line*, p. 179.
29. Interview with Douglass Cater, April 29, 1969 (Lyndon B. Johnson Presidential Library); Daley quoted from interview with Wilbur Cohen.
30. Unsigned memorandum to Lyndon Johnson, October 3, 1965 (executive file HU2–5/ST13 LG/Chicago, Lyndon B. Johnson Presidential Library); interview with Wilbur Cohen; memorandum, Nicholas Katzenbach to Lee White and Douglass Cater, December 17, 1965 (executive file HU2–5/ST13 LG/Chicago FG135 FA2, Lyndon B. Johnson Presidential Library); Orfield, *The Reconstruction of Southern Education*, pp. 195, 203; Anderson and Pickering, *Confronting the Color Line*, p. 181.
31. *Chicago Daily News*, October 6, 1965; interview with Douglass Cater; interview with Francis Keppel, April 21, 1969 (Lyndon B. Johnson Presidential Library); Orfield, *The Reconstruction of Southern Education*, pp. 152–53, 200.
32. Radio interview with Richard J. Daley, April 16, 1965 (Len O'Connor Papers, box 57, tape 4, Chicago Historical Society); King quoted from Garrow, *Bearing the Cross*, p. 448.

6. Confrontation with King

1. Bruce Cook, "King in Chicago," *Commonweal* 84 (April 29, 1966), pp. 175–76; Bayard Rustin quoted in Stephen B. Oates, *Let the Trumpet Sound: The Life of Martin Luther King Jr.* (New York: New American Library, 1982), p. 379; Royko, *Boss*, p. 150.
2. Daley quoted from Kennedy, *Himself!* p. 201, from Anderson and Pickering, *Confronting the Color Line*, pp. 191–92, and from Kennedy, *Himself!* pp. 200–201.
3. Garrow, *Bearing the Cross*, pp. 456–60; Paul Good, "Chicago Summer," *Nation* 203 (September 19, 1966), p. 238.
4. *Chicago Tribune*, January 27, 1966; quotations from Oates, *Let the*

Trumpet Sound, p. 388; David L. Lewis, *King: A Biography* (Urbana: University of Illinois Press, 1978), pp. 315–16.

5. Daley quoted from Kennedy, *Himself!* p. 200; King quoted from Gleason, *Daley of Chicago,* p. 42; *Chicago Tribune,* February 10, 1966; observer quoted in Ralph, *Northern Protest,* p. 86.

6. Daley and Parsons quoted in Kennedy, *Himself!* p. 201; Garrow, *Bearing the Cross,* p. 466.

7. *Chicago Tribune,* March 19, 1966; Oates, *Let the Trumpet Sound,* p. 393; Daley quoted from Kennedy, *Himself!* p. 202.

8. King quoted from Oates, *Let the Trumpet Sound,* p. 394; Lewis, *King,* pp. 314–15.

9. *Chicago Tribune,* June 13, 14, 1966; Daley quoted from Royko, *Boss,* p. 152.

10. Anderson and Pickering, *Confronting the Color Line,* pp. 193–94.

11. Oates, *Let the Trumpet Sound,* p. 406; Andrew Young quoted in Lewis, *King,* p. 331.

12. Lewis, *King,* pp. 331–32; Gleason, *Daley of Chicago,* p. 45; *Chicago Tribune,* July 11, 1966; *Chicago Daily News,* July 11, 1966; Lewis, *King,* pp. 332–33 (King quoted on p. 332).

13. *Chicago Tribune* and *Chicago Daily News,* July 12, 1966; Garrow, *Bearing the Cross,* p. 492; Daley quoted from Kennedy, *Himself!* p. 206.

14. King quoted from *Chicago Tribune,* July 12, 1966; Anderson and Pickering, *Confronting the Color Line,* p. 208; *Chicago Defender,* July 12, 1966; Daley quoted from Kennedy, *Himself!* p. 207.

15. *Chicago Defender,* July 12, 1966; Daley quoted from *Chicago Tribune,* July 12, 1966, and from Garrow, *Bearing the Cross,* p. 493.

16. Royko, *Boss,* p. 153; Gleason, *Daley of Chicago,* p. 46; Ralph, *Northern Protest,* p. 112.

17. Daley quoted from *Chicago Tribune,* July 16, 1966; Gleason, *Daley of Chicago,* p. 47.

18. Joe Califano to Lyndon B. Johnson, July 15, 1966, memorandum (executive file, HU2/ST13, Lyndon B. Johnson Presidential Library, Austin, Texas); Good, "Chicago Summer," p. 240.

19. *Chicago Tribune,* August 1, 4, 1966; Ralph, *Northern Protest,* pp. 119–22; Daley quoted in Garrow, *Bearing the Cross,* p. 499.

20. *Chicago Tribune,* August 1, 6, 1966; King quoted in Oates, *Let the Trumpet Sound,* p. 413; Ralph, *Northern Protest,* pp. 132–33.

21. Good, "Chicago Summer," pp. 238, 241; King quoted in Kennedy, *Himself!* p. 209.

22. Kathleen Connolly, "The Chicago Open-Housing Conference," in David J. Garrow, ed., *Chicago 1966: Open Housing Marches, Summit Negotiations, and Operation Breadbasket* (New York: Carlson, 1989), p. 65; "Victory in the North," *Newsweek* 68 (September 5, 1966), p. 21; Lemann, *The Promised Land,* p. 238; Daley quoted in Royko, *Boss,* p. 156.

23. Anderson and Pickering, *Confronting the Color Line,* p. 235.

24. King quoted in Oates, *Let the Trumpet Sound*, p. 414; Cicero politician quoted in Royko, *Boss*, p. 156.

25. Lewis, *King*, p. 341; Garrow, *Bearing the Cross*, p. 503; *Chicago Tribune*, August 13, 15, 17, 1966.

26. *Chicago Tribune*, August 18, 1966; Daley's opening remarks quoted in Garrow, *Bearing the Cross*, pp. 503–4; King and Daley quoted in David J. Garrow, *Chicago 1966*, p. 116.

27. Daley, McKnight, and Charles Swibel quoted in John McKnight, "The Summit Negotiations: Chicago, August 17, 1966–August 26, 1966," in Garrow, *Chicago 1966*, p. 122; Daley to Beatty quoted in *Chicago Daily News*, August 27, 1966.

28. *Chicago Tribune*, August 18, 1966; real estate board quoted in Garrow, *Bearing the Cross*, p. 509; Beatty quoted in McKnight, "The Summit Negotiations," p. 123; Daley quoted in Garrow, *Bearing the Cross*, pp. 509, 512.

29. Albert Raby quoted in Garrow, *Bearing the Cross*, p. 512; King quoted in Anderson and Pickering, *Confronting the Color Line*, p. 255; Connolly, "The Chicago Open-Housing Conference," p. 79.

30. Ralph Metcalfe quoted in Connolly, "The Chicago Open-Housing Conference," p. 84; King quoted in *Chicago Sun-Times*, August 20, 1966; Daley quoted in McKnight, "The Summit Negotiations," p. 143.

31. *Chicago Tribune*, August 22, 24, 25, 1966.

32. Judy Coburn, "Open City," *New Republic* 155 (September 17, 1966), p. 10; King and Daley quoted in "Still King," *Christian Century* 83 (September 7, 1966), p. 1071. The *Chicago Tribune*, August 27, 1966, contains the full text of the agreement. A march was held in Cicero on September 4, led by the Chicago chapter of the Congress on Racial Equality (CORE). Neither King nor Daley participated (*Chicago Tribune*, September 5, 1966).

33. *Chicago Sun-Times*, August 30, 1966; Coburn, "Open City," p. 10; civil rights activist quoted in Oates, *Let the Trumpet Sound*, p. 416; Thomas Keane quoted in Anderson and Pickering, *Confronting the Color Line*, p. 297.

34. Garrow, *Bearing the Cross*, pp. 535–36; *Chicago Daily News*, December 6, 1966; Raby quoted in Oates, *Let the Trumpet Sound*, p. 418.

35. Good, "Chicago Summer," *Nation*, pp. 237–42; "Still King," *Christian Century*, pp. 1071–72; "Victory in the North," *Newsweek* 68 (September 5, 1966), p. 21.

36. Oates, *Let the Trumpet Sound*, pp. 418–19; Good, "Chicago Summer," p. 242 (King quoted on p. 240).

37. Anderson and Pickering, *Confronting the Color Line*, pp. 323–24; Ralph, *Northern Protest*, pp. 204–6, 311 n. 29.

38. Rakove, *We Don't Want Nobody Nobody Sent*, pp. 279–91; Royko, *Boss*, pp. 160–63 (committeemen quoted on p. 160); Condit, *Chicago, 1930–1970*, p. 129; *Chicago Daily News*, April 5, 1967. The *Chicago Defender*, the city's primary black newspaper, endorsed Daley (*Chicago Defender*, April 3, 1967).

39. Daley quoted in *Chicago Tribune*, April 5, 1967; O'Connor, *Clout*, p.

196; *Chicago Daily News,* April 5, 1967.

40. O'Connor, *Clout,* p. 196; William J. Grimshaw, "The Daley Legacy: A Declining Politics of Party, Race, and Public Unions," in Gove and Masotti, *After Daley,* 65–66.

41. Daley quoted in Cunningham, *Urban Leadership in the Sixties,* p. 43, and in Royko, *Boss,* p. 164.

42. Daley quoted in Royko, *Boss,* p. 164; Earl Bush quoted in Grimshaw, *Bitter Fruit,* p. 125.

7. The Law and Order Mayor

1. The National Advisory Commission on Civil Disorders, *Report of the National Advisory Commission on Civil Disorders* (New York: Bantam, 1968), pp. 112–16; Matusow, *The Unraveling of America,* p. 363.

2. George A. Ranney Jr., "Illinois," *Atlantic* 221 (May 1968), pp. 22–28; Royko, *Boss,* p. 164.

3. Victor De Grazia, Roman Pucinski, and reporter quoted from "A City Run by a 'Machine,'" *U.S. News and World Report* 64 (February 12, 1968), p. 47; Daley quoted in Kennedy, *Himself!* p. 213.

4. Jerry Lipson, "Fear and Force in Chicago," *Reporter* 38 (May 2, 1968), pp. 29–30; Dan Cordtz, "Mayor Daley Battles a New Chicago Fire," *Fortune* 78 (July 1968), pp. 71, 112; O'Connor, *Clout,* p. 201; "Chicago Regrets," *New Republic* 158 (April 20, 1968), pp. 13–15.

5. Orfield, *The Reconstruction of Southern Education,* p. 204; Herrick, *The Chicago Schools,* pp. 343–49; Peterson, *School Politics Chicago Style,* p. 144.

6. Daley quoted in *Chicago Tribune,* September 6, 1967, and January 30, 1968; Lipson, "Fear and Force in Chicago," p. 30.

7. Herrick, *The Chicago Schools,* pp. 358–62; O'Connor, *Clout,* pp. 204–5.

8. Lemann, *The Promised Land,* p. 245.

9. Fish, *Black Power/White Control,* pp. 139–62; Leon Despres quoted in *Chicago Tribune,* August 1, 1968.

10. Daley quoted in Lipson, "Fear and Force in Chicago," p. 29, and in Gleason, *Daley of Chicago,* pp. 51–52; Jackson quoted in Gleason, *Daley of Chicago,* p. 52.

11. "Report of the Chicago Riot Study Committee to the Honorable Richard J. Daley," August 1, 1968, pp. 6–12; David Sullivan quoted in Kennedy, *Himself!* p. 215; Daley quoted in *Chicago Tribune,* April 6, 1968.

12. Gleason, *Daley of Chicago,* p. 59.

13. Ibid., p. 57; "Report of the Chicago Riot Study Committee," pp. 16–18; Daley quoted in Kennedy, *Himself!* p. 217.

14. Daley quoted in Gleason, *Daley of Chicago,* p. 62; "Report of the Chicago Riot Study Committee," pp. 36–37; Frank Sullivan, *Legend: The Only Inside Story about Mayor Richard J. Daley* (Chicago: Bonus Books, 1989), p. 32.

15. *Chicago Tribune,* April 16, 1968.

16. Ibid.

17. *Chicago Daily News*, April 17, 1968.

18. *Chicago Tribune*, April 16, 17, 1968; "Report of the Chicago Riot Study Committee," pp. 38–41.

19. Daley quoted in *Chicago Sun-Times*, April 18, 1968; Earl Bush quoted in Dan Cordtz, "Mayor Daley's Mouthpiece," *New Republic* 159 (September 21, 1968), p. 17; Kennedy, *Himself!* p. 221.

20. Gleason, *Daley of Chicago*, p. 80; Royko, *Boss*, p. 170.

21. Cop quoted in David Farber, *Chicago, '68* (Chicago: University of Chicago Press, 1988), p. 135; Daley quoted in Royko, *Boss*, p. 173.

22. Farber, *Chicago, '68*, pp. 115–17; Theodore H. White, *The Making of the President, 1968* (New York: Atheneum, 1969), p. 260.

23. White, *The Making of the President*, p. 260; Royko, *Boss*, p. 172; Farber, *Chicago, '68*, pp. 116–17; interview with Tommy Lyons.

24. *Chicago Tribune*, April 28, 1968; Royko, *Boss*, pp. 173–77; Joseph L. Sander, "A Study in Law and Order," *Nation* 206 (May 20, 1968), p. 657.

25. Report quoted in Farber, *Chicago, '68*, p. 96; Daley quoted in Kennedy, *Himself!* p. 223; Clark Kissinger quoted in Sander, "Study in Law and Order," p. 657.

26. *Yippie* was a light-hearted acronym for the Youth International Party, a new organization formed by Abbie Hoffman and Jerry Rubin to merge anti-war politics with the hippie lifestyle.

27. Lewis Chester, Godfrey Hodgson, and Bruce Page, *An American Melodrama: The Presidential Campaign of 1968* (New York: Viking Press, 1969), p. 120; Kennedy, *Himself!* p. 212; White, *The Making of the President*, p. 159; Daley quoted in *Chicago Sun-Times*, "Mayor Daley Remembered," special reprint, undated, p. 9.

28. Royko, *Boss*, p. 179; Gleason, *Daley of Chicago*, pp. 190–91; Farber, *Chicago, '68*, p. 153; Daniel Walker, *Rights in Conflict: The Violent Confrontation of Demonstrators and Police in the Parks and Streets of Chicago during the Week of the Democratic National Convention of 1968* (New York: Signet, 1968), pp. 67–68, 105–6.

29. Walker, *Rights in Conflict*, pp. 52–56; Earl Bush quoted in Farber, *Chicago, '68*, p. 151.

30. Walker, *Rights in Conflict*, pp. 45–51; Farber, *Chicago, '68*, pp. 101–12, 176.

31. Royko, *Boss*, pp. 180–81; Daley quoted in Farber, *Chicago, '68*, p. 157; *Chicago Tribune*, August 21, 1968; Walker, *Rights in Conflict*, p. 46.

32. Farber, *Chicago, '68*, pp. 41, 135 (quotation), 147, 150; Lois Wille, "The Secret Police in Chicago," *Chicago Journalism Review* 2 (February 1969), pp. 7–9.

33. *Chicago Tribune*, August 15, 18, 1968; Chester, Hodgson, and Page, *An American Melodrama*, p. 522; Yippies quoted in Walker, *Rights in Conflict*, p. 113.

34. *Chicago Tribune*, August 15, 1968; Royko, *Boss*, p. 182.

35. *Chicago Tribune*, August 23, 1968.

36. Gleason, *Daley of Chicago*, pp. 187–88, 212–13; *Chicago Tribune*, July

23, 1968; Daley quoted in *New York Times,* July 23, 1968.

37. Gleason, *Daley of Chicago,* pp. 238–39; *New York Times,* August 23, 1968; Kennedy, *Himself!* pp. 228–29; Walker, *Rights in Conflict,* p. 267.

38. Kennedy quoted in Kennedy, *Himself!* p. 214.

39. Royko, *Boss,* pp. 183–84; Kennedy, *Himself!* pp. 225, 229–31; White, *The Making of the President,* p. 283.

40. Royko, *Boss,* p. 183; Eugene McCarthy quoted in Norman Mailer, *Miami and the Seige of Chicago: An Informal History of the Republican and Democratic Conventions of 1968* (New York: World Publishing Company, 1968), p. 100.

41. Walker, *Rights in Conflict,* pp. 84–88; *New York Times,* August 25, 1968; White, *The Making of the President,* p. 326.

42. Walker, *Rights in Conflict,* pp. 131–37; *Chicago Tribune,* August 26, 1968; policeman quoted in Farber, *Chicago, '68,* p. 185; Daley quoted in Royko, *Boss,* pp. 186–87.

43. Police quoted in Royko, *Boss,* p. 187; Gleason, *Daley of Chicago,* pp. 314–15; Walker, *Rights in Conflict,* pp. 140–59; Todd Gitlin, *The Sixties: Years of Hope, Days of Rage* (New York: Bantam Books, 1987), p. 327; Daley quoted in Gleason, *Daley of Chicago,* pp. 315–16.

44. Gleason, *Daley of Chicago,* p. 322; Farber, *Chicago, '68,* pp. 192–93; Walker, *Rights in Conflict,* pp. 162–78.

45. Matusow, *The Unraveling of America,* p. 416.

46. Royko, *Boss,* pp. 183–84; Gleason, *Daley of Chicago,* pp. 289–94.

47. Bill Gleason, *Daley of Chicago,* pp. 319–20.

48. Walker, *Rights in Conflict,* pp. 190–202; Chester, Hodgson, and Page, *An American Melodrama,* p. 582; Gleason, *Daley of Chicago,* pp. 330–31.

49. Walker, *Rights in Conflict,* pp. 207–54; Gleason, *Daley of Chicago,* p. 331; *Chicago Tribune,* August 29, 1968.

50. White, *The Making of the President,* p. 300; Gitlin, *The Sixties,* p. 333.

51. Colorado delegation chairman quoted in Royko, *Boss,* p. 188; Gleason, *Daley of Chicago,* p. 334; Abraham Ribicoff quoted in Mailer, *Miami and the Seige of Chicago,* p. 180.

52. *Chicago Sun-Times,* "Mayor Daley Remembered," p. 7; Ribicoff quoted in Mailer, *Miami and the Siege of Chicago,* p. 181; Frank Mankiewicz quoted in Royko, *Boss,* p. 190.

53. "A Statement by Mayor Richard J. Daley to the Delegates of the Democratic National Convention, August 29, 1968," Records of the National Commission on the Causes and Prevention of Violence (series 59, box 8, folder A 231–44, Lyndon B. Johnson Library, Austin, Texas); Gleason, *Daley of Chicago,* pp. 343–48; Royko, *Boss,* pp. 190–91; Daley quoted in *Chicago Daily News,* September 6, 1968.

54. Rakove, *Don't Make No Waves,* p. 59.

55. White, *The Making of the President,* pp. 308–10; Walker, *Rights in Conflict,* pp. 310–13.

56. "Chicago: The Reassessment," *Time* 92 (September 13, 1968), p. 20;

Daley quoted in *New York Times*, August 30, 1968, and in "Daley's Defense," *Time* 92 (September 20, 1968), p. 27; O'Connor, *Clout*, pp. 206–9; Chester, Hodgson, and Page, *An American Melodrama*, pp. 601–2; Walker, *Rights in Conflict*, pp. 316–19; official report quoted in O'Connor, *Clout*, p. 207.

57. Chicago businessman quoted in "Chicago: The Reassessment," p. 21; *New York Times*, August 30, 1968.

58. Walker, *Rights in Conflict*, pp. ix, xix; Daley quoted in Chester, Hodgson, and Page, *An American Melodrama*, p. 603.

59. Farber, *Chicago, '68*, p. 205; "Chicago: The Reassessment," p. 21; Gleason, *Daley of Chicago*, p. 350.

60. Gleason, *Daley of Chicago*, p. 349; Nelson Algren quoted in "The Fear of Violence," *Nation* 207 (September 16, 1968), p. 228.

61. Daley quoted in Sullivan, *Legend*, p. 54; interview with Adlai E. Stevenson III.

62. O'Connor, *Clout*, p. 212; Royko, *Boss*, p. 195.

63. Humphrey quoted in *New York Times*, September 1, 1968; Humphrey and Daley quoted in "Of Hearts and Spleen," *Time* 93 (March 14, 1969), p. 28; Royko, *Boss*, pp. 195–96.

64. Interview with Tommy Lyons; interview with Ken Sain, May 7, 1991, Chicago, Illinois.

65. Interviews with Adlai Stevenson III, Tommy Lyons, and Ken Sain; Kennedy, *Himself!* pp. 222–38.

66. Daley quoted in Kennedy, *Himself!* p. 244.

8. Daley on Trial

1. Dr. Eric Oldberg quoted in "Chicago's Daley: How to Run a City," *Newsweek* 77 (April 5, 1971), p. 83; "Democrats against Daley," *Time* 93 (February 21, 1969), p. 20.

2. Royko, *Boss*, p. 195; "Chicago Voters Tilt Mayor Daley's Machine," *Commonweal* 90 (April 25, 1969), pp. 157–58; *New York Times*, March 12 (Dawson quote), April 9, 1969; Daley quoted in Kennedy, *Himself!* p. 242; "Porcupine Power," *Newsweek* 73 (April 21, 1969), p. 61; *Chicago Tribune*, April 9, 1969.

3. *New York Times*, April 9, 1969; "Chicago Voters Tilt Mayor Daley's Machine," pp. 157–58.

4. HUD quotation in Fish, *Black Power/White Control*, p. 240; Lemann, *The Promised Land*, p. 250.

5. Daley and Despres quotations in Fish, *Black Power/White Control*, pp. 268–69; Washnis, *Municipal Decentralization*, p. 128; Lemann, *The Promised Land*, p. 250.

6. Romney and Hyde quotations in Fish, *Black Power/White Control*, p. 273; Fuchs, *Mayors and Money*, p. 265.

7. Erwin France quoted from Lemann, *The Promised Land*, p. 250.

8. Ibid., p. 251. See also William Julius Wilson, *The Truly Disadvantaged*

(Chicago: University of Chicago Press, 1987).

9. Elizabeth Warren, *The Legacy of Judicial Policy-Making: Gautreaux v. Chicago Housing Authority, the Decision and Its Impacts* (New York: University Press of America, 1988), pp. 12–18; Bowly, *The Poorhouse*, p. 189.

10. Quotations are from Warren, *Legacy of Judicial Policy-Making*, pp. 24, 30; Bowly, *The Poorhouse*, p. 190.

11. *Chicago Tribune*, July 2, 1969; Swibel and Daley quoted in "Public Housing in Black and White," *Commonweal* 90 (May 16, 1969), p. 254.

12. *New York Times*, July 2, 1969; Bowly, *The Poorhouse*, pp. 190–91; "A Landmark Ruling," *Newsweek* 74 (July 14, 1969), p. 74; deVise, "Descent from the Summit," p. 65.

13. "A Landmark Ruling," p. 74.

14. U.S. Congress, House Committee on Government Operations, *The Gautreaux Decision and Its Effect on Subsidized Housing: Hearing before a Subcommittee of the Committee on Government Operations, Held in Chicago*, 95th Cong., 2nd sess., September 22, 1978 (Washington, D.C.: Government Printing Office, 1979), p. 7; Swibel quoted in Condit, *Chicago, 1930–1970*, p. 166; interview with Devereaux Bowly Jr.; Kleppner, *Chicago Divided*, pp. 47, 49 (Judge Austin quotation).

15. Larry David Nachman, "'The Conspiracy' on Trial," *Nation* 208 (June 16, 1969), p. 752; Gitlin, *The Sixties*, p. 342.

16. "A Mockery of Justice?" *Newsweek* 74 (October 27, 1969), p. 41.

17. "Back to Chicago," *Newsweek* 74 (October 6, 1969), p. 81 (first and second quotations); "Julius the Just," *Time* 94 (October 24, 1969), p. 75 (third quotation); "A Mockery of Justice?" p. 41 (fourth and fifth quotations).

18. *Chicago Daily News*, October 9–10, 1969; *Chicago Tribune*, October 9–12, 1969; "Poor Climate for Weathermen," *Time* 94 (October 17, 1969), pp. 24–25.

19. "Disorder in the Court," *Time* 94 (November 7, 1969), pp. 27–28; Harry Kalven Jr., "Chicago Howler," *New Republic* 162 (March 7, 1970), p. 23.

20. *New York Times*, January 7, 1970; Hoffman quoted in "Witness for the Defense," *Time* 95 (January 19, 1970), p. 17.

21. Daley quoted in *New York Times*, January 7, 1970; *Chicago Daily News*, January 7, 1970; Foran and Daley quoted in "Daley on the Stand," *Newsweek* 75 (January 19, 1970), p. 24.

22. Harry Kalven Jr., "Chicago Howler," p. 23; Daley quoted in Gleason, *Daley of Chicago*, p. 363.

23. *Chicago Tribune*, December 5, 1969; "Shoot It Out," *Newsweek* 74 (December 15, 1969), p. 37; Jon R. Waltz, "Mayor Daley's Way with Justice," *Nation* 213 (November 8, 1971), p. 461; Sergeant Groth quoted in *New York Times*, December 6, 1969.

24. "Shoot It Out," p. 37; *New York Times*, December 6, 1969.

25. *Chicago Tribune*, December 6, 1969; Christopher Chandler, "Black Panther Killings in Chicago," *New Republic* 162 (January 10, 1970), p. 24; "Shoot It Out," p. 37; Waltz, "Mayor Daley's Way with Justice," p. 461.

26. Waltz, "Mayor Daley's Way with Justice," pp. 461–62.
27. *Chicago Tribune,* May 16, 1970; Nathan Lewin, "Justice Cops Out," *New Republic* 162 (June 6, 1970), p. 14; grand jury report quoted in "Questions Remain," *Time* 95 (May 25, 1970), p. 26; Waltz, "Mayor Daley's Way with Justice," p. 462; Chandler, "Black Panther Killings in Chicago," p. 23.
28. Lewin, "Justice Cops Out," p. 18; "Questions Remain," p. 26; Kenneth O'Reilly, *"Racial Matters": The FBI's Secret File on Black America, 1960–1972* (New York: The Free Press, 1989), pp. 314–15.
29. Waltz, "Mayor Daley's Way with Justice," pp. 462–65; O'Connor, *Clout,* p. 223; *Chicago Tribune* quoted in Waltz, "Mayor Daley's Way with Justice," p. 466.
30. Waltz, "Mayor Daley's Way with Justice," pp. 463–68; *Chicago Tribune,* August 25, 1971; "Victory for Fast Eddie," *Time* 100 (November 6, 1972), p. 50.
31. "Clearing the Slate," *Newsweek* 79 (January 3, 1972), p. 14; Ralph Whitehead Jr., "All in the (Daley) Family," *Commonweal* 95 (February 11, 1972), pp. 437–38; "Mangled Machine," *Time* 99 (April 3, 1972), p. 14; O'Connor, *Clout,* p. 254.
32. Interview with Adlai E. Stevenson III.
33. Ibid.
34. *Chicago Tribune,* November 4, 1970; Royko, *Boss,* pp. 201–3.
35. Kleppner, *Chicago Divided,* p. 48; "Chicago's Daley: How to Run a City," *Newsweek* 77 (April 5, 1971), pp. 81–82; Warren, *Legacy of Judicial Policy-Making,* p. 41.
36. Squires, Bennett, McCourt, and Nyden, *Chicago,* p. 81; "Daley's Magic," *Newsweek* 77 (January 25, 1971), p. 52.
37. "A Challenge to Daley," *Time* 97 (April 5, 1971), p. 14; Rakove, *We Don't Want Nobody Nobody Sent,* p. 293; Richard Friedman quoted in "Chicago's Daley," p. 83; *Chicago Tribune,* April 7, 1971.
38. "Mayor Daley's Flip-Flop," *New Republic* 164 (May 29, 1971), pp. 15–16; "Chicago's Daley," pp. 81–84; Daley quoted in *Chicago Tribune,* April 7, 1971; IVI quoted in Allswang, *Bosses, Machines, and Urban Voters,* p. 139; *Chicago Daily News,* April 5, 1971. Despite the mayor's opposition to desegregation, he received the *Chicago Defender's* endorsement (*Chicago Defender,* April 5, 1971).
39. "Chicago's Daley," pp. 81–82 (Louis Masotti and Earl Bush quoted on p. 82); *Chicago Tribune,* April 7, 1971; Allswang, *Bosses, Machines, and Urban Voters,* pp. 139–40; wag quoted in Royko, *Boss,* p. 215.
40. Quotation from "Chicago's Daley," p. 84.

9. Awash in a Sea of Scandal

1. Mathewson, *Up against Daley,* p. 184.
2. Daley quoted in *New York Times,* July 25, 1971; interview with Dick Simpson.

3. Fuchs, *Mayors and Money*, p. 255; Erie, *Rainbow's End*, pp. 152–53; Anne Freedman, "Doing Battle with the Patronage Army: Politics, Courts, and Personnel Administration in Chicago," *Public Administration Review* 48 (September–October 1988), pp. 847–49.

4. Fuchs, *Mayors and Money*, p. 255; Erie, *Rainbow's End*, pp. 152–53; Anne Freedman, "Doing Battle with the Patronage Army," pp. 847–49; Alfredo S. Lanier, "Disbanding the Patronage Army," *Chicago* 32 (December 1983), p. 234.

5. *Chicago Tribune*, March 22, 1972; "Clearing the Slate," *Newsweek* 79 (January 3, 1972), p. 14; Whitehead, "All in the (Daley) Family," pp. 437–38; "Mangled Machine," *Time* 99 (April 3, 1972), p. 14; David L. Protess, "Banfield's Chicago Revisited: The Conditions for and Social Policy Implications of the Transformation of a Political Machine," *Social Service Review* 48 (June 1974), p. 197; "Chicago's Daley: 'His Back to the Wall,'" *U.S. News and World Report* 72 (April 3, 1972), p. 28; Daley quoted in O'Connor, *Clout*, p. 222.

6. Robert E. Hartley, *Big Jim Thompson of Illinois* (Chicago: Rand McNally, 1979), pp. 43–44, 59; O'Connor, *Clout*, p. 223; Kennedy, *Himself!* p. 258.

7. Daley quoted in "The Foot-Dragging in Daley's Chicago," *Business Week* (October 9, 1971), p. 24; Warren, *Legacy of Judicial Policy-Making*, p. 53.

8. *Chicago Tribune*, May 12, 1972; "A Precedent-Setting Ruling in Chicago," *Business Week* (January 8, 1972), p. 22; Warren, *Legacy of Judicial Policy-Making*, p. 53.

9. Suttles, *The Man-Made City*, p. 189.

10. *Chicago Tribune*, July 11, 1972; Mathewson, *Up against Daley*, p. 203; Anna Langford quoted in Ken Bode, "The Chicago Challenge," *New Republic* 166 (May 27, 1972), p. 15.

11. O'Connor, *Clout*, pp. 213–14.

12. Daley quoted in *Chicago Tribune*, July 9, 1972; *Chicago Daily News*, July 11, 1972; Bode, "The Chicago Challenge," p. 15.

13. Daley quoted in *Chicago Tribune*, July 1, 1972; Singer quoted in O'Connor, *Clout*, p. 214; Daley quoted in Kennedy, *Himself!* p. 248.

14. Royko quoted in Mathewson, *Up against Daley*, p. 213; interview with Tommy Lyons.

15. Kennedy, *Himself!* pp. 248–50; O'Connor, *Clout*, pp. 215–16.

16. *Chicago Tribune*, July 9, 1972; Kennedy, *Himself!* pp. 249–50.

17. O'Connor, *Clout*, p. 216.

18. Ibid., p. 217; *Chicago Daily News*, July 11, 1972; *Chicago Tribune*, July 12, 15, 17, 1972.

19. *Chicago Tribune*, July 15, 1972; John Touhy quoted in Kennedy, *Himself!* p. 251.

20. O'Connor, *Clout*, p. 219; interview with Tommy Lyons.

21. "Daley's Debacle," *Newsweek* 80 (November 20, 1972), p. 31; Suttles, *The Man-Made City*, pp. 188–89; Protess, "Banfield's Chicago Revisited," pp. 196–97; Michael Howlett quoted in O'Connor, *Clout*, pp. 226–27.

22. Milton Pikarsky, "Chicago's Crosstown Expressway: The Team

Concept in Action," in National Academy of Engineering, *The Engineer and the City* (Washington, D.C.: National Academy of Engineering, 1969), pp. 65–75; Elliott Arthur Pavlos, "Chicago's Crosstown: A Case Study in Urban Expressways," in David R. Miller, ed., *Urban Transportation Policy: New Perspectives* (Lexington, Mass.: Lexington Books, 1972), pp. 61–64; O'Connor, *Clout*, pp. 242–45; Black, "The Renewed Negro and Urban Renewal," p. 66; interview with Dick Simpson.

23. Daley quoted in *Chicago Tribune*, January 18, 1973; ibid., February 15, 1973; Kennedy, *Himself!* pp. 253–54 (Daley quoted on p. 254);

24. *New York Times*, October 11, 1973; O'Connor, *Clout*, p. 243.

25. *New York Times*, February 8, 1974; Marshall and Daley quoted in Kleppner, *Chicago Divided*, pp. 85–86.

26. Hartley, *Big Jim Thompson of Illinois*, p. 61.

27. Ibid., p. 62; *Chicago Sun-Times* clipping, December 21, 1973 (BGA Papers, box 56, folder "Daley, Richard J., 1973," Chicago Historical Society, Chicago, Illinois); *New York Times* clipping, April 16, 1974 (BGA Papers, box 56, folder "Daley, Richard J., 1974*-"); Daley quoted in O'Connor, *Clout*, p. 250.

28. Hartley, *Big Jim Thompson of Illinois*, p. 62; Kennedy, *Himself!* pp. 258–59; Daley quoted in Michael Kirkhorn, "Chicago Looks beyond Daley," *Nation* 218 (June 29, 1974), p. 812.

29. Daley quoted in Kennedy, *Himself!* p. 259; interview with Tommy Lyons.

30. O'Connor, *Clout*, pp. 228–33; Kennedy, *Himself!* pp. 263–64.

31. O'Connor, *Clout*, pp. 236–38.

32. Ibid., pp. 239, 246; Hartley, *Big Jim Thompson of Illinois*, p. 63.

33. Daley quoted in "Daley's Halo Slips," *Economist* 252 (July 20, 1974), p. 46; *Chicago Sun-Times*, July 11, 1974; *Chicago Tribune*, September 4, 1974; "Statement of J. Terrence Brunner, Executive Director," July 12, 1974 (BGA Papers, box 56, folder "Daley, Richard J., May, 1964*-").

34. *Chicago Tribune*, September 4, 1974; Hartley, *Big Jim Thompson of Illinois*, p. 63.

35. *Chicago Tribune*, October 10, 12, 1974; Singer quoted in O'Connor, *Clout*, p. 255.

36. O'Connor, *Clout*, pp. 251, 256.

37. Ben Heineman quoted in "Challenging Hizzoner," *Time* 105 (February 24, 1975), p. 18; *Chicago Sun-Times* quoted in Sidney Lens, "Mayor Daley's Last Hurrah," *Progressive* 39 (April 1975), p. 18.

38. O'Connor, *Clout*, p. 254.

39. Ibid., p. 253; Metcalfe quoted from interview with Don Rose; Grimshaw, *Bitter Fruit*, p. 137.

40. Michael Kirkhorn, "Daley Does It," *New Republic* 172 (March 8, 1975), pp. 10–11; Grimshaw, *Bitter Fruit*, p. 126.

41. Daley quoted in "Challenging Hizzoner," p. 18; *Chicago Tribune*, February 26, 1975; Kleppner, *Chicago Divided*, p. 83.

42. Rakove, *We Don't Want Nobody Nobody Sent*, pp. 298–305; Royko quoted in Lens, "Mayor Daley's Last Hurrah," p. 16; Allswang, *Bosses, Machines, and Urban Voters*, p. 132; *Chicago Tribune*, April 2, 1975; John Hoellen quoted in *Chicago Daily News*, April 2, 1975.

43. Suttles, *The Man-Made City*, pp. 193–94; Daley quoted in "The Last of a Breed," *Newsweek* 89 (January 3, 1977), p. 60. From 1955 to 1975 Daley received an annual salary of $35,000; in 1975, the sum was increased to $60,000 (*New York Times*, December 5, 1979).

10. The City That Works

1. Teaford, *Rough Road to Renaissance*, p. 170; Fuchs, *Mayors and Money*, p. 273. On Lindsay, see John V. Lindsay, *The City* (New York: W. W. Norton, 1969); Nat Hentoff, *A Political Life: The Education of John V. Lindsay* (New York: Alfred A. Knopf, 1969); Clarence N. Stone, "Complexity and the Changing Character of Executive Leadership: An Interpretation of the Lindsay Administration in New York City," *Urban Interest* 4 (fall 1982), pp. 29–50; and Robert Caro, *The Power Broker: Robert Moses and the Fall of New York* (New York: Random House, 1974).

2. Lindsay, *The City*, p. 21; Teaford, *Rough Road to Renaissance* (Teaford quoted on p. 183, Schaeffer quoted on p. 259); Virgil Martin quoted in "Dick Daley: The Business Candidate," *Business Week* (April 10, 1971), p. 82. See also Raymond D. Horton, *Municipal Labor Relations in New York City: Lessons of the Lindsay-Wagner Years* (New York: Praeger Publishers, 1972); and David W. Abbott, Louis H. Gold, and Edward T. Rogowsky, *Police, Politics, and Race: The New York City Referendum on Civilian Review* (New York: American Jewish Committee, 1969).

3. Fuchs, *Mayors and Money*, pp. 86–93; Daniel J. Walkowitz, "New York: A Tale of Two Cities," in Bernard, *Snowbelt Cities*, pp. 200–204. Also see Ken Auletta, *The Streets Were Paved with Gold: The Decline of New York—An American Tragedy* (New York: Random House, 1975).

4. Teaford, *Twentieth-Century American City*, pp. 144–46; Teaford, *Rough Road to Renaissance*, pp. 229–30.

5. Funchion, "Political and Nationalist Dimensions," p. 88.

6. Interview with Clark Burrus, May 16, 1991, Chicago, Illinois; Michael P. Conzen, "American Cities in Profound Transition: The New City Geography of the 1980s," in Raymond A. Mohl, ed., *The Making of Urban America* (Wilmington, Del.: Scholarly Resources, Inc., 1988), pp. 277–89.

7. "Chicago after Daley," undated newspaper clipping (Leon Despres Papers, box 69, folder 8, Chicago Historical Society, Chicago, Illinois); Woods Bowman, "Paying Big City Bills" (paper presented at the Richard J. Daley Conference, October 14, 1977, Chicago, Illinois); *Chicago Tribune*, May 2, 1976; interview with Clark Burrus; *New York Times*, September 9, 1975; Fuchs, *Mayors and Money*, pp. 144–45. As of 1975, eight governments (in addition to corporate Chicago) levied taxes on city residents—the Board of

Education, the Park District, the Cook County Board, the Cook County Forest Preserve District, the Metropolitan Sanitary District, the Cook County Health and Hospital Governing Commission, the Chicago Urban Transportation District, and the City Colleges of Chicago (*Chicago Tribune*, August 17, 1975).

8. Peterson, *School Politics Chicago Style*, pp. 116–18; Granger and Granger, *Lords of the Last Machine*, pp. 165–66; Fuchs, *Mayors and Money*, p. 196.

9. Bowman, "Paying Big City Bills"; Fuchs, *Mayors and Money*, p. 123.

10. Bowman, "Paying Big City Bills"; Fuchs, *Mayors and Money*, pp. 173–74, 197–98.

11. "Powers, Duties, and Purpose of the Chicago Public Building Commission," Fort Dearborn Project Papers (University of Illinois at Chicago Library, file 41); *Chicago Sun-Times*, July 2, 1956; Bowman, "Paying Big City Bills"; Fuchs, *Mayors and Money*, p. 201.

12. Leon Despres quoted in "Chicago after Daley"; *New York Times*, September 9, 1975; *Chicago Tribune*, June 25, 1978; Fuchs, *Mayors and Money*, p. 33.

13. Rakove, "Jane Byrne and the New Chicago Politics," p. 220; interview with Clark Burrus; interview with Adlai Stevenson III.

14. Aide quoted in "Dick Daley," p. 82; interview with Clark Burrus.

15. Fuchs, *Mayors and Money*, pp. 163–65.

16. Len O'Connor, *Requiem: The Decline and Demise of Mayor Daley and His Era* (Chicago: Contemporary Books, 1977), pp. 134–35; *Chicago Tribune*, June 25, 1978; Bowman, "Paying Big City Bills."

17. Teaford, *Rough Road to Renaissance*, pp. 183–90.

18. Grimshaw, "The Daley Legacy," pp. 63–64, 68–71; Derber, *Labor in Illinois*, p. 241; "Chicago after Daley"; *Chicago Tribune*, May 2, 1976.

19. Derber, *Labor in Illinois*, p. 237; Peterson, *School Politics Chicago Style*, pp. 188–92; Grimshaw, "The Daley Legacy," p. 70; William J. Grimshaw, *Union Rule in the Schools: Big-City Politics in Transformation* (Lexington, Mass.: Lexington Books, 1979), p. 112 n. 24.

20. Daley quoted in Peterson, *School Politics Chicago Style*, p. 202; Grimshaw, *Union Rule in the Schools*, pp. 48–51, 136; Grimshaw, "The Daley Legacy," pp. 80–82; Squires, Bennett, McCourt, and Nyden, *Chicago*, p. 81; A. F. Ehrbar, "Financial Probity, Chicago Style," *Fortune* 101 (June 2, 1980), p. 102; deVise, "Descent from the Summit," p. 23.

21. "The City That Survives," *Economist* 274 (March 29, 1980), p. 23; Ehrbar, "Financial Probity," p. 106; Fuchs, *Mayors and Money*, p. 258; Sidney Lens, "The City That Doesn't Work Anymore: Chicago in the Crunch," *Progressive* 44 (April 1980), p. 36.

22. "The City That Survives," p. 21; "Chicago after Daley"; Lens, "The City That Doesn't Work Anymore," p. 37.

23. Lens, "The City That Doesn't Work Anymore," pp. 36–37; interview with Don Rose; Ehrbar, "Financial Probity," p. 101; interview with

Dick Simpson.

24. Fuchs, *Mayors and Money*, p. 7 (quotations from p. 311 n. 32 and p. 29).

25. Haider quoted from Donald H. Haider, "Capital Budgeting and Planning in the Post-Daley Era," in Gove and Masotti, *After Daley*, p. 169, and in Eugene Kennedy, "Hard Times in Chicago," *New York Times Magazine*, March 9, 1980, p. 34.

26. Don Rose quoted in *New York Times*, December 19, 1979.

27. Grimshaw, "The Daley Legacy," pp. 71–75; "Wounded Lion," *Time* 108 (November 22, 1976), p. 26.

28. Suttles, *The Man-Made City*, pp. 12–13, 146–47.

29. Grimshaw, *Bitter Fruit*, pp. 134–35; Grimshaw, "The Daley Legacy," p. 77; Warren, *Legacy of Judicial Policy-Making*, p. 57.

30. *New York Times*, February 8, 1974, January 11, December 10, 1976; interview with Dick Simpson.

31. Ralph Metcalfe quoted in "How the Daley Machine Rolls," *Time* 107 (March 29, 1976), p. 14; Grimshaw, *Bitter Fruit*, pp. 136–38.

32. Kennedy, *Himself!* pp. 1–15.

33. Ibid., pp. 16–29.

11. The Battle for Chicago

1. Melvin G. Holli, "Daley to Daley," in Paul M. Green and Melvin G. Holli, eds., *Restoration 1989: Chicago Elects a New Daley* (Chicago: Lyceum, 1991), pp. 194–96; U.S. Civil Rights Commission quoted in Peter d'A. Jones, "Samuel William Yorty," in Holli and Jones, *Biographical Dictionary of American Mayors*, p. 401. See also Fine, *Violence in the Model City*; Carl B. Stokes, *Promises of Power: A Political Autobiography* (New York: Simon and Schuster, 1973); Charles R. Morris, *The Cost of Good Intentions: New York City and the Liberal Experiment, 1960–1975* (New York: W. W. Norton, 1980); and Teaford, *Rough Road to Renaissance*.

2. Kathleen A. Kemp and Robert L. Lineberry, "The Last of the Great Urban Machines and the Last of the Great Urban Mayors? Chicago Politics, 1975–1977," in Gove and Masotti, *After Daley*, p. 1; Paul M. Green, "The Chicago Political Tradition: A Mayoral Retrospective," in Green and Holli, *The Mayors*, pp. 212–14; Melvin A. Kahn and Frances J. Majors, *The Winning Ticket: Daley, the Chicago Machine, and Illinois Politics* (New York: Praeger, 1984), p. 107. On LaGuardia, see Thomas Kessner, *Fiorello LaGuardia and the Making of Modern New York* (New York: McGraw-Hill, 1989).

3. Kemp and Lineberry, "The Last of the Great Urban Machines?" p. 3; Holt, "Urban Redevelopment"; "The City That Survives," p. 24; interview with Don Rose; Pierre de Vise quoted in Lens, "Mayor Daley's Last Hurrah," p. 18; Ira Katznelson quoted in newspaper clipping (Leon Despres Papers, box 69, folder 8, Chicago Historical Society, Chicago, Illinois).

4. Rakove, "Jane Byrne and the New Chicago Politics," p. 220. On the

Kelly-Nash machine, see Biles, *Big City Boss.*

5. The classic statement of structural reform is found in Melvin G. Holli, *Reform in Detroit: Hazen S. Pingree and Urban Politics* (New York: Oxford University Press, 1969).

6. Lens, "The City That Doesn't Work Anymore," p. 37; *New York Times,* May 16, 1971; John Knight quoted in O'Connor, *A Reporter in Sweet Chicago,* p. 287.

7. Douglas Bukowski, "Big Bill Thompson: The 'Model' Politician," in Green and Holli, *The Mayors,* p. 80; deVise, "Descent from the Summit," p. 143; Condit, *Chicago, 1930–1970,* p. 141.

8. Squires, Bennett, McCourt, and Nyden, *Chicago,* p. 58; Despres quoted in Rakove, *Don't Make No Waves,* pp. 78–79; Lynn Williams quoted in Rakove, *We Don't Want Nobody Nobody Sent,* p. 256; Studs Terkel quoted in Rakove, *Don't Make No Waves,* pp. 16–17.

9. Joseph Epstein quoted in Rakove, *Don't Make No Waves,* p. 17; Halberstam, "Daley of Chicago," p. 30.

10. Funchion, "Political and Nationalist Dimensions," pp. 89–90.

11. Erie, *Rainbow's End,* p. 167.

12. Milton L. Rakove, "Observations and Reflections on the Current and Future Directions of the Chicago Democratic Machine," in Melvin G. Holli and Paul M. Green, eds., *The Making of the Mayor: Chicago, 1983* (Grand Rapids, Mich.: William B. Eerdmans, 1984), pp. 133–34; Whitehead, "The Organization Man," pp. 355–56; Hirsch, "Chicago," pp. 63–64; Kemp and Lineberry, "The Last of the Great Urban Machines?" pp. 18–23; "Chicago without a Boss," *Economist* 261 (December 25, 1976), p. 22; Protess, "Banfield's Chicago Revisited," p. 190; board of education quoted in Kleppner, *Chicago Divided,* p. 51.

13. Warren, *Legacy of Judicial Policy-Making,* p. 59; U.S. Congress, House Committee on Government Operations, *The Gautreaux Decision and Its Effect on Subsidized Housing,* pp. 126–28 (Collins and Master quoted on p. 102).

14. Bowly, *The Poorhouse,* pp. 221–23; Hirsch, *Making the Second Ghetto,* pp. 17–54.

15. Report quoted in Hirsch, "Chicago," p. 78; interview with Adlai E. Stevenson III; interview with Devereaux Bowly Jr.

16. Ehrbar, "Financial Probity," p. 102; *Chicago Sun-Times* quoted in Lens, "Mayor Daley's Last Hurrah," p. 18.

17. Ralph Whitehead, "Daley the Broker," *Chicago* 26 (February 1977), p. 186.

18. On black mayors, see Roger Biles, "Black Mayors: A Historical Assessment," *Journal of Negro History* 77 (Summer 1992), pp. 109–25.

19. Paul M. Green, "Michael A. Bilandic: The Last of the Machine Regulars," in Green and Holli, *The Mayors,* pp. 164–66.

20. Ibid., pp. 166–67; Harold Washington quoted in *Chicago Tribune,* April 18, 1977; Daniela Cornescu and Peter d'A. Jones, "Michael A. Bilandic,"

in Holli and Jones, *Biographical Dictionary of American Mayors*, p. 27.

21. Paul M. Green, "Michael A. Bilandic," pp. 168–69.

22. Roger Biles, "Jane M. Byrne," in Holli and Jones, *Biographical Dictionary of American Mayors*, p. 54; Paul M. Green, "Michael A. Bilandic," p. 169.

23. Biles, "Jane M. Byrne," p. 54.

24. Melvin G. Holli, "Jane M. Byrne: To Think the Unthinkable and Do the Undoable" in Green and Holli, *The Mayors*, pp. 174–77; *Chicago Tribune*, April 5, 1981.

25. Grimshaw, *Bitter Fruit*, pp. 147–49, 156–64.

26. Ibid., pp. 167–68.

27. Edward Vrdolyak quoted in Travis, *Autobiography of Black Politics*, p. 593; Paul M. Green, "The Primary: Some New Players—Same Old Rules," in Holli and Green, *The Making of the Mayor*, pp. 21–36; Grimshaw, *Bitter Fruit*, pp. 178–82; Holli and Green, *Bashing Chicago Traditions*, pp 9–18.

28. Grimshaw, *Bitter Fruit*, pp. 184–86, 189 (*Wall Street Journal* quoted on p. 186).

29. Ibid., pp. 190–92; Holli and Green, *Bashing Chicago Traditions*, chaps. 4 and 5.

30. Holli and Green, *Bashing Chicago Traditions*, p. 181.

31. Ibid., pp. 193–95.

32. Paul M. Green, "The 1989 Mayoral Primary Election," in Green and Holli, *Restoration 1989*, pp. 10–31.

33. Ibid., pp. 31–51 (31).

34. Holli, "Daley to Daley," in Green and Holli, *Restoration 1989*, pp. 204–6; Holli, "Daley to Daley: Richard J. to Richard M.," pp. 16–19.

35. Holli, "Daley to Daley," pp. 204–6; Holli, "Daley to Daley: Richard J. to Richard M.," pp. 16–19; Condit quoted in Suttles, *The Man-Made City*, p. 18.

BIBLIOGRAPHICAL ESSAY

Any study of the Daley mayoralty must begin with a thorough perusal of Chicago newspapers. I read the *Chicago Tribune* comprehensively and the *Chicago Daily News, Chicago Sun-Times,* and *Chicago Defender* selectively. The *New York Times* is useful in understanding how people outside Chicago viewed the mayor and his leadership. Similarly, national journals and periodicals presented a look at Daley's city from a distance. Mass-circulation magazines such as *Time, Newsweek, Life, Nation, U.S. News and World Report, Saturday Evening Post, Atlantic,* and *New Republic* frequently reported on Daley's activities. Specialized journals with smaller circulations such as the *Reporter,* the *Progressive, Christian Century, Commonweal,* and *American City* often published incisive commentaries on Chicago events.

I sought interviews with a number of politicians and government officials who lived during the Daley era. The vast majority declined to talk with me, and a good number did not even respond to my inquiries. The interviews I found most helpful—and the ones I cite in the book—were with Devereaux Bowly Jr.; Clark Burrus; Tommy Lyons; Don Rose; Ken Sain; Dick Simpson; and Adlai E. Stevenson III. The tapes and transcripts of these interviews remain in my possession.

The Daley family retains whatever papers the mayor left behind, and they are not presently accessible to scholars. Fortunately, other manuscript collections contain documents about Chicago's mayor. I contacted the Dwight D. Eisenhower, John F. Kennedy, Lyndon B. Johnson, and Richard M. Nixon Presidential Libraries in search of such materials but uncovered relatively little beyond routine correspondence. I found the most useful items in the Johnson Library, especially in correspondence and interviews dealing with the Chicago schools' desegregation crisis and in the Records of the National Commission on the Causes and Prevention of Violence. Other worthwhile manuscript collections were the CORE Papers, Cyrus Adams Papers, Leon Despres Papers, Len O'Connor Papers, and Better Government Association Papers at the Chicago Historical Society, as well as the Fort Dearborn Project Papers and a collection of Richard J. Daley speeches at the University of Illinois at Chicago Library.

Richard J. Daley has been the subject of several biographies, each of which contributes some insights into our understanding of his career. Mike Royko's *Boss: Richard J. Daley of Chicago* (New York: Signet, 1971) is beautifully written and great fun to read. Published during Daley's mayoralty by one of his most severe contemporary critics, the book has the strength of good journalism but lacks the perspective of history. Len O'Connor's *Clout: Mayor Daley and His City* (New York: Avon, 1975) was also published when Daley was still in office. More detailed if not as well written as *Boss*, it is every bit as harsh in its depiction of Daley. O'Connor's sequel, *Requiem: The Decline and Demise of Mayor Daley and His Era* (Chicago: Contemporary Books, 1977), covers the last months of the mayor's life and adopts a similarly negative tone. By contrast, Eugene Kennedy's celebratory *Himself! The Life and Times of Mayor Richard J. Daley* (New York: Viking Press, 1978) portrays Daley as a heroic Irish chieftain whose actions were determined by the need to defend his tribe. Bill Gleason's *Daley of Chicago: The Man, the Mayor, and the Limits of Conventional Politics* (New York: Simon and Schuster, 1970) is a more balanced treatment that deals perceptively with the tension between blacks and white ethnic Chicagoans. Frank Sullivan, who served for a short time as the mayor's press secretary, offers few original insights in *Legend: The Only Inside Story about Mayor Richard J. Daley* (Chicago: Bonus Books, 1989). Also see the following shorter biographical sketches: Peter J. O'Malley, "Richard J. Daley," in Melvin G. Holli and Peter d'A. Jones, eds., *Biographical Dictionary of American Mayors, 1820–1980: Big City Mayors* (Westport, Conn.: Greenwood Press, 1981), pp. 92–94, and John M. Allswang, "Richard J. Daley: America's Last Boss," in Paul M. Green and Melvin G. Holli, eds., *The Mayors: The Chicago Political Tradition* (Carbondale: Southern Illinois University Press, 1987), pp. 144–63. (Allswang's chapter in *The Mayors* is derived from his *Bosses, Machines, and Urban Voters* [Baltimore: Johns Hopkins University Press, 1986].) David Halberstam's "Daley of Chicago," *Harper's* 237 (August 1968), pp. 25–36, was an incisive profile of the mayor in his most turbulent year. Ralph Whitehead's "The Organization Man," *American Scholar* 46 (Summer 1977), pp. 351–57, analyzes how Daley balanced shifting bases of support to keep the Democratic machine in control. Edmund F. Kallina Jr.'s *Courthouse over White House: Chicago and the Presidential Election of 1960* (Orlando: University of Central Florida

Press, 1988) details Daley's role in John F. Kennedy's election. Peter Yessne's *Quotations from Mayor Daley* (New York: G. P. Putnam's Sons, 1969) is a compendium of Daley's malapropisms. Studies of the Daley machine abound, most of them written by political scientists and journalists. Milton L. Rakove, a political scientist at the University of Illinois at Chicago and a precinct captain in the Cook County Democratic organization, wrote about the political machine from an insider's perspective. His *Don't Make No Waves, Don't Back No Losers: An Insider's Analysis of the Daley Machine* (Bloomington: Indiana University Press, 1975) remains the most detailed description of how the machine operated. His *We Don't Want Nobody Nobody Sent: An Oral History of the Daley Years* (Bloomington: Indiana University Press, 1979) is a revealing collection of interviews with Daley friends and foes. Joe Mathewson's *Up against Daley* (LaSalle, Ill.: Open Court, 1974) provides the reformer's perspective. Bill Granger and Lori Granger's *Lords of the Last Machine: The Story of Politics in Chicago* (New York: Random House, 1987) is a lively and anecdotal—if not especially scholarly—account of Daley's hegemony. Steven P. Erie's *Rainbow's End: Irish-Americans and the Dilemmas of Urban Machine Politics, 1840–1985* (Berkeley: University of California Press, 1988) and Edward M. Levine's *The Irish and Irish Politicians* (Notre Dame: University of Notre Dame Press, 1966) contain some material on the Daley machine. So does Michael F. Funchion's "The Political and Nationalist Dimensions," in Lawrence J. McCaffrey, Ellen Skerrett, Michael F. Funchion, and Charles Fanning, *The Irish in Chicago* (Urbana: University of Illinois Press, 1987). David K. Fremon's *Chicago Politics Ward by Ward* (Bloomington: Indiana University Press, 1988) offers a wealth of colorful detail about Chicago politics but relatively little on Daley and his leadership. Melvin A. Kahn and Frances J. Majors's *The Winning Ticket: Daley, the Chicago Machine, and Illinois Politics* (New York: Praeger, 1984) casts the Chicago Democratic machine in the context of state politics. Some material on Daley can be culled from three broader studies by political scientists: Edward C. Banfield and James Q. Wilson, *City Politics* (Cambridge: Harvard University Press and MIT Press, 1963); James Q. Wilson, *The Amateur Democrat: Club Politics in Three Cities* (Chicago: University of Chicago Press, 1962); and Edward C. Banfield, *Political Influence* (New York: Free Press of Glencoe, 1961).

Since the mayor's death, a number of studies have contemplated the fate of the Cook County Democratic machine in the post-Daley era. See, for example, Samuel K. Gove and Louis H. Masotti's, eds.,

After Daley: Chicago Politics in Transition (Urbana: University of Illinois Press, 1982). On Chicago's first black mayor, Harold Washington, see Melvin G. Holli and Paul M. Green, eds., *The Making of the Mayor: Chicago, 1983* (Grand Rapids, Mich.: William B. Eerdmans, 1984); Melvin G. Holli and Paul M. Green, *Bashing Chicago Traditions: Harold Washington's Last Campaign* (Grand Rapids, Mich.: William B. Eerdmans, 1989); and Paul Kleppner, *Chicago Divided: The Making of a Black Mayor* (DeKalb: Northern Illinois University Press, 1985). The election of the second Mayor Daley is the subject of Paul M. Green and Melvin G. Holli's, eds., *Restoration 1989: Chicago Elects a New Daley* (Chicago: Lyceum, 1991).

Much has been written about race and politics in Chicago. For background on the Daley era, consult Allan H. Spear, *Black Chicago: The Making of a Negro Ghetto, 1890–1920* (Chicago: University of Chicago Press, 1967); Charles Branham, "Black Chicago: Accommodationist Politics before the Great Migration," in Melvin G. Holli and Peter d'A. Jones, eds., *The Ethnic Frontier: Group Survival in Chicago and the Midwest* (Grand Rapids, Mich.: William B. Eerdmans, 1977), pp. 211–62; James R. Grossman, *Land of Hope: Chicago, Black Southerners, and the Great Migration* (Chicago: University of Chicago Press, 1989); St. Clair Drake and Horace R. Cayton, *Black Metropolis: A Study of Negro Life in a Northern City* (Chicago: University of Chicago Press, 1993); Thomas Lee Philpott, *The Slum and the Ghetto: Neighborhood Deterioration and Middle-Class Reform, Chicago, 1880–1930* (New York: Oxford University Press, 1978); William M. Tuttle Jr., *Race Riot: Chicago in the Red Summer of 1919* (New York: Atheneum, 1977); Harold F. Gosnell, *Negro Politicians: The Rise of Negro Politics in Chicago* (Chicago: University of Chicago Press, 1967); James Q. Wilson, *Negro Politics: The Search for Leadership* (New York: Free Press, 1960); Otis Dudley Duncan and Beverly Duncan, *The Negro Population of Chicago: A Study of Residential Succession* (Chicago: University of Chicago Press, 1957); Roger Biles, "'Big Red in Bronzeville': Mayor Ed Kelly Reels in the Black Vote," *Chicago History* 10 (Summer 1981), pp. 99–111; and the relevant sections of Roger Biles, *Big City Boss in Depression and War: Mayor Edward J. Kelly of Chicago* (DeKalb: Northern Illinois University Press, 1984), and John M. Allswang, *A House for All Peoples: Ethnic Politics in Chicago, 1890–1936* (Lexington: University Press of Kentucky, 1971).

On black politics during the Daley era, begin with William J. Grimshaw's *Bitter Fruit: Black Politics and the Chicago Machine, 1931–1991* (Chicago: University of Chicago Press, 1992), which offers a comprehensive interpretation of black politics in twentieth-century Chicago. Also see his earlier *Black Politics in Chicago: The Quest for Leadership, 1936–1979* (Chicago: Loyola University, 1980). Dempsey Travis's *An Autobiography of Black Politics* (Chicago: Urban Research Press, 1987) contains some useful information. In *Making the Second Ghetto: Race and Housing in Chicago, 1940–1960* (Cambridge: Cambridge University Press, 1983), Arnold R. Hirsch insightfully discusses the Daley machine's role in ghetto expansion. His "Chicago: The Cook County Democratic Organization and the Dilemma of Race, 1931–1987," in Richard M. Bernard, ed., *Snowbelt Cities: Metropolitan Politics in the Northeast and Midwest since World War II* (Bloomington: Indiana University Press, 1990), is a broader-based discussion. Karl E. Taeuber and Alma F. Taeuber, *Negroes in Cities: Residential Segregation and Neighborhood Change* (Chicago: Aldine Publishing Company, 1965), complements Hirsch. For additional background on the fair housing question in Chicago, see the Chicago Commission on Human Relations, "A Report to the Mayor and City Council of Chicago on the Present Status and Effectiveness of Existing Fair Housing Practices Legislation in the U.S. as of August 31, 1967" (Chicago: The Commission, 1967). The mayor's role in housing matters is considered in Devereaux Bowly Jr.'s *The Poorhouse: Subsidized Housing in Chicago, 1895–1976* (Carbondale: Southern Illinois University Press, 1978); Thomas M. Landye and James J. Vanecko's "The Politics of Open Housing in Illinois," in Lynn W. Eley and Thomas W. Casstevens, eds., *The Politics of Fair-Housing Legislation: State and Local Case Studies* (San Francisco: Chandler, 1968); Elizabeth Warren's *The Legacy of Judicial Policy-Making: Gautreaux v. Chicago Housing Authority, the Decision and Its Impacts* (New York: University Press of America, 1988); and U.S. Congress, House Committee on Government Operations, *The Gautreaux Decision and Its Effect on Subsidized Housing: Hearing before a Subcommittee of the Committee on Government Operations,* 95th Cong., 2nd sess., September 22, 1978 (Washington, D.C.: Government Printing Office, 1979). On William Dawson, see James L. Cooper, "South Side Boss," *Chicago History* 19 (Fall–Winter 1990–1991), pp. 66–81. On Ralph Metcalfe, see Ralph Whitehead Jr., "Black Politics in Cook County," *Nation* 215 (July 10, 1972), pp. 14–16. Daley also plays a major role in Nicholas Lemann, *The Promised Land: The Great Black Migration and How It Changed America* (New York: Alfred A. Knopf, 1991).

Daley's resistance to the civil rights movement is described in a number of sources. Begin with James R. Ralph Jr.'s *Northern Protest:*

Martin Luther King Jr., Chicago, and the Civil Rights Movement (Cambridge: Harvard University Press, 1993), and Alan B. Anderson and George W. Pickering's *Confronting the Color Line: The Broken Promise of the Civil Rights Movement in Chicago* (Athens: University of Georgia Press, 1986). On the 1966 summit with King, see David J. Garrow, ed., *Chicago 1966: Open Housing Marches, Summit Negotiations, and Operation Breadbasket* (New York: Carlson, 1989); Pierre deVise, "Descent from the Summit: Race and Housing in Chicago since 1966" (Ph.D. dissertation, University of Illinois at Chicago, 1985); and the relevant portions of the following King biographies: David J. Garrow, *Bearing the Cross: Martin Luther King Jr. and the Southern Christian Leadership Conference* (New York: William Morrow, 1986); David L. Lewis, *King: A Biography* (Urbana: University of Illinois Press, 1978); and Stephen B. Oates, *Let the Trumpet Sound: The Life of Martin Luther King Jr.* (New York: New American Library, 1982). On the racial disturbances following the King assassination, see "Report of the Chicago Riot Study Committee to the Honorable Richard J. Daley," August 1, 1968. Daley's clashes with The Woodlawn Organization are detailed in John H. Fish, *Black Power/White Control: The Struggle of The Woodlawn Organization in Chicago* (Princeton: Princeton University Press, 1973), and Sanford D. Horwitt, *Let Them Call Me Rebel: Saul Alinsky—His Life and Legacy* (New York: Alfred A. Knopf, 1989). Kenneth O'Reilly's *"Racial Matters": The FBI's Secret File on Black America, 1960–1972* (New York: The Free Press, 1989), considers the Black Panther raid and subsequent legal contests.

The battle over race and public education in Chicago is one of the primary topics in Paul E. Peterson's *School Politics Chicago Style* (Chicago: University of Chicago Press, 1976), and Mary J. Herrick's *The Chicago Schools: A Social and Political History* (Beverly Hills, Calif.: Sage Publications, 1971). The Chicago situation is also covered in Gary Orfield's *The Reconstruction of Southern Education: The Schools and the 1964 Civil Rights Act* (New York: Wiley-Interscience, 1969), and John E. Coons's "Chicago," in *Civil Rights USA: Public Schools in the North and West* (Washington, D.C.: Government Printing Office, 1962). Also see U.S. Congress, House Committee on Education and Labor, *Investigation of DeFacto Racial Segregation in Chicago's Public Schools: Hearings before a Special Subcommittee of the Committee on Education and Labor,* 89th Cong., 1st sess., July 27, 28, 1965 (Washington, D.C.: Government Printing Office, 1965).

Several studies deal with Chicago's anti-poverty programs during the Daley years. Consult U.S. Congress, House Committee on

Education and Labor, *Hearings before the Subcommittee on the War on Poverty Program of the Committee on Education and Labor*, 88th Cong., 2nd sess., 1965, and U.S. Congress, House Committee on Education and Labor, *Hearings before the Subcommittee on the War on Poverty Program of the Committee on Education and Labor*, 89th Cong., 1st sess., Examination of the War on Poverty Program, held in Washington, D.C., April 12–15, 29, 30, 1965 (Washington D.C.: Government Printing Office, 1965). Also see Seymour Z. Mann, *Chicago's War on Poverty* (Chicago: Loyola University Center for Research on Urban Government, 1966); Trudy Haffron Bers, "Private Welfare Agencies and Their Role in Government-Sponsored Welfare Programs: The Case of the War on Poverty in Chicago" (Ph.D. dissertation, University of Illinois at Urbana-Champaign, 1973); J. David Greenstone and Paul E. Peterson, *Race and Authority in Urban Politics: Community Participation and the War on Poverty* (New York: Russell Sage Foundation, 1973); J. David Greenstone and Paul E. Peterson, "Reformers, Machines, and the War on Poverty," in James Q. Wilson, ed., *City Politics and Public Policy* (New York: John Wiley and Sons, 1968), pp. 267–92; Paul E. Peterson, "Forms of Representation: Participation of the Poor in the Community Action Program," *American Political Science Review* 64 (June 1970), pp. 491–507; James V. Cunningham, *Urban Leadership in the Sixties* (Waltham: Brandeis University, 1970); and George J. Washnis, *Municipal Decentralization and Neighborhood Resources: Case Studies of Twelve Cities* (New York: Praeger, 1972).

Daley was one of the big city mayors who took full advantage of the federal government's generous financial assistance for urban renewal in the 1950s and 1960s. Jon C. Teaford's *The Rough Road to Renaissance: Urban Revitalization in America, 1940–1985* (Baltimore: Johns Hopkins University Press, 1990) is an excellent introduction to the topic. Chicago is the subject of Peter H. Rossi and Robert A. Dentler, *The Politics of Urban Renewal: The Chicago Findings* (New York: The Free Press of Glencoe, 1961); Gregory D. Squires, Larry Bennett, Kathleen McCourt, and Philip Nyden, *Chicago: Race, Class, and the Response to Urban Decline* (Philadelphia: Temple University Press, 1987); Gerald D. Suttles, *The Man-Made City: The Land-Use Confidence Game in Chicago* (Chicago: University of Chicago Press, 1990); and Larry Bennett, "Postwar Redevelopment in Chicago: The Declining Politics of Party and the Rise of Neighborhood Politics," in Gregory D. Squires, ed., *Unequal Partnerships: The Political Economy of Urban Redevelopment in Postwar America* (New Brunswick, N.J.: Rutgers University Press, 1989). Daley's partnership with private interests is explored in

Pastora San Juan Cafferty and William C. McCready, "The Chicago Public-Private Partnership Experience: A Heritage of Involvement," in R. Scott Fosler and Renée A. Berger, eds., *Public-Private Partnerships in American Cities: Seven Case Studies* (Lexington, Mass.: D. C. Heath, 1982). George Rosen, *Decision-Making Chicago-Style: The Genesis of a University of Illinois Campus* (Urbana: University of Illinois Press, 1980), is a thorough case study of one of Daley's most famous urban renewal projects. Daley's flawed campaign to build the Crosstown Expressway is detailed in Milton Pikarsky, "Chicago's Crosstown Expressway: The Team Concept in Action," in National Academy of Engineering, *The Engineer and the City* (Washington, D.C.: National Academy of Engineering, 1969), and in Elliott Arthur Pavlos, "Chicago's Crosstown: A Case Study in Urban Expressways," in David R. Miller, ed., *Urban Transportation Policy: New Perspectives* (Lexington, Mass.: Lexington Books, 1972). The best source on the mayor's role in the completion of O'Hare International Airport is Richard Paul Doherty, "The Origin and Development of Chicago-O'Hare International Airport" (Ph.D. dissertation, Ball State University, 1970). Daley's centrality in remaking the Chicago cityscape is analyzed by a leading architecture critic in Carl W. Condit, *Chicago, 1930–1970: Building, Planning, and Urban Technology* (Chicago: University of Chicago Press, 1974). Harold M. Mayer and Richard C. Wade's *Chicago: Growth of a Metropolis* (Chicago: University of Chicago Press, 1969) includes a wealth of photographs of the construction projects completed during Daley's tenure in office.

Daley's relations with organized labor are considered in J. David Greenstone's *Labor in American Politics* (New York: Vintage Books, 1969) and Milton Derber's *Labor in Illinois: The Affluent Years, 1945–1980* (Urbana: University of Illinois Press, 1989). In *Union Rule in the Schools: Big-City Politics in Transformation* (Lexington, Mass.: Lexington Books, 1979), William J. Grimshaw studies the attempt to unionize the public school system during the Daley years.

The mayor's controversial performance at the 1968 Democratic National Convention is evaluated in David Farber's definitive *Chicago, '68* (Chicago: University of Chicago Press, 1988). Norman Mailer's *Miami and the Siege of Chicago: An Informal History of the Republican and Democratic Conventions of 1968* (New York: World Publishing Company, 1968) vividly re-creates the climate of chaos and protest at the Chicago convention. Supplement these monographs with a reading of such general studies as Theodore H. White, *The Making of the President, 1968* (New York: Atheneum, 1969); Lewis

Chester, Godfrey Hodgson, and Bruce Page, *An American Melodrama: The Presidential Campaign of 1968* (New York: Viking Press, 1969); and Todd Gitlin, *The Sixties: Years of Hope, Days of Rage* (New York: Bantam Books, 1987).

Daley's financial machinations have become a subject of some interest in recent years. The most complete discussion of the topic appears in Ester R. Fuchs, *Mayors and Money: Fiscal Policy in New York and Chicago* (Chicago: University of Chicago Press, 1992). Also see A. F. Ehrbar, "Financial Probity, Chicago Style," *Fortune* 101 (June 2, 1980), pp. 100–106; "The City That Survives," *The Economist* 274 (March 29, 1980), pp. 5–28; and Sidney Lens, "The City That Doesn't Work Anymore: Chicago in the Crunch," *The Progressive* 44 (April 1980), pp. 34–38. A copy of "Paying Big City Bills," an unpublished paper presented by Woods Bowman at the Richard J. Daley Chicago Conference on October 14, 1977, is in my possession.

The best sources on the Daley administration scandals are the Chicago newspapers, which investigated enthusiastically. The Summerdale scandal plays a prominent role in Richard C. Lindberg's *To Serve and Collect: Chicago Politics and Police Corruption from the Lager Beer Riot to the Summerdale Scandal* (Westport, Conn.: Praeger, 1991) and William J. Bopp's *"O. W.": O. W. Wilson and the Search for a Police Profession* (Port Washington, N.Y.: Kennikat Press, 1977). Robert E. Hartley's *Big Jim Thompson of Illinois* (Chicago: Rand McNally, 1979) describes Thompson's role in prosecuting Daley's cohorts in the Democratic machine.

INDEX

Carmichael, Stokeley, 123
Carroll, Patrick J., 26
Carter, Jimmy, 222
Cater, Douglass, 116
Cavanaugh, Jerome, 109, 140, 223
Cayton, Horace R., 8
Cermak, Anton J., 15, 23–24
Chatham, 86
Chatters, Carl, 46, 213
Chicago American, 41
Chicago Board of Education, 97,
   109, 115, 142, 183, 210, 216, 229
Chicago Central Area Committee,
   47–48
Chicago Commission on Human
   Relations, 9, 96, 111, 132–33, 141
Chicago Committee on Urban Op-
   portunity, 104, 143
Chicago Conference on Religion
   and Race, 129, 131
Chicago Daily News, 9, 28, 107, 141,
   184, 203, 226
Chicago Defender, 36–37, 99, 204, 261
   n.38, 267 n.38
Chicago Department of City Plan-
   ning, 47
Chicago Eight (Seven) Trial, 169–77
Chicago Federation of Labor, 46, 53
Chicago Federation of Teachers,
   215–16
Chicago Freedom Movement,
   120–24, 129–31, 133, 135, 137–38
Chicago Heights, IL, 133
Chicago Home Rule Commission,
   56
Chicago Housing Authority, 10, 11,
   13–15, 87–91, 130, 133, 171–73,
   182–84, 190, 230–31
Chicago Human Rights Commis-
   sion, 11
Chicago Land Clearance Commis-
   sion, 13, 77
Chicago Metropolitan Home
   Builders Association, 14
Chicago Metropolitan Housing

Council, 9, 11, 50, 171
Chicago Mortgage Bankers Associ-
   ation, 14
Chicago Plan Commission, 11, 47,
   171, 182
Chicago Real Estate Board, 14, 95,
   129–30, 132–33
Chicago Sanitary District, 79, 87
Chicago Skyway, 49
Chicago Sun-Times, 108, 198, 200–1,
   203, 231
Chicago Transit Authority, 27, 49,
   60, 210–11
Chicago Tribune, 34, 37, 49, 142, 147,
   153, 178–79, 203, 236
Cicero, IL, 10, 23, 45, 88, 120, 129,
   196, 261 n.32
Citizens of Greater Chicago, 17
Civic Federation of Chicago, 14
Clark, Jim, 120
Clark, John S., 25
Clark, Joseph, 44
Clark, Mark, 177
Clark, Ramsey, 146, 152
Cleveland, OH, 209, 223
Cobo, Albert, 44
Cody, Archbishop John P., 122,
   128–29
Cohen, Wilbur, 116, 142
Collins, Cardiss, 230
Community Action Program (CAP),
   104, 108
Condit, Carl W., 227, 241
Congress on Racial Equality, 123,
   261 n.32
Conlisk, James, 149, 152, 155, 164,
   178, 180, 190, 197
Connelly, Hugh, 25, 29
Connor, Eugene "Bull", 120, 163–64
Connors, Botchy, 27, 30
Coogan, Dr. Thomas, 199, 222
Cook County Board of Commis-
   sioners, 23, 31, 213
Cook County Physicians Associa-
   tion, 99

From his first election in 1955 to 1976, Mayor Richard J. Daley dominated Chicago's political landscape. A product of the Irish Catholic working class, Daley never lost touch with his roots as he rose through the Democratic party machine—whose workings he perfected—to become one of the most enduring and influential political figures. Hard work and party loyalty earned him his place, and his public image as a devout family man dedicated to Chicago turned out the voters repeatedly.

The story of Daley is also the story of Chicago. Faced with issues confronting many American cities in the twentieth century—civil rights, integration, race riots, fiscal crisis, housing, suburban flight, urban renewal—Daley conducted Chicago's business with a steadfast resolve to withstand the many changes that threatened to engulf his city. In particular, his atavistic approach to racial issues, typified in his opposition to Martin Luther King's campaign to desegregate schools and housing, moderated social change. Through such policies shaping the development of Chicago, he resisted social forces and preserved his city, effectively slowing the pace of change.

Even as Daley resisted social change, he was building a new Chicago that under his guidance became known as "the city that works." Daley earned this title for the city by championing civic infrastructure projects that modernized the skyline and improved the quality of life for those who lived and worked there. He rebuilt Chicago's downtown Loop, introduced striking modern architecture, improved street lighting downtown as well as in residential areas, completed a network of expressways, constructed the University of Illinois at Chicago, modernized the organization of the police and fire departments, and improved delivery of services such as garbage and snow removal. At the same time, his fiscal management of the city during the urban financial crisis of the 1970s was considered exemplary, the envy of other American cities.

On the national front, in the meantime, Daley was gaining a reputation. Though as a fellow Irish Catholic Daley had enjoyed high visibility for his